29261

D0972636

BLACK MAN'S

RELIGION

Can Christianity Be Afrocentric?

Glenn Usry & Craig S. Keener

InterVarsity Press
Downers Grove, Illinois

InterVarsity Press® is the book-publishing division of InterVarsity Christian Fellowship®, a student movement active on campus at hundreds of universities, colleges and schools of nursing in the United States of America, and a member movement of the International Fellowship of Evangelical Students. For information about local and regional activities, write Public Relations Dept., InterVarsity Christian Fellowship, 6400 Schroeder Rd., P.O. Box 7895, Madison, WI 53707-7895.

All Scripture quotations, unless otherwise indicated, are the authors' own translation.

Cover photograph: Joseph McNally/The Image Bank
ISBN 0-8308-1983-5

Printed in the United States of America ∞

Library of Congress Cataloging-in-Publication Data

Usry, Glenn.
    Black man's religion: can Christianity be Afrocentric?/Glenn
Usry and Craig S. Keener.
        p.   cm.
    Includes bibliographical references.
    ISBN 0-8308-1983-5 (pbk.: alk. paper)
    1. Afro-Americans—Religion. 2. Afrocentrism—Religious aspects—
Christianity. I. Keener, Craig S., 1960- . II. Title.
    BR563.N4U87   1996
    270'.089'96073—dc20
                                                        96-381
                                                        CIP

17	16	15	14	13	12	11	10	9	8	7	6	5	4	3	2	1
10	09	08	07	06	05	04	03	02	01	00	99	98	97	96		

Preface

The main title of this book is meant to be provocative more than precise. It responds to the historically inaccurate White idea (circulated today by some African-Americans as well) that Christianity is a "White man's religion." This is why our book is called *Black Man's Religion*—not, of course, to imply that non-Blacks are excluded, but to point out that biblical Christianity is a Black religion as much as a White one. Further, because the book addresses Black women as well as Black men, a more accurate title would be "Black *People's* Religion"—but choosing this title would have meant losing the deliberate contrast to the traditional phrase "White man's religion," which its users originally applied generically to White people. Although we intentionally address both men and women in our heritage, we retain the less accurate phrase solely to underline the contrast, because this book is a response to the charge that Christianity is a European and White American religion.

As most students of history recognize, the idea that Christianity originated as or remained primarily a European religion is unfounded. Christian history includes Asian, African and other representatives. In fact, we could never imagine that Christianity was ever strictly a European religion if we knew the facts of history—about the ancient church in East Africa, about the faith of our community's forebears on the plantations (though it was a Christianity quite different from that of the plantation owners) and so on. That is what this book is about: reminding African-American Christians of our firm place in history.

The authors of this book originally set out to write a brief manual on Afrocentrism and African-American history for use by New Generation Campus

Ministries, an African-American Christian student movement. We especially wanted to respond to ill-informed objections against the Black church and self-consciously African-American Christianity—objections raised both by White supremacists and by some Afrocentric ideologies that have opposed the Bible and biblical Christianity. The manual quickly grew in size and scope, and eventually, with NGM's blessing, we decided to make it available to a wider audience.

Although we have endeavored to make this book's answers as accurate as possible, we have also tried to make sure that it addresses the right questions. This is not a complete survey of Christians of color in history (a task both impossible in one volume and beyond our own training), nor do we address every issue raised by Afrocentric historians today. We choose to deal with a particular set of questions we are currently hearing among urban youth and college students. We also do not focus on the historic racism of many professed Christians; although the failure of many Christians to practice Jesus' teachings calls for serious comment, our work responds to those who associate Christianity more with White supremacy than with Jesus, so we are emphasizing the side of the evidence which our accusers have neglected. For the same reason, we have cited popular works of interest to the subject alongside scholarly works, and have focused less on scholarly theological works and more on works most relevant to the subject of the book. This is neither to denigrate the sources omitted nor to rank all works cited on the same level; it is to say that, as far as possible, we have focused on the purpose for which we wrote the book.[1]

To a great extent, the selection of information in this book thus reflects the original purpose for which the book was written: providing African-American Christian students with a deeper awareness of both their ethnic and their spiritual heritage, especially where those heritages coincide. One of the biggest issues is the objection (from members of the Nation of Islam and others) that Christianity is "a White man's religion"; second to that is the general accusation (held by White supremacists but not by the Nation of Islam) that everything noble in history is White. We respond to both, with most attention to the former objection. Too often we have found Christians unprepared to answer the objections that the Nation of Islam raises, despite the abundance of evidence that could answer these objections. But even though we respond to the Nation of Islam's critique of Christianity, we agree with them that African-Americans are *right* to affirm their African-American heritage.[2] And as we respond to what we believe to be an inaccurate portrayal of our history, we do not intend any personal attack against those who hold contrary positions.[3]

We are in the process of completing a second volume responding to various specific objections to African-American Christianity, but we have devoted this entire first book to answering the inaccurate complaint that historically Christianity is not Black. This book thus grapples with two basic issues. The first, as noted above, locates precedents for our African-Christian heritage in history. The second issue is one we sometimes miss when discussing our heritage. If we are to identify with peoples in history, on what basis do we identify with them? We cannot very well write Afrocentric history (by which we mean history from an African-American perspective) unless we have decided the basis on which we as African-Americans actually identify with peoples in history. In actuality we identify with others on a number of grounds, and these various grounds will provide the different angles from which we can examine our place in history.[4]

To some extent we identify on the basis of common geographical origin (Africa), to some extent on the basis of common skin color (Black), to some extent on the basis of a common heritage of oppression and discrimination, and finally to some extent on the basis of a shared commitment to fight oppression and discrimination. Thus this book will address our heritage as African-American Christians in the following chapters: our African heritage (chapter two), race and U.S. history (chapter three), race and ancient Egyptian and Israelite history (chapter four), oppression, including medieval Arab and later Western slavery (chapter five) and justice through reconciliation (chapter six).

In all these respects Christianity still remains part of our heritage. If we identify with our heritage geographically, Christianity originated close to Africa and has maintained a strong presence in Africa from the beginning. If we identify with our heritage racially, Black Africans appear in prominent roles in the Bible (such as Jeremiah's rescuer and the first Gentile Christian), as well as in subsequent Christianity. If we identify with others who have been oppressed or who join with us in working for justice, the biblical gospel resonates most of all with the oppressed and summons its followers to work for justice. But of course ultimately we must choose Christianity not simply for these reasons but because we embrace its message of a God who embraced the need of all humanity in the cross.

Chapter six is more directly practical and constitutes the conclusion of our defense: to produce justice in a society where ours remains a minority voice, we ultimately must join ranks with others who share our concern for justice. At the same time we cannot provide a defense for African-American Christianity without responding to those who attack the Christian agenda of reconciliation as subversive to the cause of racial justice. Those who call themselves Christians have often lived contrary to Jesus' teachings, but while their lifestyle confirms biblical testimony about human selfishness, it says little about Christianity's real power to transform the world when practiced truly.

In studying the history of Christianity we find warnings and disappointments as well as encouragements. History reveals the truth of Jesus' warning that not all those who professed to follow him would genuinely obey his teachings (Mt 7:15-23). True Christianity, however, is not about Christians but about Jesus, and it rises or falls with him. Our second book will address some of the specific objections raised against Jesus and the Bible and will make a brief case for the biblical portrait of Jesus. The present volume has not enough space to argue the truth of Christianity, nor does it deny that professed Christians have often behaved in non-Christian ways (when enforcement is left to the individual's heart, most religions produce an ample supply of hypocrites). We believe that this work does, however, conclusively respond to the charges that followers of Jesus generally were historically European and White and identified with the cause of slavery. Those charges are either misinformed or dishonest.

Different people will read this book for different reasons. Because most readers consult the documentation only for further research, we limit our documentation to the endnotes and bibliography; this keeps the actual text of the book shorter and more readable. The book is also arranged so that the reader may skip ahead to the sections that interest him or her most.

We should add one final but essential note. This book is a collaborative effort by two friends who saw a need and brought different skills to the task. Glenn knows best the popular questions and literature the book needs to address; Craig is already a published scholar and did the "grunt work" of research. Glenn is African-American, a graduate of a Black college and Black seminary; Craig is European-American, though he currently lives and teaches in the Black community (for the last four years at Hood, the seminary of the A.M.E. Zion Church) and holds ordination in the National Baptist Convention, the largest Black American denomination. We hope that Craig's involvement will refute the charge of "bias" from some White people inclined to dismiss any Afrocentric or Black idea, or to ignore our research. Glenn is responsible for the book's editorial "we," as an African-American Christian addressing other African-American Christians, our main audience. But we needed each other's expertise in writing the book. Others would be far more capable of writing a book like this one than we are, but we trust that this work will serve the purpose for which it was written in the time in which it was written.

Acknowledgments and Dedication

We express our appreciation to the library of Livingstone College, a historically Black institution founded in North Carolina by the A.M.E. Zion Church shortly after the Emancipation; and to Hood Theological Seminary, the A.M.E. Zion seminary where one of the authors teaches.[5] We are grateful for access to the Black Studies collection there and for the library staff's kind procurement of other works for us through interlibrary loan. We also express our gratitude to New Generation Campus Ministries, for reminding us of this work's importance and prodding us to complete it.

Among those who have read the manuscript and provided helpful insights are the Reverend Dean Nelson, national director for New Generation Campus Ministries; Dr. Harold Dean Trulear of New York Theological Seminary; Tony Warner of InterVarsity Christian Fellowship; Brenda Salter-McNeil of the Chicago Urban Project; and Dr. William Pannell, author of *The Coming Race Wars?* and professor at Fuller Theological Seminary. We also thank Dr. Catherine Clark Kroeger for lending us her helpful bibliography—though, due to our deadlines, we managed to accommodate only a few of her extra sources—and to Rodney Clapp and Ruth Goring, our editors at IVP. When our book was becoming much too long, it was Dr. Leonard Lovett who gently warned us to divide it into two volumes, and in time we recognized the wisdom of his counsel.

This book is dedicated to the Black church. Both Glenn and Craig are indebted to the heritage of the Black church, which is Glenn's by birth and Craig's by adoption. The Black church remains the most prominent social institution in the African-American community today,[6] and though parts of the church need reform, we believe that no institution in our community is better equipped to provide moral leadership in this hour. The historic strength of the Black church can also provide wisdom far beyond the Black community if we will let it speak to the broader American church, society and nation.

1
Why History Belongs to Us

IN RESPONSE TO OBJECTIONS THAT CHRISTIANITY IS A "WHITE MAN'S RE-
ligion," we affirm that it is also a "Black man's religion." But what does it mean
for Christianity to be "Black"? Different people would give different answers
to that question. The heart of this book begins in the next chapter (some readers
may wish to start there), but here we will introduce the basic issues we must
address. A "Black" perspective can mean an African perspective, a perspective
based on skin tone or a perspective based on a shared history of being enslaved
and oppressed. This book addresses all these perspectives.

However, we find it necessary to limit our focus. Though important racial
issues need to be addressed in many parts of the world, our book deals primarily
with the racial situation in the United States. The U.S. population includes
many peoples with diverse histories, such as White European peoples that came
in successive waves to flee religious repression or political oppression, or to find
economic opportunity; immigrants from the East and South who often came
for the same reasons; and Native Americans, whose land was seized and who
were forcibly repressed and restricted to special "reservations" by White settlers.
American history also includes the history of Africans whose very lives were
seized, who (if they survived the long passage across the Atlantic Ocean
crammed into dark cargo holds) were forced to work as slaves for generations

and, after slavery, were usually restricted from participation in a society controlled by White peoples. We acknowledge and lament the hardships suffered by other immigrant groups; without playing those hardships down, our book focuses on the distinctive situation of African-Americans who did not immigrate to North America willingly. As one evangelical work points out, "The predominant distinguishing factor for African Americans is the history of social, economic, and political oppression experienced because of color discrimination," and this aspect of their experience "pervades every aspect of social institutions within which they participate."[1]

Traditional history books in the United States (including those the authors used in school) did not grapple with these different histories. Some newer texts attempt to remedy this lack; however, it is still true that Black Americans know far more about European involvement in the nation's history than most White Americans know about the involvement of all other peoples put together. Many White Americans still assume that "being American" means assimilating the values of the dominant White majority (a "privilege" usually more available to some ethnic groups than others). Yet some of the same members of the dominant culture object when African-Americans desire to learn more from their own heritage or focus efforts for betterment on their own people.[2] Racial unity is important, but one should not call for racial unity while defining unity in terms that suppress rather than welcome backgrounds different from one's own.

What We Are *Not* Saying

Nothing in this book should be taken to imply that we think that White Americans should not reflect on their own heritage or share it with others—an impression some White people get when people of color want to affirm a distinctive heritage. When African-Americans claim a desire to express their own heritage, they are not denying anyone else the right to theirs. Focusing on an aspect of history that concerns one's own heritage is not the same thing as repressing other views or insights, as some extreme advocates of "political correctness" have been known to do. Thus it is not fair for some White readers to dismiss an African-American perspective out of hand by simply associating it with a political or social "camp."

We believe that some Whites associate any Black self-affirmation or rehearsal of racism's history with radical anti-White sentiments, as if Martin Luther King Jr., SNCC, Malcolm X and the Black Panther Party all represented precisely the same cause. As legal scholar Derrick Bell protests, "We want nothing more than our rightful share of opportunities long available to whites," but "many whites view black claims for justice . . . as unjustified bellyaching."[3]

Whereas many Whites fear that Black talk about their heritage is separatist, many Blacks want to give up the discussion because they feel as if Whites never really listen to what they are saying. Yet as long as we share the same society we have no choice but to seek grounds for discussion. And this goal requires each voice to make a reasonable case for its position.

So in this book we seek to demonstrate that our community has a heritage to appreciate; but even when we record injustices we have experienced, we are not seeking to disparage others' heritage or those elements of U.S. heritage that all of us have in common.[4] Most African-Americans do not object to learning *more* than our own history, but we do insist that the history we learn must *include* our own distinctive history.

This book is not advocating an impractical separatism, like the massive "back to Africa" movements of the past or some extreme forms of Black nationalism today. In the nineteenth century, both Black slaves and Whites recognized that when slaves were freed, Whites often feared their presence and wanted to send them back to Africa.[5] Yet the United States was built in part on the backs of Black labor, and it belongs to Black people as much as to White people; White supremacists will not get rid of us that easily! Our purpose is not to *reject* our history—whether the African part or the American part—but to *reclaim* it. Like David Walker, the revolutionary Black leader who issued his *Appeal* to Black Americans against White racists in 1830, we affirm that African-Americans have *earned* the right to be called Americans, whether racists like it or not.[6]

But because our history has traditionally been denied to us, many of us have a special desire to affirm our heritage—a desire that the White community (which has always owned its own history) sometimes does not recognize. We agree that national unity is a good goal, but genuine unity comes by consensus, not by force. Consensus presupposes reconciliation, which in turn presupposes honestly confronting our history of fragmentation. To members of the dominant White culture, it may have seemed as if everyone was more unified when fewer African-Americans openly protested racism. But as plenty of widely known historical documents now testify, that was never a relationship based on honesty.

We freely acknowledge other peoples' contributions in history, but here we emphasize especially the contributions of people with whom many of our people identify. As one White writer lamented, in most parts of the country White children can still grow up assuming that their history is the only history worth studying, that the mantles of Egypt and all truly great civilizations are theirs.[7]

In other words, they are socialized into a passive racial bias that affects how they think of other peoples whether or not they overtly engage in racism. Psychological studies indicate that as early as age four White American children can begin assuming that the world is White-centered, and this brings various psychological and emotional complications when they confront the real world.[8] On the other hand, many White students, if given the chance in learning environments when they are young, can develop an appreciation for diverse cultures.[9] Nannie Helen Burroughs (1883-1961), a spiritual and educational leader among our people who also emphasized racial reconciliation, underlined "the duty the Negro owes to himself to learn his own story and the duty the white man owes to himself to learn of the spiritual strivings and achievements of a despised but not an inferior people."[10] Thus we ask that fair due be offered the histories of all peoples, for the sake of this nation's White citizens as well as our own.

What We *Are* Saying

While some outspoken groups have been wrong to advocate racial separatism, they have been right to respond to a need for affirmation within our communities, and we cannot challenge their error without acknowledging where they are also correct. Granted that history does not exclusively focus on Africa or African-Americans, one would hope that European-Americans would not suppress our contribution while extolling only their own. Contrary to racist assumptions held by some Americans, not all great civilizations were White and European. Contrary to many of the same people's assumptions, people of color have not always been objects of oppression (incapable of ruling ourselves, as Richard Nixon reportedly suggested!).[11] Nor is it likely that the main characters of the Bible, including Moses and Jesus, looked like Anglo-Saxon Europeans. World history is also our history, the Bible is also our book, and the history of this country is also our history, though whatever advances we have made here have generally come against apparently insuperable odds.

None of us can undo history, whether we like all of our history or not. We can not undo our presence in the United States any more than we can undo the United States's untimely separation from England. (We call it "untimely" because the British Empire abolished the slave trade first. Had the United States still been part of the British Empire at that time, it might have later averted the Civil War.) We can undo our presence here no more than we can undo the fall of various African empires, or the conquest of one kingdom by another repeatedly throughout history. Yet we learn our history not to change or avenge the past, but to understand our present so we can have a say in our future. As Marcus Garvey put it, "Black men, you were once great; you shall be great again."[12]

Although legislation and education have helped the situation considerably, they have not been able to abolish prejudice. Advancing socially at our optimum rate (as in the Reconstruction era) has sometimes provoked merely resentment and backlash. Legal integration has often produced only Black-to-White assimilation without genuine cultural tolerance. The current state of our inner-city communities sometimes generates despair and disgust.

A Harlem Renaissance or a Spike Lee can have some positive influence on the larger society's perspectives, but changing our status must include transforming our own perspectives. Centuries of history provide eloquent evidence of what we can do and how the tragic plight of the ghettos is *not* our natural state. Those tempted to succumb to playing by society's rules may gain courage for the battle by remembering that we are a race of ancient civilizations and noble dignity in the face of hardships—a people for whom God has a purpose and destiny.

In this book we seek to examine history from an African-American Christian perspective: the history of biblical times, the history of Africa, the history of our ancestors in this land. But our attempt to look at history from an African-American perspective forces us to ask, "What *is* an African-American perspective?" What kinds of different questions might we ask of history as opposed to, say, the questions asked by Americans of European or Asian or Latin descent?

The question is relatively simple to answer when we examine the history of our own country, but more complicated as we study ancient civilizations in Africa and the Middle East. Can we claim only the darkest of Africans as our moral forebears, or can we, as Europeans have done in the past, identify with many of the other socially or spiritually great nations of history? We will examine several useful grounds for identification, evaluating the strengths and weaknesses of each one in turn.

The Basis for Identification

We identify with characters in history or in any story on the basis of points we have in common with them. The points of identification depend mainly on the issues that matter most to us and shape the world in which we think.

Many of us can identify with a character just on the basis of that character's feelings—in other words, because we share a common humanness. But we can also identify on the basis of other more particular characteristics. Members of any minority culture within a larger culture will look for precedents that help define and socially validate their own culture. African-Americans might identify on the basis of a character's geographical origin—that is, we might identify with someone African. Culturally, however, we have become quite different from most Africans who have spent their whole lives in Africa (as Africans also regularly note),[13] and most of us think of ourselves as in some sense *Americans* of African descent. Thus geography, while significant, is not the strongest point of contact.[14]

We are more likely to identify with characters on the basis of the main characteristic that sets us apart in this country: our color. Yet our complexions vary from the lightest to the darkest hues, and even in Africa complexions vary from light-brown Amharas to dark black Amaswazi to reddish and other pigmentations. What makes our color significant to us does have something to do with the level of melanin in our skin (which God gave us eyes to appreciate); but the special significance of our color that sets us apart also has to do with what racists have done to us on the basis of our Black African heritage. A person of one-quarter Black blood may be three-quarters White genetically, but even if this person can pass for White, he or she is Black socially as long as he or she chooses to be identified with us. In the days of slavery, the person with one-quarter Black blood would have been a slave just as much as the person with one hundred percent Black blood.

In other words, a deeper characteristic of our identity than our pigment itself is our experience of being part of the Black community in America, a heritage that has usually included simple dignity in the face of oppression. Historically, the African-American community knows what it is like to have our pride crushed, to be wounded by people who have power over us although we have done nothing to hurt them. Our community knows what it is like to find strength in the face of that adversity, to carry on anyway, to express the nobility of an often silent yet always persevering resilience, the true depth of which our oppressors could never begin to understand unless they were in our place. We are Africans by descent, but we are Africans whose experience as an oppressed people for the past few centuries has shaped us uniquely.[15] When we see black skin, we identify with one another as sharers in the same community of experience, whatever shade of black our skin is. Yet what bonds us together most as African-Americans is the shared experience of suffering and perseverance in this land; thus we can identify with those who are oppressed.

Finally, as Christians we identify with those who genuinely share our Christian faith, regardless of color or background. (We do venture to doubt, of course, whether overt racists genuinely share the Christian faith.) To some degree this faith is also a part of our heritage, though Jesus is for all peoples and can never be tied down to one heritage alone. Although most were not yet Christians when our ancestors came from Africa, some believed in only one God; most believed in many gods and spirits but acknowledged one supreme God who ruled over all.[16] In the subsequent, distinctive experience of African-Americans, we have found a special strength in the Black church that has enabled us to stand against oppression. Some of our preachers, like the Baptist revolutionary Nat Turner, were in the forefront of armed resistance; most, however, preferred nonviolent alternatives, which brought less immediate suffering to all parties involved.[17] In either expression, faith in God has always given us both the strength to survive and the motivation to make things different.

Most of the Black abolitionists were church people—Frederick Douglass, for instance, was an ordained A.M.E. Zion deacon, and Sojourner Truth and Harriet Tubman were ministers. Similarly, Black educators like Mary McCleod Bethune (who attended Moody Bible Institute) and Nannie Helen Burroughs (whose training school may have sent out more women missionaries than any other school in the country) were motivated by Christian convictions.

Mary McLeod Bethune (1875-1955), founding president of Bethune-Cookman College and the leading black educator and activist of her time, embraced the gospel mandate with great seriousness throughout her career. She was the first African American to enroll in the Moody Bible Institute, where she received, according to her biographer C. G. Newsome, a "mighty baptism of the Holy Spirit. This experience, she confessed later, made her effective in all that she thought, said, or did thereafter."[18]

Most Black Civil Rights leaders, like Martin Luther King Jr., Ralph Abernathy and Jesse Jackson, were or are ministers.

Values and Our History

Yet "Black" does not necessarily imply "Christian."[19] And it is increasingly difficult to speak of "African-American social values," as if we all held the same values: the traditional values of our community have been ebbing away. Most African peoples had a more highly evolved social system than most European peoples did. In contrast to current American values, most of our African ancestors upheld the sanctity of marriage and provided a stable family structure and education for the nurture of children; we emphasized loyalty to the community as a whole and not just self-interest.[20]

The same held true after our arrival on this continent. When African slaves were brought to this country, slave traders purposely separated peoples of the same tribes and languages so they would not be able to pass on their culture. Although marriages were often permitted, they could be dissolved at the master's whim, if the master chose to sell away the husband or wife (who did not always live on the same plantation). Despite the obstacles of continually broken families, our people took up the challenge and as a community raised the children and kept their families strong whenever it was in their own power to do so. Divorce remained relatively rare and our family structures strong through most of the twentieth century.

Only in recent decades has the Black family been devastated on a wide scale; this devastation has reflected social trends that have hit the ghettos hardest, but it certainly does not reflect our historic values. Rather, it reflects the widespread impact of modern secular American values of placing the self before the community, as well as sexual and drug crises originally spawned by White free-thinkers in the universities in the sixties.

Likewise, our people historically maintained a high work ethic and valued education. During Reconstruction after the Civil War, we made what may well have been faster progress than any immigrant population in the history of this country has made. The promise of a new America lured us to hope and labor—until White northern Republicans cut a deal with White southern Democrats and withdrew the federal troops protecting Reconstruction.

In the years that followed we were forced down by the murder of over ten thousand of our leaders and, by the turn of the century, new laws designed to bar us from voting or advancing economically. Eventually our people had a harsh reality beaten into them: no matter how hard you work, "the White man" will only let you get so far.[21]

Some thought the traditional welfare system would liberate many people from poverty. Yet by its lack of provisions to get people into the work force, it actually seemed designed to keep its clients from getting jobs, cars or their own homes, much less an education. We will soon know whether currently proposed alternatives will make matters better or worse.

The Challenge Today

To many, current challenges to acquiring an education, a job and a voice in society appear even more daunting. Confronted with a history of White flight, discrimination and changing economic and educational structures, some members of a newer generation have come to wonder whether it is worth trying to work within the system. Our ancestors worked hard, but some African-

Americans today are questioning whether such hard work will get us anywhere anyway. Why bump your head on a glass ceiling? they ask. Meanwhile drug dealers—probably the leading killers of our youth today—merely mimic the larger society's values. Like TV network executives and other American purveyors of a free enterprise without moral boundaries, they cry, "We just give people what they want; it's not our fault if what they want is not what's good for them." No clear moral consensus remains concerning a "work ethic" in the African-American community or the U.S. society as a whole—especially among those who have never seen much hope firsthand.

Trends in the present generation indicate that we can no longer speak of even family ideals shared by everyone in the Black community. When we identify with people in history on the level of values, then, some values may reflect our heritage—the values of our grandparents and their parents before them. But in the end an identification on the basis of values must go beyond the prevailing attitudes of our culture and demand a personal choice. We believe that both the God and the values of our grandparents' generation are desperately needed in modern society—but they can be recovered only by our personal choice.

In the light of the various positions on such issues that now exist among us, it may be almost presumptuous anymore to call something a "Black thing." Christianity is not a "Black man's religion" in the sense that all African-Americans will embrace it or that it speaks to African-Americans alone. But Christianity is an integral part of our heritage, and a part of our heritage that can eloquently address some of the family, employment and other crises in our communities.[22] Many of our people today look for precedents in history, and if we look for such precedents for Black Christianity we will find that there are many. The heritage of the Black church—our African Christian heritage, our African-American Christian heritage and our solidarity with others who have suffered in history—provides a renewing source of hope for the Black community today, and for anyone outside the Black community who wishes to be revitalized by it. May the Black church and its vibrant historic experience of the gospel be a source of renewal to our land.

2
Back to Africa: Geographical Identification

I N RECENT YEARS MANY HAVE ARGUED THAT CHRISTIANITY CAME TO AFRICA only under European colonialism, whereas the Nation of Islam, a growing alternative to Christianity in the Black community, claims that its heritage is indigenously African. Actually historic Islam *has* been in Africa for a long time, but Christianity has been there longer.

Although this chapter focuses on Christian history in Africa, White racism provides a reason to also survey briefly the history of some other African civilizations in which few if any Christians lived: African history provides a response to those Whites who think Europeans genetically superior to Africans. In the now notorious book *The Bell Curve,* for example, some White American researchers argued that Blacks on average have lower IQ scores than Whites because of their genes.[1] The authors did concede that exceptional individuals exist in all races and thus that some African-Americans are smarter than most Whites. Nevertheless, the study's claims could have serious impact on an African-American student who is already wondering whether the pressure of academics is worth it, especially if he or she gets little reinforcement at home or among peers. Children's self-image is often shaped by others' stereotypes of them.[2]

A more basic question, however, is whether *The Bell Curve*'s conclusions are *correct.* Racists and a few geneticists were quick to embrace the study. Other scholars, however, responded by noting the different values and socialization that start in infancy, the inferior prenatal and postnatal care among the poor that can affect brain development, and so on.[3] In twenty test countries, major gaps appeared in IQ scores between *generations,* again suggesting social rather than genetic origins.[4] Studies also show that Black students raised in academically affirming homes do as well as White students, until they face the racial divide of our culture.[5]

Further, scientists whose primary field is genetics (in contrast to the authors of *The Bell Curve*) have provided data that readily refute *The Bell Curve* (unintentionally—their work appeared at roughly the same time). Princeton University Press's recent one-thousand-page *History and Geography of Human Genes,* the most massive study of global genetics yet offered, demonstrates conclusively that external traits like skin color bear little relation to most internal genetic traits. For example, Australian aborigines, who are black in color, are genetically more like Southeast Asians than like Africans who share their pigment patterns.[6] Harvard biologist Richard Lewontin, who analyzed seventeen genetic markers in 168 diverse peoples, discovered "more genetic difference within one race than . . . between that race and another. Only 6.3 percent of the genetic differences could be explained by the individuals' belonging to different races."[7]

Because the genes that determine mental processes are not those that determine race, one cannot make scientific predictions based on race. "If there are intelligence 'genes,'" anthropologists conclude, "they must be in all ethnic groups equally."[8] Culture and opportunity are responsible for far bigger differences. After observing data from half a century of European immigrants, one study "found that as ethnic groups rose categorically in socioeconomic status, so did their I.Q. scores."[9] Clearly, IQ test scores are not the same thing as inherited intellectual capacities. (We will discuss the nature of "race" more fully in chapter four.)

Although some might be satisfied to argue that more African-Americans would score higher on IQ tests if social conditions were better, we should not settle for an "if." Two methods allow us to *prove* that Americans of African descent are capable of the highest academic achievements. First, we can keep working to improve the social conditions that inhibit academic advancement, and hence improve the test scores. But second, and more to the point of this chapter, history testifies that no group of people has a permanent monopoly on learning. If academic intelligence is largely genetic, the gene pool has shifted from some races to others quite often in history! In this chapter we survey some African empires and focus especially on the heritage of the church in Africa.

Why Africa's Heritage Matters to Us

Although most of us identify with certain public figures for other reasons than solely a shared African heritage, we do have a special interest in Africa. When Western history books focus on the European civilizations of White Americans' ancestors, seeming to confirm racist genetic arguments, it encourages us to know that our ancestors were equally inventive. Africans adapted to their environment and produced intricate social networks no less complex than those of Europeans. Likewise, contrary to some popular current misconceptions, Europe has never been ethnically united any more than Africa has been—as two "world wars" and recent events in the former Yugoslavia have reminded us. As William Pannell, an African-American scholar and author of *The Coming Race Wars?* reminds us, the Balkan battles demonstrate "that Europeans behave just like those uncivilized Africans just as soon as they are released from communist colonialism," except that when Europeans engage in warfare it is called a "struggle for democracy"![10]

One of the greatest African-American leaders of the twentieth century, W. E. B. Du Bois, pointed out that

there was not a single year during the nineteenth century when the world was not at war. Chiefly, but not entirely, these wars were waged to subjugate colonial peoples. They were carried on by the Europeans, and at least one hundred and fifty separate wars can be counted during the heyday of the peace movement. What the peace movement really meant was peace in Europe and between Europeans, while for the conquest of the world and because of the suspicion which they held toward each other, every nation maintained a standing army which steadily grew in cost and menace.

Du Bois believed that it was the Europeans' participation in the African slave trade that ultimately degraded their respect for humanity.[11]

It was only in recent centuries that Europeans discovered (or borrowed—such as gunpowder from the Chinese) technology that enabled them to "colonize" the rest of the world. (Even then the Europeans were hardly advanced by contemporary urban standards; computer technology has advanced information exponentially, so that the advantage of colonial Europe appears rather marginal from a modern vantage point.) Although we have learned a number of useful values from European societies, in many other ways (for instance, respect for parents, familial intimacy or commitment to the community) African societies have often reflected more humanitarian ethical values than traditional European societies. Some of these values are now breaking down in African society as well—perhaps largely under the influence of urbanization and Western culture.

When the relative dominance of European societies in the most recent two centuries of world history convinces some Whites of their innate superiority, we need to remind them, and all those influenced by them, that their assumptions are historically shallow. As one scholar notes, the Egyptians were a mixture of Black African and Semitic peoples; African and Asian kingdoms "were at the forefront of civilization when Caucasoid Europeans were hunting in forests and living in caves." Even the Roman Empire succumbed to Asian invaders.[12] Today many East Asian societies are rapidly surpassing Western economic machines in productivity. History is capricious in its favoritism; it never bestows eternal dominance on any people.

Many White historians and scientists in the nineteenth century contended that Black people had always filled inferior positions in human history (for example, they claimed that White Egyptians held Black slaves).[13] In response, the Reverend Thomas Smyth offered abundant historical and anthropological data to show that Black people "were in the earliest period of their known history cultivated and intelligent, having kingdoms, arts, and manufacturers," and that the specific enslavement of Blacks as a race was of more modern origin.[14]

Knowing some African history helps us precisely because it reminds us that the oppression our race has experienced need not remain a permanent state. In the words of Garvey mentioned in the last chapter, "Black men, you were once great; you shall be great again."[15] Or as Du Bois declared, "Let then the Dreams of the Dead rebuke the Blind who think that what is will be forever."[16]

Africa's History and Europe's History

Africans began building a civilization in Nubia by 3000 B.C., and Africa has never been without some powerful societies since that time. The de-Africanization of history was simply a byproduct of Eurocentric historiography—that is, Europeans looked (perhaps somewhat naturally at the time) only for their own heritage in history, and then assumed that their resulting ethnocentric position represented the only evidence that has survived in history.[17] Europeans supposed Africa the "dark continent" because it was the final continent whose interior opened itself to their gaze. This delay was, however, in large measure due to the sophisticated civilizations that had kept them at bay! Most Africans by that period were farmers working with iron tools, "organized into states and communities powerful enough to deter invaders and migrants from overseas until late in the nineteenth century."[18]

Yet if Europe lays claim to empires, Africa also had empires. If Europe lays claim to education and technology, it must be recognized that Europe took the lead in such areas only during certain periods of history (Arab and Chinese civilizations far surpassed it during Europe's Middle Ages). If Europe lays claim to higher morality, the continual feuds and wars within Europe, and the Crusades beyond it, challenge its moral supremacy in history. Can peoples who often abandoned babies, following the ancient Roman custom,[19] condemn Africans for the much rarer practice of twin-murder?[20] Likewise, the generally tolerant Romans found it necessary to suppress the Druid barbarians of ancient France and Britain because they practiced human sacrifice,[21] a custom practiced but rare in most ancient African societies.[22] If African peoples had some superstitious practices, some European customs to this day reflect pagan and superstitious roots (including elements of the modern wedding ceremony)—though now such practices for many Africans and Europeans alike are simply time-honored "customs" without particular religious significance.[23]

European colonialism hardly exhibited itself in the most moral of fashions. In the early 1800s a British Quaker reported with horror that he had found British agents ripping off Indian women's breast nipples and practicing other forms of torture to acquire money for the British government.[24] Later in the century, British officials jailed educated Africans for proposing self-government in the Gold Coast.[25] It cannot be denied that Africans themselves practiced certain kinds of bondage (often like European serfdom) before Arabs and European empires enslaved them on a more widespread scale.[26] Nor should it be denied that North Africans owned many White slaves (the Mamelukes) for a period of time (a matter of historical interest unfortunately neglected by some Eurocentric scholars).[27] Yet Europe also practiced debt bondage and serfdom before it learned the use of African slaves from the Arabs, and neither African nor Arab slavery could be compared with the frequently fatal horrors of Europe's transatlantic slave-cargo ships. All peoples have elements of their history we would now acknowledge to be unconscionable.

More to the central point of this book, despite the majesty of Europe's medieval cathedrals, Europe cannot lay claim to a superior knowledge of Christianity. The idea that Christianity is a White or European religion is a myth fostered by the narrow memories of White racists, who do not distinguish between cultural adherence to a religious doctrine and full-hearted commitment to Christ as rightful Lord of one's life. The extent of one's "Christian" heritage is irrelevant in a faith that demands that each listener must *personally* accept Christ. Biblical Christianity teaches that Jesus is relevant to all peoples and not bound to Western cultural forms.[28]

But if one wishes to compare Africa and Europe for the record, Africa had Christianity earlier, parts of Africa preserved it longer, and church attendance is currently higher in most countries of Black Africa than in nearly any country of continental Europe.[29] Indeed, even in the European colonial period, relations between pragmatic colonial authorities and more committed Christians were sometimes quite strained. The authorities were often at odds with Protestant missionaries[30] and worked to suppress African Christian revival movements when these threatened Europe's economic advantage. (In 1916, for example, they arrested Prophet Braide, who preached, healed and caused rain to fall in the name of the God of Israel, when he denounced liquor and hence cut into colonial profits on the three-million-gallon-a-year rum and gin industry in West Africa.[31]) Because the majority of European traders in the colonial era were irreligious, they tended to turn Africans *away* from Christianity rather than toward it.[32]

Colonial authorities in Africa often opposed missionaries, both African-American missionaries and Whites.[33] Uncomfortable with the morally conservative lifestyles of evangelical Christians, "many British administrators were critical of the missionaries, and hostile to Christian-educated Africans."[34] Many colonial authorities in West Africa preferred Muslims over Christians as well as over adherents of traditional religions, discriminating against Christians in hiring practices.[35]

Though Western missionaries in Africa were usually ethnocentric, they tended to be less so than other Europeans,[36] perhaps because of their closer work with Africans. In other words, it was their culture, not their faith, that generated the ethnocentrism. Even when they were mistaken in supposing that Western commerce would raise Africans' standard of living and undercut the slave trade, Western missionaries like David Livingstone were among the leading opponents of African slavery, and their reports of its horrors particularly stirred the conscience of the West against it.[37]

Even so, African Christians quickly learned to read the non-European Bible for themselves; they were not solely dependent on the missionaries. After massive revival movements (like the indigenous East African revival, independent from mission churches) the African churches were often more radical than the Western missionaries. Even some of the missionaries seemed threatened by the Africans' intense devotion to Christ.[38]

Meanwhile, within Europe and the United States, Christianity led many of its true adherents into the forefront of the British and American antislavery movements—although those whose commitment to religion was more nominal "sighed with relief," as Du Bois says, when such religion "could base its denial of the ethics of Christ and the brotherhood of men upon the science of Darwin" and other European thinkers.[39] Or as the mid-twentieth-century African Pentecostal prophet Nicholas B. H. Bhengu put it, "Many Europeans are far greater heathen than can be found amongst the Bantu."[40]

Africa's Empires

Mighty kingdoms in various parts of Africa carved out empires like those in Asia and Latin America long before most of Europe north of the Mediterranean region formed such complex societies.[41] Ancient Greek, Egyptian and other sources indicate that Nubia and Egypt constituted powerful civilizations before Europeans ever emerged from barbarism.[42] Medieval Europe, in fact, drew many classics from North Africans who were translating Greek works, and many examples show that Europe in this period highly respected African civilization; a tenth-century European emperor, for instance, chose an African as his nation's patron saint.[43] Negative attitudes arose only later.[44]

Egyptian evidence shows that the Nubians south of Egypt constituted one of the oldest empires in extant history[45] and sometimes subdued Egypt itself. Israelite texts in the Bible show that the Israelites respected the "military might, political stability, and wealth" of African kingdoms.[46] (Indeed, they announce that Egypt would ultimately share Israel's hope and that many inhabitants of "Cush," their term for Africa as a whole, would ultimately join Israel in the worship of Israel's God: Psalm 68:31-32; 87:4; Isaiah 19:21-25.) The Romans and others had trade ties with West Africa and with East Africa even south of Kenya. The Roman Empire itself was not so much European (as we today define European) as Mediterranean, and far more of it was North African than northern European.[47]

Ancient Abyssinia, now called Ethiopia, was a kingdom of apparently mixed racial heritage (Arabian and African),[48] and Greek, Roman and Arab expansions could not subdue it.[49] In the sixth century the Ethiopians allied themselves with the Byzantines against the Persians and established their rule in South Arabia to protect its Christians against the Persians.[50] (Eventually, however, Ethiopia was driven out of South Arabia, the only remaining Ethiopians being slaves of the Arabs.[51] Although the Ethiopians had brought prosperity, their conquests in Arabia may have contributed to later Arab Muslim antipathy toward Christians after the rise of Muhammad.[52]) This kingdom provided what may have been the longest dynasty in world history. The ruling line claiming descent from the Queen of Sheba may have continued for nearly two thousand years before it was finally cut off by Marxist revolutionaries in the twentieth century.[53]

Blacks besides Nubians and those we might today consider mulatto were prominent during the period of Roman dominance. Some have suggested that the Carthaginian general Hannibal, who defeated Rome many times before Rome conquered Carthage,[54] may have been Black, though his wife was Spanish. Carthage, on the North African coast, was of mixed ancestry and included not only immigrant Phoenician but also indigenous African elements.[55] North Africans were trading with Africans farther south as early as 1000 B.C., and there is much evidence for Carthaginian trade with the south as early as the fifth century B.C.[56] While there may be insufficient evidence to clearly substantiate Hannibal's ancestry, other evidence for Roman contacts with Black peoples is stronger. Rome had to contend with a Black kingdom in Numidia, a great civilization that succumbed to the Vandals only in A.D. 428 and to the Arabs in the eighth century.[57] Much information remains of other African empires as well, some of them (especially those in East Africa) with a significant Christian heritage.

West African Kingdoms

The West African empire of Ghana "was old when the Arabs first mentioned it in A.D. 800."[58] It reached its apex in the eleventh century. A primary source of gold for North Africa and Europe, the kingdom was so wealthy that the Arab geographer El Bekri reported in 1067 that Ghana's army was made up of 200,000 men and the ruler's castle boasted sculpture and painted windows.[59] This empire flourished until it was crushed in 1076 by Sanhaja Berbers who had been converted to Islam. It managed to continue in a weakened state for some time afterward.[60]

Similarly, the West African kingdom of Songhay ruled an area perhaps the size of Europe throughout the Middle Ages. It had advanced communication, literature, roads and so forth, and its slavery was less exploitive than Europe's came to be.[61] Its leading city, Timbuktu, was one of the greatest intellectual centers of medieval times, housing about one hundred thousand residents.[62] The city celebrated its orchestras and music, jewels and gold, fencing, poetic recitations, chess tournaments and so forth.[63] Its university (the University of Sankoré) had contacts on the Mediterranean coast,[64] trained scientists, physicians, lawyers, geographers, artists, and members of other academic disciplines.[65] The university also preserved manuscripts in various languages (scholars went there to check their Greek and Latin manuscripts). Even centuries after Songhay's destruction, a European traveler found there a man who owned and read an Arabic translation[66] of parts of Aristotle and Plato.[67]

Sunni Ali became ruler in 1464 and "became a nominal Muslim for the same economic reasons that influenced other black kings": the Arabs controlled all trade northward to Europe and to Asia. Most of his people, however, maintained their traditional African religions and resented Islam. African kings often faced the dilemma of "how to be a Muslim without alienating the people. Sunni Ali was powerful enough to play it both ways," but the Arabs and Berbers recognized "his real loyalty . . . to the traditional religion of the Africans."[68] While pronouncing the Muslim creed and showering benefaction on some Muslim scholars, he destroyed many other Muslim scholars and forbade "the observance of Islamic law among members of his court, placing an interdict, for example, on the keeping of Ramadan."[69] His paradoxical stance reflected both political and trade realities and traditional African pluralism: African society could tolerate Islam, but Islam claimed civil authority over the state and the right to forbid all other religions, and the ruler feared for Songhay's sovereignty.[70]

West Africa had first known Islam as a religion of foreign traders; many leaders eventually found Islamic identification expedient for trade with Arabs to the north, but support for traditional religions politically expedient among their own people. From around 1100 to 1600, Islam maintained itself in West Africa through "the patronage of the older African traditions" that hosted it, and only a minority elite were truly Islamized. (This undoubtedly suited some Berber and Arab Muslims. Because one should not enslave those who were already Muslims, many propagators of Islam in Africa avoided proselytizing too much, lest they reduce "the potential reservoir of slaves."[71]) From around 1700 to 1900, Muslim reform movements seeking to Arabize West African Islam would spread through the region,[72] but West Africans would continue to mix Islam with more traditional African beliefs[73] (indeed, African Muslims in the 1600s and 1700s often combined their Islam with Christianity[74]). When African Muslims retained local practices, slave traders counted their Islam inauthentic and viewed them as legitimate targets for enslavement; neighboring peoples were often accused of apostasy so they could be enslaved.[75]

Under Sunni Ali, Timbuktu launched a counteroffensive, directed not against individual Muslims but "against the influence of the ideology they professed which was regarded as incompatible with traditional African values."[76] The lack of ultimate success of the program became evident shortly after Ali's death. Ali's successor, unwilling "to compromise with Islam at all," was quickly deposed and replaced with a strong Muslim.[77] The sultan of Morocco invaded Songhay in 1582, equipped with cannons from the north. Although Songhay continued its resistance for seven decades, its feeble vestige of strength finally collapsed under the pressure.[78]

The last Black president of the university, Ahmad Babo (1556-1627), who wrote over forty works, was one of the sixteenth century's greatest scholars, but Songhay's conquerors deported him to the north to use his learning for the Moors. Because his biographies of earlier Black scholars in his kingdom were destroyed along with his other works, even the names of these scholars were obliterated from recorded history. In his *Destruction of Black Civilization,* Chancellor Williams observes:

> In the Muslim destruction of the Songhay empire, the main centers of learning with all of their precious libraries and original manuscripts were destroyed first. Then the age-old practice was adopted of seizing all the men of learning and skilled craftsmen for enslavement and service to the conquerors.[79]

Contrary to Islamic law, non-Black Muslims enslaved Black Muslims as well as Black non-Muslims, leaving mulattos furiously protesting that they were White.[80] In this case and others, the North African slave trade was so dependent on raids that when pagan slaves were in short supply, the traders enslaved even Muslim Africans who had long supplied their northern neighbors with non-Muslim slaves.[81] Williams finally mourns, "The armies of Islam continued their triumphant march in Africa, destroying its basic institutions wherever they could do so."[82]

Finally perishing from open view in the seventeenth century, Songhay was forgotten by Europe until excavations at Timbuktu and neglected Arab records brought it again to the West's attention. Had the African empire of Songhay survived, the world today might be a different place, but as Du Bois observes,

> First came the Mongol and the Turk from Asia. The Turk seized the Eastern Roman Empire and in the west drove Arab and Berber from the coast down into Africa and below the barrier of the desert sand. Armed with gunpowder, these fugitives fell on Songhay and overthrew their state and culture at Tenkadibou in 1591.[83]

Du Bois thinks that had Europe and Ethiopia not been separated, Ethiopia might have "rescued the Songhay culture"; but as it was, a once great culture fell into oblivion.[84]

Songhay and the other kingdoms mentioned above were not the only long-standing African empires. The enduring rule of the Bantu in Central Africa is well known.[85] The Portuguese also encountered a mighty and ancient empire in Benin in 1486.[86] Archaeological evidence has revealed "a 2,500 square-mile complex of earthen ramparts" in the area, dating from about 800 A.D. until that culture's conquest by the Benin kingdom; this represents "the world's second-largest man-made structure (after China's Great Wall)."[87] Mali traces its history back to the seventh century but became more famous under Gonga Musa (also "Mansa Musa"), who came to the throne in 1307. Although Malians mixed their Northwest African Islam with many traditional African beliefs,[88] they had plenty of power to exhibit outside their kingdom. Musa reportedly took sixty thousand people in his entourage to Mecca in 1324, allegedly including twelve thousand servants.[89] (Slaves regularly accompanied masters on their pilgrimages; "as late as 1960, some Tuareg notables were reported to have sold some slaves in Arabia to defray part of the expenses of the pilgrimage."[90]) But Mali declined in the fifteenth century.[91]

Other prominent kingdoms include that of Behanzin, king of Dahomey, who repeatedly defeated French imperialists until he was himself defeated by a Senegalese mulatto acting in the service of France.[92] Learning from the fate of neighboring peoples, the Mossi Empire allowed Muslims in the land only for trade, not proselytizaton (which often became a first step toward Arab control of a land). But their stand against Arab imperialism only delayed their fall; struggling in the 1890s against insuperable odds, they finally fell under control of the French instead.[93]

Southern African Kingdoms

Southern Africa had powerful empires as well, although the focus of this book does not invite us to address them in detail. The empire of Zimbabwe reportedly ruled an area the size of modern Mexico.[94] Due to overcrowding in the north, the first Bantu people migrated to the southeast Africa region between 1000 and 1200; other Bantus arrived around 1440.[95] Under Emperor Mutote and his son Matope, the whole land from Zambia to South Africa was united, hindering further Arab imperialist expansion southward.[96] At Matope's death, however, the empire splintered.[97] Once the Africans were divided, Arabs advised and funded both sides, pitting them against one another to weaken them and gain power for themselves.[98] They might have succeeded in their plan had not the Portuguese arrived before the Arabs could reap the benefits of their own tactics.[99] But the Portuguese eventually broke the kingdom, despite much war and continued uprisings.[100]

Mutote and Matope were not the only famous warrior-kings of southern Africa. The Zulu monarch Chaka was one of the most powerful—though also one of the most brutal and tyrannical—conquerors in history.[101] And Moshesh, king of the Basutos, outwitted and defeated both the British and the Boers in South Africa.[102]

North and East African Kingdoms and Christian History[103]

Not only Africa's military and economic power but also its social and religious history rivaled or surpassed that of contemporary Europe. During the time of the Roman Empire, which (after the overthrow of Carthage) encompassed a sophisticated and flourishing civilization in North Africa as well as southern Europe, Europe north of the Mediterranean consisted chiefly of warring barbarian tribes. When northern barbarians sacked Rome in the fourth century A.D., Roman civilization collapsed in the western Mediterranean, setting back southern European civilization. In time the barbarians began to appreciate some elements of the civilization they had overrun; they even began to listen to the teachings of Christian missionaries (although they generally had martyred the first of them).[104]

Although urban civilization showed fewer signs of life in Europe over the next thousand years or so, monasteries sprang up as centers of learning, and many European tribes were gradually Christianized at least in name. The Roman Catholic Church began to exercise authority in Europe; this was sometimes good and sometimes bad, depending on how corrupt or devout the church's leaders were in a given generation. Sometimes true Christians who spoke out against injustice or tried to translate the Bible into the language of the common people were killed, just like members of other faiths who ran up against the church hierarchy. But there were always movements of genuine Christians, many seeking reform within the church and many affecting the thinking of others.

Western history books often report such developments in Europe but neglect important religious developments in other parts of the world. The Eastern Orthodox Church, for example, had meanwhile sent missionaries eastward; there is now solid evidence that these missionaries established churches in China and probably traveled as far east as Korea, Japan and Southeast Asia by the ninth century.[105]

North Africa

The North African theologian Tertullian is usually credited as the creator of

Latin Christianity in its traditional form.[106] By the end of the second century North Africa was so thoroughly Christianized that Tertullian could protest to the emperor: "We have left nothing to you but the temples of your gods!" And, to paraphrase his following argument, "Why do you think we Christians want to take over the empire? If we wanted to, we would have done so by now— we already outnumber your legions!"[107] Christianity developed earlier and spread faster in North Africa than in most other parts of the Empire; while the main language of the Roman church remained Greek, Latin Christianity originated there, ultimately shaping the thought of the Roman church.[108] Martyrdom only further inflamed the zeal of the North African Christians.[109]

Even in the nineteenth century, European scholar Theodor Mommsen acknowledged that "through Africa Christianity became the religion of the world."[110] Nearly half of the most prominent church leaders in the first few centuries (such as Origen, Cyprian, Athanasius and Augustine) were North African,[111] and probably a fair number of these were dark in complexion.[112] Christianity spread in Egypt so strongly that that nation remained majority Christian into the tenth century,[113] and to this day at least 10 percent of its population remains Christian,[114] despite the historic obstacles this Coptic people, representing Egypt's pre-Arab population, has had to face.[115] Their numbers "declined to their present minority position" especially in the thirteenth through sixteenth centuries, through massive Arab immigration and repression by the Mamelukes (formerly White slaves), partly in reprisal for Europe's Crusades.[116]

North Africa was one of the gospel's securest homes. As John S. Mbiti puts it, "Christianity in Africa is so old that it can rightly be described as an indigenous, traditional and African religion. Long before the start of Islam in the seventh century, Christianity was well established all over north Africa, Egypt, parts of the Sudan and Ethiopia."[117]

But shortly after Rome fell to northern European barbarian hordes, the barbarians streamed into North Africa, devastating its civilization (c. 429).[118] The Donatist Berbers of North Africa initially welcomed the Germanic invaders, anticipating deliverance from Roman rule.[119] But the European invaders were Arians, who often persecuted and repressed the orthodox teachers of North Africa.[120] As centers of teaching disintegrated, the North African church grew weaker. (Of course even from the start, *some* North African Christianity, like much Roman Christianity then and much North American Christianity today, had been Christian in name alone.[121]) Thus when Muhammad began his conquests, the North African church was so disunited that Islam's armies readily began their sweep across North Africa in the seventh century.[122]

Egypt, in fact, tired of Byzantine rule (especially its repression of Monophysites),[123] welcomed the Arabs in A.D. 641. The initial treaty promised Egyptian Christians religious freedom provided they would pay a poll tax.[124] But in the eighth and ninth centuries Muslims destroyed centuries of Coptic art; heavy financial pressures, including on the monasteries, also made life difficult for the Copts.[125] During most of this period, however, persecutions were only intermittent, and the successor of a persecutor of Christians "even permitted Copts who had been forced to accept Islam to return to their Christian faith."[126] Beginning in 1250, however, the (White) Mamelukes seriously repressed the Copts, till by the fourteenth century they had become only a small portion of Egypt's population.[127] A revival of the Coptic church's self-esteem came in the mid-nineteenth century.[128]

In time all of North Africa, which had been mainly Christian, fell to Islam. Preceding centuries of internal strife (the Donatist schism), repression over secondary doctrinal issues by others who claimed the same Christian faith (Rome and Byzantium) and repression imposed by advocates of more serious distortions of the Christian faith (the Arians) had rendered the North African Christians weak and susceptible to collapse.[129] In a very real sense it was professed Christians rather than Muslims who undermined Christianity in North Africa; to some extent the Arabs were just cleaning up after them.

Under Islamic law Christians were welcome to convert to Islam; otherwise they were given the status of second-class citizens and charged a tax that many peasants could not afford to pay. Muslims converting back to Christianity could be (and sometimes have been) tortured or killed.[130] In 1048 Arab invaders took Cyrenaica, Tripoli and Tunis, and some pressed on into Morocco.[131] Muslim rulers permitted some Christian communities to continue in Mauritania and port cities because of trade with Europe, but though they allowed Christians to have churches and priests, they forbade sharing Christianity with non-Christians.[132] Outside influences were not particularly potent in this environment. Some members of European religious orders who traveled to North Africa to discuss Christianity with Arabs in the thirteenth century were welcomed (for instance, St. Francis of Assisi); others were martyred.[133]

Some local Christians persisted for many centuries, but outside of Egypt, most were eventually stamped out. When the Turks took Tunis in 1583, they dethroned the more tolerant Muslim ruler; violently hostile toward Christianity, the new rulers reportedly forced the remaining Christians to choose Islam or die.[134] Thus most of North Africa became Muslim in faith and came to be dominated especially by Arab peoples and civilization.[135]

Nubia

Farther south in Africa, however, Christianity continued to grow—as it had for some time, indeed from the very beginning of the Christian mission. According to the Bible, the very *first* Gentile Christian (the first Christian who was not Jewish) was an Ethiopian, a Black African official of Queen Candace (*kandak'e*—Acts 8:27). Because he was a "eunuch," he would have probably reminded early readers of Acts of another African eunuch in the Old Testament— a foreign official in the royal court of Judah, who was one of the prophet Jeremiah's only two faithful allies.[136] The author of Acts probably intends this account to symbolize the great spread of Christianity in Africa, which he expected and which has in fact happened.[137]

This first non-Jewish Christian in the New Testament was plainly from Africa. In ancient Greek and Roman usage, "Ethiopia" did not mean only what it means today (that land was traditionally called Abyssinia).[138] In ancient Mediterranean literature "Ethiopians" meant all Black Africans, and other texts mention a particular African kingdom whose queen was titled "the Candace."[139] This kingdom was an ancient and powerful Nubian civilization with its capital in Meroe, which had continued since around 750 B.C.[140] and whose people were so dark-skinned that they became the standard by which the Mediterranean world defined blackness.[141] Archaeology attests both this kingdom's magnificent splendor as an empire in its own right and its relations with Rome.[142]

The official's witness might have been more significant in African history had the empire of Meroe not begun declining by the mid-first century A.D., "almost certainly" because of "the rise of a rival trading empire, with its centre at Axum" in East Africa.[143] The Nuba people invaded the territory of Meroe in several waves, until the Axumites finished Meroe off in the mid-300s and the Nubians began to form new kingdoms in the region.[144] Yet Christianity spread southward into Nubia again in the 300s and 400s, this time from Egypt, till Nubia became predominantly Christian.[145] The Ballana rulers, practicing human sacrifice, were not Christian but tolerated the spread of Christianity until the kings themselves were converted in the 500s.[146] One of the most renowned monks of the earliest centuries of Christianity was a tall Black African Christian called Father Moses.[147]

Unlike many other peoples, Nubia adopted Christianity without coming under the sway of Roman law;[148] having done so, Nubia clung to it tenaciously. Despite organizational weaknesses of Nubian Christianity, the church survived the Islamic conquest of much of North Africa. Nubia's skilled archers repelled the Arabs twice at Dongola,[149] and unable to conquer Nubia after taking Egypt in 641, the Arabs made an unusual treaty (Arabic *Baqt*) in 652.[150] Notably, this was "the *only* treaty in which the Arabs recognized the independence of a non-Muslim state; Aswan was their only officially accepted frontier."[151] One writer suggests that the Arabs intended this treaty "to make their failure appear to the world as a victory of some sort."[152] The treaty was "a compromise guaranteeing the Nubians independence and freedom in return for an annual tribute of 360 slaves and the obligation to maintain a mosque. . . . This agreement remained in force for six hundred years and enabled the Nubian states to prosper and develop unhindered."[153] Lest the treaty appear to the Nubians to be demanding tribute, however, the Arabs portrayed it as a commercial exchange, "agreeing to pay in exchange wheat, barley and wine at a value in excess of the gifts by the Africans."[154] The Arabs wanted to build mosques in Nubia and gain access for Arab traders, and reciprocally they permitted Nubians the right to build churches in Egypt. But of course churches in Egypt were being converted to mosques anyway, and the Arabs knew that the Nubians had no expansionist aims toward the north, in contrast to their own expansionist aims into the Sudan.[155] The Arabs were looking out for their own interests; besides the slaves acquired under the treaty, the Arabs took other Nubian slaves by trade.[156]

Whereas Egypt's Christians virtually invited their Arab conquerors in to liberate them from the Eastern Roman Empire, the Black Nubians refused submission and even tried to help free the now-oppressed Egyptian Copts from the new Arab empire.[157] The Nubian resistance was spirited; the story is told of a Black virgin who preferred beheading to capture, and tricked her Muslim captors into slaying her.[158] One may understand the Nubians' resistance when one pictures the conditions to which Egypt's Copts were ultimately subjected. Egyptian Christians were forced to wear identifying clothing that set them apart, "were required by state policy to pay tribute [and] offer hospitality to Muslims," and "were forbidden to erect new churches or monasteries or to display any aspect of Christian practice."[159]

Chancellor Williams recounts the intervention of the Nubian kingdom of Makuria on behalf of the now-persecuted Christians of Egypt in 745, when Omar, initiating a de facto holy war, imprisoned the patriarch and began "destroying churches or converting them into mosques."

Since the Patriarch of Egypt was the head of all Christian churches in Africa, the Africans regarded this latest onslaught against the churches as an insult as well as a breach of the peace treaty, now almost a hundred years old. . . .

When the arrogant Omar ignored all protests and pleas, the African king headed an army of 100,000 men and marched on the Arab center of power in Lower Egypt. The governor of Egypt quickly freed the Patriarch and promised to leave the Christians and their churches alone.[160] The Nubian king on various occasions protected the patriarch of Alexandria, but Arab rulers also sometimes grew suspicious of the Coptic Egyptian church's African ties. Al-Yazuri (ruled 1047-1058) increased the economic burden on the Copts and imprisoned Christodulus, the patriarch, when he was "falsely accused of inciting the Nubian king to withhold" tribute.[161] In 1074 Christodulus was again arrested, accused "of having ordered Buqtar, the archbishop of Nubia, to destroy the mosques there"; he was, however, found innocent, and his accuser was executed.[162]

From reading Arab reports from the seventh through the fifteenth centuries about the Black civilizations to the south,[163] one might think that Christianity was Africa's indigenous religion and wonder how aware these Arabs were of Christianity elsewhere; the churches were thoroughly Africanized. But this African civilization, more prosperous and advanced than that of the Arabs, had invited their conquest.[164]

Arab Egypt implemented policies designed to erode Nubia's strength, hoping to make it a vassal kingdom.[165] Far less united than Arab Egypt, Nubia could not provide a long-range response. Du Bois points out that Islam's flood "was held back for two centuries by a solid Christian phalanx in Abyssinia and Nubia.... It was not until 1270 that Saladin crushed the Nubians and annexed Nubia," and even then Nubia regained its freedom and remained free until the sixteenth century.[166] (Moreover, most Black peoples who initially succumbed to Arab imperialism did not do so willingly. The early period of Arab expansion in North Africa witnessed many Black revolts against Arab rulers; in 869, for example, tens of thousands of Black slaves revolted, and subsequently they controlled the Euphrates Delta for over a decade.[167])

The Christian era in Nubia was marked by prosperity and, till the later part of the period, unity; in contrast to Nubia's former assumption of the divinity of kings, the Christian period also introduced a separation between church and state.[168] Christian Nubia was a brilliant civilization, largely forgotten by history until archaeologists in the second half of the twentieth century began to bring its remarkable accomplishments to light.[169] The Nubian church perished only in the late fourteenth or early fifteenth century, as its influence declined and that of hostile Islamic neighbors increased.[170] "In the fifteenth century, the once powerful kingdoms broke up into a maze of warring principalities, and the coup de grace to medieval Nubian civilization was dealt by the invasion of hordes of Arab nomads."[171]

Once the Arabs had finally subdued Nubia and placed a Muslim king on the throne, he immediately signaled Nubia's new direction by turning a church in the capital into a mosque.[172] Christianity lingered, but eventually Islam prevailed, "sustained by the influx of marauding Arab tribesmen."[173] The nearby Christian state 'Alwa was also in decline, unable to secure trained priests from Alexandria or Abyssinia to teach the people, until it too succumbed.[174]

Abyssinia

Abyssinia, or Ethiopia, in East Africa also holds a very significant place in Christian history; Christianity became the religion of that land at roughly the same time that it became the religion of the Roman Empire. Abyssinia's Axumite king Ezana (also spelled Aezanas) converted to Christianity sometime around 333 and made that the state religion. Many Christians already lived in Axum when Frumentius and Edesius began working to spread the Christian message there, and Ezana, who counted these ministers among his friends, had supported their efforts even before his conversion.[175] This East African church accepted the same doctrines (such as the Trinity—a term coined by Tertullian, a North African theologian[176]) as the North African, Greek and Roman churches—doctrines formally recognized at Nicea (A.D. 325), Constantinople (381) and Ephesus (431).[177] The East African Christians maintained close relations with Egyptian and Syrian Christianity and functioned as part of the Eastern church.[178]

Ethiopia's rapid and solid conversion to the Christian faith will give pause to anyone familiar with the history of Christian mission. The barbarians of northern Europe martyred most of the early missionaries sent to them, as did the Roman Empire; both of these regions were won over only slowly and then often only nominally. Ethiopia, by contrast, may have been the most open and ready soil in which Christianity ever took root.[179]

Inscriptions from Ezana's time state that his empire stretched across much of central Africa into Arabia and on the Nile as well.[180] After the same king reconquered Saba in South Arabia, about 335-370, Christianity spread freely in South Arabia, though facing a period of deadly persecution (it had already spread peacefully in much of Arabia, however; six Arabian bishops were present at the Christian Council of Nicea in 325).[181] After the rise of Islam, it was this East African empire in what is now Ethiopia (alongside Nubia) that had to defend the rights of oppressed Christian minorities in Muslim lands. As William Leo Hansberry, the founding scholar of Howard University's African history program, points out:

> Between 1322 and 1327 the Byzantine emperor and Pope John XXII sent deputations to the sultan of Egypt to plead the cause of the Christians in that country. An appeal of the same character was also dispatched to Egypt by the Ethiopian king Amda Tseyon, warning the sultan that unless the repressive measures being imposed on the Egyptian Christians were revoked, he would institute a similar program of proscriptions against the Muslims in Ethiopia. In addition, the Ethiopian king threatened to divert the course of the Nile, which would have had the effect of transforming much of Egypt into a desert.[182]

Amda Tseyon's threat worked, but during the reign of his successor (Newaya Krestos, 1344-1372) the sultan had Abba Mark, the Alexandrian Christian patriarch, imprisoned. Newaya Krestos again threatened the sultan, who "not only freed the patriarch but also abrogated his harsh measures against his Christian subjects."[183]

This African empire probably remained more solidly Christian than Europe did.[184] Medieval Europe remained aware of its existence,[185] and Christianity continues in this region today. When we read about Christianity in the medieval period we usually think of Europe, because that is what we have been taught by White Christians contemplating their own heritage; but Christianity was no less an African faith, and in contrast to some other faiths, it began there without conquests or force of arms.

In the following centuries Islamic opposition ultimately did separate Ethiopia from its Christian siblings elsewhere in the world, isolating two streams of Christianity from each other to the impoverishment of both.[186] The initial relations between Arab Muslims and African Christians had been positive; Axum's ruler welcomed Muslims fleeing from Mecca, which was originally hostile to them. Ethiopians also allowed Muslims to settle on their coast.[187]

But Arab Muslims were exerting severe pressure on Axum in the tenth century,[188] and in time the Arab regime in Egypt "blocked attempts by Christian Ethiopia to establish contacts with the outside world" because it feared that Ethiopia might make common cause with professedly Christian medieval Europe, where anti-Arab sentiments were building toward the terrible era of the Crusades.[189] Ethiopian "pilgrims in Jerusalem in 1345-7 complained that the Sultan of Egypt had imposed a ban on Ethiopian travellers through his country" to keep them from contacting Europeans.[190] In the sixteenth century the forces of Islam stepped up their imperialistic advances southward. Ahmed ibn Ibrahim el Ghazi, the emir of Harrar, invaded Ethiopia and persecuted its church; Lebna-Dengel, Ethiopia's emperor (1508-1540), fought valiantly against the invaders and finally sought Portugal's help, but the Ethiopian scholar Ephraim Isaac mourns that the help came too late. By the time it arrived,

> the Ethiopian Church lost not only many of its great teachers, writers and leaders but also many of its treasures of literature and art. It was this second phase of Moslem onslaught that brought the golden age of monastic life in Ethiopia to a close. Once again, as after Islamic pressure of the seventh century the Ethiopian Church sank into eclipse.

But the Ethiopian Church "regained internal stability" in the mid-seventeenth century, establishing itself against both Arab and Portuguese influences; from this point Ethiopia remained strong.[191]

Isaac points that the three largest monotheistic religions dominate the traditions of three major Semitic groups in that region: Judaism is central to Jewish tradition, Islam to Arab tradition, and Christianity to Ethiopian/East African tradition.[192] Most recently Ethiopian Christians have survived repression from a harsh Marxist regime; instead of shriveling under sometimes deadly persecution, however, the churches grew.[193]

While Ethiopian Christianity prevailed, however, it historically exerted little missionary vision to expand elsewhere in Africa or beyond.[194] Nubia had likewise exerted little missionary vision beyond its borders and in time, having depended on Alexandria for trained clergy, lacked teachers to continue instructing its own people in the Christian faith.[195] In military terms, no matter how strong one's defense, eventual defeat is nearly inevitable when an army has no offense.

If many European missionaries stirred the gospel anew in Africa, it was not because no African Christians had existed before their arrival. It was because in that period only the European Christians had discovered Christ's command to evangelize all nations (Mt 24:14; 28:18-20; Acts 1:8). They brought to us again a gift that should have been our birthright long before. As one writer points out, no one would even think of calling Christianity a "White man's religion" today if more Egyptian, Ethiopian and Nubian Christians had spread the gospel to the rest of Africa.[196]

Egypt

Although we have discussed some of Egypt's Christian and Arab history, we have said little about Pharaonic Egypt in this chapter; we reserve that discussion primarily for chapter four. Afrocentric scholars have laid claim to Egypt as part of Africa, whereas some other scholars have disputed this claim. The reasons for the dispute are complex, though Afrocentric arguments are sensible: in the geographical sense, Egypt has been part of the African continent for as long as the continents have been divided according to their current classification. In the cultural sense, Egypt has always had ties with Black peoples to the south and west as well as with Asian civilizations to the northeast.[197] The skin of the lighter northern Egyptians was darker than that of most peoples to the north, though lighter than that of most peoples to the south. Because of the way our nation's history has defined "Black," we can identify with lighter as well as darker people of color in history (many of them looked just like some of us do).

Various modern peoples (foremost among whom are the modern Egyptians themselves) lay claim to the heritage of ancient Egypt. This heritage includes both positive points in which we can take pride—such as technological and military supremacy that would be comparable to the position of the United States in today's world—and some moral flaws with which we would not want to identify, including brutal group slavery and the oppression of the large peasant class.[198] Although for the purposes of our work we regard Egypt as African, and according to the modern division of continents Egypt is indisputably African, we will discuss it as a special issue later under the question of color, because many people still dispute the ancient Egyptians' complexion.

Suffice it to say, however, that even apart from the special case of Egypt, Africa has a history no less glorious than any other people on any terms. Like Egypt and other mighty empires, Africans controlled great civilizations in periods when Europe consisted of disorganized tribes warring against one another. Yet like other non-European peoples, Africans did not have the sudden technological advances that permitted certain European powers to colonialize the rest of the world in recent times. Today, when almost everyone admits that colonialism and empires were morally wrong, the fact that non-Europeans were not responsible for establishing the inhuman empires of modern centuries can hardly be viewed as a fault. (Of course, the inhuman non-European empires of some previous centuries may likewise require reevaluation.[199])

Is the Geographical Division of Humanity Useful?
In any case, the very practice of dividing humanity by continent is open to question. The abuse of such divisions is evident when a White writer claims that Europe is "the *unique* source" of ideas like individual freedom.[200] Presumably the writer links his mainly northern European ancestors (mentioned elsewhere in his book) with civilizations like ancient Greece because Europe now includes both—despite the fact that Greece belonged to an ancient Mediterranean cul-

tural continuum rather than one defined by modern definitions of Europe. Would this writer allow us the same privilege of treating Egypt as a purely African civilization because it is on the modern continent of Africa? Elsewhere in his book he seems to balk at such a proposal.[201]

What is the objective boundary between Africa and Asia? If it is the Sinai desert east of Egypt and south of Israel/Palestine, the boundary seems arbitrary. Arabia could be viewed as part of Asia, and Egypt as part of Africa. Yet the ancient inhabitants of South Arabia were ethnically closer to East Africans than say, to East Asians. And what is the boundary between Europe and Asia? Whereas most continents are separated from others by water, the only boundary between Europe and Asia is the Caucasus Mountains. So why are Europe and Asia separate continents? Perhaps simply because earlier Europeans, loath to associate themselves with the culturally distinct peoples of Asia, wanted Asia on a separate continent when they drew the map. Europeans drew the maps that are used today, and they drew them for their own cultural purposes; there is nothing sacred about the boundaries of the continents as they are currently divided.

Should we then divide continents by culture instead of by arbitrary geographical boundaries? Russia straddles Europe and Asia, both in its location and in its cultures. Arab culture exerts a heavy influence throughout North Africa, so that many thinkers today classify North Africa culturally with the Middle East, just as Guyana, which is located in South America, is classified as part of the Caribbean rather than as part of Spanish-speaking Latin America. This problem of examining cultural spheres becomes even more acute as we move back in time.

Assigning Egypt to only one cultural sphere is more complicated than we might at first guess. Ancient Egyptian literature defines the different cultural worlds within which Egypt moved in various periods of its history. In the second millennium B.C., Egypt's sphere of diplomatic and military exchange included especially the Hittites to the north, the Babylonians to the northeast and the Canaanites (whom Egypt often controlled) in the same direction. Yet although these borders were threatened more rarely, Egypt also had interests to the west in Libya and to the south in Nubia. After the Hyksos were expelled Egypt reconquered both Nubia and Syria-Palestine; although Syria-Palestine was allowed its own officials under Egypt, the Egyptians controlled every level of government in Nubia. Displaying "little respect for the indigenous way of life," they "pursued a policy of deliberate acculturation, attempting to break down the ethnic identity of the Nubians by forcing them to adopt Egyptian manners and customs."[202] They ruled Nubia for nearly five centuries, till the final century of the New Kingdom.[203]

Nubia also subdued Egypt a number of times, in one period earning a widespread reputation in the ancient world for its just and merciful rule. In contrast to Egypt's earlier policy of replacing Nubian culture with Egyptian culture, the Nubian rulers brought peace to Egypt, respecting and even observing Egyptian customs while ruling there.[204] Egypt had active borders on all sides: the primary continuum of culture in which Pharaonic Egypt participated stretched from north, especially northeast, Africa (Nubia northward) to the eastern region that is now Iraq. This was the same cultural setting in which Israel moved in the Old Testament.

By the time of Augustus Caesar, however, the cultural framework in which Egypt functioned was different. Now Egypt was oppressively controlled by Rome. The Roman Empire stretched throughout the Mediterranean world, and the eastern regions once controlled by Babylonia and Assyria were now under the control of Parthia. Egypt and Israel had become primarily Mediterranean, rather than Near Eastern, societies.[205] Documents from this period give evidence of considerable mobility between North Africa and other parts of the empire; the whole Roman Empire was a Mediterranean culture with large North African and southern European elements.[206]

Under Arab domination, Egypt became part of yet another cultural continuum. Molefi Kete Asante, a leading Afrocentric scholar, points out that the Arabs who controlled Egypt from 641 on had

little respect or appreciation for the classical civilization they found in the Nile Valley. Having destroyed the organic structure of the African society they found in Egypt, reinstituted the ban on the Egyptian language, and allowed the great ancestral holy places to lie in ruin, the Arabs created the perfect opportunity for the distortion of the African heritage of Egypt.[207]

Coptic peasants had preserved much of the language of ancient Egypt until the Arab period,[208] but by the twelfth century Arabic was replacing Coptic as Egypt's primary language.[209] Even agricultural practices that had been part of Egyptian culture since prehistoric times were suppressed by Arab domination.[210] As throughout the Arabs' medieval expansion, Islamization inevitably produced Arabization.[211]

Under the empire of the Ottoman Turks and under the British Empire, Egypt again came under different and culturally unsympathetic spheres.[212] Today Egypt retains some of its Arab, Coptic and African orientations, though one element sometimes comes to the fore and suppresses the others. (For example, the killings of Coptic Christians by Islamic fundamentalists and the torture of prominent Muslim converts to Christianity by some police forces have aroused international ire.[213] Egypt's destruction of Nubian-African culture to the south, occasioned especially by flooding necessitated by dams, has been less publicized but has similarly hurt indigenous culture.[214]) Egypt is African, but Egypt is not African *alone,* nor are all (or most) Africans Egyptian.

All this is to say that if we divided the continents by culture, the divisions would change every century or two. This is one of the problems with merely geographical identification. Further, Africa includes many peoples and diverse cultures, and our ancestors, derived from many of those cultures in West Africa, forged a new culture in the Western Hemisphere. While we rightly identify with Africa and our heritage there, the unique heritages of African-Caribbean culture and African-American culture are no less valid and important to us than the various African cultures of our brothers and sisters who remained behind. Our own history as a people of African beauty and spirit, forced to adapt to and survive in a new environment, has demonstrated the strength and resiliency of our people in special ways. Consequently, we do identify with the land from which we spring; but we also identify with the cultural community of which we are a part, the Black American community. We too have some special gifts to offer the world.

Conclusion
We identify to some extent with our history on a geographic basis, but that is not the sole or most prominent basis for identification today. Africa's history and culture are in no way inferior to those of Europe, contrary to earlier European propaganda. Though imperfect like that of all cultures, much of Africa's history is also noble and beautiful. Indeed, as former slaves, we African-Americans of all people know some of *European* history's moral flaws! No culture has been above criticism.

But if geographic identification is not adequate, we should explore color or race as a basis for identification. First (in chapter three) we will turn to the question of racial identification: why is it important to us? Second (in chapter four) we will turn to Egypt and Israel, two non-European peoples significant in the history of Western civilization. After we examine those peoples, we must return to the question of racial identification. Contrary to categories established by nineteenth-century Eurocentric thinkers, we will find that a deeper bond unites us than merely the color of our skin.

3
Black Is Still Beautiful: Identification by Color

AFTER POLICE MISTAKENLY SEARCHED A *BLACK ENTERPRISE* MAGAZINE executive, they explained that they had been looking for a short-haired Black man. "Well, that narrows it down to about 6 million people," he replied.[1]

This provides one typical example of what it means to be Black in the United States of America. A less typical but more frightening reminder that racism is a reality today is the rapid spread of Neo-Nazi and other White supremacist groups. Not all groups have proved as deadly as the terrorists (with alleged White supremacist connections[2]) responsible for the 1995 bombing in Oklahoma City, but hate crimes, including murder, are on the rise. Lest any readers assume they live in a "safe" part of the country, Klanwatch has identified such groups in nearly every state of the Union, including in northeastern states (for example, three groups in Massachusetts, four in Delaware, six in New Jersey, nine in Michigan, twelve in Illinois, thirteen in Ohio and seventeen in Pennsylvania).[3] In one year Aryan Nations, a White supremacist group some of whose followers have been convicted of armed robbery and murder, has spread from three to twenty-two states and seeks to infiltrate antigovernment militias.[4] One of the biggest dangers of such groups, however, is that they allow the more common expressions of racism to appear mild by comparison.

Why do people judge one another on the basis of skin color? One reason we identify people on the basis of their skin color is that the first characteristic we notice in a person we meet is his or her appearance. Only after we get to know the person do more important characteristics challenge our initial impressions. Skin color is one of the most obvious physical characteristics to our eyes. Yet the obviousness of skin color does not explain why our society is divided on the basis of color, or why its most conspicuous dividing line (in areas such as employment and marriage) is between Black people and White people, not simply among various shades of color from the darkest black to the palest white.

This division of society cannot be attributed to a mere notice of complexion differences (which could be appreciated as beautiful as easily as used for separation). This societal division can be attributed only to racism. And racism based on color is not a universal phenomenon; it is rooted in the particular histories of the societies that practice it. To explain why identification on the basis of race is important to us, we must survey briefly the history of race in U.S. society.

If a Christian Afrocentric work does anything with regard to color, it must examine the question of color in ancient Egypt and Israel. (This is partly because the question constitutes a major theme in popular contemporary books on "Blacks in the Bible.") We will turn to that question at length in chapter four. Before we can do so, however, we must explain why the issues of identification by color and a common background under oppression are important to us.

Some suppose that even addressing the issue of racial identification is itself racist. Due to this nation's racial history, however, racial identification occurs automatically, consciously or unconsciously; to address the issue properly, we must describe this current state of affairs before prescribing appropriate ways to engage in such identification. This chapter is thus an introduction of sorts to chapters four through six, and a reader who already understands the nature of the question may feel free to skip directly to the next chapter.

Racism and Color: Inextricably Linked?
Racism in the sense of preferring one's people to other peoples is as old as recorded history, but racism in the sense of dehumanizing others on the basis of their *skin color* is a modern phenomenon.[5]

The ancient Greeks, for instance, thought of themselves as the noblest of peoples, and the Greek philosopher Aristotle said that others were fit only to be enslaved.[6] But no one despised other peoples simply on the basis of the color of their skin. Egyptians came in various shades and had no conception of race in the modern sense;[7] Herodotus spoke of certain Ethiopians as the most handsome of all peoples; and Greco-Roman literature in general expressed positive views of Africans, starting from Homer, who emphasized that Africans were an especially pious and just people, favored by the gods.[8] Arabs enslaved Africans, but not originally on the basis of race. Even the British who enslaved Africans initially viewed the slavery of a given people as a matter of chance rather than a matter of color,[9] and intermarriages produced mulatto nobles in continental Europe (such as the chevalier de St. Georges and General Alexander Dumas).[10]

Racism and Slavery in Early U.S. History

In the United States, however, the situation was different, although it started in the same way. Slavery already existed among some West African peoples, but Arab slave traders first introduced African slaves into Europe among the Spanish and Portuguese.[11] The British colonies initially permitted a different practice: indentured servitude, a seven-year term of service after which the servant was to be freed and awarded land to make his own living. (This was based on an Old Testament practice meant to wean the Israelites, newly freed from slavery themselves, away from practicing slavery at all.[12]) Poor British people voluntarily entered into indentured servitude, hoping to find more economic prosperity in the New World at the end of their service; African slaves were procured from the Spanish and Portuguese and brought into indentured servitude as well.

The first Africans in English America thus were not slaves, but arrived on these same socioeconomic terms on which many English and Irish settlers came.[13] In August 1619—one year before the *Mayflower* landed and over a century before George Washington's birth—twenty African Christians captured from a Spanish slave ship arrived in Jamestown. Two of them, Anthony and Isabella, married, and they named their first son William Tucker in 1624. William was the first African-American in the modern sense, and he was not a slave.[14] Over the next four decades, Black Americans bought land, "voted, testified in court and mingled with whites on a basis of equality. They owned other Negro servants. And at least one Negro imported and paid for a white servant whom he held in servitude."[15]

The colonists quickly learned, however, that it was more economically advantageous to exploit African servants than European ones. If they oppressed British subjects by extending their term of service or refusing to give them their due at the end, the servants could appeal to the king for help. African servants, however, had no one to whom to appeal; further, they could not blend into local populations if they escaped, and this distinction made their recapture easier.[16] Consequently, the exploitation of African slave labor was imported into British territory. The basis was economic; racism—dehumanizing African peoples based on their skin color—was simply an ideology created to justify economic exploitation and relieve "tender" European consciences.[17]

Once economic motives supported racism, it quickly became the law of the land, affecting primarily Africans but by extension all those not clearly from Europe. As Ellis Cose notes:

> Americans have always defined themselves largely on the basis of race. The nation's first citizenship statute, passed in 1790, limited naturalization to "aliens being free white persons." That law (though amended to grant citizenship rights to blacks after the Civil War) stood until 1952. It forced generations of nonwhite petitioners, including natives of India and Japan, to try to prove—as late as the 1940s—that they were white.[18]

Other racist policies followed in the wake of Africans' enslavement; some of these policies remain part of American society to this day. Interracial marriages had existed among Black and White indentured servants (as among Blacks and Whites through much of history), but once slaveholders saw to it that any children of such unions were reckoned as slaves, interracial marriages gradually became illegal throughout the southern states.[19] Such prejudice against interracial marriage (as opposed to rape and seduction) hardened a barrier between the races that did not exist in other slave societies which had no such rules (such as Portuguese Brazil and the Spanish empire).[20] It also became a volatile cultural issue that political race-baiters associated with the dangers of integration.[21] After the Civil War southern legislators gradually enacted racial "purity" laws defining as Black those with merely one Black great-great-grandparent.[22]

Discriminatory customs were not limited to the South. Even after slavery was abolished in the North, northern Blacks could not attend schools unless they had their own, and Black men were rarely granted employment, with more recent White immigrants preferred.[23] Although there were many notable exceptions of northern Blacks who advanced economically, White society even in the North refused to treat our ancestors as equals[24]—though there were always some exceptions who paid a great price to help us.[25] In the eighteenth century Richard Allen eventually began the A.M.E. Church after being confronted with segregation and prejudice among White Methodists in Philadelphia. Philadelphians later burned a meeting hall to the ground because Black and White abolitionist women had met there together (the next morning, however, these abolitionists reaffirmed their resolve as Christians to continue meeting together regardless of color.)[26]

Antislavery sentiments began to stir among Whites in this country as early as the late 1700s, but regional lines hardened in time, polarizing the nation and preventing liberation until the Civil War of the 1860s. Thomas Jefferson's clause attacking England's slave trade was deleted from the Declaration of Independence to avoid offending slaveholders;[27] its inclusion would have indicated hypocrisy anyway, since Jefferson held slaves during his lifetime and at times denied that Blacks could survive in America without White help.[28] But slavery ended in the North within a few decades after the Revolution,[29] especially due to the protests of religious leaders.[30]

Despite similar sentiments in the South, however, inventions like the cotton gin (which reinforced the economic value of slavery to the South) ultimately yielded a conservative reaction to preserve slavery there.[31]

Racism After the Abolition of Slavery

After slavery was abolished, Black Americans made faster progress throughout the South than almost any other people has made in this nation's history, both politically and educationally. So great was the hunger for education that as soon as churches sent books from the North, Black schools begin to develop immediately, even around Union army camps.[32] Much of this progress, however, was short-lived.[33] When Republicans and Democrats in Congress deadlocked over the presidency, Republican Rutherford B. Hayes gained the presidency through a compromise that gave the southern Democrats what they wanted: "home rule," allowing the South to deal with the Black population in its own way. In short, the Black community's political patrons sold them out for political advantage.[34]

After federal troops were withdrawn from the South, signaling the end of Reconstruction, White racists gradually began to regain power; at the same time many *thousands* of the most courageous African-American leaders and their followers in the South were lynched.[35] After high hopes and motivation, we were forced down by murder and intimidation. "Uppity" Blacks had become too successful for some White power brokers in the late nineteenth-century South to tolerate.

Around the turn of the century "Jim Crow" laws were instituted, which totally segregated Blacks from Whites—something even slavery had not accomplished.[36] Slaveholders with smaller estates in more northward states like Virginia and North Carolina had often grown to know their slaves personally;[37] but postslavery segregation effectively excluded White people from most contact with Black people and allowed racial caricatures to develop further.

Beginning in the early 1900s, disfranchisement deprived African-Americans even of the legal right to vote for which so many had risked their lives in the early years of Reconstruction. In 1896 there were over 130,000 African-American voters in Louisiana, but just eight years later the same state had only 1 percent of that figure.[38] The basis for disfranchisement was color, pure and simple. Historians report the story of a Black Harvard graduate who sought to register to vote in Mississippi; passing the literacy requirement in English, he successfully translated texts of various languages (such as Latin and Greek) presented to him until his White examiner stumped him with Chinese.[39] Black people had been coercively and forcibly removed from the political process.

From this point forward we were forced into a strategy of "temporary" accommodation, a strategy that reduced opposition but severely limited our advancement as a race.[40] The success of accommodation was quite limited, reducing opposition but also limiting advancement and chances for integration. Many Whites began to take for granted that Black people were satisfied with their status in American society. But Black people weren't.

Thus the early twentieth century witnessed the largest mass migration movement in this nation's history, as rural Blacks began to move to the cities of the North, hoping to find jobs and a less hostile environment.[41] Whereas Atlanta witnessed a 21 percent increase in African-American residents between 1910 and 1920, Philadelphia (with its already burgeoning Black population) witnessed a 58.9 percent increase in the same period; New York, 66.5 percent; Chicago, 148.2 percent; and Detroit, 611.3 percent.[42] Rural southern Blacks (90 percent of the U.S. Black population at the beginning of the twentieth century) considered White northerners as allies in some sense. Although northern troops, decimating the economy of the South, had brought the slaves hardship—often greater economic hardship than slavery itself had entailed[43]—they had also brought liberation and supposedly the opportunity for economic and social advancement through integration into free American society.

Many abolitionists in the North had meant well, but they thought that "freedom" (as opposed to equality) was enough; they ignored biblical teachings about restitution for economic injustice, in this case to a people forcibly kidnapped, dislocated and deprived of economic capital and education.[44] Making the South free the slaves was one thing; investing one's own money in advancing the cause of freedpeople was another. Although many individual White philanthropists responded to northern Black appeals to join in funding educational and missionary outreaches to southern Blacks, it could never have been enough for the whole southern Black community,[45] and some Whites shared from the standpoint of paternalism—"good" Whites helping "poor coloreds."[46]

What this meant was that the Blacks migrating northward for jobs met not open arms but weary resistance.[47] Although Black spending was welcome, Black employees were often unwelcome (that meant the flow of cash went one way, from us to them), and Whites quickly withdrew from neighborhoods in which Blacks settled. Northern labor agents often lured uneducated Black girls from the South, promising domestic work, then employing them in brothels when they arrived.[48] It should also be noted that the Federal Housing Authority met the housing shortage in the 1950s by providing loans for new homes, but Blacks and members of other non-White groups were specifically excluded from the loans; "one black person in a block could result in having loans cut off for the entire block." Both Black and White families grew, but Black families were trapped in decaying, overcrowded cities, where resources became scarcer.[49] (No one should dismiss these observations as simply the complaints of rankled "radicals" or assume that discrimination in housing remains solely a relic of the past. Not only Black liberals but also Black conservatives have found even White "progressives" who systematically excluded Black applicants from housing once their "quotas" were met.[50])

Impoverished life in an urban ghetto does not keep people from feeling, from loving, from hoping; but it does limit their options and horizons, and ultimately can shape their character and destiny if they never encounter realistic alternatives to the role models it presents as normative. Although we are each responsible for the choices we make, our choices affect other people too, and ghetto life can shape its citizens to force them to survive there. Thus only a month after Martin Luther King Jr. moved to inner-city Chicago, his own children began to take on the hostile attitudes of their ghetto, and King had to send them back to the kind of middle-class neighborhood from which they had come. This is not to blame Dr. King for removing his children from a potentially damaging environment—but to lament that most of our people in the projects still do not have that option.[51]

Thus White racism created the cycle of poverty in the North's urban ghettos, creating with it a de facto segregation that remained even after racial barriers began to collapse throughout the South in the wake of the Civil Rights Movement.[52] (Even today, 86 percent "of white suburban Americans live in neighborhoods that are less than 1% black, meaning that the prospects for the country depend largely on how its cities fare in the hands of a suburban electorate."[53]) Martin Luther King's nonviolent tactics brought change throughout the South, but his greatest failure came against the ethnic power structures of Chicago.[54] To this day Malcolm X (whose "By any means necessary" is usually quoted out of context) is the icon of many northern ghettos; likewise, the creeds of Black Power and Black Nationalism seem to make more sense than nonviolence in many cities because most Whites seem too protective of their own interests to heed Dr. King's nonviolent approach. (Though only a few Whites find sufficient incentive or connection to the Black community to risk challenging stereotypes by joining our poorer communities, the police forces and public administrations of such communities are often disproportionately White.[55]) Even King himself realized the failure of the earlier Civil Rights approach for urban ghettos toward the end of his abruptly terminated life. But unfortunately, the people who usually get hurt when we turn to violence are our own businesses and those non-Blacks who are on our side.[56]

The Lessons: Color and Beyond Color

This history of racial tension illustrates two points for us. First, it illustrates the importance of color in this country; our history *forces* us to look at our situation through the prism of color. Whites may pretend that color does not matter, because the dominant society as a whole reflects their perspectives and color does not need to matter to them; but we do not have that luxury. Second, however, this history of racial tension illustrates that the real issue goes beyond skin tone: the issue is not color but power. Those with the power want to protect their vested interests. Those with the power in this nation have traditionally been White people. But the powerful do not abuse their power because their skin lacks pigment; society's power brokers oppress other people because that is what selfish people with power normally do, unless they genuinely submit to strong religious, moral or social deterrents which would prevent them from doing so.

Color does not necessarily guarantee unity, even for us. Just as freed slaves in the Roman Empire acquired slaves whenever they could,[57] some slaves in the United States, once freed, acquired slaves, despite the much worse conditions to which American slaves were generally subjected.[58] Jawanza Kunjufu notes that "in 1830, there were 3,777 African Americans who were slave owners."[59] By that year 1,556 Black masters in the Deep South (where the larger agricultural plantations were located) held 7,188 slaves;[60] 753 Black slaveholders who held ten or more slaves each lived in New Orleans alone.[61] In South Carolina, meanwhile, 59 free Blacks held 357 Black slaves in 1790; by 1830, 450 held 2,412.[62] So "widespread was black slaveholding in the city of Charleston that the majority of free black heads of household owned slaves from 1820 to 1840."[63] Evidence also suggests that most Black slaveholders treated their slaves the same way White slaveholders did; some were kind, but most treated them "as chattel property."[64] The numbers declined after this period, but mainly because the number of Black masters declined in the South and those who remained became more urbanized, needed fewer slaves and sold those they did not need.[65]

Likewise, by serving the interests of White slavers, Black slave traders like Hamed bin Muhammed, headquartered in Muslim Zanzibar, became prosperous in nineteenth-century Central Africa.[66] Better known as Tippu Tib, he was "the most murderous of the Mulatto slave traders"; without him and other Black slave traders, Arab and European alike could have made little progress.[67] The Arabs established their own outposts throughout the Manyema region of the eastern Congo, where ivory was abundant.

Armed with rifles and aided by local people such as the Myamwezi, the Arabs carried out devastating raids for ivory and slaves. One of the greatest traders in ivory and an unrepentant slaver, Muhammid bin Hamid, better known as Tipu Tib, carved out a political empire in the upper Congo where he reigned supreme during the 1880s and early 1890s. This system of raiding and trading endured until the Belgians of the Congo Free State defeated the Arabs in battle and destroyed the last vestiges of their power.[68]

With what may represent only slight exaggeration, a writer on the slave trade laments:

The worst cruelties, the widest ravages, the greatest loss of human life in the slave trade occurred during the 1870s and 1880s, after the Atlantic trade had been effectively abolished. Those were the years when the famous Tippu Tib, with his Arab companions and black mercenaries, had literally depopulated most of the Upper Congo forest.

Tippu Tib's aim was to kill as many men as possible so as to enslave as many women and children as possible. This in turn provided King Leopold's excuse for an "equally disastrous exploitation of the Congo."[69] Whereas some African tribes vigorously opposed the slave trade regardless of the cost to themselves, others were the source of many *slattees,* laborers for the foreign slavers.[70]

Although it is the exception rather than the rule, skin color has not always defined allegiance historically. For some, moral convictions or immoral desires take precedence over the community into which they were born. Thus we might ask who is of greater service to Black Americans: a proverbial "Uncle Tom" or White Americans who participated in slave revolts or risked their lives to help the Underground Railroad?[71] John Brown is a well-known White abolitionist, but less known is George Boxley, leader of a slave revolt in 1816. Both Brown and Boxley were visionary White Christians who identified with and died for the Black community.[72] African-Americans supported Brown, some died fighting alongside him, and African-Americans throughout the North publicly honored Brown and his companions as martyrs, advocating more open armed resistance against slavery.[73] White missionaries were suspected of complicity in other slave insurrections as early as 1741,[74] and in 1831 the governor of Virginia even blamed White Christian perspectives for influencing Nat Turner's revolt, although Black biblical perspectives were recognized as still more influential.[75] At the same time, it is widely known that most slave revolts that were thwarted failed because a slave betrayed the plot to his or her master![76]

Color by itself does not guarantee loyalty to one race or another. Loyalty to our race and to the broader cause of justice for which we contend matters more than skin tone. The United States is in fact unusual in identifying persons of mixed descent as "Black" (the Arab world classifies them as White,[77] although some Arabs present themselves to Black Americans as "people of color"[78]). But in the words of Chancellor Williams,

> even if the United States did attempt to reclassify this group as either white or coloured, the millions who are bound to the African race by unbreakable ties of love would fight such a move. For like the late Congressman Adam Clayton Powell, who could have passed for "white" anywhere in the world, they would say, "Call me Black!"—knowing full well that "Black" refers not to anyone's color (for which none is responsible), but "Black" defines one's attitude toward the homeland of his ancestors.[79]

Thus in the end "Blackness" in America has as much to do with allegiance as with complexion. (We will treat this issue of allegiance in chapters five and six.) But this emphasis does not rule out the social impact of skin color.

While Blackness in the end addresses allegiance, in the beginning pigmentation is an inescapable social factor. When a White racist sees an Uncle Tom, the first thing the racist sees is the color of Uncle Tom's skin. Even Tom is to that extent one of us.[80] In the same way, it is often hard for those who have experienced repeated betrayals by racism to be sure they have found a trustworthy (not prejudiced) White person until they have gotten to know that person.

Complexion is less significant finally than allegiance, but in this society it still defines us at first sight. We may debate whether that should be the situation, but as long as it remains the situation—as long as we are even initially judged by the color of our skin rather than by the content of our character—we need to provide historic and current Black role models for our people. This is why the next chapter surveys current discussions about how Black the Egyptians and the Israelites might have been.

One more question remains to be asked before turning to the Egyptians and Israelites, however: how useful is identification based on race?

Racial Identification: Useful?

Because our history as a race in the United States has isolated us from the mainstream of White society, some racial identification is helpful to us.[81] One purpose of Black studies is to focus on our history, as it has been neglected by the broader society, and so to provide more respect for and understanding of our culture in that society.[82] But learning our heritage also provides a crucial context for our own young people to discover from relevant role models the potential they have.[83] It is wrong for Black boys to grow up in the projects looking to drug dealers as role models, simply because most successful Black men grow up outside the projects or move out as soon as they are able. More of us need to identify with our race enough to go back to the projects after we have achieved success, to provide role models for our Black boys and tell them that we can make a difference in the world—and start by making a difference for them. Why should drug dealers—destroyers who often target our people no less than the Klan did—provide better role models than those who want to get a good education and raise families and do good for our communities and our world?[84]

Racial identification occurs *automatically* in U.S. society; as long as this situation continues, we must point to *appropriate* racial role models. It is unspeakably tragic for Black boys in the inner city to grow up alienated by a school system they feel is irrelevant or afraid of them, unaware of the great risks our slave ancestors took to learn how to read when it was illegal for slaves to do so[85] (and unaware of the brilliance of a Black Phillis Wheatley, whose teenage command of written English would shame most college graduates today,[86] and who sought to dedicate her talents to God's glory[87]). Nineteenth-century Black activist David Walker observed,

> I would crawl on my hands and knees through mud and mire, to the feet of a learned man, where I would sit and humbly supplicate him to instill into me, that which neither devils nor tyrants could remove, only with my life— for colored people to acquire learning in this country, makes tyrants quake and tremble on their sandy foundation.[88]

Many of our youth likewise remain unaware of or disinterested in the great achievements of Black scientists and thinkers of the past—Benjamin Banneker, George Washington Carver, Charles Drew, Garrett Morgan and others. Scholars have noted how inner-city youth are like youth elsewhere until they begin to realize what life's options appear to be for them.[89] Understanding more history and seeing more firsthand role models can help convince them that society cannot limit their options so easily. If our ancestors could achieve, raise solid families and impart values to their children during times of White oppression greater than today's, what is our excuse but a lie we have swallowed from past generations of oppressors, a blow to our self-esteem that cries out, "We can't do any better"?[90] Our history does not allow us the luxury of that excuse.

In the past the White community perpetuated negative images of Black women,[91] and "the sexual harassment of African-American women by white men contributed to images of Black women as fair game for all men."[92] In recent decades certain studies showed that very young Black girls prefer Black dolls, but as they grew older and more influenced by White society's values, many of them preferred White dolls because they had come to view them as "prettier." This suggested that for them Black might be beautiful, but it appeared less beautiful than White.[93] At present, values seem to be shifting in a healthier direction in the African-American community,[94] but evidences of low self-esteem remain on some other counts. Perhaps some young women have sold themselves so cheaply—for a kind word, for a fleeting favor from a man who will not commit his own life to a woman in marriage before getting her pregnant—because they do not value themselves highly enough.[95] And sometimes they do not dare to value themselves because we have created a society that does not value them—indeed, a society that does not know how to value anyone as a person of infinite worth, as a person made in God's image. African-American scholar Cornel West rightly protests our culture's reduction of "individuals to objects of pleasure."[96] But Black men should affirm Black women, remembering among other things the historic strength of Black women in times of trouble for our people.[97] Likewise, we must address those men who sell themselves cheaply to drug dealing, to impregnating without fathering and so on because they too have not learned to value themselves.

In such a situation, some reports from outside our community can encourage those tempted to doubt their worth: that the Greek historian Herodotus called a certain tribe of Africans the "handsomest men in the world"; that the Roman poet Ovid declared that a dark-skinned African woman conquered the heart of the hero Perseus with her extraordinary beauty; that many Greco-Roman writers preferred Black beauty to White beauty, though these writers were White.

Partly for such reasons none of the lighter peoples in the ancient Mediterranean opposed "interracial" (intercolor) marriage (it was considered a matter of personal taste)—one of the strictest tests of a culture's racism.[98] (Although some point out that the Qur'an describes as black the faces of apostates in the judgment, as opposed to the whitened faces of the faithful,[99] and some other Arab Muslim writers described Black Africans as ugly and stinky,[100] this is not the usual image from the ancient or most of the medieval world. Ancient Europeans often regarded Black Africans as beautiful, different as their own standards were; so did many Arabs, who also favored interracial unions.[101])

Likewise, the Israelites, who were darker than most White Americans but lighter than most Black Africans, could appreciate the beauty of a dark-complexioned Israelite turned still darker by the sun. "I am black and beautiful," declares Solomon's beloved in Song of Solomon; in the context she is hailed as the world's most beautiful woman.[102] The Bible thus praises a woman Black in color as the world's most beautiful woman. (In a pure, brotherly and not misleading way, some of us brothers may want to make sure our sisters know that we think so too.)

But racial identification is important to us because it has been denied to us, not because particular physical characteristics unite us. In Africa we would identify more with our tribe than with our complexion, because in Africa most people are Black anyway; we would identify on the basis of kinship ties, local customs and tribal or national allegiances. Here, however, we share a common heritage and common suffering that set us apart from the White community. For this reason racial identification by color is not enough by itself. To define ourselves only on the basis of our race is to accept categories some White people originally established to oppress us. Unless we unjustly judge the least pigmented Blacks as inferior to the most pigmented Blacks, dividing ourselves by gradations of Blackness and perhaps excluding those who have too much "White" blood, color alone cannot be the basis of unity and identification. (In times past, accepting traditional White views of beauty, we sometimes regarded light-skinned Blacks more highly.[103] But because of our shared history, the African-American community dare not allow categories others have imposed on us to divide us. Our ancestors all suffered together, for U.S. slave codes always treated mulattos as Black.[104])

The lightest shades of Black overlap with the darkest shades of White. Being Black in America is a social category, not just an issue of how much pigment any of us has. Thus a few dark-skinned Caribbean friends have complained to us that White and Black Americans do not regard them as "Black"—not because of their pigment but because their cultural experience is different (despite their heritage as survivors of slavery as well). Similarly, a White Canadian we know, when stopped by a hostile Black militant, replied that he was Canadian and had nothing to do with the U.S. race problem; he was not "White" in the social sense in which we have often used the term.

As one proponent of multicultural education puts it:

Race is a socially determined category that is related to physical characteristics in a complex way. Two individuals with nearly identical physical characteristics, or phenotypes, can be classified as members of different races in two different societies. In the United States, where racial categories are well defined and highly inflexible, an individual with any acknowledged or publicly known African ancestry is considered Black. One who looks completely Caucasian but who acknowledges some African ancestry is classified as Black. Such an individual would be considered White in Puerto Rico.[105]

In this country a person with only one-quarter Black blood was considered Black and kept in slavery; a person with one-quarter Black blood who was free and could pass as White, but still chose to identify with our race, we recognized as Black. Blackness as we define and celebrate it in the African-American community is not just a matter of pigment, but a matter of identification with the community. We have historically embraced those who were willing to become part of us—even the few Whites who would join us (like George Johnson in Alex Haley's *Roots*[106])—because we were not willing to judge on the same terms of pigmentation on which the White community judged. Thus A.M.E. bishop Daniel Alexander Payne (1811-1893) not only protested White discrimination against Blacks but also protested "an A.M.E. church that prohibited a white woman from joining the congregation." When some African-American colleagues reacted angrily, he responded by declaring that "the pastor who would turn away from God's sanctuary any human being on account of color was not fit to have charge of a gang of dogs."[107] (Never mind, of course, what that says about a few of the White ministers as well.)

As Cornel West insists, purely racial reasoning plays into the hands of Whites who use this reasoning; in this sense, he argues, many gangsta rap artists share aspects of the ideology propagated by David Duke and other Aryan supremacists.[108] We must instead build on moral reasoning, "to understand the black freedom struggle not as an affair of skin pigmentation and racial phenotype but rather as a matter of ethical principles and wise politics."[109] Black "authenticity," he argues, is thus not just a matter of color—though anyone Black can become an object of racism—but of commitment to the interests of the Black community as a whole. "In short, blackness is a political and ethical construct."[110]

Further, though we have argued above that African-American history provides crucial role models, we must also concede that even the best Afrocentric role models from history may prove inadequate if youth lack *accessible* role models in their personal lives—something a book cannot provide, but the church ought to.

Conclusion

Racial identification happens automatically in the United States, because race is a category African-Americans have to live with every day. At the same time, our unity as a people has less to do with pigment than with shared history. Thus without neglecting the important matter of color, we must look beyond skin tone to a much deeper basis for identity—a shared cultural experience, a shared heritage of dignity in the face of oppression. Before we turn to this, however, we will examine two ancient peoples with whom many of our people are identifying ethnically—peoples who became significant to all Western history.

4
Was Egypt or Israel Black?

NEITHER GEOGRAPHY NOR SKIN TONE IS OUR ULTIMATE BASIS FOR IDENtification, as we noted earlier in this book. Nevertheless, history has made color an important issue to those who have been oppressed on the basis of their color. It is therefore encouraging to note that many mighty empires respected even by White Americans were dark peoples. It is likewise important for those who are alienated from White society to recognize that our first forebears in Christianity were not White Europeans. (Many African-Americans have felt alienated from Christianity because of White artists' portraits of biblical figures as well as past racist propaganda against African participation in the biblical story. As we will observe in chapter five, the attempts to exclude Blacks from Christianity began with slaveholders who wanted to withhold the gospel from slaves because it promised good news of freedom.)

This is not to imply that anyone should think White Europeans are excluded from historic Christianity; it is rather to say that (in contrast to the views of some) Christianity did not start with them and does not "belong" to them. In comparison to Europeans and White Americans, in fact, none of our people, not even the most race-conscious, should feel as if we are latecomers to the biblical story. After all, Christians of European descent share with us a faith that began closer to our homeland than to theirs. Until White Europeans drew the maps, no conscious continental boundaries existed between Israel and

North Africa, and Afroasiatic peoples migrated freely between what we call Africa and Asia through ancient Palestine.[1]

Egypt and Israel are two examples of peoples in history who were closer to our homeland than to that of the northern Europeans who later appropriated their heritage. Indeed, Israelites and Egyptians were darker than most northern Europeans, most Egyptians could have passed for Black by the common U.S. definition, and many Egyptians were Black Africans by anyone's definition.

Do We Identify with Egypt as a "Black" Civilization?

As noted in chapter two, we do not identify with everything that Egyptians said or did in history. But Afrocentric scholars have emphasized our heritage in Egypt—a heritage that, if not wholly African in every traditional sense, is certainly more African than European! China, Mesopotamia and Egypt have all laid claim to the title "cradle of civilization"[2]; yet the peoples of these lands were not White Europeans. Because White society has often portrayed the history of civilization as a story of White civilization, it can encourage us to know that these civilizations were generated by peoples of color.

Besides Egypt's own accomplishments, some have credited it with those of Greece. While some popular arguments rely on late sources and give Egypt credit for something of questionable merit (Greek philosophy),[3] the arguments of Martin Bernal are much more careful and nuanced, appealing to early Greek traditions as well as contemporary archaeological and documentary evidence.[4] Regardless of whether in the end one accepts all of Bernal's historical conclusions,[5] his analysis of historiography is difficult to dispute: many modern theories concerning Egypt and Africans rest on foundations of the nineteenth-century racist ideology that birthed them.[6] Despite weak links in some of his specific arguments, Bernal has persuasively demonstrated important formative Egyptian influences on early Greek civilization.

In any case, no one disputes that Egyptian civilization antedates Greek civilization by over two thousand years. Thus a classical scholar's recent work on Greek history concurs that even if one does not go as far as Bernal, "as to the Greeks, their culture would have been inconceivable without the contributions of the Egyptians, Babylonians, Syrians and Phoenicians."[7] The degree of Egypt's influence is, however, disputed, as is a more central question for our study: were the Egyptians Black?

Scholarship Divided by Presuppositions

Some Afrocentric scholars have gone further than saying that peoples of color generated the earliest civilizations; these scholars argue that at least the Egyptians and possibly the Babylonians and Assyrians were *Black Africans.*[8] How strong is the evidence? Although the evidence for the Babylonians and Assyrians is questionable and somewhat peripheral to our point, the evidence for Egypt naturally commends itself for examination. After all, at least our modern division of continents places Egypt squarely in Africa. No natural boundaries separate Egypt from the rest of Africa.

Few casual readers of history are aware that the primary prejudices against Egyptians' being Black Africans remain those conceived by nineteenth-century scholars whose bias is well known. Because nineteenth-century European "science" temporarily declared Blacks to be subhuman, historians had to find ways to harmonize their own findings with those of "science." "The first was to deny that the Ancient Egyptians were black; the second was to deny that the Ancient Egyptians had created a 'true' civilization; the third was to make doubly sure by denying both."[9] Thus, for example, the famous Egyptologist Sir Flinders Petrie (1853-1942), trying his best to find a rational explanation for clear evidence of Black elements in Egypt's population, suggested that an obviously Black queen "might be of an inferior race and not of the 'high type.' "[10] Early-twentieth-century historical-critical scholars also made comments most of us would today regard as astonishing—such as Martin Noth's criticism of "the ancient Egyptians for having incorrectly portrayed and classified the Nubians as Negroes"![11]

Current scholarship is not so monolithically Eurocentric. Most readers will not simply dismiss without investigation heavily documented works such as those by Cheikh Anta Diop, a Senegalese scholar who has argued that Egypt was a Black African civilization. Diop thinks that Egypt not only affected Mediterranean and ancient Near Eastern civilization but also influenced the rest of African civilization for centuries after its ascendancy. He contends that the desertification of the Sahara, coupled with the uninhabitability of most of Central Africa, drove most Africans to settle in the Nile Valley around 7000 B.C.[12] The focus of Egyptian civilization in southern Egypt until later periods of its history,[13] parallels between Egypt and other African societies,[14] the kinship of Egypt with Meroitic Sudan[15] and similarities between Egyptian and some other African language systems[16] suggest a strong African component in Egypt. Diop produces references from Greek and Roman authors attesting that the Egyptians were "Black"[17] and points to ancient Egyptian paintings and the skin of some mummies.[18]

A Survey of the Evidence Outside Paintings
While Diop's breadth of research is impressive, scholars dispute some details,

and not always for racial reasons.[19] African components in a population need not rule out other components in addition to them.[20] Thus, for example, the Egyptian language may reflect African roots or influences without excluding other influences (such as clearly Semitic elements) as well. The Egyptian language belongs to a language group found in both East Africa and West Asia but distinct from those found in Central Africa. Some far less nuanced work takes linguistic "parallels" much too far: John Jackson produces sixteen alleged parallels between English and Egyptian (such as *abode* and *abut; autumn* and *atum; write* and *ruit*—which could easily enough be coincidental in view of the large number of words in a language) to contend for otherwise undocumented Egyptian influence "among the ancient Britons"![21]

While some ancient Mediterranean authors described the Egyptians as dark, this darkness was a relative term (words with the *melan-* root do not always mean coal-black). The Egyptians were darker than the Greeks, but in Greek and Roman views they fell into a broader middle range of Mediterranean peoples when contrasted with the epitome of Whiteness, the Scythians,[22] and the epitome of Blackness, the "Ethiopians." Frank Snowden has produced a voluminous survey of Greek and Roman literature on the Ethiopians, who clearly included Black Africans of different skin tones (the so-called black, copper and red complexions). Yet Ethiopians were always described as the "blackest" of peoples, and Egyptians, though darker than peoples to the north, were usually distinguished from Ethiopians in the Greek and Roman period.[23] Likewise, Arabs described themselves as "black" in contrast to the lighter Persians (whom they considered "red") but depicted themselves as "red" or "white" when comparing themselves with Africans, whom they regarded as "black."[24] In Arab paintings most of the slaves are clearly Black and African, and most Arab and Persian masters are clearly White;[25] the Arabs' battle enemies are often Black as well.[26] Further, Arabic *sudan,* meaning "black," "sometimes includes Ethiopians, but not Egyptians, Berbers, or other peoples north of the Sahara."[27] Thus the designation "black" did not always mean the same thing in all contexts.

Skeletons likewise tell an ambiguous story.[28] According to Du Bois, physical anthropologists found "fully Negroid" features in only about a quarter of Egyptian skeletons studied.[29] These would indicate a sizable Black presence in Egypt, but one's evaluation of the rest of the Egyptians depends on how one physically classifies races (a question discussed in our next section, below). Because racial classification on skeletal grounds is notoriously fallible (most Black African peoples are not "fully Negroid" by some definitions), this evidence does not help much either way. It presupposes an arbitrary division of races that does not actually fit the physical evidence (see "Division by Race," the final section of this chapter).[30]

The other evidence is no less mixed. Against the contentions of some writers, when the Egyptians called themselves "inhabitants of the Black Land" they were referring to the land itself, not to their own complexion. "The Black Country" referred "to the rich alluvial soil along the banks of the Nile, in contrast to *dasre(t)*, 'red land,' the desert region on either side of the fertile Nile Valley."[31] Their land was "black" only in the sense that the deserts were, as they put it, "red."

At the same time, having observed that Egyptians were not all as "Black" in color as the peoples to their south, we may also observe that they were considerably darker than peoples to their north—*dark enough, in fact, that almost any of them could pass for African-Americans today.* It is clear that Black Africans of dark black hue made up a significant proportion of Egyptian society, and that the Black Egyptians (especially Nubians) from the south intermarried freely with lighter Egyptians from the north,[32] making the Egyptian people as a whole far darker than most peoples to their north. Du Bois notes that African and Asian peoples both migrated to Egypt and mixed freely, eventually producing "an Egyptian mulatto race differentiated in color and other physical characteristics from the Central Africans."[33]

It is thus fair to say that most Egyptians had some "Black" blood, although it would not be fair to say that all Egyptians lacked non-Black blood, since Asiatic peoples had also settled in the land in various periods and had likewise intermarried. In some periods of Egypt's history, explicitly Nubian pharaohs sat on the throne (for instance, Tirhakah, a powerful ruler also mentioned in the Bible, apparently as an ally of the righteous king Hezekiah[34]); but in other periods, lighter pharaohs from the Lower (northern) Kingdom reigned.[35] The original inhabitants of Egypt were Africans in southern Egypt (c. 3000-5000 B.C.), but the northern Egyptian population included a mixture of elements with Syria and Palestine; in time these peoples were united in one kingdom.[36]

Most Egyptologists concur that the Egyptian people,[37] like their language[38] and culture,[39] included a mixture of African elements from the south (by 3200 B.C.), Semitic elements from the northeast and western elements from Libya (though the Arab conquests later introduced more Semitic elements into the population).[40] Most scholars agree that the Hyksos were Asiatic Semites.[41] Egyptians and Nubians were ethnically related but linguistically distinct; "Whereas Ancient Egyptian was an Afro-Asiatic language (a family found in

North and East Africa and in Western Asia), the Nubian tongues belonged to the Nilo-Saharan group, found only in the central part of the continent."[42] Thus no one should deny the African character of Egypt; but affirming its African character need not mean denying its other elements. In a world that did not divide continents as we do, African and Semitic cultures mixed freely.

Egyptian Self-Depictions in Art

In their paintings some Egyptians are black in color;[43] most are dark red to reddish-brown (like very dark Native Americans).[44] Because interpreters have raised objections to this evidence, we will first summarize their objections and then respond to them.

One might object that the colors on these paintings are not relevant. Some scholars have observed that in some statues women are lighter in hue than men, suggesting characterizations that did not reflect reality.[45] Egyptian artists usually followed strict conventions—for instance, which way a person's arm was to point, the angle of one's shoulders and the like.[46] Sometimes they had conventions for coloring as well.[47] Thus it could be argued that these artists were employing idealized colors for men and women: men, who worked outside, were bright and dark, while in some scenes women, more confined to the home, were portrayed as lighter.[48] Old Kingdom painted sculptures typically portrayed men as reddish-brown and women as a light yellow.[49] If Egyptian art followed this convention consistently, both hues would have to be exaggerations, for all men and women could hardly have descended from entirely different races.[50]

The suggestion that complexions on paintings in most periods merely reflect artistic convention, however, would be misleading. In most of the pictures Egyptian women are dark-skinned—bright red, dark brown and so forth—just like the men.[51] In some portrayals women are darker than men,[52] and a woman can be darker than her husband in the same picture.[53] The exceptions suggesting a different artistic convention are mainly from sculpture from the Old Kingdom[54] or from scenes of the dead.[55] Various shades of pigment on men in the same paintings indicate that Egyptian artists were quite aware of varied shades in pigment and quite capable of reproducing these realistically in their artwork;[56] Egyptian artists had a great variety of shades at their disposal.[57]

Even in the Roman period, when most of those who could afford to commission portraits of themselves were Romans or (more often) Greeks who belonged to the former colonial elite,[58] artistic portrayals of *native* Egyptians continued using dark hues.[59] In all periods Egyptians appear darker than typical Western Asiatics (Semites) like the Syrians;[60] in the same way, northern Egyptians also normally can be distinguished from the dark Black Nubians to the south.[61] We thus suggest that in most periods the complexion depictions are realistic[62]—some men had darker, and some lighter, wives—but like modern light-skinned Black people who do not get much sun, even most "pale" Egyptians maintained a relatively dark complexion compared to White Americans.[63]

Range of Egyptian Complexions

The most likely reading of the evidence from art fits our evidence from other sources: some Egyptians were black in color, whereas others were various shades of brown; very few would have been as light as northern Europeans. One scholar writing for the Brooklyn Museum points out:

On an average, between the Delta in northern Egypt and the Sudd of the Upper Nile, skin color tends to darken from light brown to what appears to the eye as bluish black, hair changes from wavy-straight to curly or kinky, noses become flatter and broader, lips become thicker. . . . All of these people are Africans. To proceed further and divide them into Caucasoid and Negroid stocks is to perform an act that is wholly devoid of historical or biological significance.[64]

The gradual change in shade applies even to the Nubians, as a top scholar concerning ancient Nubia notes

the gradual if superficial change in the physical characteristics of the population from north to south, skin becoming darker in colour, facial features flatter, hair more tightly curled and skeletons increasingly slender. The ancient Egyptians observed these differences and faithfully reproduced them in painting and sculpture, distinguishing the "brown"-skinned inhabitants of Lower Nubia from the black people living further to the south.[65]

Although ancient writers and artists took notice of such differences, it was never in a prejudicial manner.[66] All ancient evidence suggests that prejudices were sometimes based on culture or nationality (for instance, many Greeks regarded all non-Greeks as inferior, and in the Ptolemaic period Greeks ruled Egypt arrogantly)[67] but never on skin tone. Prejudice based on color had to await the rise of Arab and northern European civilizations.[68]

The Ambiguity of Racial Distinctions and Ancient Egyptians' Complexion

Africans are not homogeneous in complexion or other physical features, any more than Europeans or Asians are. Different African peoples throughout the continent exhibit their own easily distinguishable physical features.[69] Although nearly all ancient Egyptians could pass for Black in modern North America, the gradations of skin tone and other features suggest that the entire modern conception of racial categories is misleading. History in fact indicates that it is racist (see "Division by Races," the final section of this chapter), and for this reason many modern anthropologists have abandoned it. The verdict of Bernal, best known for his case in *Black Athena* that Egypt heavily influenced Greek civilization, is reasonable: "To what 'race,' then, did the Ancient Egyptians belong? I am very dubious of the utility of the concept 'race' in general because it is impossible to achieve any anatomical precision on the subject." We will comment further on the ambiguity of racial distinctions later in the chapter. Despite biases among researchers, however, Bernal is convinced

> that, at least for the last 7,000 years, the population of Egypt has contained African, South-West Asian and Mediterranean types. . . . I believe that . . . the African element was stronger in the Old and Middle Kingdoms, before the Hyksos invasion, than it later became. Furthermore, I am convinced that many of the most powerful Egyptian dynasties which were based in Upper Egypt—the 1st, 11th, 12th and 18th—were made up of pharaohs whom one can usefully call black.[70]

Our modern U.S. racial categories do not fit the situation in Egypt, because our categories are an artificial response to our nation's racist history. Having said that, however, we must frankly admit that *had* ancient Egyptians been forced into modern U.S. racial categories, their complexions from reddish-brown to black are the complexions represented in our Black communities, not in the White community.[71] Perhaps a higher percentage would have fallen in the "light" range than in most of our communities, but by the White standards used to evaluate color in the United States (any Black blood making a person Black), many of them could not have "passed" as simply White people with a nice tan. White racists who traditionally sought to claim all great civilizations of the past as White have no factual foundation for their position; indeed, they would have rejected as "non-White" most ancient Egyptians had they met them.

As Bishop Dunston points out, Herodotus's view that the Egyptians were somehow "black" indicates that "whatever mixture there was still represented some shades of black in his eyes."[72] And as Lerone Bennett puts it,

> Great Negro scholars (W. E. B. Du Bois, Carter G. Woodson, William Leo Hansberry) have insisted that the ancient Egyptians, from Menes to Cleopatra, were a mixed race which presented the same physical types and color ranges as American Negroes—a people, in short, who would have been forced to sit on the back seats of the busses in Mississippi. "If the Egyptians and the majority of the tribes of Northern Africa were not Negroes," Carter

Woodson said, "then there are no Negroes in the United States."[73]
African-American scholar Charles Copher, whose influence is celebrated by the
many students he instructed at ITC (Interdenominational Theological Center)
in Atlanta, likewise puts the matter quite accurately:

> The evidences testify that, according to American sociological definitions of
> Negro, the ancient Egyptians were Negroes; that according to modern an-
> thropological and ethnological definitions the ancient Egyptian population
> included a large percentage of so-called Negroes, possibly 25% as an average
> across the long period of time that was ancient Egyptian history.[74]

Because the primary reason that Americans today ask about the Egyptians' race
is our own situation in the history of U.S. race relations, buses in the pre-Civil
Rights South provide a useful standard for evaluating the answer. When the
question is framed in these terms, it takes little imagination to guess that the
skin of ancient Egyptians would have appeared black in the spectrum of American color codes.

Were the Israelites Black?

Some religious groups, from sectors of African-American Islam to the Church
of the Living God (a Black Pentecostal group) have portrayed Jesus, David and
other biblical heroes as having dark skin.[75] Others have gone so far as to claim
that Black peoples today are the true descendants of the ancient Jews.[76] Some
modern Afrocentric writers point to the revelation of Jesus in Revelation 1:14-
15 to claim that Jesus was Black, noting the hair like wool and feet like polished
bronze.[77] But the hair is said to be "*white* like wool"; if this is not clear enough,
the writer adds "like snow." Because "white" included many shades from white
to gray, John, the recipient of this revelation, explains *how* white: white like
wool or like snow.[78] This applies not to the white hair of old age alone, for
Jesus' whole head is said to be white, not only his hair (1:14).

Does this mean that Jesus is Caucasian in this revelation? Hardly. His eyes
are like fire (1:14), and his feet are like bronze in the sense that they glow as
if heated in the fire (1:15). In other words, "white" refers not to Jesus' complexion but to the blinding light of his glory. The image is borrowed directly from
the symbolic description of God's glory in Daniel 7:9-10, alongside other glory
imagery from Daniel 10:6.[79] In other words, Jesus is so bright that he shines
like lightning or like the sun (Rev 1:16).[80] One would not expect John to be able
to measure Jesus' pigment in such a state (see similarly Mark 9:2-3).[81]

So what color was Jesus when he walked with his disciples on earth? Probably the same light-brown color as most other Jews who traveled a lot in the

hot Mediterranean sun. After all, Jesus did not stand out in a crowd when he wasn't glowing (Jn 7:10-11).[82] This is not to say that Jesus and his other Jewish contemporaries were Black Africans; it is merely to say that they were not White Europeans either.[83]

Unless one is Jewish, a Bible reader's identification with the biblical characters will be on the basis of similar situation (a common bond of oppression or faith) rather than identical ethnicity. Nevertheless, people of African descent have an ethnic heritage in ancient Israel as well as a spiritual one. Some writers today overstate the case, and we must survey their position before we go on to warn against *understating* the case.

Overstating the Case

One noted writer, whose research is sounder in some other respects, claims that Hebrew religion today is "controlled by converted Europeans who are not semitic and who have absolutely no relationship to the biblical Jew at all. I doubt if there is anybody on the face of the earth who is a direct descendant of the biblical Jew except African people." He then proceeds to explain that modern Jews are descended from thirteenth-century European converts to Judaism who wanted to avoid the extremes of Islam and Christianity: "they studied the religion and projected themselves onto the world as though they had invented it."[84] Unfortunately, this theory concerning the origin of modern Jews is incontestably wrong: hundreds of documents throughout the Middle Ages indicate the continuity of the ethnic Jewish community in Europe from the Roman period.[85]

But while it is not fair to say that the Israelites were Black Africans, arguing this would be no more prejudiced than pretending that they were British or German, as White American pictures in many popular Bible storybooks imply.[86] If some Afrocentric scholars have gone overboard in darkening ancient Israel, their zeal may be misinformed but remains understandable. Noting that Whites often acted as if God were White, Garvey responded, "Whilst our God has no color, yet it is human to see everything through one's own spectacles, and since the white people have seen God through white spectacles, we have only now started out (late though it be) to see God through our own spectacles."[87]

Given the psychological and social damage done by centuries of European art (some of it unfortunately hung even in Black churches), the point that Jesus was not European needs to be made graphically. Perhaps a few traditional Ethiopian Orthodox paintings in church windows would help let it be known that Black Christians have identified with ancient Israel just as long as White Christians have. But those of us who would prefer to do without artwork in the church windows, or who identify with our spiritual forebears spiritually rather than racially, can grasp the point. Of course it is especially Jewish people who identify ethnically with ancient Israel; non-Jewish Christians identify with the biblical characters mainly morally and spiritually. But we cannot be faulted for taking note that ancient Israelites looked considerably more like many of us than many modern Eurocentric artists' blond portraits of them suggest!

Some Afrocentric works go beyond contending that the Egyptians were Black to argue that Babylonians, Canaanites and other ancient Near Eastern peoples were Black,[88] often on evidence that remains disputed.[89] Some of this evidence includes the assumption that all Ham's descendants (as listed in the table of nations in Genesis 10) were Black.[90] Yet this view can be turned for or against African-Americans; White racists previously exploited the same assumption in this country for the purpose of using Canaan's curse to enslave Blacks.[91] (Some White supremacists still exploit the curse of Canaan today.[92])

Although especially exploited by White racists, the tradition transferring the curse of Canaan's subjugation to all Hamite, hence (on their reading) African, peoples predates its abuse by Europeans. Jewish tradition from the second century and later,[93] developed further by ninth-century Islam,[94] associated the tradition of Ham's blackness with the thesis that Ham was "cursed" with black-ness. Many Muslims used this "curse" to justify enslaving Africans, even when they were fellow Muslims.[95] Although Genesis speaks of Canaan's rather than Ham's enslavement, Arabs transferred the curse of slavery to Ham's descen-dants, whom they took to be Black Africans.[96]

Yet this tradition about the cursing of Ham bears little resemblance to what the biblical text *says!*[97] It is remarkable that some Afrocentric writers, appar-ently unwittingly accepting the teaching of White racists, would assume that the Bible cursed the descendants of Ham (an assumption they believe militates against taking the Bible literally),[98] when in fact the text of Genesis said no such thing. The "curse of Ham" was a postbiblical myth borrowed from Islam and especially developed by White supremacists in Europe,[99] then by their succes-sors in the United States[100] and among the Boers (Afrikaaners) in South Afri-ca.[101] In the Bible, Ham himself and his other sons (including clearly African ones like Africa/Cush and Egypt/Mizraim) were never cursed.[102] Christian Afrocentric biblical writers are correct that the curse on Canaan was fulfilled in the time of Joshua and his successors and ceased to be applicable later as descendants of the Canaanites assimilated into other peoples.[103] Genesis was written to encourage Israel in possessing the land, but even the curse on Canaan was clearly not permanent; in later times Jesus acted on behalf of a Canaanite (Mt 15:21-28).

Some writers who argue that non-Israelite Near Eastern peoples were Black then seek to show that the Israelites intermarried with these Black peoples and therefore had Black offspring, by the U.S. definition of Black (having any Black blood). This approach, however, may argue for more than is necessary for our case. For the argument to be necessary, one would have to assume that before intermarriage the Israelites were lighter than their enemies, and this is not favored by the evidence. After all, Abraham himself was from Mesopotamia, so the Israelites' complexion would have been close to that of the Mesopotamians.

Other complications may also challenge this approach. The Canaanites may have been Hamites according to Genesis, but (against some authors) it is simply untrue that they learned a Semitic language only from contact with Israel.[104] Ugaritic tablets from Ras Shamra plainly show that they spoke a Semitic language almost identical to Hebrew long before Israel settled there.[105] Further, that the Cushites were darker than most Egyptians (both also Hamites) indicates that Hamites varied in color; northerly Hamites like the Canaanites may have been no darker than dark "Semites."[106]

This is important to note for historical reasons, but theologians should also take note: painting the Canaanites Black but the Israelites White reads Israel's conquest of Canaan as an account of a "White" civilization overthrowing a "Black" one, a proposition that would not please any Black monotheists who value God's historic revelation to Israel (be they Christian, Jewish or Muslim).

An honorable objective (such as encouraging our young people about our heritage) does not force us to flirt with inaccurate scholarship.[107] There is plenty of real evidence for Black presence in the Bible (as Afrocentric Christian writers like Walter Arthur McCray, William Dwight McKissic Sr., Charles Copher and Cain Hope Felder have accurately noted), and evidence that cannot hold up under scrutiny only undermines the credibility of our whole approach with those who wish to dispute it. White academicians have already begun reacting against inaccurate and overstated Afrocentric claims that seek to appropriate all of history's greatness and none of its failings for our people. One such writer laments that "the excesses of Afrocentrism are now threatening to discredit the whole field of African-American studies."[108] While such a severe backlash has not yet appeared in biblical studies, it can best be avoided, and the cause of valid Afrocentric pursuits can best be served, by reserving our fervor for the many claims that can be adequately documented.

This is not so much a criticism of what our writers have written so far—early works in any field of study will have to be revised, including this one—as a warning to writers in the future. Saying that "Simon the Canaanite" was a Black apostle[109] implies that the Canaanites were substantially darker than the Israelites, an assumption that (as we have noted) must be (and in our view has not been) proved. More disconcerting about the assertion, however, is that it is simply not what the biblical text the writers are using says: Matthew 10:4 does not say "Canaanite" (which Matthew knew how to say—Mt 15:22) but the differently spelled "Cananaean," or *Kananaios,* the Aramaic word for Zealot.[110] Thus Luke calls this same person "Simon the Zealot" in his parallel passage (Lk 6:15). Similarly, the "wise men" are probably not from the south, from Africa, as some have insisted;[111] they are literally "Magi" from the East (Mt 2:1-2, Greek text and most translations), and Magi were almost by definition from Babylonia/Persia.[112]

Whether we like it or not, we cannot claim all ancient Near Eastern peoples as Black. We should not simply claim that "the Hittites spoke a Bantu (African) language"[113] without seeking to substantiate our position at length, given that many specialists in the language contend that it was Indo-European.[114] A better case could be made for the Sumerians, who possessed Mesopotamia around 4000 B.C. and thus constituted a center of early civilization roughly simultaneous with those of the Egyptians and Nubians. Calling themselves the "blackheaded" people, and admitted by White scholars to be "swarthy," or black, these people were probably darker than their neighbors and may have been immigrants from Black Africa.[115]

But Abraham's migration from Mesopotamia does not connect him with Black African Sumerians. Runoko Rashidi, who connects Sumerians with Africa, concedes that they were always a minority in the region where they ruled;[116] further, the Akkadians under Sargon conquered Sumer around 2355 B.C.,[117] four centuries before Abraham's quest. By the time of Abraham, descendants of Sumerians had long been assimilated into the indigenous population. If the Sumerians were Black, many Mesopotamians (presumably including Abraham) would have had some Black blood, after four centuries of intermarriage. But Mesopotamians simply were not all Africans, as some popular apologists for Afrocentric biblical interpretation have implied.

Black Blood in Israel
Yet some other aspects of this approach are valid. The Egyptian population was

extremely mixed and generally darker than peoples to their north (including Israelites and probably Canaanites, Babylonians and other peoples to the northeast as well, just as those peoples tended to be much darker than Europeans and others to the north of them). Further, the Israelites did intermarry among the Egyptians during certain periods. The Bible explicitly declares that Joseph fathered two tribes for Israel by an Egyptian wife, automatically making Israel nearly 10 percent Egyptian (Gen 41:50).[118] (Joshua was from one of these two half-African tribes, Ephraim; in later years it became so dominant that the northern tribes of Israel were sometimes simply called "Ephraim." But even from the beginning God meant good for Joseph's sons—Gen 49:22-26.)

Not only Hagar[119] but also many of Abraham's servants were Egyptian (gifts to him from Egypt's ruler, Gen 12:16), and in this period it is fairly likely that some of the servants Pharaoh gave him would have been Black Nubians.[120] Jacob's grandfather Abraham had large numbers of herdsmen (Gen 13:6-8), and 318 male servants were born in his house (Gen 14:14), not including those acquired later.[121] Abraham's son Isaac inherited all that was in Abraham's household (Gen 25:5), and Jacob in turn received Isaac's inheritance (Gen 25:31-34; 27:29). The descendants and households of Jacob and his brother Esau both grew into large peoples while still in Canaan (Gen 36:6-7).

When the Israelites were subjected to slavery under the Egyptians, they and their former servants were now all defined as Israel together; this means that much intermarriage must have taken place.[122] Thus the vast numbers listed for Israel's tribes in Moses' day were descended not only from Jacob's seventy physical descendants (Ex 1:5) but also from the even larger number of servants who would have intermarried with them. So although Israel as a people descended from Abraham, individual Israelites by Moses' day also had genetic roots in both northeast Africa and southwest Asia,[123] placing them in the broad category "Afroasiatic."[124]

The "mixed multitude" from Egypt also means that many more Egyptians accompanied Israel when they left Egypt;[125] since Israel as a whole was numbered by tribes, it must be assumed that these Egyptians assimilated into the tribal populations through intermarriage. God certainly approved of Moses' marriage to an Ethiopian (Cushite—that is, Black African) woman, and one of his servants who opposed it was temporarily turned completely white with leprosy as a divine judgment (Num 12:1-16).[126] Although the text in Numbers reads as if Moses had recently married the woman (since the criticism appears recent—12:1), it remains possible that the "Cushite" here is the Midianite wife Zipporah mentioned earlier in Exodus 2:21.[127] *If* this is the case and these

Midianites were of African descent, an African whom Moses respected not only recognized Moses' God as the only true one but also provided Moses with wisdom for organizing the ranks of Israel (Ex 18:11-26). If it is not the case, it still shows us how Moses could respect a wise foreigner; and his later father-in-law in Numbers 12 is *surely* African.

Because of how American history defines "Black," some modern Israelis, darkened by the Mediterranean sun, could pass for light-skinned Black people (or vice versa), just as most Egyptians could have passed for light- or dark-skinned Black people. Some have even suggested that ancient Jewish people were often darker than many American Jewish people today, because most American Jews are descended from Jewish people who lived in Europe in Jesus' day and the centuries immediately following. In that period many Greeks, Romans and other southern Europeans converted to Judaism and intermarried among themselves and with darker Jews descended from Abraham, who was from the Middle East; thus European Jews as a whole may have become somewhat lighter.[128] (Some have similarly suggested that many North Africans may have become lighter during the centuries of Germanic Vandal presence in North Africa, starting in the fifth century A.D.,[129] and perhaps under Arab rule as well.)

Many Semites (to the extent that such categories objectively exist) are dark-skinned, and some Semitic peoples are closer in certain respects to some African peoples than to Europeans (compare the blend of ethnic elements among the Amharas in East Africa). Because racism against Jewish people has persisted through history despite the Crusades, the Inquisition and the Nazi Holocaust, we have a moral responsibility to add a caveat here. Regardless of whether the above evidence is sufficient to imply that ancient Israelites were probably often darker than most modern ones, it does *not* imply that ancient Jews were wholly African, as some have wrongly contended. Nor do the widely known facts about conversion and intermarriage during the Roman Empire challenge modern Jews' Jewishness, as some anti-Semites would seek to argue—many of us too have mixed-race ancestry.

Besides their general darkness compared to White northern Europeans, most ancient Israelites also had some African blood, as we have argued above, although it may often have been much diluted. By traditional White American definitions, anyone with any Black blood is to be viewed as Black; if our history in this nation has so defined us, then we might be able to identify ethnically with biblical characters—many of whom had some African blood by this definition—more than Eurocentric portrayals of them would suggest.[130] The Bible, however, never deals with these characters' color, for color—whether light or dark—was never an issue in their social environment. The Bible also indicates that obedience to God's standards of justice and mercy was far more significant.

White churches often use pictures of a White Jesus and White Bible characters, probably to make their children feel at home with the characters. But if we evaluated the Bible characters' real complexion on the standard for race we use in this country, many of them might not have fared well on Mississippi's buses before desegregation. Most of them surely appeared more like North Africans than like northern Europeans.

We would never imply that the Bible is irrelevant for White people; but we join Felder, McKissic, McCray and others in opposing claims that the Bible relates to people conscious of their light complexion more than to those of us who are conscious of our dark complexion. Our basis for identifying with biblical characters must go deeper than skin color (which was a nonissue in the ancient world), but illustrations in White Bibles and films should not alienate us from the Bible itself as if peoples of color were latecomers to the Christian faith.

The God of the Bible actually was never exclusively concerned with Israel; he chose Abraham in order to bless all peoples (Gen 12:3) and commissioned the first Christians to bring their message to all peoples (Mt 28:18-20; Acts 1:8). Although God's continuing love for Israel testifies to his faithfulness and his plan for all peoples to learn of him (Rom 11:25-32), God worked in the history of all peoples. "Are you not like the children of Cush [Africa] to Me, people of Israel?" the Lord declares. "Didn't I lead Israel up from Egypt—but likewise the Philistines from Crete and the Arameans from Kir?" (Amos 9:7)

The Bible repeatedly affirms that God, who is not flesh and not made in our image, is the rightful God of all peoples—whatever their nationality or complexion. Thus we dare not seek to deny him to others, but rather we intend to refute implicit claims by some others which would deny him to us or imply that we are at best secondary heirs of his kingdom. As stated before, the first non-Jewish Christian was an African court official (Acts 8:26-39). God and the early church did not share the modern world's fixation with color boundaries, but had they done so, Africans would not have been the ones excluded. Jewish Christians initially had problems with Gentiles, but their biggest recorded problems with Gentile Christians were with Greeks and Romans—the Bible's closest cultures to Europeans.

The Bible Is Our Book

More of the Bible is set in the region of northeast Africa than in Europe, even southern Europe; whereas Rome is mentioned about twenty times and Greece twenty-six, Ethiopia appears forty times and Egypt over seven hundred.[131] For the sake of those who want to claim Rome for the heritage of Europe as a continent (though it ruled more territory in North Africa than in northern Europe) while rejecting Egypt as part of Africa, we should note: *northern Europe nowhere* appears in the Bible!

The Bible was an African book far longer than it was a northern European book; most of it makes more sense from an African cultural standpoint than from a northern European one. And notwithstanding the prejudices some White Christians, reflecting their culture's attitudes, displayed in the past, God never made White people the guardians of Christendom. Biblical Christianity is spreading fastest now in Africa, Latin America and Asia; the only continent weaker in Christian evangelism than Europe now is Antarctica (and that is because barely anyone lives there). Even in North America, the Black, various Spanish-speaking, Korean, Chinese and other minority communities supply much of the impetus for revival.

The day when Black Christians must play a significant role in evangelizing White America may be coming sooner than most of us think. History in fact supports the plausibility of such a thought. Although financial considerations prevented most Black American churches from doing as much as we wanted in overseas missions after the Civil War[132]—despite the fact that we would have usually accomplished it more sensitively than Whites[133]—we were among the first to recognize the importance of sharing Christ's hope among all peoples.[134]

Indeed, although William Carey of England, a pioneer in crosscultural sensitivity who worked among the people of India and often struggled with colonial authorities there,[135] is often called the father of modern missions,[136] it is a matter of historical record that African-American missionaries preceded him. The radical African-American minister George Liele founded Jamaica's first Baptist church in 1782, eleven years before Carey left the British Isles. By 1791 Liele's church in Kingston had nearly 350 members, most of whom were slaves, but some of whom were free Blacks and Whites.[137] His churches, incidentally, also became quite involved in insurrections against slavery.[138]

Slaveborn African-American David George (1743-1810) started a Baptist church in New Brunswick in 1782, and in 1793 he led much of his congregation to Sierra Leone, where he established the first Baptist church in West Africa and helped establish the modern nation of Sierra Leone. There he encouraged missions and continued to minister till his death in 1810. Like many other Black ministers, he was persecuted for interracial ministry—in his case, for baptizing a White person.[139]

Leaders in the nineteenth-century evangelical missions movement included Black women such as Amanda Berry Smith (1837-1915). Influenced by Phoebe Palmer's holiness teachings in New York City, Smith ran orphanages and was an itinerant preacher in the United States, England, Liberia and India.[140] To go back much further: long before Europe sent missionaries or even responded to the gospel, three African missionaries from Egypt were martyred for their witness in Switzerland. After Christianity spread in that region these missionaries came to be honored, and continue to be honored, as saints.[141]

Even though the goal in reaching White people is to bring them to Christ, Lord of all peoples, not to make them Black, we should not accommodate the sin of racial prejudice by pretending that Christianity has ever been a distinctly "White religion"! Christ's absolute claims allow no prior loyalties (see, for example, Mt 10:14-39; Mk 1:16-20; 8:34-38; Lk 12:33; 14:25-35; 18:22-30; Jn 12:23-26; 13:12-17)—including commitment to one's race, nation or tribe. A day is therefore coming when we will have to find creative ways to cross racial barriers not for our sake but for the sake of reaching *others* with the gospel. Our final chapter will propose some suggestions along these lines.

Division by Races?

By color definitions used to define Blackness in the United States, Egypt was largely a Black African people, although it included other elements; Israel also included elements of a Black African heritage. Yet the entire discussion of this issue has been fraught with a recurrent semantic question which relativizes the whole issue for both sides of the debate. As we have been hinting in our discussion of Egypt and Israel, our categories of racial division are inadequate. It is relatively easy to refute older Eurocentric claims that Egyptians and Israelites were essentially White Europeans; but careless Afrocentric claims that make all Egyptians "coal-black" or the Israelites full-blooded Black Africans are no more accurate historically than the older Eurocentric excesses, and simply invite skeptics to dismiss our far more credible genuine claims.

Some ancient kingdoms, particularly in Africa, were purely Black kingdoms. Others, like Egypt, were mixed kingdoms, not belonging to a single race as modern categories define race. That some modern readers are obsessed with proving Egyptians either "Black" or "White," however, only shows the weakness of our categories—categories originally created by our oppressors to define and control us. When we buy into a system of dividing races that ignores gradation of skin tone and intermarriage among races, we accept a system that was created by Whites in the nineteenth century, when Whites believed that they were the most highly evolved race, the newest product of evolution. The whole classification of black versus white versus yellow (African versus European versus Asian) was their construct, partly so they could claim for themselves the histories of powerful peoples with whom they chose to identify.

Lacking sufficient data, nineteenth-century ethnographers created three major racial classifications on the basis of prejudices, regarding "intermediate" characteristics as due to mixing of pure races, an idea exploited not only by U.S. slavery advocates[142] but also eventually by Hitler and others.[143] Some of this prejudicial design undoubtedly stems from racist European philosophers like Hegel (who thought his own German people and culture were the highest products of the spirit of history so far; Hegel of course could not have propagated such ideas after Hitler took German nationalism to its logical conclusion).

In the mid-1800s scientific racism was common in the United States, and Harvard scientist Louis Agassiz went so far as to maintain that Blacks and Whites originated separately rather than from common ancestors. Agassiz's position "offered to the anxious South the perfect defense of its peculiar institution: an ethnological defense of slavery."[144] From Aristotle on, the inequality of "nature" had been used to justify slavery; henceforth it could be made to justify racism as well.[145] Agassiz thus considered interracial marriage a sin against nature as serious as incest and sought to avoid all personal contact with Blacks.[146]

In the face of supposedly scientific data justifying slavery, two nonabolitionist clergymen, horrified by the theory, began to use their knowledge of science to challenge it.[147] More seriously, Asa Gray, an evangelical biology professor at Harvard, took Agassiz on.[148] Gray admittedly had more at stake in the issue than purely biological interest: "from evangelicalism he had learned the moral worth of every member of the human race, and did not hesitate to go against the opinions of his peers in expressing distaste for slavery."[149]

Economic motives of European powers who were "colonizing" Native American, African and Asian civilizations also contributed to racist thinking. W. E. B. Du Bois observed that

the scientific basis of race difference . . . appeared increasingly difficult as observation and measurement became more accurate. Three, five, twenty races were differentiated, until at last it was evident that mankind would not fit accurately into any scientific delimitation of racial categories; no matter what criteria were used, most men fell into intermediate classes. . . . The theory of absolutely definite racial groups was therefore abandoned, and "pure" racial types came to be regarded as merely theoretical abstractions which never really or very rarely existed. Whereas anthropologists discarded most other types early, however, "Negroid" was long retained; differentiating this stock of people from others was helpful for those needing to rationalize the slave trade.[150]

European colonialists, insistent that "thick lips, broad nose" and "wooly hair" had to accompany black skin to fit their racial scheme of "Black," regarded Black African "bushmen" as non-African![151] After reviewing various tribal physical types in Africa, Du Bois more reasonably concluded that in the *strictest* sense "there is thus no one African race and no one Negro type."[152] Yet misconceptions persist today based on racial categories rooted in our history of racism rather than in objective scientific fact. As a modern historian complains, "While the scientific basis for these studies has long been discredited (e.g., Collins 1968), specific ideas and much of the terminology survive and continue to influence interpretations of African prehistory."[153]

Objective historians today have become less comfortable with traditional racial classifications, recognizing that the modern classifications are rooted in White racism:

> Today, most physical anthropologists do not believe that pure races ever existed. . . . While one characteristic may increase in frequency from north to south, another will do so from west to east, or from the center to the periphery of its range. . . . It is therefore meaningless to choose a particular region within a range of continuous variation and to label its inhabitants a race.[154]

Biology has likewise brought racial categories into question, as Sharon Begley points out in a *Newsweek* article:

> "Racial" traits are what statisticians call non-concordant. . . . [This] means that sorting people according to *these* traits produces different groupings than you get in sorting them by *those* (equally valid) traits. When biologist Jared Diamond of UCLA surveyed half a dozen traits . . . he found that, depending on which traits you pick, you can form very surprising "races."[155]

So-called Asian dental features characterize both Native Americans and Swedes; biochemically, Norwegians and northern Nigerian Fulanis fall into one race, whereas Japanese and most Africans fall into another; by blood types Germans and New Guineans form one race whereas Japanese and Estonian Europeans form another. Although Somalis and Ghanaians both have dark complexions, in most genetic traits they could be as distant as either group is from the Greeks.[156] Cheikh Anta Diop observes that "the nasal indices of Ethiopians and Dravidians would seem to approximate them to the Germanic peoples, though both are black races."[157] Thus roughly 70 percent of cultural anthropologists today and half of physical anthropologists no longer accept race as a biological category.[158]

The growing recognition that racism permeated early racial classifications has naturally brought about a reaction, as modern archaeologists point out:

A major reason for the lack of integration between archaeology and physical anthropology in the decades immediately after World War II was the question of race. During the 19th and early 20th centuries some scholars (and many politicians) attempted to use physical anthropology to help prove their theories of white racial superiority.[159]

Today's physical anthropologists concentrate more on the "age, sex, and health of deceased," aware that skeletal measurements are inadequate for differentiating human populations, although genetics research promises to provide clearer genealogical links.[160] Material culture (such as ruins and artifacts) is no more objective as a tool for ethnic classification. Because different aspects of material culture (agricultural, military and other practices) provide different regional configurations, scholars admit that it is no longer easy to reconstruct "supposed ethnic groups."[161] Nor do any correlates exist between physical racial categories on one hand and linguistic or cultural spheres on the other.[162] Thus one scholar warns that general racial categories

are neither exhaustive nor mutually exclusive. The Australian aborigines, for example, with Negroid skin and Caucasoid hair, are sometimes classified as a fourth "race." . . . Both the longest human heads and the roundest are found among American Indian tribes. The tallest and the shortest people in the world, the Watusi and the Pygmy, live within a few miles of each other; both have black skin and kinky hair.[163]

There was simply too much overlap in most areas to permit the cut-and-dried categories traditionally advocated by scholars inclined toward racism.

As should now be clear, sharp racial divisions are artificial categories, just as geographical boundaries are.[164] Racial characteristics (skin tone, hair, nose) vary among the same "race" and overlap among diverse peoples, and even if races were "pure" (that is, if each fell into one of three categories with no overlap) to begin with, intermarriage among peoples throughout history has skewed the categories. As Raymond Mack notes of the biological data,

The basic physical structure of all human beings is the same. Furthermore, differences within categories are greater than differences between them; the categories are based on gross averages. There is more difference between the lightest and the darkest Negroid, or between the lightest and the darkest Caucasoid, than between the lightest Negroid and the darkest Caucasoid.[165] To argue the case in racial terms is thus in a sense to capitulate to the very line of thinking White racists devised, as Cornel West points out: "The basic aim of black Muslim theology—with its distinct black supremacist account of the origins of white people—was to counter white supremacy. Yet this preoccupation with white supremacy still allowed white people to serve as the principal point of reference." Elijah Muhammad simply "imitated" the line of reasoning White racists had created.[166]

For the same reason West both praises contemporary Afrocentrism, for its focus on genuine Black issues, and critiques it, for its fear of cultural mixing and for sometimes reinforcing "the narrow discussions about race."[167] The Nazis who turned the New Testament into an Aryan document and its leading characters into non-Jewish Aryans distorted history for perverse ends. What we currently intend as noble ends cannot justify distorting history in a different direction, especially if someone could later use our words in perverse ways in which we did not intend them. Turning all famous personages of the past Black will not do, just as turning them all White has not done.

The importance of the degree of Egypt's or Israel's Black ancestry may be further relativized by another point. Many anthropologists think that humanity originated in Africa[168]—which would make the whole human race of African descent. Further, since dark people can have lighter offspring but White people do not have dark offspring, it makes sense to suppose that the primordial Adam and/or Eve was Black.[169] If this is true it would mean that everyone has *some* Black blood. Following evidence from the most thorough and up-to-date study of global genetics so far, a writer for *Time* magazine explains that "all Europeans are thought to be a hybrid population, with 65% Asian and 35% African genes."[170] In other words, not only do most of us have some White ancestry, but *all* Whites have some significant African ancestry.

This revelation may be disconcerting to Aryan purists like Hitler and the Klan, but our community has accepted it for a long time. *We* didn't invent racism. White racists drew the lines of our community to keep our ancestors down. Our ancestors banded together for survival, and we must continue to uphold one another for the survival of our people. But the very emphasis on dividing peoples by race is an historical byproduct of *racism*. We come in different complexions and other physical features, but what unites us as a people in America is less our skin tone than our shared history.

If our boundaries were drawn by our recent history, but the same boundaries did not exist through all of human history, we cannot demonstrate that the boundaries are permanent. Because the modern world's racial categories are not permanent or inherently natural lines of demarcation, we turn in the next chapter to a discussion of a deeper basis for identification.

Conclusion

To the extent that Black is defined by skin complexion, nearly all Egyptians seem to have been dark enough that in this country they could pass for the darker or lighter of *us*. In other words, if we are going to ask a modern question about ancient peoples who did not think in such terms, the Egyptians were us. The Israelites were probably not usually as dark as the Egyptians, but in the hot Mediterranean sun, they too were dark, and many might have passed for lighter-skinned African-Americans if suddenly transported to North America.

But helpful as this question is for encouraging those of our people annoyed by contrary portrayals, it does not go far enough. Throughout history it has been culture rather than physical features that united most peoples. Color has become an issue to us today mainly because the Euro-American community historically forced it to be an issue for us.

We must look to a deeper basis of identification, an identification based on the bond of suffering. Indeed, it was on this basis that our ancestors most often identified with the characters in the Bible. The Israelites in Egypt, for instance, were slaves like we were, regardless of their skin tone. Regardless of our skin tone, we belong to the Black race and suffer together as a community. Thus we have always drawn the lines between our community and our oppressors more on social grounds (who identifies himself or herself as part of our community) than on the basis of skin tone or other physical features. This basis for identification may also allow us some other allies in the struggle for justice.

5

God of Our Weary Years: Identification on the Basis of Common Oppression

*Help us to realize that our brothers are not
simply those of our own blood and nation,
but far more are they those who think as we do
and strive toward the same ideals. . . .
Help us, O Lord, to remember our kindred
beyond the sea—all those who bend in bonds,
of our own blood and of human kind—the lowly
and the wretched, the ignorant and the weak.*

W. E. B. DU BOIS[1]

IF WE DO NOT IDENTIFY SIMPLY ON THE BASIS OF NATIONALITY OR COMMON skin color, on what basis do we identify? One basis on which we can identify is a heritage of common oppression.[2] Oppressed peoples have something in common, and we who have experienced particular kinds of oppression (slavery and racism on the basis of our skin color) experience a particular bond with others who have experienced the same kinds of oppression.[3] (Thus, for example, Black Consciousness in South Africa analyzed the political situation in terms of race, but meant this racial perspective "not in an ethnographic sense but in the sense that the oppressed group in South Africa was black."[4])

Racism was created as an ideological justification to oppress others. To fail to recognize that the issue behind racism is oppression is to buy into the very lie by which the oppressors have sought to define the situation of the oppressed. This broader approach of identifying with the oppressed in general also provides a practical basis for cooperation to achieve justice, helping us combat racism in a society impatient with racially specific claims. Thus, for example, the policies of radical Republicans after the Civil War benefited lower-class Blacks and Whites alike, but then White powerbrokers in the South appealed to *racial* divisions to unite lower-class Whites with themselves and regained power.[5] After examining all other strategies for countering racism, Derrick Bell concludes that the most effective way to help our own people will be a broader societal coalition to "seek justice for all through a systematic campaign of attacking poverty as well as racial discrimination."[6] (Leading up to this conclusion, the rest of Bell's book illustrated how Whites in the United States have historically opposed any programs aimed only at the Black community. Bell himself paid a costly personal price to challenge racial injustice[7] and hence has earned the right to suggest that we oppose mistreatment of others regardless of race.)

A Black Civil Rights activist in the seventies denounced White racists in the United States for degrading Black people's worth: "Violence is a country where property counts for more than people."[8] But his rage is applicable far beyond the United States. Because oppression is rampant in every society where human selfishness allows some people to gain power over others—that is, in virtually every society—it is helpful for us to survey some forms of serious oppression in history and especially today. We focus especially on the oppression of Black Africans, although we list other examples as well.[9] Although minority peoples are often more sensitive to other minority perspectives without being so urged,[10] minorities must remain vigilant against the temptation, generally favored by oppressors, to divide the oppressed from one another.[11]

This chapter especially focuses on slavery, its history before and beyond the American practice of slavery with which we are most familiar, and some early Christian responses to slavery. When some members of the Nation of Islam have identified Christianity with slavery, they have severely misrepresented the historical evidence (although some professed Christians *did* fit their stereotype). We begin this chapter by looking at non-Western slavery in history, especially in what Western history calls the medieval period. In this period the Arabs were beginning the transcontinental slave trade.

Slavery in the Arab World

Most empires throughout history held slaves—the Egyptians, the Assyrians, the Babylonians and the Romans, as well as Asian, African, and pre-Columbian American civilizations.[12] What surprises many people today, however, is how widespread hard-core slavery remains in modern times. For example, the last region to officially abolish slavery was the Arabian peninsula in 1962,[13] but even then official proclamations seem to have had little effect.[14] In the mid-sixties it was still being estimated that Saudi Arabia alone held a quarter of a million slaves.[15] Besides such traditional, hereditary slaves (to whom some would limit the designation "true slaves"), many migrant workers in that region (especially from predominantly Islamic countries, but also non-Muslims from poorer Asian countries) likewise continue to be *virtually* enslaved—bound to their masters, unable to leave or complain, and paid only about thirty dollars each month.[16] Many of these servants are raped and beaten; one Filipino guest worker fleeing the country had seventy-two injuries, including skull fractures.[17] In many parts of the world slavery remains a reality even today.

The first part of this chapter will focus on this and related examples, examining Arab slavery in history, then the racial question and finally attempts to abolish slavery. After this we will turn to examining slavery and other kinds of oppression elsewhere in the contemporary world, before returning to the question of slavery and religion in the United States.

Arab Slavery in History

We focus on Arab slavery in this part of the chapter because apart from the Western slavery with which we are familiar firsthand, the largest enslavement of Africans in history unquestionably involved the Arabs. This is not to imply that Arab slavery was harsher than other kinds of slavery. Indeed, it was rarely comparable to the racial oppression and slavery practiced in the West in more recent centuries.[18] Islamic law offered slaves some significant humane protections absent from Western slavery (for example, it forbade the splitting of families) and encouraged slaveholders to free slaves[19] (although this act was considered much less meritorious than many less expensive acts of charity[20]). Islam actually "improved the position of the Arabian slave":

> The Qur'an recognizes the basic inequality between master and slave and the rights of the former over the latter (XVI:71; XXX:28). It also recognizes concubinage [slave sexual partners] (IV:3; XXIII:6; XXXIII:50-52; LXX:30). [Yet also] it urges, without actually commanding, kindness to the slave (IV:36; IX:60; XXIV:58).[21]

But the Arab trade in African slaves introduced significant aspects of oppression into human history worthy of note in this chapter. Despite the prevalence of slavery in the early Roman Empire,[22] it had mostly vanished from Europe in the early Middle Ages.[23] It was the Arab slave trade that paved the way for Western slavery of Africans. The Arab slave trade has a much longer history than the European slave trade, although its geographical distance has made that history less known in our country. Under Arab leadership, slavery moved from a local or regional level to a much wider mercantile trade.

The Arab world's involvement in expanding the slave trade was not purely coincidental. As one specialist in the field notes, "Islam, by sanctioning slavery, gave tremendous impetus to its growth and, as a consequence, sparked the development of the slave trade along transcontinental lines."[24] We think unlikely the view of some experts that Muhammad wished to legitimize slavery;[25] custom had already established it, and Muhammad instead *regulated* it.[26] But the fact that Muhammad himself held slaves[27] made the institution impossible to challenge, and subsequent centuries of Islamic law regarded slavery as required by the Qur'an itself.[28] Although Arab slavery was generally more humane than Western slavery, these assumptions about Islamic law made the abolition of slavery more difficult. Muslims objected that "to forbid what God permits is almost as great an offense as to permit what God forbids."[29]

Contrary to what one might guess from propaganda traditionally circulated by the Nation of Islam,[30] slavery in Arabia and the Gulf region has an old and continuous history for centuries. In contrast to the West African slave trade, the slave trade in East Africa picked up as the British and French were finally working to abolish the slave trade on the seas; most slaves from East Africa were sent to Arabia and the Persian Gulf area.[31] Indeed, because Arabs, Berbers and Persians pioneered the long-distance slave trade to begin with,[32] and because "the importation of Black slaves into Islamic lands" over twelve hundred years may have involved more slaves than the European slave trade did, some African writers have suggested that both the West and the Middle East should pay reparations to Africa.[33] The Arab world had slavery for a thousand years before the Europeans used slaves in the Americas and continued it over a century after the West abolished it; they employed as many as eleven million slaves during this period.[34]

After the Arabs conquered the Sassanian empire in 642 they took over the slave trade in East Africa.[35] Their *jihad,* or holy war, "served as a convenient license to wage war against unbelievers" and, after winning such wars, to enslave these unbelievers.[36] Even in later times, the slave raiders conveniently assumed all West Africans to be idolaters, therefore subject to enslavement.[37] Meanwhile, the Barbary states captured Christians and sold them for ransom; Jews and Christians who defaulted on their tribute to Muslim conquerors were also enslaved.[38]

Thus the slave trade spread along with the armies of Islam. Arabs initially imported slaves from Europe as well as Africa; the Ottoman Empire later reduced many Christians in the Balkans to slavery and then turned to the Caucasus as a source for White slaves.[39] But by the nineteenth century Africa was providing no longer simply a large proportion but the "overwhelming majority of slaves used in Muslim countries from Morocco to Asia."[40]

The slave trade was vicious, and though briefer than transport in cargo holds across the Atlantic (in which as many as 40 percent of slaves from inner Angola perished before reaching the Americas[41]), Arab transportation of captured slaves was also costly. The mortality rate for those marched across the Sahara may have been as great or greater; stragglers, weakened by malnutrition, were either killed or left to die on their own.[42] Male slaves may have suffered most, "yoked together with forked sticks or chained together so as to prevent them from escaping."[43]

Even after arriving at their destination some slaves, such as those assigned to remove salt from soil and prepare it for cultivation, found their oppression intolerable:

> Consisting principally of slaves imported from East Africa and numbering some tens of thousands, they lived and worked in conditions of extreme misery. They were fed, we are told, on "a few handfuls" of flour, semolina, and dates. They rose in several successive rebellions, the most important of which lasted fifteen years, from 868-883, and for a while offered a serious threat to the Baghdad Caliphate.[44]

But in contrast to Western slavery, with its exploitation of slaves for plantation and mine labor, the Arab market usually preferred young women and girls, who generally sold for higher prices than male slaves did. Women were used especially as household servants and concubines.[45] By contrast, Arabs neutered male African slaves to become eunuchs in prestigious households, a practice that grew with the Turkish sultans.[46] But the sexual double standard was evident; Arab men used Black women slaves, but their wives dared not use male slaves. One account in *The Thousand and One Nights* reflects Arab male fears: having forgotten something, King Shahzaman returns from a journey unexpectedly to find his wife and a Black slave asleep together; he kills them in their sleep with his sword, then proceeds with his journey.[47] Such stories seem to reflect the stereotypes of Africans in medieval Arab literature as possessing "immense potency and unbridled sexuality"; the texts portray both Black men and women "as creatures of immense sexual appetites and powers."[48] When one has access to a large number of sexual partners from another race, it is not difficult to guess why one would stereotype that race in exaggerated sexual terms. The sexual use of slaves, regardless of race, has been a common historic practice.[49]

Judaism and Christianity, which had earlier existed in cultures practicing slavery (albeit on a smaller scale), had opposed the sexual use of slaves (Christian law mandated excommunication from the church for this offense). Islam, however, did not consider slave concubinage morally objectionable. Arab masters regularly kept and sought slave concubines.[50] An Islamicist observes that mating with Black slave women was sanctioned by Islamic law "and indeed by the Qur'an itself."[51] "A Muslim was strictly forbidden from marrying his slave. . . . A Muslim, however, was free to acquire as many concubines as his purse allowed. Under Islamic law, it was both legally and morally correct for a man to have sexual relations with his female slaves as with his wives."[52] This improved the mother's legal status and created a mulatto population.[53]

Although mulattos are common, one may speculate why Arab countries did not become darker than they are; the demographic growth of mulattos seems to have been lower than for the strictly Arab population. If we may believe a nineteenth-century report, infanticide explains why, for example, the many Black concubines of Turkish gentlemen produced so few mulatto children.[54]

Racism and Arab Slavery

Although some American Muslims have exploited the image that Islam historically escaped the curse of racial prejudice, nineteenth-century Western thinkers created this image merely as a foil to challenge Western racism.[55] The image was never more than propaganda, as even the most basic acquaintance with medieval Arab literature demonstrates.[56] Given the respect for Africa evident in many Greek and Roman sources,[57] Western prejudice against Africans may have even derived in significant measure from attitudes of Arab slave traders.[58]

Early Christianity emphasized the equality of all, specifically including Africans, and, like the cult of Isis, swept aside racial distinctions in its common fellowship.[59] Islam could function as a multicultural brotherhood as well, but the economic temptation involved in slavery ultimately gave way to a period with many examples of prejudice.

Arab prejudice itself did not begin with color, however, but with culture; the color prejudice does not derive from the Qur'an itself or seem to stem from Muhammad's day.[60] Arabs respected their rivals in the East, the great civilizations of China and India, and their rivals in Christian civilizations as well. But they believed that by contrast the "barbarians" to the north and south were most easily enslaved.[61] Although Islamic law prohibited enslaving fellow Muslims, Islam (in contrast to nominally Christian Europeans) held no scruples about holding fellow religionists as slaves if they converted after their enslavement.[62]

Although Arab slavery was multiracial and Arabs favored White slaves, they especially came to associate slavery with Blacks. For instance, the term *'abd,* originally applied to Black slaves (White ones were called *mamlūks*), eventually applied to slaves in general.[63] Whereas European military forces resisted Muslim slave raiders, many parts of Africa were unable to provide a united front. "Lamentably, many African chiefs often became middlemen in the trade by rounding up inhabitants of nearby villages and exchanging them for an assortment of manufactured wares." Arab traders found buying slaves easier than capturing them for themselves.[64] Whether as a result of the relative ease with which they acquired them (partly for geographic reasons) or because Arabs were impressed with the quality of their initial Nubian slaves,[65] one writer concludes that "the Arabs had always considered Africans as especially suited to be their servants."[66]

Indeed, although the Qur'an rejects any racial basis for slavery, some Muslims adopted this idea from Aristotle. By the tenth century, they justified the enslavement of northern peoples (the Turks) and southern peoples (Black Africans).[67] With a racial theory in hand, despite the southward advance of Islam into West Africa in the 1300s, "the perception remained, disputed but widespread, that African Muslims were somehow different from other Muslims and that Africa was a legitimate source of slaves."[68] Nevertheless, nineteenth-century Muslim reports, similar to those of American slaveholders, claim that their Black slaves were *happy* to be Muslim slaves; this had made them human beings.[69]

Arabs usually preferred White slaves when they could acquire them[70] (perhaps to some degree because they were rarer by virtue of their location and political factors). Arabs paid much higher prices for White women (whom they obtained from areas like Turkey and southern Russia near the Black Sea) than for Black women.[71] (The price of White slaves rose still higher in 1829, when Russia cut off much of the supply, until Turkish attacks moved Russia to look the other way to some extent.[72]) Yet once the Russians had cut off the supply of most Georgian and Circassian slaves, the Muslim nations increased still further the scale of their enslavement of Blacks from East and West Africa.[73]

Color also affected one's social mobility. White slaves regularly became "generals, provincial governors, sovereigns, and founders of dynasties," but whereas Black slaves rose so high in Muslim India, they barely ever did so in the central Muslim lands.[74] Until the supply for White slaves was reduced in the nineteenth century, Blacks had fewer opportunities for advancement and "were most commonly used for domestic and menial purposes, often as eunuchs," and to work the salt and copper mines of the south.[75]

Possibly because more slaves were Black and they were often given less prestigious positions, other prejudices appear frequently in Islamic literature of the Middle Ages.[76] Thus Arab texts often report Africans to be stupid, dishonest, unclean and stinky, and sometimes call their women ugly.[77] "The black's physical appearance is described as ugly, distorted, or monstrous."[78] Thus Ibn Qutayba (828-889), undoubtedly following earlier traditions on this point,[79] explains that Blacks "are ugly and misshapen, because they live in a hot country. The heat overcooks them in the womb, and curls their hair."[80] In the eleventh century Sa'id al-Andalusi (d. 1070) similarly explained that cold makes extreme northerners stupid, but temperature extremes also affect Black Africans, who "lack self-control and steadiness of mind and are overcome by fickleness, foolishness, and ignorance."[81] Further examples include writers from throughout the Arab world, such as the tenth-century Iraqi Arab Ibn al-Faqih al-Hamadani.[82] Many accounts remain of "insult and humiliation" suffered by those with dark complexion, whereas other Arab texts speak of Whiteness "as a mark of superior birth."[83]

As in many cultures,[84] though non-Arab converts were equal in theory, in practice they "were regarded as inferior and subjected to a whole series of fiscal, social, political, military, and other disabilities. They were known collectively as the *mawali* . . . a term the primary meaning of which was 'freedman.' "[85] A good Black slave was not without hope, however; in *The Thousand and One Nights* a good Black slave was allowed to turn White at his death as a reward![86]

In one clear respect, however, Arabs held a higher view of Black slaves than Europeans and their American descendants did. Lacking a specific doctrine of African racial inferiority, Arabs did not view race as a barrier to marriage, although social class was.[87] Even this rule was not always followed, however; the Bedouin considered marriages with Blacks shameful, as did the Arab nobility. It was normally concubinage—mating with Black slave women—rather than interracial *marriage* that was practiced.[88] And while Arab masters slept with concubines of any complexion, their racially mixed servant armies proved a matter of tension, leading to racial segregation. (Ibn Tulun built the first separate Black quarter for soldiers, known as *al-qata'i*.[89])

Attempts to End the Trade

After Christian abolitionists gained political influence in Britain and the British Empire abolished slavery, growing abolitionist sentiments there led to British opposition to the slave trade in the Arab world as well.[90] After Britain had abolished slavery, France, the Netherlands and Russia followed suit. Britain then exerted diplomatic pressure where possible and eventually naval power where necessary to try to stem the slave trade elsewhere.[91] Arab leaders warned that their societies depended so heavily on the slave trade that attempts at abolition would jeopardize their thrones and possibly their lives as well.[92] Convinced that Islamic law permitted and therefore established slavery, "the most conservative religious quarters," especially in Mecca and Medina, opposed the reforms most fervently.[93]

Thus when the British persuaded the Turks (the Ottoman Empire) to reduce the slave trade,[94] Shaykh Jamal issued a *fatwa* from Mecca in 1855 declaring the Turks now apostate from true Islam. As a consequence, he declared, it was "lawful to kill them without incurring criminal penalties or bloodguilt, and to enslave their children."[95] Arabs revolted, attacking the Ottoman authorities, who finally agreed to permit the slave trade in the Hijaz. Elsewhere, Arabs ignored both the Turks and the British, except in Egypt, Tunisia and Algeria (which were by then under British and French control). Libya and Arabia, free from foreign domination, remained centers of the slave trade long after it was shut down elsewhere.[96] Although other motives of ill-fated British colonialism were less noble (and colonial companies in some areas practiced virtual slave labor of which most British abolitionists were unaware[97]), one motive of colonialism was to stop the African slave trade, forcibly if need be.[98]

Abolitionism gradually made some progress. Thus the bey of Tunis, needing British help to fight off the French and Turks, officially abolished slavery in 1846 (although slavery continued illegally, including the enslavement of many Muslim women contrary to Islamic law).[99] The sultan of Morocco insisted that abolition was unrealistic, since slavery was part of the Moroccans' religion as well as their culture;[100] but Britain succeeded in most of North Africa except Morocco and with the Ottoman Empire except the Hijaz.[101] Iran outlawed slavery in 1906, although the prohibitions were enforced only by laws that were enacted later.[102] In time many Muslim leaders also concluded that the spirit of Islam did not support slavery.[103]

Official decrees were helpful, but the struggle to end the slave trade was far from ended. Egypt's ruler allowed Samuel Baker, a British explorer, to try to shut down the slave trade in the upper Nile region, where "5000 Arab slave traders . . . were shipping some 50,000 slaves a year down the Nile." Despite some small victories, however, Baker could not suppress them, and British attempts continued long after Baker's decease.[104] The slave trade in the Sudan was heavy in the 1850s and 1860s, but the new ruler Khedive Ismail outlawed it and in the 1870s appointed Europeans as officials in his government, trusting them to enforce the antislavery laws. In 1875 General Charles Gordon cracked down on slavers, but after two years Muslim resentment against his interference as a non-Muslim eventually forced him to withdraw.[105]

The sultan of Oman and Muscat found the slave trade particularly profitable. From 1818 on, the sugar plantations of the Mascarene Islands required a continuing supply of slaves; in the decade following 1835, Omani businessmen there controlled large estates of two to three hundred slaves each.[106] To better control his profitable and growing empire in East Africa, the Omani sultan Seyyid Said actually moved his seat of authority from Oman to Zanzibar.[107] East Africans had turned to Oman to help them in ousting the Portuguese, but "the new imperialists [the Omanis] turned out to be no less grasping and rapacious than their predecessors."[108]

While acknowledging Britain's interest in Seyyid Said's "commercial empire" in Zanzibar and the interest of both scientists and evangelical missionaries, one scholar points to the slave trade as the key factor in British intervention in East Africa. The English were horrified by accounts of dead and live slaves crammed together as tightly as possible in Arab cargo holds, "one mass of smallpox." "Had the slave trade not existed, it is very doubtful whether the British would have become deeply interested in East African affairs in the middle of the nineteenth century."[109]

Various British officials placed polite pressure on Arab allies, especially when the slave trade passed through British territories. Thus when they learned that Seyyid, who by now controlled much of the East African coast and the Arab slave trade there, was shipping slaves to India, they quietly objected to him.[110] When quiet diplomacy failed to produce concrete results, the British warned that "British friendship," on which the Omanis depended, "had to be repaid in the hard currency of slave trade reform," and the British navy began searching ships heading for India.

After realizing that the British could not intercept most of the ships, the Omanis continued breaking the treaty, until finally Seyyid needed British help too much not to cooperate. In the end, Britain forcibly shut down the East African slave trade, closing it down in Zanzibar in 1897 and in Kenya in 1907.[111] The British finally succeeded in Zanzibar by a show of force yielding five hundred Arab casualties, but the Arab plantations there were able to survive into the twentieth century anyway, since most ex-slaves remained as tenants working plots of land on their former masters' estates.[112] The show of force against the Omani slave trade was British imperialism, but in this case it served the good cause of checking Arab imperialism against Africa.

In the nineteenth century about forty thousand slaves were being shipped to Zanzibar each year, then reshipped north. A diplomatic impasse with the profiting rulers of Zanzibar frustrated the British officers (who by this period were firmly antislavery) in their attempts to stop the trade.[113] On one occasion as a British frigate gave chase to an Arab pirate vessel, the slaver pirates reportedly cut 240 slaves' throats and threw them overboard to lighten the ship and hasten their escape.[114] The Arab slave traders were from Oman, not Zanzibar, so they also exploited Zanzibar, kidnapping its own citizens if too few slaves were available.[115]

Thus Chancellor Williams, an African-American historian especially proficient in this area of African history, expresses his concern over the confusion of many U.S. youth who "are dropping their white western slavemasters' names and adopting, not African, but their Arab and Berber slavemasters' names!" He laments that "Blacks are in Arabia for precisely the same reasons Blacks are in the United States, South America, and the Caribbean Islands—through capture and enslavement."[116] He notes that many African historians, still reacting to more recent European colonialism, have emphasized the evils of

European imperialism in Africa while ignoring the most damaging developments from the Arab impact before the general European takeover in the last quarter of the nineteenth century, a relatively recent period. . . . From the earliest times the elimination of these [African] states as independent African sovereignties had been an Asian objective, stepped up by Muslim onslaughts after the seventh century A.D.[117]

"The Islamic advance was three-pronged," he reports: "proselytizing missions claiming one brotherhood; widespread intermarriages and concubinage with African women, due to the Muslim system of polygamy; and forceful conversions at sword point."[118] North African mulattos called themselves White and helped Arab slave traders enslave Black peoples, fearful of the consequences of being considered Black.[119] In the Sudan of more recent times, converted Africans quickly counted themselves ethnically Arab and rejected their Black African identity.[120] Further,

as Arabization spread among the Blacks so did slavery and slave raiding. The Arabs' insatiable and perpetual demands for slaves had long since changed slavery from an institution that signaled a military victory by the number of captured prisoners to an institution that provoked warfare expressly for the enslavement of men, women and children for sale and resale.[121]

The Ottoman Turks in the early-nineteenth-century Sudan were no less repressive than the Arabs. Their leader Muhammed Ali not only brought down the Funj kingdom but massacred more African men, women and children than any ruler before him—so much "that even the white world protested."[122] Although some today have glossed over the earlier period,

> very simply . . . the Arab screams against Western imperialism are the screams of outrage against Western imperialists for checking and subduing Eastern imperialists in the very midst of the Blacks they had conquered. There are still countless thousands of Blacks who are naive enough to believe that the Arabs' bitter attack on Western colonialism shows their common cause with Black Africa.[123]

Western and Arab colonialists actually seem to have made more of a common cause. Most European colonial governors in the 1800s were *encouraging* Islam as a healthy alternative to traditional religions and practices in Sierra Leone.[124] Not only colonial governors and companies but also many early Christian missionaries viewed Islam favorably and worked with Muslims where possible.[125] John S. Mbiti points out that Western colonial rulers actually helped finance the building of mosques and pilgrimage to Mecca, and generally "created conditions which facilitated the spread of Islam."[126] It appears that in some sense Western and Arab powers thus joined forces in a manner that—often intentionally though perhaps sometimes only inadvertently—exploited Africa.

Slavery Today

Outright slavery continues to occur in many nations such as Pakistan (where Christians and lower-caste Muslims are particular targets); some have estimated that as many as twenty million Pakistanis are held in bondage.[127] Those who speak out against the oppression, such as twelve-year-old former slave Iqbal Masih, risk death (Masih was gunned down April 16, 1995).[128] The Dominican Republic in the Caribbean uses as many as one million Haitian workers in similar ways.[129] A 1993 newspaper report in India's state of Orissa complained that some people there are selling children "for the price of a bowl of chicken curry"—65¢ in U.S. money.[130]

In the Sudan, the Arab Muslims of the north have been systematically starving the Black African adherents of traditional African religions and Christianity in the south, who rebelled because the north imposed Islamic law over the whole land.[131] The conflict and the inflexibility of the northern rulers have led to as many as two million deaths in the past ten years.[132] Government troops have begun "ethnic cleansing" among the Nuba mountain people, especially the

Christians there.[133] In the wake of this civil war, raids have reportedly included taking slaves, a practice the Sudan had once abolished.[134]

Slavery and slave-raiding, which never fully died out in the Sudan, have reappeared on a large scale. . . . According to this source, as well as accounts by journalists and scholars, hundreds if not thousands of people have been carried off by slave traffickers. The great majority of the victims are children between the ages of eight and fourteen who are forced to march from their native lands to the North where they are sold into slavery. . . . A Sudanese historian from the University of Khartoum who had the courage to write about [the subject] was arrested by the police.[135]

Amnesty International reports that the Sudanese government has ignored human rights to maintain its power: "virtually every kind of human rights violation known to Amnesty has been perpetrated by the political and security establishments, including arbitrary arrest and detention without charge or trial, torture and ill-treatment, [and] extrajudicial executions," among other offenses.[136] Besides thousands of extrajudicial executions in government raids on villages, Amnesty reports the enslavement of many women and children for domestic use.[137] Likewise, Sudanese professor Ushari Ahmad Mahmoud reports that the Arab militias burn villages, killing the men and seizing women and now-orphaned children to perform chores and to serve as concubines. Slaves are also shipped to the Persian Gulf, Libya, Chad and Mauritania.[138] A Sudanese lawyer noted that northern armies recruit children to convert them to Islam so they can join in fighting their homeland. "They are also used as a living blood bank for northern soldiers. Six miles from Khartoum, there is a camp called Um al-Gus where hundreds of children are being held. Every time there is a major battle, they are rounded up to donate their blood."[139]

In the Islamic Republic of Mauritania, Arab-Berber Muslims from the north hold many Black African slaves from the south.[140] As *Newsweek* reports, "More than 100,000 descendants of Africans conquered by Arabs during the 12th century are still thought to be living as old-fashioned chattel slaves. Aside from the shantytowns and a strip of land along the Senegal River, virtually all blacks are slaves, and they are more than half the population."[141] Some Mauritanian masters deny the existence of slavery when talking with outsiders—it is, after all, officially illegal—but many slaves do not mind admitting that they are slaves, though some will add hastily, "But only the children get beaten." Stirring our grief for a brainwashed brother, one slave interviewed declared, "Naturally, we blacks should be the slaves of the whites."[142] More common than this outright slavery is debt bondage, sometimes on contrived grounds, which can also enslave families for generations.[143]

In Bangladesh, slave traders kidnap three- to six-year-old boys or buy them from parents for the equivalent of twenty years' wages and empty promises of hope for the boys. The boys are then used as camel jockeys as gamblers watch in Persian Gulf nations: they are tied to the camel's back, and their screams make the camels run faster. Many die or are maimed. Residents of Gulf nations buy twelve- to twenty-five-year-old Bangladeshi females at auctions as well: those considered more beautiful may fetch as much as two thousand dollars from sheiks, while brothels employ those considered less attractive, who typically bring a price of two hundred dollars.

Because the Gulf nations employ half a million Bangladeshis, Bangladesh is reticent to crack down on this slave trade. A Muslim and a Christian have teamed up to rescue as many children as possible from this system. The Muslim complains that as Islamic nations, Bangladesh, Pakistan and the Gulf states should by all rights oppose slave prostitution, since Islam prohibits adultery.[144]

One Gulf nation, Saudi Arabia, a U.S. ally, represses its own 10 percent Shiite population and has arrested many practicing Christians as well, including hundreds of workers from developing countries.[145] In 1953 a high-level witness reported that some Saudis, usually African-born and pretending to be "missionaries," were sent to the Sudan and West African regions like Upper Volta (Burkina Faso) and Niger. There they promised to take fellow Africans to Islamic holy sites "so that they may make the pilgrimage and teach them the Koran in Arabic." Once in Saudi Arabia, these pilgrims were being enslaved.[146]

(The ideals of religion have always been easily ignored or exploited by those who value money more than faithfulness to their religion; the history of every religion is replete with examples.[147] For example, Western colonialists practiced apartheid throughout Africa, while often mouthing a religion whose original values they ignored by refusing to live with Africans as equals.[148] The teachings of true Christianity, whose founder emphasized just and loving treatment of one's neighbor, have generally been neglected by insincere professing Christians more concerned with their own agendas in life. Indeed, the lives of most North American churchgoers today reflect all too little influence from Jesus' teaching and all too little evidence of his lordship.[149])

Mozambican refugees are sometimes sold into virtual slavery to White farmers in South Africa and to Black men in the townships seeking concubines.[150] The Soviet KGB is now known to have supplied slave labor for government mines.[151] Since the end of World War II most people have known of the Nazi enslavement in labor camps of prisoners of war and people from occupied territories.[152]

Unofficial slavery also includes child labor. Perhaps one hundred thousand carpet weavers in India, one-third of the market, are children forced to work there. About half of the fifty thousand children forced to work in Pakistan's carpet industry die by the age of twelve.[153] Portugal has about two hundred thousand full-time child laborers who could otherwise be in school.[154] Jungle gold miners in Peru have reportedly enslaved thousands of children.[155] Over one thousand girls are currently slaves of traditional fetish priests in the North Tongu district of Ghana, where they are worked from dawn to dusk and also serve the priests sexually once they reach puberty.[156] A Sudanese-backed resistance movement in northern Uganda sells kidnapped children in exchange for Arab weapons.[157]

Amnesty International has documented other deadly injustices besides slavery in many of these lands.[158] In Mauritania, "government troops killed hundreds of unarmed villagers, shooting some of them dead simply because they were fishing during curfew hours. As tensions escalated between black and Arab-Berber communities in Mauritania, hundreds of blacks taken into custody 'disappeared.' "[159] A later Amnesty report documents that the government killed at least 399 political prisoners, Black men from the southern part of the country. Tortures included urinating on prisoners, burning out eyeballs with cigarettes, and various other cruel acts conducted in the midst of corpses.[160] The Arab-Berber Mauritanian government had also expelled thousands of Black Africans after a border dispute with Senegal, the nation to the south.[161]

Such repression is frequent in today's world. As is widely known, Sunni Muslim Iraqis sought to implement genocide against Sunni Muslim Kurds, a minority population (20 percent) they controlled.[162] Arab Islamic fundamentalists are gradually working to expand their own influence (and ultimately, they hope, control) in East Africa.[163] Sadly, though the West's proxy battles through African states declined after the end of the Cold War, violence remains rampant. Intertribal war led to one of the most rapid holocausts in history as hundreds of thousands of Rwandans—mostly unarmed, many women and children—were massacred by Rwandans of a rival group in 1994.[164]

States such as India and Pakistan continue to threaten one another's borders; young girls from the hills are still sold as prostitutes in Bangkok's brothels; political dissidents are still suppressed in many African nations. Whether through Islamic fundamentalists, Western strong-arm tactics or the internal repression of dissident indigenous peoples in Central America, Central Asian Republics and elsewhere (shall we compare the unredressed treatment of Native

Americans and others in the United States?), colonial imperialism is alive and well in the world, even among some parties that most loudly protest against imperialism.

If we want to protest oppression today, there is plenty of it to protest all over the world, including bona fide slavery, torture and genocidal racism. Merely protesting past injustices while ignoring those of the present takes little courage. But if we can use the past to teach us strategies for the present, we can change life for the better for many people in our generation.

Identifying with the Oppressed

Those who want to side with justice must favor the oppressed. This is a principle in the Bible—so pervasive in the Bible, in fact, that we look especially to the Bible to find the best historical arguments for it. This may be one reason the Bible has been such an important instrument of liberation and strength in the heritage of our people (see especially chapter six).

The Bible tells us that when Pharaoh enslaved the Israelites and they cried out to God because of their suffering, their cries arose to God, and he raised up Moses to deliver them. Then God gave Moses laws for his people—very similar to the laws of other nations except without adjusting punishments variously for people of different social classes, as most other ancient Near Eastern nations (which favored nobility) had.[165] Justice was essential to Israel's tradition—but Israel did not always live by it.

Again and again, when Israel turned from God and went its own unjust way, it lost God's protection and became oppressed by other nations. Again and again the Jews' suffering would move them to cry out to God, and he would deliver them. Themes of liberation like this (found in biblical law, psalms, proverbs, prophets, Jesus' life and teachings and so on) were cited regularly by the evangelical Christian abolitionists in their nineteenth-century crusade against slavery.[166] But before looking at the Bible's teachings directly, we should survey how the Bible was applied and exploited regarding the slavery of our ancestors.

Slaves, Slaveholders and Christ

Throughout the history of slavery in the United States, "white slaveholders did little to promote the evangelization of blacks."[167] It is now well documented that the first American slaveholders didn't want their slaves to hear about the Bible, because they were afraid the slaves would understand that Christianity made them their master's equals before God.[168] Thus as African-American Princeton

professor Albert Raboteau, the leading researcher in slave religion, puts it,
   The danger beneath the arguments for slave conversion which many masters
   feared was the egalitarianism implicit in Christianity. The most serious ob-
   stacle to the missionary's access to the slaves was the slaveholder's vague
   awareness that a Christian slave would have some claim to fellowship, a
   claim that threatened the security of the master-slave hierarchy. . . . A
   continual complaint of masters was that Christianity would ruin their slaves
   . . . since they would begin to think themselves equal to white folks.[169]
The masters "feared that Christianity would make their slaves not only proud
but ungovernable, and even rebellious."[170] And history shows that they turned
out to be right—slaves assumed that Christianity did make them their masters'
equals.[171] Some slaves who became Christians also became abolitionists, quickly challenging the Western churches' complacent acceptance of—and at times
complicity in—slavery.[172] Slaveholders thus had reasonable fears, and for the
first century and a half of North American slavery, until religion gained a
stronger hold in the southern colonies,[173] most slaves heard little about Christianity.[174] During this period the Black church was strongest in the North (one
may examine the history of the A.M.E. and A.M.E. Zion churches there).[175]

But many more slaves heard about Christianity in the time of the Great
Awakening, when the evangelical revival (especially among Baptists and Methodists) "fostered an inclusiveness which could border on egalitarianism" (equality), because it stressed conversion rather than a merely intellectual approach
to Christianity.[176] Inspired Black preachers began to preach to White as well
as Black audiences, at times even planting interracial churches.[177] Black poet
Phillis Wheatley praised revivalist George Whitefield, in her first published
poem, for the hope his message inspired among her people.[178] As Lerone Bennett Jr., historian and senior editor of *Ebony* magazine, points out concerning
the late 1700s, "Baptists and Methodists strongly condemned slavery," and
Blacks "like Joshua Bishop of Virginia and Lemuel Haynes of New England
pastored white churches."[179]

Black authority and interracial ministry disturbed supporters of the status
quo who had no personal commitment to Christ. Sometimes Black ministers
were persecuted for their Christian preaching, but they retorted that they would
even die for the sake of the gospel and were often able to make White critics
back down.[180] Thus in 1788 former slave Andrew Bryan, baptized by the Black
Baptist minister George Liele, joined forces with a White and another Black
Baptist minister to start Savannah's "Ethiopian Church of Jesus Christ."

For slave owners eager to clamp down after the more liberal treatment of the British, exhortation was one thing, but a free-standing church was another. Bryan was continually harassed, and in 1790 he was imprisoned along with about fifty members of his congregation. As their white friend Abraham Marshall reported, "the whites grew more and more inveterate; and taking numbers of them before magistrates—they were imprisoned and whipped . . . particularly *Andrew, who was cut and bled abundantly.* . . . He held up his hand, and told his persecutors that he rejoiced not only to be whipped, but *would freely suffer death for the cause of Jesus Christ.* "[181] Bryan was still a slave at the time, but he purchased his freedom and that of his wife after his master died. By 1800 his church had seven hundred members, he was often baptizing between ten and thirty people, and other Baptist churches sprang from his own. The White Baptist churches of Savannah praised him for his work.[182] Other Black Baptists in the South "participated in the rapid growth of legal biracial congregations," some of which belonged to local Baptist associations.[183] By 1844, just under one-quarter of Baptists in this country may have been Black—around 170,000 Black Baptists.[184]

After slave insurrections motivated by Black preachers, however, southern Whites often feared slaves' assembling for religious meetings, and many southern states passed laws restricting such meetings.[185] Still, separate Black churches continued to exist in many parts of the South.[186] Northern Blacks, very many of whom had practiced Christianity since the 1700s free from slavery,[187] hence found a strong Christian population among southern Blacks when they sent missionaries to evangelize them after the Civil War, but the numbers of Christians jumped dramatically after the end of slavery through northern Black Christians' efforts.[188] The greatest growth of the churches thus came after slavery, from the impetus of African-Americans who had already been free.[189]

Slavery and Free Readers of the Bible

As most of us today recognize, enslaving people never made sense for honest readers of the Bible. Northern Black Christians issued calls for emancipation[190] and noted that the Bible, which teaches the brotherhood of humanity, obligates Christians to oppose slavery.[191] It was in fact a fiercely committed Black Christian, David Walker (not the Black Muslims over a century later), who first called hypocritical White Christians "devils" (in 1829),[192] though he also advocated reconciliation where possible and praised the Whites who had genuinely joined Blacks in the cause of freedom.[193] Predominantly northern Black churches like the A.M.E. and the A.M.E. Zion were strongly abolitionist,[194] and Black Methodist leader Richard Allen was president of the first national Black political organization, which grew from his Bethel Church.[195]

The Scriptures proved essential in the Black church's battle against slavery.[196] But Black Christians were not alone in their fight, as one African-American scholar points out:

For the most part, northern black Christians adhered to the Protestant revivalist doctrines of the antebellum period. Those doctrines tended to brand slavery a sin, thereby making opposition to slavery a sign of holiness and a Christian duty. . . . The American antislavery and reform movements were directly related to the evangelical movement of the early nineteenth century.[197]

The earliest American arguments against slavery were religious.[198] As early as 1710, an Anglican bishop, William Fleetwood, had bitterly attacked American slaveholders for withholding Christianity from their slaves and had gone on to attack slavery itself.[199] Quakers like John Woolman (1720-1772) articulated Christian antislavery arguments.[200] Despite opposition, Samuel Hopkins, preaching and writing as early as 1776, fervently denounced slavery, persuading some slaveholders to free their slaves.[201]

With much more significant impact, John Wesley and all the other early Methodist leaders were vehemently opposed to slavery;[202] Bishop Francis Asbury noted North Carolina slaveholders' consequent fear concerning Methodist influence over the slaves.[203] The 1784 Methodist General Conference, which declared slavery "contrary to the golden laws of God," garnered support among southern evangelicals as well as those in New York and Philadelphia.[204] The 1812 General Conference of the Methodist Church declared that "no slaveholder should be eligible to the office of local elder."[205] By 1824 any minister who acquired slaves, except for the purpose of freeing them, lost his ministerial credentials. The Maryland conference of 1826 unanimously denounced slavery and said laypersons should not hold slaves. In 1825 even the bishop of Georgia considered requiring all Methodists there to free their slaves.[206]

Reports in 1827 indicate that the Methodists and the Friends were the most active antislavery denominations, but many Baptists,[207] Presbyterians[208] and others were also involved in the work.[209] The few minutes of Baptist meetings and letters of Baptist missionaries from the 1700s reveal Baptist opposition to slavery; the minutes of Virginia Baptists in 1789, for example, declare:

Slavery is a violent depredation of the rights of nature and inconsistent with a republican government, and therefore, we recommend it to our brethren to make use of their local missions to extirpate this horrid evil from the land; and pray Almighty God that our honorable legislature may have it in their power to proclaim the great jubilee consistent with their principles of good policy.[210]

Itinerant missionaries sometimes found a good hearing but at other times faced mobs or arrests from hostile Whites.[211]

But though the gospel is pure, that does not prevent many who profess it from compromising it to accommodate their culture. Nominal Christians are more apt to interpret the Bible in light of their own culture than to read their culture in light of the Bible. When one begins converting slaveholders to the faith, does one require them to renounce slavery before receiving baptism? Churches in the nineteenth century, like churches today, generally welcomed those who came, hoping to improve their moral condition through biblical instruction. The complication, of course, is that the behavior of unchanged churchgoers soon comes to dominate and hence to corrupt the church. We may question whether unchanged churchgoers have been genuinely converted to faith in Jesus; that problem is one churches must address today, just as churches should have better addressed it then.

The intensity of public opposition to the antislavery movement was pronounced well into the middle of the nineteenth century. Most Americans viewed abolitionists as supporters of an extremist, unpopular cause; supporting abolition then may have required something of the conviction manifested by the more vocal and often similarly unpopular prolifers who picket abortion clinics in the United States today.[212]

Some of the Methodists' initial compromises in the early 1800s came because slaveholders, mistrusting the Methodists' antislavery reputation, allowed them no access to the slaves.[213] At the same time the highly evangelistic and rapidly growing Methodist church once led by Francis Asbury was becoming somewhat more traditional and bureaucratic, as large movements usually eventually do, losing some of its earlier fervor.[214] Despite continuing antislavery efforts, the Methodists began to water down their earlier demands for immediate freedom for slaves to favor a policy of merely *gradual* abolition.[215]

In the eighteenth and early nineteenth century, southern Baptists and Methodists exhibited considerable antislavery sentiment. Many slaveholders were therefore reluctant to have the preachers and missionaries of these denominations work among their slaves. But when the southern wings of these churches changed their positions, when southern clergymen became ardent defenders of slavery, the master class could look upon organized religion as an ally.[216]

Proslavery sentiment became so strong in the South[217] that many southern ministers who advocated immediate abolition were forced to emigrate northward to the free state of Ohio, sometimes taking their congregations with them.[218] Resentment of northerners' smuggling antislavery tracts into the South likewise grew intense. For instance, in July 1835 a northern minister who was selling books had wrapped them in antislavery papers. The papers themselves were taken as evidence that he intended to distribute them, and the minister was convicted and whipped, and fled the South without either his books or his vehicle.[219]

Slaveholders felt that religion reduced social problems on their plantations. But as one historian notes, "The master class understood, of course, that only a carefully censored version of Christianity could have this desired effect. Inappropriate biblical passages had to be deleted; sermons that might be proper for freemen were not necessarily proper for slaves."[220]

Those who favored slavery could simply cite the practice of slavery throughout history, including in Bible times, to support the idea that slavery is natural, without grappling with whether the biblical writers favored or disapproved of the institution.[221] Although abolitionist preachers like La Roy Sunderland soundly refuted the proslavery arguments slavery supporters did offer from the Bible,[222] opponents of abolishing slavery were free to disregard them. Those with economic incentives to maintain slavery would embrace the view that profited them more (in this their moral commitment resembled that of most North Americans today). As religion gained a wider hearing in the southern colonies, some preachers who supported the slaveholders' cause found a way to leave out parts of the Bible that sounded like they made the slaves equal; different catechisms were provided for slave and free.[223]

Thus the preachers would quote Ephesians 6:5, "Slaves, submit to your masters," out of context.[224] A few verses down, in verse 9, Paul says, "And you, masters, do the same things to them, because you also have a Master in heaven"—but the southern preachers chose to skip these words. In antiquity only a small number of people said that slaves and masters were equal before God; those who went as far as Paul generally believed that slavery was immoral.[225] Paul's words were some of the most deliberate antislavery words of his time, yet by quoting out of context a verse that in context meant something quite different, slaveholders could make slavery sound more acceptable.[226]

The slaveholders misrepresented Paul on several counts. First, Paul was addressing a situation so different from slavery in the Americas that we are reluctant to describe both with the same term. Roman slavery was nonracial, and among the household slaves (the only slaves Paul addresses in his "household codes") manumission (achieving freedom) was common. Household slaves actually had more social and economic mobility than free peasants, and slaves of prestigious persons held such status and power that some free aristocrats married into slavery to improve their status!

Second, had Paul written a critique of societal injustice he would have needed to start with the heaviest issues first: mine slaves, field slaves and landless peasant farmers (something like sharecroppers) rather than house slaves. Paul *may* have addressed such issues in his teaching, but only his few letters to urban congregations remain, and there he writes practical pastoral counsel for situations that members of these congregations faced.

Third, Christians were a persecuted minority sect; Romans considered Christians and other "Eastern cults" socially subversive and worried (with some historical reason) that such groups gave women and slaves dangerous ideas of freedom. Writing from a Roman prison cell, Paul had to be strategic as well as radical. Although he urged slaves to seek freedom when they had the opportunity (1 Cor 7:21-23), he was also aware that no slave revolution in Roman history had been successful, nor had even the most radical thinkers of his day devised any other way to end slavery.[227] To condemn Paul for his lack of militancy would also be to condemn the majority of nineteenth-century Blacks, who yearned for slavery's abolition but not necessarily a violent means to achieve it! Yet what Paul *did* write, including his call for mutual submission between masters and slaves, undermined the moral foundation of slavery—a point not lost on the abolitionists.

The Bible itself is no more the cause of its abuse by those who twist its meaning than a warm refrigerator is the cause of spoiled food belonging to those who never plugged the refrigerator in (as Tom Skinner, a Black Christian writer, pointed out in his *Words of Revolution* in 1970[228]). Yet counterfeits have rarely managed to suppress the true spirit of the Christian faith from emerging to challenge them. Abolitionism has distinctively, perhaps uniquely, arisen in societies directly influenced by Christianity; most other societies and philosophers in history have merely taken the institution of slavery for granted.[229]

Slaves in America quickly recognized "that the Bible had more to say about Jesus lifting burdens than slaves obeying masters" and thus "discovered a secret their masters did not want them to know."[230] It is to the credit of our forebears that they could discern real Christianity from the perverted form of it their masters sought to enforce on them.

The Bible and Abolitionism
At the same time that southern slaveholders were exploiting the Bible and

twisting Christianity for their own purposes, a revival movement was sweeping through the North. As people began to actively believe the Bible's teaching, they began to recognize its declarations about injustices—about kidnapping people, enslaving people and so on. These abolitionists could follow the example of William Wilberforce and the Clapham Sect in Great Britain. Fueled by the Wesleyan revival movement surrounding early Methodism,[231] the British abolitionists had lobbied Parliament until finally slavery was abolished in the British Empire. Wesley opposed British conquest and colonialism and strongly opposed slavery.[232] He argued that by economically maintaining the slave trade, plantation owners were guilty of all the murders the slave trade involved and thus were bringing judgment on their heads.[233] He demanded the release of slaves and advocated political transformation by abolition.[234] The evangelicals were staunchly antislavery; thus "in the 1790s the evangelical was marked out as much by a desire for the abolition of the slave trade as by an interest in missions."[235] In this period people generally recognized that biblical arguments supported and furthered antislavery more than anything else.[236] Wilberforce passed the mantle of British abolitionism on to William Lloyd Garrison for the United States, raising Garrison's stature in the U.S. movement.[237]

Ministers turned up on all sides of the abolition issue, some supporting immediate emancipation, others advocating gradual emancipation and still others merely supporting humane treatment while maintaining the status quo.[238] That some defended the status quo (which we would regard as inhumane under any circumstances) is not surprising; most people in most cultures support the prevailing sentiments of their society. What is more significant, however, is how Christian faith became a driving force for abolition, a moral cause that societies without Christian teaching have rarely birthed.

Abolitionist preachers like La Roy Sunderland, Dr. Willis and especially Theodore Weld argued that the Bible was against slavery,[239] and Sunderland and others wrote angry tracts demanding the abolition of slavery and promising God's swift judgment against the nation if it were not done.[240] Most denounced slavery as a sin, some books bearing such titles as *God Against Slavery . . . the Duty of the Pulpit to Rebuke It as a Sin Against God.*[241] The evangelical humanitarian Lewis Tappan explained that abolitionists did not pass judgment on whether a slaveholder was truly a Christian, which God alone could judge, but they did

> hold that no slaveholder, professing to be a Christian, is entitled to Christian FELLOWSHIP, *because* slaveholding is a sin, and should subject the offender to discipline. . . . The apostle Paul directed that Christians should not

eat with an *extortioner*. A slaveholder is an extortioner. If, then, a Christian may not eat a common meal with such an offender, may he sit at the Lord's table with him? I trow not.[242]

The evangelical revival in western New York, Pennsylvania and Ohio became a primary source of antislavery workers. Charles Finney, an evangelical revivalist who led as many as half a million people to Christ, was influential in this movement. As old-school Calvinist notions of the fixed social order waned and revivalism's emphasis on the individual will's devotion to God's purpose gained ground, the emphasis shifted from salvation as primarily an ultimate goal to salvation as primarily the beginning of a transformed life seeking to transform the social order.[243] Asa Mahan and other holiness leaders associated with this revival insisted that believers needed the Spirit's power "to tackle concrete problems of politics and social morality."[244] Finney's revivals planted the seeds of women's emancipation[245] and produced new leaders for the antislavery cause like Theodore Dwight Weld[246] and the Jamaican-born retired Captain Charles Stuart.[247] Finney likewise influenced the wealthy Tappans, who devoted their economic resources to the abolitionist cause.[248] He may have won as many converts to the antislavery cause as William Lloyd Garrison.[249]

Lyman Beecher, one of the most prominent clergymen of the day, tried to steer a safe course between the traditional scholars and the radical new revivalists crusading for salvation and social reform. But Finney's successes in the East, from Philadelphia to Boston, forced Beecher to invite Finney into his own pulpit.[250] One of Beecher's main projects was to start Lane Seminary to properly school the new ministers on the western frontier; the Tappans agreed to support the school because Theodore Dwight Weld was going there to advocate the abolitionist cause. Once the seminary was established, however, and Weld began agitating for abolition, the trustees tried to force the students to leave the issue alone. Asa Mahan, a Finney associate, dissented from the other trustees and along with Weld and forty students—mostly converts of Finney's revivals—withdrew from the school, leaving it empty.[251]

Beecher was enraged, but most of his own children eventually went over to the revivalists' abolitionist cause. This included his daughter Harriet Beecher Stowe; Weld's work constituted the primary source for the plot of her famous abolitionist novel *Uncle Tom's Cabin*.[252]

Meanwhile, a Finney disciple who had founded Oberlin Institute in 1833 contacted Mahan, who contacted the Tappans. They agreed to support the new school provided it took an official antislavery stand. Radical for its time, it became the nation's first coeducational school and the first school where Black and White students enrolled together.[253] Some Oberlin abolitionists felt that this stance was too radical even for Oberlin, lest it precipitate undue opposition; but the Tappans were even more radical, preaching "amalgamation"—complete mixing of Blacks and Whites.[254] Led by Finney and Weld, the Oberlin students now precipitated another national revival—this one for the abolition of slavery.[255]

White abolitionists worked to end slavery, but Black Christians voiced still stronger convictions. David Walker denounced slavery in God's name in terms that terrified most Whites.[256] Various Black churches served the Underground Railroad;[257] "the most vigorous organizers of networks 'to freedom' were black churchmen."[258] Northern Christians saw the Civil War as a religious war,[259] and Black troops marched into Charleston, South Carolina, singing Methodist hymns.[260]

Slaves and Bible Interpretation

The Black and White abolitionists understood the Bible correctly on slavery, but they were not alone. Our few records of what the slaves believed show us that the slaves knew from the Bible stories they did hear that their preachers weren't telling them the whole story, and they reconstructed a more just version of Christianity on their own. As one African-American scholar points out, instead of simply accepting the form of Christianity delivered to us by racist church institutions, African-Americans accepted a Christianity whose "truth was authenticated to them in the experience of suffering and struggle . . . to produce an indigenous faith that emphasized dignity, freedom, and human welfare."[261] Or as Cheryl Sanders, a womanist theologian at Howard Divinity School, summarized her findings in her Harvard dissertation, "Conversion introduced the slave to a gospel of freedom which contradicted the gospel of submission they were taught by whites."[262]

Some slaves were able to learn to read before Nat Turner's rebellion and discovered the truth directly from Scripture itself:

When my master's family were all gone away on the Sabbath, I used to go into the house and get down the great Bible, and lie down in the piazza, and read, taking care, however, to put it back before they returned. There I learned that it was contrary to the revealed will of God, that one man should hold another as a slave. I had always heard it talked among the slaves, that we ought not to be held as slaves. . . . But in the Bible I learned that "God hath made of one blood all nations of man to dwell on all the face of the earth."[263]

For slaves who could not read, the work of learning genuine Christian ethics was more difficult; they had to reconstruct Christianity based on the pieces of it they were allowed to hear. The slaveholders wanted their preachers to explain about submission, but they also frequently allowed these preachers to tell the slaves "harmless" Bible stories, like the story of Moses or the story of Samson—not realizing that the slaves were able to fathom the message of such stories better than the White preachers were. The slaves heard about Moses leading an oppressed people out of slavery, and they lifted their voices in prayer to the God of the Israelites to do the same for them. "Oh, Mary, don't you weep, don't you moan," they sang; "Pharaoh's Army got drownded."[264] As Frederick Douglass pointed out, many of the slave spirituals were coded with messages about escape to the North;[265] they functioned as protest songs providing divinely sanctioned hope.[266] Gabriel Prosser, leader of a major slave revolt, saw himself as a new Samson called to battle the White Philistines and liberate his people.[267] The slave church understood that Daniel and his three friends, who had been given Babylonian names by their captors (just as Kunta Kinte was renamed Toby), found strength in their situation through their faith in God.

The gospel of personal salvation assumed the equal worth of each individual, an evangelical idea that many preachers to the slaves tried to tone down, lest they be forbidden to preach altogether. Still, they found it impossible to avoid texts that spoke of all Christians as spiritual priests.[268] Of course even those White preachers who, to gain access to the slaves, preached submission to masters recognized that the parts of the Bible they did preach were "potentially subversive to the institution of slavery."[269] Sometimes they avoided altogether the stories about God smiting Pharaoh to lead his people out of slavery.[270] But even these preachers could not evade pervasive themes of human dignity in the Bibles they used; preaching about Adam and Eve, they sometimes declared that all humans ultimately shared the same ancestors, that all were sinners, that God demanded submission from masters as well as slaves and that Jesus became a servant himself.[271] They likewise had to preach that all people come to God on the same terms, whether they are Black or White.[272]

The implications should have been obvious to the White slaveholders and the preachers themselves: they were trying to preach a religion that was never built to accommodate slavery or oppression. But the Bible points out that sinful people have a propensity for self-deception: the problem isn't with the truth, but with those who twist it so they can fit it into the way they and their peers are already living (Jer 17:9-11; Jas 1:21-27). The Gospels show that the religious folk of Jesus' day (such as the Pharisees) needed to be born again too (Jn 3:1-8). That was why Jesus called his hearers not only to believe but also to *live by* his ethics. One need not agree with all of Marcus Garvey's proposals to appreciate his stinging critique of professing Christians who ignore Jesus' values:[273]

> A form of religion practised by the millions, but as misunderstood and unreal to the majority as gravitation is to the untutored savage. We profess to live in the atmosphere of Christianity, yet our acts are as barbarous as if we never knew Christ. He taught us to love, yet we hate; to forgive, yet we revenge; to be merciful, yet we condemn and punish, and still we are Christians. If hell is what we are taught it is, then there will be more Christians there than days in all creation. To be a true Christian one must be like Christ and practice Christianity, not as the Bishop does, but as he says, for if our lives were to be patterned after the other fellow's all of us, Bishop, Priest and Layman would ultimately meet around the furnace of hell, and none of us, because of our sins, would see salvation.[274]

Who would be damned to hell more than ministers who justified slavery or other injustices, Francis Grimké demanded?[275] Similarly, Du Bois, hated by many Whites for his unflinching resistance to injustice, prayed, "Incarnate Word of God . . . we are not Christians because we profess Thy name and celebrate the ceremonies and idly reiterate the prayers of the church. . . . We must be . . . merciful and not oppressors. . . . The cause of our neighbor must be to us dearer than our own cause."[276]

The slaveholders couldn't identify with most of the characters in the Bible the way the slaves could. They couldn't understand the Bible as clearly as their slaves could. This is because the Bible is a book that resonates with the wounds of the oppressed, that tells of a God who cares for the oppressed. It tells us of a God of justice, who is angry with the hypocrites who twist his Bible into a book of injustice.

What does the Bible really say about injustice? Does this book really contribute to our pursuit of a solution to injustice and racial prejudice? To this question our next chapter must turn.

Conclusion

Some minimize the importance of race in shaping our identity; others find in it *the* defining issue of our identity, even above personal faith or our common humanity. We must recognize race as an essential issue in defining who we are, but do so with a very large *because* attached. Race shapes who we are and how we perceive the world especially because of the racial history of this nation, the shaping of our nation's experience of racial and cultural diversity in largely *negative* ways.

We hope for a better vision of racial and cultural diversity, where allegiance to a God who created all peoples in his image provides appreciation of rather than distaste for diversity. This is the vision of hope portrayed in Revelation 7:9: "After these things I looked, and behold a great crowd which no one could count, from every people and tribe and nation and language, standing before God's throne and before the Lamb . . ." Revelation warns of a perverse unity among peoples for the purposes of evil in this world (13:7-8, 16) but promises that those who share God's kingdom will also share in the ultimate expression of multicultural diversity in unity before God's throne.

All people and all societies need work, and we who care about our people can do more for our people than anyone else can. Yet this admission does not imply that White people who still control most of our society's power structures are justified in looking the other way. Even if it seems hard for us to sacrifice on behalf of our people, we know that most Black people sacrifice for our community more than the vast majority of White people do. Is it really possible for a White person to follow a God of justice, a God who cares for the rights of minorities, a God who in history will ultimately vindicate the oppressed?[277] And once a White person already following this God genuinely understands the racial barrier and its history in this country, can he or she really join us— become socially or spiritually "Black" enough to be on our side, whether as an advocate for justice in the White community or as an adopted member of our own? If we really want any cooperation from the White community, we must be ready to embrace and teach those who genuinely answer our call. The next chapter explores this issue of White repentance and Black forgiveness: justice through reconciliation.

6
Militant Christianity: Justice Through Reconciliation

ALTHOUGH SELFISH PEOPLE HAVE TWISTED THE BIBLE, LIKE EVERYTHING else, for perverse ends, the fact that the abolitionists used the Bible as a moral authority to combat prejudice suggests that it may be put to similar use for justice today. The Bible actually has more to say about justice than one might guess from many contemporary churches' selective use of it.

Once we have surveyed some of the Bible's teaching on justice, we may look to one final basis for identification. While racial identification is important for those who have been made to feel like second-class citizens on the basis of their race, we have been arguing that it is not the only basis for identification or unity. Identification on the basis of common oppression (chapter five) invites us to identify on a deeper ground of shared commitment to justice.[1] Identification should never be a barrier to reconciliation; reconciliation embraces those who make common cause with us for combating oppression.

The Bible's Denunciations of Injustice
In the first decade of the twentieth century Francis Grimké, a prominent Black preacher in Washington, D.C., warned that self-effacement would never work. There would be no peace in the land until the Black community received justice, for Blacks would not be satisfied with being treated as less than human beings.

That, he cried, is "God's law"; and the century that followed has confirmed his witness.[2]

Sometimes Israel's priests and false prophets justified and supported the social status quo, which oppressed the poor. Then God's true prophets, like Amos, thundered against the injustice with the word of the Lord:

> For three sins of Israel—no, for four,
> I will not turn back their judgment:
> For they sell the innocent into debt slavery for money;
> They sell the poor because they could not pay for their shoes! (Amos 2:6)

> Bad news, you who are looking forward to the Lord's coming!
> That day . . . will be as dark as night with no light for you.
> I am disgusted with your religious meetings. . . .
> Your best religious rituals are unacceptable to me. . . .
> Just let justice flow like water,
> And let doing right flow like a stream! (Amos 5:18-24)

Such announcements by Amos were not favorably received by the comfortable establishment; the high priest denounced Amos and suggested that he leave town. Amos responded by crying judgment against the high priest:

> So now listen to God's message! You're saying, "Don't prophesy against Israel." . . . Because of this, this is what God says to you: "Your wife will become a prostitute to earn a living, the Assyrians will kill your children, and you will die in captivity in Assyria." (Amos 7:16-17)

The prophets had more important concerns than winning friends and influencing people. They spoke for justice, and if their own generation didn't listen to them, a later generation would remember them when judgment finally came. Jeremiah was thrown into a well and left to die; he was rescued only by one of his two faithful allies, a foreigner from Nubian Africa (Jer 38:1-13). What was his crime? Lines like the following:

> To defend the rights of the distressed and poor, . . .
> Isn't that what it means to know God? (Jer 22:16)

When his people determined to free fellow Jews they were holding as slaves, but then changed their mind and decided to keep them in slavery, Jeremiah rather unpatriotically pronounced a divine sentence of death against the slaveholders, destruction against the city and judgment upon the king (Jer 34:8-22).

Amos and Jeremiah were not alone—consider these samples from earlier prophets like Isaiah and later ones like Ezekiel, calling for the justice God had already ordained in the law of Moses:

> Hear God's message, you rulers of Sodom . . .
> "Why do you bother with these sacrifices to me? . . .
> Stop bringing these useless offerings! . . .
> Stop doing evil—learn how to do right.
> Seek justice: stand up against the oppressor;
> Stand up for the needs of fatherless children,
> Defend the rights of the widow![3] (Is 1:10-17)

> Don't you know the real kind of "fast" I demand?
> Free those oppressed by the wicked,
> *Let the slaves and oppressed go free,*
> *Break every chain!*
> Don't you see that my fast is to share your food with the person
>   who is hungry,
> To take the homeless street people into your home,
> To give clothes to the person who has nothing to wear,
> And not to run when you see a needy relative coming your way?
>   (Is 58:6-7)

> Take heed! This was your sister Sodom's sin: Sodom and her people were full of pride, had plenty of food and had life just fine—but did not help the poor. (Ezek 16:49)

Where are the righteous spokespeople of God today, who will denounce the injustices of our land, not just when it is convenient but when it will cost something? Where are those who will dare to proclaim the wrath of a just God against the oppression of people, not only of our own race but also of others? Isaiah, Amos and other prophets said that the true sacrifice God requires of us is justice for the oppressed and compassion for the broken. This is the sacrifice our free Black ancestors in the North made in the days of slavery and afterward; though they had little, they put together what they did have, and they used it to help their people. They lived as simply as they could and formed charitable societies to better their race, to fund schools for their education, to advance the cause of abolition. Christianity was something they lived and not just something they talked about on Sunday morning.

Some people today say that the Bible favors oppressors, because it gave the oppressed strength to endure their situation. Some say that had the oppressed not had strength to endure, they would have revolted. This objection ignores the simple fact that the slaves often *did* revolt and that the Bible was their source of strength for much of their resistance.[4] Leaders of slave revolts, from Nat Turner, a Baptist preacher,[5] to Denmark Vesey, with help from fellow African Methodist Episcopal conspirators,[6] to Gabriel Prosser, the "new Samson,"[7] found strength in their faith.[8]

White slaveholders often recognized the danger; for instance, hostility toward Methodism, toward missionaries working among slaves and toward anyone suspected of wishing to improve conditions for the slaves grew in the wake of Vesey's revolt.[9] Religious assemblies of slaves without White supervision were made illegal.[10]

Of course, many more Bible believers advocated other forms of resistance and disobeyed their oppressors to meet for worship and to pray and work for freedom.[11] But in each case models from the Bible and Christianity provided slaves with ideological equipment for their resistance. Northern leaders of the resistance, from Frederick Douglass, the A.M.E. Zion deacon and fierce advocate of abolition,[12] to Harriet Tubman, the "Moses of her people" who on various trips led over three hundred people to freedom,[13] to preacher Sojourner Truth—all were motivated by their understanding of the gospel of Christ.[14]

Even after slavery, it was faith that sustained our people in the face of unrelenting trials.[15] As one Black theologian puts it, "The Christian faith gave the black man a sense of 'somebodiness' in spite of circumstances to the contrary."[16] This is what gave us strength to fight on. Thus as Ida B. Wells passionately fought for justice on behalf of her people, she found her only refuge in prayer: "O God, is there no redress, no peace, no justice in this land for us? Thou hast always fought the battles of the weak & oppressed. Come to my aid at this moment & teach me what to do, for I am sorely, bitterly disappointed."[17]

In the 1960s historian Lerone Bennett Jr., senior editor of *Ebony* magazine, pointed to various strands of resistance before the middle of the twentieth century and observed, "In 1955, Martin Luther King fused these elements and added the missing link: that which has sustained and bottomed the Negro community since slavery—the Negro church."[18] Religion has been used to oppress the masses, but this is not how Nat Turner, Martin King, Malcolm X— or Jesus Christ—used religion.[19] Jesus condemned the hypocrites of his day, and hypocrites cannot be his true representatives today.

Jesus and the Oppressed

Evangelical Christian women of Africa declared in their PACWA[20] Covenant, which also emphasizes evangelism and discipleship, "Where God is biased, it is in favour of the oppressed, the widows, the orphans, the aliens and the poor, the majority of whom are women."[21] Whereas some middle-class White Christians have been able to decide whether to emphasize a personal relationship with God or social justice, most of the Black Church has never had the luxury of choosing: we needed both. Like our sisters in Africa, we can resonate with the whole message of the gospel that has come to us in Jesus Christ.

Some religions claim to side with the oppressed; most religions ignore them. But the God of biblical Christianity is surely a God of the oppressed.[22] Biblical Christianity teaches that God will set all justice right in the day of judgment, though he has allowed people time to repent and make restitution in the present. It also calls us to work against oppression in the present.[23]

But other faiths built on the ethics of the biblical prophets (such as contemporary Judaism) share these ideas no less. Where Christianity is *distinctive* is in its teaching that the one true God himself became one of the oppressed. It teaches that Jesus of Nazareth was God in the flesh, who lived a human life among us and suffered what we suffer. He moved among and defended the outcasts and oppressed of his day, like lepers, widows and even religious outcasts who needed to come back to God. His disciples included both nationalists with messianic vision like Peter (and perhaps Simon the Zealot, *if* this title suggests that he was a revolutionary) and (by contrast) a former collaborator with the Romans—but nobody from the establishment publicly took his side.

In the end, the religious and political establishment of Jesus' day did him in. His captors beat him, and his judges gave him a death sentence without a fair trial. He was stripped, beaten more, mocked more and finally publicly executed as a criminal with the lowest and most degrading form of execution known to humankind at that time.

Jesus became one of us. He joined the ranks of the oppressed.[24] That means that as deep as our pain goes, he shared that pain with us. God doesn't just condemn oppression; he shared our experience of being oppressed.

The "good news" of the story is that in the end even death could not stop him. Even if the whole world disagreed with God's verdict, God's justice had the final say: Jesus didn't stay dead. Like our ancestors used to say, "God may not come when you want him, but he's always right on time." Some people consider that "pie-in-the-sky" theology that keeps the oppressed down. We call it hope—a motivating hope that enables us to make a genuine difference in the world.[25] For example, it has been demonstrated that far from inhibiting militancy, the Black church in the 1960s provided most of the moral purpose and participation in the Civil Rights Movement.[26] As Black theologian James Cone has pointed out, "The idea that Jesus made blacks passive is simply a misreading of the black religious experience. He was God's *active* presence in their lives, helping them to know that they were not created for bondage but for freedom."[27]

But it is not enough to make God a God of justice in theory. Many White slaveholders were content to have a God who was theoretically just; they could define justice the way some Greek philosophers did—giving everybody what the "wise" person in power deemed appropriate, rather than allowing everybody what they need. Jesus taught something utterly different: he taught identifying with the oppressed.

In Jesus' day, his people felt powerless, oppressed by the Romans. No one, however, was more powerless than the children. Yet when Jesus' followers were hoping that Jesus was on his way to Jerusalem to overthrow the Romans, he stopped their excited procession so he could bless some children. At that time he warned, "Whoever does not accept God's kingdom as a child cannot enter it" (Mk 10:15). His disciples didn't quite catch his point; when Jesus turned away a man who was rich and powerful in society by telling him, "If you want to be saved, you have to give up all your wealth for the poor," they became confused (Mk 10:17-31).[28]

Right after Jesus explained that his mission was to come and die, his disciples went back to jostling for power in the church (not unlike some of their successors today), and Jesus had to remind them of his mission again: "If you want to be really great in the kingdom, learn how to serve others; I did not come to be served, but to be a servant, and to give my life to save others" (Mk 10:32-45). Still wanting Jesus to hurry to Jerusalem, to get on with the business of setting up his kingdom, the disciples didn't want a blind beggar to slow Jesus down or waste his time. But Jesus stopped and healed the beggar, because caring for human need—whether a child or a blind beggar—is what his kingdom is all about (Mk 10:46-52).

Jesus taught that one must become "like a little child"—powerless—to enter his kingdom (Mk 10:14-15). This teaching inverts the entire social order. It implies that according to the Bible, White slaveholders needed to become like their slaves to be saved.[29] It would imply that White politicians in Mississippi who funded state-run White schools five times better than state-run Black ones[30] weren't saved. *Perhaps* God shows some mercy to those who do not know what they are doing (although one might suspect that most of these politicians knew exactly what they were doing). But whether or not this is the case, Jesus' words leave no doubt as to whose side he is on. It is not enough to talk about Jesus being "Savior"; what the Bible says Jesus saves people from is their sins, and if people have not stopped oppressing and started identifying with the needy, then they are still living in sin.

But what about us? As some theologians have observed, we too have to become "Black" in this sense. We may be members of an often oppressed race, but to challenge that oppression requires more than just pointing out the White community's many failings. We must identify with the oppressed ourselves. Thus, for example, the Bible says that Moses as an Egyptian prince could have enjoyed the "temporary pleasures of sin"—the wealth of Egypt amassed by the unjust exploitation of Israelite slaves. But because Moses had a future hope—because he believed that God had a higher reward for him—Moses chose not to be part of the Egyptian royal family, but to identify with his oppressed people (Heb 11:24-26).[31] As Vernon Johns, King's predecessor at Dexter, reminded his congregation, Moses "rejected his status as the adopted grandson of Pharaoh to lead the Hebrew slaves out of Egypt."[32] Johns likewise preached on "segregation after death," noting that the rich man who failed to acknowledge Lazarus was consigned to hell; but Johns applied this parable not only to Whites but also to wealthy Blacks if they turned their backs on less affluent members of their race. (Though agreeing with Du Bois's strategy of active confrontation, he took exception to his "talented tenth" proposal.[33])

Likewise, Martin Luther King Jr. called on the Black middle class of his day "to rise up from its stool of indifference . . . to bring its full resources—its heart, its mind and its checkbook to the aid of the less fortunate brother."[34] And Dr. King was not the first to remind us of our responsibility to the genuinely needy among our people. One prominent Black woman in the nineteenth century exhorted others by her example of living as simply as possible so she could contribute more to the betterment of her people.[35] Another pleaded with our ancestors not to waste money on gambling or other useless pursuits: "O ye sons of Africa, turn your mind from these perishable objects. . . . Let our money, instead of being thrown away as heretofore, be appropriated for schools and seminaries of learning for our children and youth."[36] Harriet Tubman, once free, understood that the gospel obligated her to work to free others.[37]

African-American minister Artis Fletcher has provided warning reminders along these lines. He tells of meeting a man in the Los Angeles ghetto who could not get a job and complained that the Whites were keeping him down. After the man finished trade school, however, he rapidly advanced economically, until he was finally making over two thousand dollars a week. Fletcher visited him again, but this time the man complained, "Black people in the ghetto are lazy! They just won't work!" He had no intention of trying to make things better for those he had left behind. He had

bought himself a home in a nicer community . . . put a fence around it . . . bought a Cadillac—and three dogs to protect it! He's a good example of how economics alone is not the answer. You see, without Christian values, without the commitment to make life better for people in his community, without the commitment that Christ had, all he wanted was to get what he wanted for himself.

In short, Fletcher warns, "if we have political success and we have economic success but don't have Christian values, we'll become oppressors." Fletcher knows, of course, that merely attending a church does not guarantee these Christian values; it was surely no accident that he delivered these remarks in a church.[38]

Since desegregation, some of us have moved up economically and educationally and have moved out of the ghettos—Du Bois's "talented tenth" (in this case closer to one-third or half)—leaving our poorer brothers and sisters behind in an even worse state than they were before.[39] If some of us want to combat oppression, we cannot just fight the stereotypical "White man"; we also have to repudiate some of White America's values, like the non-African practice of placing personal advancement before the needs of our communities. To adapt the popular expression, we need to put our money and time where our mouth is and serve our people in the projects, with the life-changing gospel, with education and with positive male and female Black role models. In other words, we need to really value the betterment of our people above the White man's definition of "success."

In the words of Du Bois, who suffered much for the African-American community, "let us value achievement not for what it brings to us but for what it gives to a starving struggling world."[40] Of course, such an idea may be *too* revolutionary for armchair revolutionaries who are satisfied to make money and fame by criticizing others without making sacrifices of their own time and income.

Jesus' disciples didn't catch his meaning right away, but he let them keep following him till they did begin to get it, shortly after the resurrection. Apparently Jesus accepts followers willing to do his will even long before they can think through the specific implications of his lordship for every situation. That is fortunate for us, since many of us have been slow, just as Jesus' disciples were, because we fail to understand what sin and oppression are really all about.

"Sin" is disobeying God's law; this means not loving him or our neighbors as we should. Sin means that we are selfish, that we exploit power over other people when we have it. It also means that when we don't have power we wish we did, so we could do to others what they've done to us—though this brings us down to their moral level. Such desire to achieve power for destructive (as opposed to constructive) ends contradicts both reason[41] and the very spirit of our people historically.[42]

It's the kind of exploitation by which White people have sinned against Black people and against Native Americans in the Western Hemisphere and against Black people in South Africa. It's the kind of genocide that the Germans used against Jews and other non-Aryan races earlier in the twentieth century. It's the kind of abuse of power that warring African or northern European tribes used against each other in the past—and some continue in the present.[43] It's the kind of oppression that the Assyrians, the Egyptians, the Babylonians, the first Islamic armies, the Mongols, the Crusaders, the Moguls, the Ottoman Turks, the Mayans and others in history have imposed on other peoples, many of them enslaving their prisoners of war. It's the kind of oppression revealed when men rape women or beat their children.[44] In his earlier days, before he renounced the Nation of Islam, Malcolm X was right: White people *are* devils. He was only wrong in thinking that the rest of us weren't.

Our people in America have never oppressed any group of people the way White people have oppressed us. In fact, we've never oppressed White people as a group—but this might be merely because we never had the chance to do so.[45] On an individual level, when one treats one's girlfriend, wife, boyfriend, husband, roommate, parent, child, friend or enemy like an object, when one uses other people, when one acts selfishly with only one's own interests in mind—one shows that same kind of devil nature that White people showed in enslaving us, only with less power to enforce it.

That's the sin, the devil nature, that the Bible says Jesus came to free humanity from. The Bible teaches that if we ask Jesus to be Lord of our life, he will free us from our past devilishness and enable us to do what's right—for God, for our people and for everybody else. He even promises to send his own Spirit to work in our hearts so that we can make a positive difference in this world for him.

Is Reconciliation Possible?

When Marcus Garvey met with leaders of the Klan, they concurred that separation of the races was the best solution for America's race problem. At the same time Asa Philip Randolph, later founder of the first Black labor union, angered both Garveyites and White racists by advocating integration; he received numerous death threats. Although the government worked much harder against Garvey, it also worked against Randolph, trying to shut his newspaper down.[46]

In subsequent decades both Randolph's "radical" advocacy of integration and Garvey's advocacy of separatism won many adherents, perhaps because history provides some support for both approaches. The history of this nation has generated distrust and discomfort in interracial settings; hence separatism seems easier for most people in the short run. But apart from the social and economic realities of our interdependence, separatism cannot hold hope for a better future. Social psychology confirms that racial tensions initially released in integration decrease in society as a whole as integration progresses.[47] (If we do not experience this as fully as we should, one reason may be that much of our society remains de facto segregated.) Our immediate history frequently produces confrontation, but such tensions are not inevitable based on inherent racial natures. "Rather, tension is the direct result of the racial separation that has traditionally characterized our society. In short, separatism is the cause of awkwardness in interracial contacts, not the remedy for it."[48] This observation invites us to consider whether partial and long-range improvements are worth the short-range pain.

Although Whites who work with or join the Black community remain the exception rather than the rule, many examples demonstrate that it can be done. Yet White cooperation will profit the cause of justice for our people only if it is offered properly, with understanding, patience and sensitivity on both sides. Such sensitivity initially requires listening above all else. The Student Nonviolent Coordinating Committee was one of the most effective Civil Rights organizations of the 1960s. Blacks and Whites in the movement worked together to break down segregation throughout the South, and they were largely effective until the movement took a different turn. Some Black leaders began to feel that the movement could be fully effective only if its staff were completely Black, and in 1966-1967 all White staff were gradually forced out. The dream of racial reconciliation for which SNCC had worked was dead.[49]

Reconciliation demands a commitment to work through differences and stand for justice even when it is costly to one or both parties. As one White writer admits, "White guilt" is merely a self-indulgent exercise that profits no one; "the real issue" is not whether one is "concerned about combating racism" but whether one is actually *doing* anything to combat it.[50] Upwardly mobile Whites must be willing to commit what some critics would call "class suicide"—to admit that discrimination against Black people exists in this country and to be prepared to become objects of that discrimination themselves, if need be, by allying themselves with the just cause of the African-American community.

A persecuted German revival sect called the Moravians initiated Protestantism's first missions movement. The Moravians so believed in the value of all people that many of their missionaries identified wholly and for their whole lives with slaves in the West Indies, where slavery was particularly brutal.[51] Their pietistic faith influenced Wesley, and through Wesley and his successors it also influenced the British antislavery movement.

Experience shows us that most North Americans of any complexion are unwilling to commit class suicide; but some Christians hold strong enough convictions that they are ready to abandon class privileges as soon as they recognize that it is their biblical responsibility to do so.

Whites often think the current uncomfortable racial situation would go away if Black people would just stop *talking* about racism. They fail to recognize that the hostility has existed for centuries, though we once publicly suppressed it, allowing Whites to feel more comfortable in their ignorance.[52] In most societies the dominant culture does not know how minority cultures within it feel because it does not need to know[53]—certainly not in U.S. society, where a dominant majority can outvote minorities and where representation is guaranteed geographically but not by social classifications more relevant to protecting minority voices today.[54] It is not surprising that when more Whites learned how we felt about racism they chose to assume that our feelings were new rather than that our feelings were something they did not know all along!

Sometimes we kept silence to keep the peace. After the Civil War, when angry southern Whites charged the freedmen's aid societies with favoring "social equality," some northern Blacks who had come to work in the South accommodated segregation to "excite the least prejudice and opposition to our whole work"—until the situation could be changed.[55] The fact that our silent compliance was repeatedly required in the nineteenth and twentieth centuries never meant that African-Americans enjoyed their state. How could "separatism" not have existed as long as Whites kept other groups out of their mainstream social experience and then cursed us "as a group for not being fully ready to enter it"?[56]

Some object to those perspectives of multicultural education that do not contribute to public unity; but true unity presupposes reconciliation, and reconciliation presupposes dealing with issues rather than pretending (as a majority culture is uniquely able to do) that those issues will go away if ignored.[57] Diversity already exists; *acknowledging* it is a necessary step toward our functioning as a united society.[58]

But only honest discussion of the issues can pave the way for reconciliation. Many Whites are afraid to hear what Blacks have to say (sometimes they accept only "hostile" reactionaries without honest arguments as representatives of our race and our views, perhaps because it reinforces a stereotype that allows them to ignore us). Many Blacks assume that all Whites already know the justice of our position and choose to ignore it. As a White writer in 1970 lamented, Whites generally "equate Color with Threat, and so react with hostility" toward Blacks; we conversely "identify Whites with oppression, and so develop hatred against them." Yet in both cases we remain captive to stereotypes that White racism created in the beginning.[59]

Racial Reconciliation in the Deep South

The White statesman Thaddeus Stevens, a far more passionate advocate for interracial justice than Abraham Lincoln was, fought in Congress for Reconstruction and was later buried in a Black cemetery. His gravestone includes the epitaph he chose for himself:

I repose in this quiet and secluded spot,
Not from any natural preference for solitude,
But finding other cemeteries limited by charter rules as to race,
I have chosen this that I might illustrate in my death
The principles which I have advocated through a long life,
Equality of Man before his Creator.[60]

Stevens lived long ago, but his heart is not without successors today. There are some examples of racial reconciliation in the secular community, but the Christian community possesses a special dynamic for racial reconciliation—even if many Christians on both sides of the racial divide have ignored this dynamic: an absolute moral conviction of the necessity for racial reconciliation, and a supernatural empowerment to carry it out.[61]

With reference to the frequent silence of White Christians, Black evangelist Tom Skinner is largely right that "true Christianity has never really been applied to the sphere of black-white relations in this country."[62] Most people have preferred their comfortable enclaves to the risk of attempting to build reconciling relationships, some of which inevitably involve painful betrayal. Meanwhile secular politicians tend to ignore the church, Black or White, except in traumatic situations. During the 1992 Los Angeles riots, for example, they pounded on the doors of inner-city churches, recognizing that the church had more power to bring peace than any of their own government-supported secular forces could. To much of the White community, religion is usually acceptable only when it makes no demands on their personal ethics.[63] As that famous Black preacher of liberation, Howard Thurman, has complained,

> Too often the price exacted by society for security and respectability is that the Christian movement in its formal expression must be on the side of the strong against the weak. This is a matter of tremendous significance, for it reveals to what extent a religion that was born of a people acquainted with persecution and suffering has become the cornerstone of a civilization and of nations whose very position in modern life too often has been secured by a ruthless use of power applied to . . . defenseless peoples.[64]

But the examples of obedience that do exist more than reinforce the reality of the dynamic potential of the gospel for those who dare to live it out. Surveys of highly committed religious Americans (as opposed to merely nominally religious Americans) indicate that those who claim to have a personal relationship with God are over 20 percent more likely than the "spiritually uncommitted" to be personally willing to cross racial boundaries.[65]

The Civil Rights struggle demonstrated that some people *would* cross racial boundaries, many of them because of committed faith. Most innocent persons murdered because of involvement in the Civil Rights Movement were Black, but some Whites also suffered. To protest construction of a segregated school in Cleveland, Ohio, the Reverend Bruce Klunder, a White minister, laid himself in the path of a bulldozer. Instead of stopping, it crushed him to death. He had always preached taking necessary risks to accomplish the purposes of Jesus Christ, which included racial unity. The Black community angrily demanded justice on his behalf; the school was eventually built, but Klunder's death mobilized both Blacks and Whites to fight for racial justice.[66]

Other White ministers were taking less serious but nonetheless important steps, risking their popularity in favor of justice (more, perhaps, than many public figures do today). Although we rarely today think of Billy Graham as a Civil Rights activist, he did make public statements even in the early 1950s, before the Civil Rights Movement was nationally known. In 1953, for instance, Graham stunned an audience in Tennessee by railing against segregation and personally removing the ropes that separated members of his audience. In 1957 he asked King to talk to his crusade team about integration and added Howard Jones, an African-American pastor from Cleveland, to the team.[67] Graham likewise supported King against some opposition at the Baptist World Alliance,[68] approved of King's messages and provided tactical advice and cooperation.[69]

The following examples of racial reconciliation provide a sample of how it can occur in our own day. Spencer Perkins, a Black minister from Mississippi, has cowritten a book with a close White friend, Chris Rice, called *More Than Equals*.[70] They argue for reconciliation, but not the superficial kind of reconciliation that many church people like to talk about.[71] Malcolm X understood the Bible rightly when he pointed out that injustice calls for restitution, not just cheap grace. Chris and Spencer describe the painful learning experiences both had to undergo to truly embrace one another as full brothers in Christ.

Spencer's father, a Mississippi preacher involved in the Civil Rights Movement, was beaten nearly to death, yet he told his son, who suffered greatly during school integration, to keep on loving.[72] Although "loving" sounds weak to some people today, it takes considerable strength to pity the sin-enslaved oppressor and thereby put him in his place, to stop letting him control our response. Spencer eventually found triumph in love.

By contrast, Chris, a White man, felt that he was not at all prejudiced. He had been raised by missionary parents in Korea, where they had worked on behalf of the Korean equivalent of the Civil Rights Movement. Chris had left college to work with Spencer and others in a poor Black community in Mississippi. He thought he wasn't racist and couldn't understand why many of his Black colleagues assumed that all White people were—until he realized that he hadn't made any close Black friends. He had come to Mississippi to "minister," but not to submit. Through the crisis of that revelation he was transformed from what Malcolm and Stephen Biko figured many White liberals are—advocates for their ideas of what's good for us—into a real servant to the Black community.[73]

Black Allegiance by Conversion

The authors of this book have a similar story to tell. Although it constitutes only one story of reconciliation among many, we narrate it at length here because it is the story we know best (it also will help explain what one of the authors is doing contributing to this book!). As noted in the preface, no one can accuse this book's research of being biased against White people, because one of the authors of this book came to his pro-Black views quite in contrast to his background. Although the author responsible for the final perspective and "voice" of this book is African-American, its primary researcher is White.

The White researcher, however, now lives in the Black community and is an ordained minister in the National Baptist Convention (which is largely African-American).

Glenn is the African-American author, and his passion for addressing Afrocentric questions and related issues arises from his own background. Although he did not grow up in an explicitly Christian home and may have attended a church at most twice, he called on Jesus as Lord at age fourteen. Still, however, he did not draw the connection between Jesus and "church," and did not begin attending church until years later. Not long after he had called on Christ, a representative of the Nation of Islam came to his home in Hempstead, New York, and persuaded Glenn that he should become a Muslim. On his way to pick up a copy of the Qur'an he sensed a voice in his heart saying, "I am the way, the truth and the life: no one comes to the Father except by me." Not even aware that these words were from John 14:6, he immediately returned home and began studying the Bible. He still questioned most things he found in the Bible but began to do historical research to examine them, and eventually he became convinced that the Bible was true. Today he pastors a rapidly growing church, most of whose congregation is young and African-American.

Craig grew up in a small Ohio town. After he was converted to Christianity from a background in atheism, he found a close friend who had converted from an equally nonreligious background in drugs at about the same time. The friend, Kyrk, was Black, and the two became best friends. This was in the late seventies, when it was not "cool" to be prejudiced in a small town in Ohio, thanks largely to the Civil Rights Movement's influence on popular thought. More important, non-Christians marginalized and often harassed Kyrk and Craig for their open witness for Christ (Craig even got beaten a few times for his witness). The opposition they faced bound them together as Christians and made any differences between them seem negligible. They did not talk about racism; they talked only about their common faith, and found themselves welcome whenever they visited each other's churches.

At that time in his life Craig would never have defined himself by his Whiteness; his identity went far deeper than his ethnicity, for he had found a purpose for his life under the lordship of Jesus Christ. Though not all people who claim to be Christians truly believe and live what they profess, real Christians are able to be agents of racial reconciliation because they recognize a common bond that goes deeper than the color of skin or patterns of culture.[74] Yet the deeper bond Kyrk and Craig shared *should* have been all the more reason to explore and listen to one another's backgrounds—rather than pretending that those backgrounds didn't matter.

As the years passed and the Civil Rights Movement's momentum waned, Craig, now a college student, quietly wondered sometimes if Black people weren't making too much of racism. Hadn't the biggest of those issues been settled in the sixties? Of course he never would have confessed these suspicions out loud; that would have made him sound racist. And besides, he respected his Black friends' feelings too much to say anything that might have hurt them. Little did he know that by doing nothing, by not seeking to learn the depth of his brothers' and sisters' pain, by not lifting a finger to challenge injustice, he was a silent participant in that pain and injustice. As C. Eric Lincoln, a prominent scholar of the Black church and a friend of Dr. King, Malcolm X, Alex Haley, Jesse Jackson and many other influential Black leaders, has declared, "Whether one is personally a racist or not becomes increasingly inconsequential, because the silent consensus which institutionalizes the racist ideology makes it normative to the whole culture and entraps us all."[75]

Scholars observe that the Jim Crow laws of the American South were not pushed through by new forces of racism but by the weary acquiescence of racism's opposition.[76] Today many White people recognize that slavery and segregation were injustices, but quickly point out that they themselves are good, unprejudiced Whites, or that slavery and segregation are sins of past generations (or of some other geographical region). But this observation does little to alleviate their guilt if they harbor the same racist sentiments that were used to justify slavery and segregation all along. As Jesus put it,

> Woe to you religious people! For you . . . say, "Had we lived in the time
> of our ancestors, we would not have joined them in killing the prophets."
> So—you identify yourselves as the heirs of those who killed the prophets.
> Go ahead then—finish off your ancestors' guilt! (Mt 23:29-32)

Craig did know from the Bible that his Black friends were right to oppose racism, and listening to them eventually convinced him that their evaluation of the situation was essentially right. But the world had many issues that needed to be addressed, and though Craig denounced racism, for him racism remained only one sin among many. Then one day early in 1987 Craig faced a tragedy that broke his heart. Injustice appeared to be ending his career and indeed, in his mind, his whole life. Although he would ultimately be vindicated, he did not know that at the time. The pain was so great that he did not know how to cope with it; he just wanted to die.

At about this time, a Black grandmother in Durham, North Carolina, who was raising her five grandchildren by herself, showed Craig great kindness.

When Craig crossed her path, she later recounted to him, God suddenly spoke to her heart and told her that it was all right to trust Craig. She and her grandchildren then unofficially adopted him into their family. He moved across the street from the project where they lived, in an almost all-Black neighborhood.

Members of one people have often transferred allegiance to another; one may take as examples Ruth, Rahab and David's Philistine bodyguard in the Bible, or even the sense in which Gentiles who come to faith in Jesus adopt the God who revealed himself through Israel's history (Rom 11:17-24; compare Is 19:24-25). Josephus thus explains why Gentiles could become part of Israel: "To all who desire to come and live under the same laws with us, [God] gives a gracious welcome, holding that it is not family ties alone which constitute relationship, but agreement in the principles of conduct."[77] The notion invented by White racists that one cannot transcend boundaries created by skin color or culture ignores history and, no matter how popular it has become on both sides of the U.S. racial divide, merely deters both reconciliation and the fight for justice.

Craig visited this family's church with them and marveled at the spirit of celebration and liberation he found there. He was impressed that the ministers dealt with everyday issues and seemed to really care what went on in the community. He noticed that in the project where they lived there were only two kinds of role models for children: drug dealers and church people. He noticed the pain this grandmother and her grandchildren had gone through, pain greater than his own; yet they found strength in their worship of God, strength he found himself sorely lacking.

Only then did he begin to understand that the Black church in its purest form, through its centuries of perseverance in suffering, had tapped into an experience with God that his White church background had neglected. In time he began to long to participate in that heritage of strength he was coming to respect so much. Although Craig had previously pastored another church, he came into Orange Grove Baptist Church in Durham as a servant, one who had been broken by his trials and came to the Black tradition because he needed its strength. The pastor of Orange Grove had studied and learned from the Black nationalism of the Nation of Islam before his own conversion to Christianity; but he took the young Bible scholar under his wing and taught him more about his new environment in the Black community.

Some of what Craig learned shocked him. His friend Arthur casually mentioned how an English professor had called him aside after the first day of class to warn him that he wouldn't pass the class if he stayed in it (Arthur chose to stay in anyway, and earned an A). The professor closed her warning with "And if you tell anyone, it will be your word against mine."

"That doesn't happen often, does it?" Craig demanded incredulously.

Arthur gently looked at Craig as if he were really out of touch. As Craig heard more stories he realized that even if only 10 percent of the White population was that blatantly racist, it would generate enough racism to torment his Black friends on a regular basis (while some Whites remained oblivious).

Craig faced some opposition; some Black people would not accept him. Although those barriers always came down with time, he knew that he would have to start over every time he walked into another Black community that did not know him. Some people judged him because of the color of his skin rather than his heart, until he could prove himself. "Now you know what Black people have to go through in a White world," he was told. It was a painful but important lesson.

But a deeper pain came as he read *The Autobiography of Malcolm X* and then turned to the slave narratives. He wept as he realized the injustice that White people—people who looked just like him—had done to Black people— his best friends, the people he loved. He became so ashamed of the color of his skin that he wanted to take a knife and rip his skin off. He also resented the White community for its wrong perception of the racial situation he had accepted, a perception for which he now felt partly responsible by virtue of having accepted it.

Yet as Craig heard his pastor preaching each Sunday that all of us were created in God's image, he began to recognize that he too was made in God's image. Christ died not only for the sins he had committed in person but also for the sins of his society that he had in the past failed to adequately recognize and thus had tolerated by default. Accepting Christ's forgiveness, he was free to simply be part of the Black community he loved and that loved him, without any dose of traditional "White guilt."

After a few years he learned to balance his newfound loyalty with Christ's demand to serve all people. He could affirm the principle of racial justice without withholding love from anyone, including members of the White community which he at first wrongly resented.

Though Craig would have to prove himself repeatedly to African-Americans who didn't know him, he knew where his allegiance lay; and for the sake of that new allegiance, he would pay the price of proving himself over and over. Now that he knew the truth about racism and God's answer to it, he could never be the same person he had been before.

If you hadn't guessed, any statements in this book that might still sound harsh to White people are Craig's statements, not those of the Black author. (Glenn, in fact, made him tone most of them down!) Reconciliation comes most readily when one can recognize one's *own* community's responsibilities to bring it about; Craig thus emphasizes the White community's responsibilities when he addresses the issue with mainly or partly White audiences. Like most ministers, however, both Glenn and Craig emphasize loving and embracing people regardless of color; the love of Christ demands that we all listen to one another humbly and serve one another even before we may agree on all the details.

Orange Grove Baptist Church ordained Craig as one of the first White ministers in the nation's largest Black denomination since World War I.[78] He is the only White person in his current neighborhood, but as his ordaining pastor put it, "We don't see Craig as white anymore. We see him as one of us."[79] Carl Kenney referred neither to his skin color nor to his background, but to his *allegiance.* Having seen both sides of the racial conflict in the United States, Craig recognized that one side was being largely honest about the conflict while the other side was not: White people as a group had oppressed Black people as a group, and the reverse was not true. Having no prior loyalties except to the lordship of Jesus Christ, Craig understood that allegiance to Jesus Christ and his values demanded that he take the right side—without for that reason compromising his Christian love for people of any race.

With some good reason Jewish people in Jesus' day mistrusted most Gentiles, but they saw a particular Gentile centurion as an "exception" (Lk 7:4-5). Ruth the Moabite constituted a similar exception in the Old Testament (Ruth 1:15-18).[80] An exception means that the rule does not apply in all cases, and points to the possibility of other exceptions to come—if we are willing to reach out as an impoverished grandmother and a pastor once influenced by the Nation of Islam were willing to do.

Successful Models of Reconciliation Justice
What was it in the hearts of those White people who have joined our ranks that made the difference? In many cases it was that they did not read the Christian Bible selectively; they dared to believe what it taught.

We may pause to note that the impetus for interracial Christian movements did not end with Black Baptist ministers like Andrew Bryan in the eighteenth century, nor is it limited to individual examples like those offered above. Thus, for example, one of the dominant Christian movements of the late twentieth century has temporarily interracial origins and the hope of an interracial future.[81] Pentecostalism grew from the Azusa Street Revival led by the Black preacher William Seymour.[82] A leading German scholar notes that Pentecostalism incorporated numerous elements of American slave religion and points out that it is the only worldwide movement "at whose foundation one black man stands and which has—although never properly recognized—learned more from this tradition than any other church [has]." For this reason, he explains, it has appealed to Third World Christians as well, and its Third World adherents now outnumber its Western ones.[83] (African-American Christianity in general includes a significant heritage of spiritual experiences[84] and seeking the empowerment of God's Spirit in Christ, what many have called "a Pentecostal power."[85])

The first official Pentecostal denomination, Church of God in Christ, was predominantly African-American but still included some White ministers until violent persecution by White Jim Crow supporters in the South forced the Whites and Blacks to meet separately.[86] When Aimee Semple McPherson, an early White Pentecostal figure, announced in 1924 that she would preach about the Klan in one of her services in Los Angeles, the audience quickly filled up; to many Whites the Klan represented traditional values. (Indeed, the Klan had reached its height of five million members in the mid-twenties—ten times its membership in 1871 and one hundred times its membership in 1920 or today.[87]) When some Klansmen seated themselves in the service, she told the story of a Black man evicted from a White church. Jesus appeared to him and comforted him, telling him that Jesus himself was not welcome there either. Then she made her point:

> You men who pride yourselves on patriotism, you men who have pledged yourselves to make America free for white Christianity, listen to me! Ask yourselves how is it possible to pretend to worship one of the greatest Jews who ever lived, Jesus Christ, and then to despise all living Jews?

On she went, but the Klansmen walked out.[88]

Many holiness and Pentecostal churches were racially integrated from their early years.[89] Many of these churches outside the "mainstream" were integrated in the South before the Civil Rights Movement began, often because they regarded color as secondary to the gospel.[90] Pentecostalism has also taken some important steps toward racial reconciliation in the 1990s.[91]

The best models of reconciliation justice, however, are Jesus and some of his early followers. Jesus in his day denounced religious hypocrites and invited nonreligious people to become his followers. Jesus is far less interested in religious rhetoric than in people who will really follow him the way he demands—

people who trust him enough to pursue love, justice and mercy.[92] Religious people of Jesus' own nation didn't like Samaritans;[93] thus they didn't like it when Jesus defined "loving your neighbor" as loving a Samaritan, and doing so in practical ways (Lk 10:25-37).[94] They would have been upset had they known that he talked with a Samaritan woman and attracted Samaritan followers (Jn 4).[95] But Jesus *lived* racial reconciliation in a culture and an era when reconciliation wasn't popular.

When Jesus entered Jerusalem a week before his crucifixion, he found moneychangers in the outer court of the temple—the place where Gentiles (non-Jews) were supposed to worship. In the Old Testament, Gentiles had been welcome in the temple alongside Jews (1 Kings 8:41-43), but by Jesus' day women were excluded from the main part of the temple, and Gentiles were kept even farther out. Now the commerce in the Gentile part of the temple marred Gentiles' worship opportunities further, and Jesus stormed through the temple courts, overturning tables and declaring, "Did not the Bible declare, 'My house will be called a house of prayer for all peoples'? But you have made it a refuge for thieves!" (Mk 11:17, quoting from Is 56:7 and Jer 7:11).

In short, Jesus led an active protest against a segregated religious institution. Jesus knew very well the price he would pay: the Sadducees, rich leaders who collaborated with the Romans, ran the temple and dealt ruthlessly with any opposition.[96] Within a few days they had brought Jesus to the Romans on trumped-up charges and had him executed as a revolutionary.[97] Jesus wasn't the kind of revolutionary they thought, but he was more subversive to the values of ancient society than any insurgent or articulate philosopher could have been—and he proved to be what Tom Skinner called "the greatest revolutionary ever."[98] He started a revolutionary movement that could change the world—if his followers have the faith to live his teachings with conviction.

At least one of his followers certainly did. Racial reconciliation wasn't a popular notion in the first century; Greeks thought they were better than other peoples, Romans knew they were more powerful, and Jews despised worshipers of false gods (which included almost all non-Jews). But like many of Jesus' other early followers, Paul took a stand for racial reconciliation. Ministering in a multiethnic church in Syria that included Africans in leading roles on its pastoral staff (Acts 13:1-3),[99] Paul and his allies forged their way into the Gentile world with a message of not only salvation but also reconciliation: Gentile Christians could be accepted into God's people on equal terms with Jewish Christians. That the pastoral staff in the first Antioch church probably included a former slave would have strengthened their class sensitivities as well.[100]

Paul's message was too much for some non-Christian Jews of his day. Some Jews from the area around Ephesus recognized an Ephesian Gentile with Paul in the vicinity of Jerusalem's temple and figured that Paul had gone all the way in living out his ideal of breaking down barriers. Even though Paul was in the temple on an errand of reconciliation, supporting Jewish concerns and affirming his Jewish identity (Acts 21:21-26),[101] his opponents lacked information and assumed they knew his motives. Wrongly convinced that he had brought a Gentile past the dividing wall into the temple beyond which Gentiles could not pass—a law that was enforced under penalty of death[102]—they rioted. Without further evidence, they accused Paul of having taken this Gentile with him, and Paul was taken into custody (Acts 21:27-37). Paul did have one opportunity not only to gain his freedom but also to preach the gospel of Christ to the entire crowd; but because Paul's gospel included racial reconciliation, he spoke that whole truth and suffered the consequences (Acts 22:21-22). Paul ended up doing time for over two years just waiting for a fair trial (Acts 24:25-27).[103]

From his confinement in Rome, Paul the inmate[104] wrote to his friends in Ephesus about racial reconciliation. He declared that Christ had built a new temple, which included both Jew and Gentile on equal terms (Eph 2:19-22). And Paul said that the dividing wall in the temple—which had become for him and his friends in Ephesus the ultimate symbol of racial hostility—had been shattered by the cross of Jesus Christ (2:14).[105]

As years passed, Paul surely continued to urge his earlier idea that "there is neither Jew nor Gentile in Christ Jesus" (1 Cor 12:13; Gal 3:28; Eph 2:11—3:10); meanwhile Jews and Syrians were soon slaughtering each other in the streets of Caesarea.[106] Paul, like Jesus, paid a price for proclaiming racial reconciliation in a world divided by ethnic hostilities, a world where most people could not *conceive* of racial reconciliation.

In an early church where slaves could rise to the office of bishop, where church income was often used to buy slaves' freedom, where Christians of Ethiopian, North African, European and other cultures could embrace in the name of one God, society's values were being challenged.[107] All this came through a movement that was persecuted by law-and-order Romans as revolutionary and subversive, but was far more revolutionary and subversive than the Romans could have guessed, as long as there were *genuine* Christians to live according to Jesus' teaching.

It doesn't take much courage to speak against the idea of racism in our society. Most people will condemn racism in principle (even those who doubt its continuing reality), and many people will agree that it is bad in practice, too.

But reconciliation is more costly than denouncing the idea of racism. Reconciliation means patiently loving both enemies and attempted friends onto the side of justice when we can.[108] It means being so sure we're right that we can work for change and not be intimidated into reacting on mere emotion every time someone says something we know is not true. In a culture where a blow to the cheek was the supreme insult (inviting legal penalties), Jesus told disciples to turn the other cheek. The ultimate contempt for an oppressor's insult is to refuse to be insulted by it because we recognize that oppressors cannot define our identity. Forgiveness and reconciliation constitute the greatest act of resistance, the supreme declaration of our liberation. Are we willing to pay the kind of price that Jesus, Paul, Martin Luther King and others have paid for reconciliation?[109]

What It Will Take

François Dominique Toussaint L'Ouverture, who led his Haitian forces to freedom against the French, at first earned the love of White as well as Black subjects by his just rule. Deceived by Napoleon's aides, Toussaint then died in a French prison, and his aide and successor proved less trusting of the French. When they massacred Haitian Blacks, he massacred Whites in reprisal. Counterviolence seemed to be the only language these treacherous Europeans understood.[110]

Chancellor Williams points out that Whites fled the cities in the wake of desegregation. While many Blacks still seek the approval of White society, White society welcomed integration only when it could use integration to achieve domination.[111] The very Whites who criticize Black separatists consistently withdraw from Blacks.[112] As evangelist Tom Skinner puts it, White flight became so dramatic in northern cities during the African-American migration there "that integration began to be defined as that period between the time that the first black family moves into a community and the last white family moves out."[113] One White writer complained in 1970 that as legal segregation was ending, "segregation by custom and pressure is actually increasing."[114]

White Harvard psychiatrist Robert Coles recounts his surprise in finding the same problems in the North as in the South during segregation; his studies demonstrated how entrenched racism is in northern White middle and upper classes, although White northerners verbalized it less. One self-styled liberal, a White attorney, felt that when Black people in Mississippi or Detroit took to the streets, they were wrongly "breaking the laws," but when the same people went hungry or could find no employment, that was merely a "social problem" lacking moral dimensions.[115] One may wonder if many northern Whites were more committed to the fight against racism in the past than today precisely because then they could pretend it was a "southern" problem.

Whites who fled the cities did not simply leave empty-handed; most jobs likewise left the cities[116]—and some Whites quickly began complaining how many Blacks do not work! While a capitalist society is ideal for generating wealth, capitalism's mechanism for distributing it equitably presupposes the equal availability of economic, social and educational capital—which is not our current social situation.

A common response to the problem today is to say that economic empowerment of the poor is the church's rather than the government's responsibility. If so, the current situation provides an ideal opportunity to show what the church is made of—a test of her moral fabric. Will U.S. Christians sacrifice their own luxuries to provide college scholarships for children from single-parent homes who otherwise could not afford it? Or will we let them remain part of the permanent underclass to which their educational status and economic background will normally consign them? (That capital is currently inequitably distributed on the basis of family and race may seem acceptable according to our culture's presuppositions; but then again, the unequal concentration of power in the hands of a hereditary nobility in many societies we would now condemn was quite acceptable to them. Neither oligarchy nor plutocracy represents the ideal of democracy we praise.[117] Capitalism itself can function justly, but only if we overcome the prejudices that have traditionally made loans, education and even hope less accessible to certain segments of our society.)

As of the mid-1980s, the economically lowest fifth of U.S. families earned 4.7 percent of the national income, whereas the top fifth earned roughly nine times that amount, 42.7 percent. Whereas the top fifth included only 7 percent of African-American families, nearly one-third of us lived below the poverty line, which was worse off than thirty years ago. These statistics reflect socioeconomic factors, not a genetic predisposition in our race: though only 54 percent of our men were employed in the mid-eighties, nearly 75 percent were in 1960.[118] Lest someone accuse us of complaining about inequity only where our own people are involved, we may note that a decade ago the median family income for Hispanics with four years of college was roughly seven thousand dollars less than for Americans of northern European descent with the same educational qualifications.

Some people respond, "See, everyone has problems." But if all injustice is wrong—and by definition all injustice is—then pointing to the injustice done to others as a way of trivializing the injustice done to us is an unjust response. Some Whites complain that we have been "down" for so long that the problem lies solely with our race. But whereas European and some other immigrants may choose to assimilate into the mainstream, dominant culture, history testifies that the dominant culture has historically barred Blacks from doing so, and experience suggests that enough racism remains to make entrance into White society a challenge even today. Further, some of us, like some Hispanics and members of other cultures, *like* distinctive elements of our culture and would like to be welcome in this society without having to discard it. If some members of our race have by now become imprisoned in a culture of unemployment and poverty and can conceive of no other life, we must never forget how they got there. That memory can fuel our efforts to improve conditions on their behalf.

After a careful analysis of history, Chancellor Williams concludes that Blacks have failed in this country precisely because they are *not* separatists. The White intelligentsia exploits the fact that American Blacks "have never really hated the whites"; we have only hated being hated.[119] Although those of us who personally know Whites who have proved to be genuine exceptions will balk at Williams's apparent solution—Black separatism—his point is well taken, and his analysis of the problem is insightful. African-Americans cannot depend on White "benevolence" but must work for the needs of our own people. *This* Reconstruction must be strong enough to survive with or without the White protection on which the first Reconstruction depended.[120]

This does not mean that we must surrender hope of communicating with White people; it does mean that integration as equals will not come merely through laws while selfish hearts are unchanged. Selfishness is, as Howard Law School graduate Garland Hunt has wryly observed, not so much a skin problem as a sin problem. People in control do not want to relinquish their power, and those whose sole defense seems to be hatred are afraid to relinquish the one means of retaliation they think they have.

"Integration" has sometimes merely created an exodus of Black business or community cohesiveness; integration is inadequate without true *reconciliation*. As essential as civil rights legislation has proved for many of us, we know now that no civil rights law will make White people embrace us. Whether the sin is racism or selling drugs, nineteenth-century chattel slavery or the modern exploitation of prostitutes by pimps and johns, laws on the books by themselves don't change people's hearts—and only a change of heart as radical as what Jesus called a new birth will do. As the Black Power movement discovered, "History simply does not support King's faith in the ultimate goodness of men, black or white."[121] Yet Black nationalists who say, "We don't need White people; we want our own country," are more utopian and less practical than King—

both because their separatist solution is unworkable in our country and because the problem isn't the color of White people's skin. The problem is the universal human problem of sin, or—in everyday terms—of selfishness, of exploiting power when we get it.

As those of us who live in neighborhoods with a lot of drugs and theft know, the drug dealers who exploit and kill our children for profit are no better than the White slave traders who exploited and killed us for profit in times past. Black preacher Wellington Boone argues that " 'selling out' is doing to your community what justifies what the White man thinks about you anyway."[122] That is true whether the offense is pulling a gun on one's brother, pressuring a young woman to have sex and then leaving her pregnant or urging her to abort the Black fetus inside her, or repudiating the right to education that our ancestors, newly freed from slavery (when Whites had forbidden us to read), worked so hard to get during Reconstruction. Our people's lives are too precious to be wasted on other people's greed, whether the oppression comes from within or without.

Just laws and just enforcement can help us, and we must continue to work for such changes; but only love can change hearts and make some enemies into allies. This kind of love is part of our heritage. Even other nations know of the kindness of the Black American community—our perseverance and ability to forgive rather than be destroyed by bitterness, the way some other peoples would have been had the roles been reversed. Because of our history, we are able to testify about God in a special way, to gain a hearing among White secularists, among oppressed peoples of color and among other Black Americans who (with some historical reason) mistrust the motives of White Christians.[123]

Indian statesman Rajmohan Gandhi, grandson of the famous Mahatma Gandhi, believes that God kept African-Americans for a reason.

> As an Indian and a Hindu, I salute the God who carried African-Americans through the fires of slavery and the stones and thorns of oppression to the grassland of life, liberty, and the greatness (and common sense) of a people who refuse to carry the sacks of bitterness on their backs. They had nothing. They only had their God. He was more than sufficient.[124]

Bitterness kills; love can heal us and our nation. Tough love it must be—a reconciliation between equals that demands justice. Love has got to be tough to persevere through the spite of the hateful and build bridges to those hearts that can yet learn love's language. But without love we will only breed more pain and send the cycle of oppression spiraling further downward inside and outside our communities.

Sources as diverse as Christian teaching and the Nation of Islam recognize that suffering has prepared us for a mission with integrity.[125] Although Joseph's brothers exploited him and sold him into slavery against God's teachings, God showed his power by bringing good from the evil (Gen 50:20).[126] God has also provided good for us from the terrible evils our ancestors suffered, and we, like Joseph, have the opportunity to use this good to help others.

Although our community's resources are fairly limited by North American standards, if the African-American community were counted as a nation and compared with other nations of the earth, our gross income would rank us higher economically than most other nations. If we choose, we can work together and use those resources to better our people as a whole, continuing to invest in our Black colleges, in the education of our youth and in other promises for a better future.

While many White Americans do not appreciate the value of our people, people of some other nations hope for our wise use of resources and even our potential voice in U.S. society. After all, our Civil Rights Movement reverberated throughout the Western world, affecting European colonialists; most African nations also threw off colonial rule while we were striving for our freedom here. By further claiming our rightful place in this society and maturely defending our own, we can join forces with our siblings of all races battling injustice on other continents. God's plan for us is as great as our history if we dare aspire to it.[127]

Thus we must serve the wounded in our own communities, offering a better sense of identity to those who value themselves cheaply (as expressed, for example, in their sexual or narcotic habits). We must point them to a higher basis for self-esteem and hope. We must likewise offer a message of love and reconciliation to the White communities, starting with the churches (where people who profess to be born again are responsible to follow a Lord who calls for a loyalty transcending color and class). Racial reconciliation is possible because a higher loyalty than color exists, a loyalty in which *all* races must find their ultimate purpose in history. This reality, like much of life, appears paradoxical: it is only our creator and rightful Lord, who demands that we make him first priority above family and even life itself (Mt 10:37-39), who gives us back our life and identity in a greater way in him (Mk 8:34-38).

We must call all people to justice, to compassion, to do the right thing. And there is no greater foundation for that mission than the message of a God who identifies with the oppressed and who paid a costly price to free us from the sin of identifying with the oppressors (the sin of seeking power over others). If we choose to identify with him, this identification goes beyond any other level of identification we have discussed, because we find our ultimate identity and purpose in serving the God of justice, liberation and hope.

Our ancestors who fought the horrors of slavery preached that we come to God by repentance—turning from sin—and by faith in God's mercy in Christ alone. They declared that this would transform our moral character and bring each of us into a personal relationship with God in Christ.[128] The slave narratives likewise recount numerous dramatic conversions and a faith that sustained believers through the most difficult of times.[129]

Conclusion

Many readers of this book recognized the power of the Bible in working for justice and reconciliation before picking the book up. We have also, however, welcomed readers who might read the book for the information it contains without a previous commitment to our own perspective as part of the Black church. At this point White Christian readers will understand the role we suggest for them: listen with an open heart to the pain of your African-American brothers and sisters in this society, and join us in affirming our dignity and role.

Some readers of the book may, however, represent neither a Black nor a White Christian perspective. Some may have never recognized that justice and reconciliation constitute one of the major agendas of the God of the Bible. If you are among these readers and would like to identify with the God of the oppressed, to enroll on his side, to make a difference in the world for justice, you can join his movement. According to God's teaching in the Bible, Jesus by dying on the cross paid the price for humanity to come back to God. That is the *ultimate* reconciliation, which can empower us to seek reconciliation with other people, even when we confront the challenging cases who resist reconciliation.

To join this movement for justice and reconciliation you must tell God that you want to return to the purpose for which he created you, that you want him to guide your life from now on. It's very simple, but there is one catch: It will cost you your life. Or to put it less provocatively: God has a purpose for your life, and he wants you to make a difference in the world for him. That means that his plans for your life are better than your own plans or anyone else's plans. You may have some right ideas in mind, and God may bless some of your plans that were actually his plans all along. But when you make Jesus the Lord of your life, you give him the right to tell you what to do—including loving all people, including defending the rights of the oppressed, including protecting our people from exploitation, including consistently "doing the right thing."

You join God's movement by sincerely telling God that you want to join. The God of justice made admission that basic because he wants you on his side so much that he sent Jesus to die for you. His purposes for your life are much bigger than your own purposes are. If you will trust him to give your life real significance for this world, then you can begin following him by acknowledging that you believe that Jesus made the way for you to be on God's side, and telling him that you want to follow him from now on.

Join up with others committed to Christ's call for justice and integrity before God. Study the Bible, his plan-book, and get ready for a real revolution that can change not only policies but also human hearts, starting with your own— though you need to recognize that change cannot come without commitment and sacrifice. Joining the movement is easy; but achieving the movement's objectives is costly. Will we be the generation committed enough to truth to take up Christ's challenge and pay that price?

The final stanza of Black minister James Weldon Johnson's "Lift Every Voice and Sing," our Black national anthem, is appropriate:

God of our weary years,
God of our silent tears,
Thou who hast brought us thus far on the way;
Thou who hast by Thy might
Led us into the light,
Keep us forever in the path, we pray.
Lest our feet stray from the places, our God, where we met Thee,
Lest, our hearts drunk with the wine of the world, we forget Thee,
Shadowed beneath Thy hand,
May we forever stand
True to our God,
True to our native land.

Notes

Preface

[1]If one speaks of "basic" and "applied" research in science, one might call this book an exercise in "applied" (rather than "basic") historiography; we grapple here with specific historical questions for a specific purpose. One of the authors tentatively plans a later work addressing primarily White audiences, most of which are still unfortunately unaware of Afrocentric questions. As Cheryl Townsend Gilkes points out, Afrocentric history is no more "inspirational" than most Eurocentric history (as when many Americans elevate Thomas Jefferson while neglecting his role as slaveholder; "We Have a Beautiful Mother," in *Living the Intersection,* ed. Cheryl J. Sanders [Minneapolis: Fortress, 1995], p. 31).

[2]Cone's view may also be relevant here: "whatever response blacks make [that troubles White racists] is nothing but a survival reaction to white racism" (James Cone, *Black Theology and Black Power* [San Francisco: HarperSanFrancisco, 1989], p. 20).

[3]Although we respect presentations that differ from our own (often due to the asking of different questions) or disagree with our own, we hope that they will respect ours as well. Attempts to keep racial or religious questions from being asked constitute an attempt to control discourse—to censor racial or religious perspectives. Examples include the attempts of southern Whites to prevent the distribution of northern antislavery tracts (see W. Sherman Savage, *The Controversy over the Distribution of Abolition Literature, 1830-1860* [n.p.: Association for the Study of Negro Life and History, 1938]) and times when religious dogma has suffocated biblically grounded prophetic dissent. Minority perspectives ought not to be excluded from the public forum.

[4]Some understand the term *Afrocentric* to apply to an exclusive emphasis on African heritage as central to human history; we apply the term in its broader usage, indicating a focus on African-American concerns because this is the community we address, not as if other communities are inherently less important (followers of Christ are christocentric, with nothing more central). For a defense of this qualified Afrocentrism, see Carl Ellis, "Afrocentrism and Christianity," *Urban Family,* Summer 1995, pp. 15-16. Our position might be called "multiculturalism," in the broad sense of sensitivity to diverse cultural perspectives; see James Breckenridge and Lillian Breckenridge, *What Color Is Your God?* (Wheaton, Ill.: BridgePoint/Victor, 1995), pp. 232-34. Some womanist scholars have also critiqued the common use of *Afrocentrism.* For example, Delores Williams ("Afrocentrism and Male-Female Relations in Church and Society," in *Living the Intersection,* ed. Sanders) notes that it is often women-exclusive (pp. 45-46, 50). Lorine Cummings ("A Womanist Response to the Afrocentric Idea," in *Living the Intersection*) hopes for more women's input (p. 61). For a more positive appraisal see Gilkes, "Beautiful Mother" (she notes nineteenth- and twentieth-century antecedents, pp. 26-27, but also that some contemporary circles define Afrocentrism too narrowly, p. 22).

[5]Livingstone boasts that it is one of the only Black colleges all of whose trustees have been Black from its inception over a century ago to the present.

[6]See, for example, "Amazing Grace: Fifty Years of the Black Church," *Ebony,* April 1995, pp. 87-96; also Dwight Perry and Ralph Hammond, "The Strategic Role of the Black Church," in *The African-American Consultation on Church Planting and Revitalization,* ed. Dwight Perry (Baptist

General Conference Annual Meeting 1992), pp. 101-19; some of the latter will appear in a forthcoming book with Baker Book House by Dwight Perry and Julie Ieron.

Chapter 1: Why History Belongs to Us

[1]Breckenridge and Breckenridge, *What Color Is Your God?* p. 217.

[2]The same people often turn their eyes from the plight of ghettos created by racism, yet object when Black Americans with more resources focus on serving our people in those communities.

[3]Derrick Bell, *And We Are Not Saved* (New York: BasicBooks, 1987), p. 73.

[4]Even a study focused on the cultural value divergences between African- and European-American students notes that (apparently due to a shared heritage in U.S. history and culture) the commonalities exceed the divergences in every matter studied (see Robert T. Carter, "Cultural Value Differences Between African Americans and White Americans," *Journal of College Student Development* 31 [January 1990]: 77). Dolores Norton contends that social workers should recognize ethnic differences but emphasize them in the broader context of "the universal goals of societal organization that underlie human behavior" ("Diversity, Early Socialization and Temporal Development," in *Perspectives on Equity and Justice in Social Work*, ed. Dorothy M. Pearson [Alexandria, Va.: Council on Social Work Education, 1993], p. 17).

[5]See the observations of both in Frederick Law Olmsted, *A Journey in the Seaboard Slave States* (New York: Dix & Edwards, 1856), reprinted in Frederick Law Olmsted, *The Slave States*, rev. ed., ed. Harvey Wish (New York: Capricorn, 1959), pp. 120-21.

[6]See especially the recent lighthearted critique of the practicality of large-scale nationalistic separatism by Lerone Bennett Jr., "Martin or Malcolm? The Hero in Black History," *Ebony*, February 1994, p. 74: no nation will take thirty million Black Americans, we might not all want to go anyway, and "anyone who believes Whites are going to give Blacks a state, or anything else, and anybody who believes Blacks can take and hold a state or even the southern end of Manhattan has not consulted Robert E. Lee or the Pentagon weapons procurement specialist." See Vincent Harding's 1968 essay "The Religion of Black Power," in *Black Theology*, ed. James H. Cone and Gayraud S. Wilmore, 2 vols. (Maryknoll, N.Y.: Orbis, 1993), 1:40-65: "For if racism rages as deep into American life as it appears and if violence is its closest brother, then a black revolution will no more solve the problem than a civil war did (even if Rap Brown gets his atomic bomb)" (p. 64). Elijah Muhammad's separatism, in contrast to Marcus Garvey's, focused on a home in the United States (see C. Eric Lincoln, *The Black Muslims in America*, 3rd ed. [Trenton, N.J.: Africa World Press/Grand Rapids, Mich.: Eerdmans, 1994], p. 68). Although White racists and Black separatists have at times joined forces for the common goal of separation, that goal is both impractical and hurtful to Black and White alike (Orlando Patterson, "Going Separate Ways: The History of an Old Idea," *Newsweek*, October 30, 1995, p. 43).

[7]Judith H. Katz, *White Awareness: Handbook for Anti-racism Training* (Norman: University of Oklahoma Press, 1978), pp. 14-15.

[8]Ibid., pp. 11, 13. See p. 21 in "What Martin Luther King Jr. Means to Me," *Ebony*, January 1994, pp. 21-25: King freed millions of Whites "from the mental shackles of assumed racial superiority that had bound them to an era that had long gone with the wind." On racial attitudes among children, see Phyllis A. Katz, "The Acquisition of Racial Attitudes in Children," in *Towards the Elimination of Racism*, ed. Phyllis Katz (New York: Pergamon, 1976), pp. 125-54.

[9]For two classroom examples, see Joan Kernan Cone, "The Urgency of Choice in the Untracked Classroom," *Teaching Tolerance*, Fall 1993, pp. 57-63; David Aronson, "The Inside Story," *Teaching Tolerance*, Spring 1995, pp. 23-29. This publication, devoted to promoting tolerance (especially racial and cultural understanding) is published by the Southern Poverty Law Center, 400 Washington Ave., Montgomery, AL 36104.

[10]Quoted in Alexis Spencer-Byers, "Unsung Heroes in Black History: Nannie Helen Burroughs (1883-1961)," *Urban Family*, Fall 1995, p. 36.

[11]"The Haldeman Diaries," *Newsweek*, May 30, 1994, p. 6, quoting from H. R. Haldeman's diaries, April 28, 1969; this assumes, of course, that Haldeman's report is accurate. (The joke about White supremacists discriminating equally against all non-Aryans might apply in this case: the entry for February 1, 1972, also includes an anti-Jewish statement.)

[12]Marcus Garvey, correctly remarking that Egypt, Ethiopia and Timbuktu were greater empires than

Europe in their day; as quoted in Joanne Grant, ed., *Black Protest: History, Documents and Analyses, 1619 to the Present* (Greenwich, Conn.: Fawcett, 1968), p. 202. History is not an excuse to stay down but a summons to empowerment (see, for example, Donald Hilliard Jr., "Does Race Matter?" sermon at the Cathedral, Second Baptist Church, Perth Amboy, N.J., November 12, 1994; Kay Coles James, *Never Forget* [Grand Rapids, Mich.: Zondervan, 1992], pp. 72, 181).

[13]For example, John S. Pobee, *Toward an African Theology* (Nashville: Abingdon, 1979), p. 39.

[14]Classifying all peoples of black skin or immediate African descent together culturally is culturally insensitive; similarly lumping different Spanish-speaking cultures together does not work well in U.S. school systems (see Christine E. Sleeter and Carl A. Grant, "An Analysis of Multicultural Education in the United States," *Harvard Educational Review* 57 [1987]: 424).

[15]This is not to enter the scholarly debate concerning to what degree slaveholders successfully suppressed our African heritage. Some argue for little continuity, whereas others have argued for much. Some degree of both continuity and discontinuity have characterized our experience, but certainly more African culture survived than White scholars previously assumed (see, for example, Melville J. Herskovits, *The Myth of the Negro Past* [Boston: Beacon, 1990]; John W. Blassingame, *The Slave Community: Plantation Life in the Antebellum South,* rev. ed. [New York: Oxford University Press, 1979]). Similarities between some traditional African beliefs and Christian traditions, especially those in nineteenth-century revivalism, also made it easier for many of our ancestors to embrace Christianity (Mark A. Noll, *A History of Christianity in the United States and Canada* [Grand Rapids, Mich.: Eerdmans, 1992], p. 107; William Pipes, *Say Amen, Brother!* [New York: William-Frederick, 1951], pp. 53-73, compares Whitefield's emotive style with that of the African shaman, despite the author's ethnocentric distaste for African religious practice). Some other elements also carried over (see Henry Mitchell, *Black Belief* [New York: Harper & Row, 1975]; and Henry Mitchell, "The Theological Posits of Black Christianity," in *Black Theology II,* ed. Calvin Bruce and William Jones [Lewisburg, Va.: Bucknell University Press, 1978], pp. 115-32). But as another writer says, "The issue of the ultimate origin of American Negro religions is still involved in polemics, and the question can be avoided entirely" in this book (Arthur E. Paris, *Black Pentecostalism: Southern Religion in an Urban World* (Amherst: University of Massachusetts Press, 1982), p. 8.

[16]On the African concept of the supreme God and intermediary spirits, see, for example, John S. Mbiti, *African Religions and Philosophies* (Garden City, N.Y.: Doubleday, 1970), especially pp. 37-118. Despite parallels, of course, differences remain, as evident for instance in the Ashanti tale "How the Lesser Gods Came into the World," in *African Myths and Tales,* ed. Susan Feldman (New York: Dell, 1963), pp. 76-82. Yet much African folk wisdom is similar to biblical proverbs; see the insightful collection by our friend Kettehkumuehn Murray, *Oral Utterances* (Charlotte, N.C.: Kilimanjaro, 1995), reflecting his explorations in his native Liberia and elsewhere in West Africa.

[17]On the significance of religion, particularly the Black church, to the Black resistance both in slave times and subsequently, see Gayraud S. Wilmore, *Black Religion and Black Radicalism,* 2nd rev. ed. (Maryknoll, N.Y.: Orbis, 1983).

[18]Cheryl J. Sanders, "Black Women in Biblical Perspective," in *Living the Intersection,* ed. Sanders, p. 127, quoting from Clarence G. Newsome, "Mary McLeod Bethune and the Methodist Episcopal Church: In but Out," *The Journal of Religious Thought* 49 (Summer 1992): 10. She also points out that Nannie Helen Burroughs (National Baptist Convention) wrote a booklet on 148 Bible women, including what we would today call an "Afrocentric" description of Queen Candace (noting that the Africans knew how to *obey* a woman!).

[19]Already two generations ago this northern urban trend away from conservative Christianity and the simultaneous growth of groups like those of Daddy Grace and Father Divine was noted by commentators outside our community; see Arthur Huff Fauset, *Black Gods of the Metropolis,* Publications of the Philadelphia Anthropological Society 3 (Philadelphia: University of Pennsylvania/London: Oxford University Press, 1944); and more recently Hans A. Baer, *The Black Spiritual Movement* (Knoxville: University of Tennessee Press, 1984; Kenneth Burnham, "Father Divine and the Peace Mission Movement," in *Black Apostles,* ed. Randall Burkett and Richard Newman [Boston: G. K. Hall, 1978], pp. 25-47). Northern urban African-American Christianity continues to flourish, however; see C. Eric Lincoln and Lawrence H. Mamiya, *The Black Church in the African American Experience* (Durham, N.C.: Duke University Press, 1990), pp. 115-63.

[20]Although traditional African societies often restricted the wife more than the husband (gender equality may be more a genuinely positive insight of modern Western culture), most prohibited adultery (usually imposing social penalties absent in the modern West). For varying practices, see, for example, William N. Stephens, *The Family in Cross-Cultural Perspective* (New York: Holt, Rinehart & Winston, 1963), p. 245; Isaac Schapera, *Married Life in an African Tribe* (Evanston, Ill.: Northwestern University Press, 1966), pp. 204-7; Monica Wilson, *Rituals of Kinship Among the Nyakyusa* (London: Oxford University Press, 1957), pp. 134, 258, 262; G. K. Nukunya, *Kinship and Marriage Among the Anlo Ewe*, London School of Economics Monographs on Social Anthropology 37 (New York: Humanities, 1969), pp. 70-71.

[21]Henry Mitchell and Emil Thomas argue that Africans and even the slaves exhibited healthy self-esteem, but that Black Americans internalized feelings of inferiority after the collapse of Reconstruction (*Preaching for Black Self-Esteem* [Nashville: Abingdon, 1994], pp. 30-33).

[22]It may be of interest to Christians that churches generally promote stability in Black families and Black earnings; see Wallace Charles Smith, *The Church in the Life of the Black Family* (Valley Forge, Penn.: Judson, 1985). On the negative side, however, it should be noted that some Black churches do suppress women (see, for example, Cheryl J. Sanders, "Afrocentric and Womanist Approaches to Theological Education," in *Living the Intersection*, ed. Sanders, p. 164). Historically, Jarena Lee had to stand firm in her call regardless of what men said (see, for example, Lorine Cummings, "A Womanist Response to the Afrocentric Idea," in *Living the Intersection*, pp. 63-66; Deborah McDowell, "Slavery as a Sacred Text," in *Living the Intersection*, pp. 81-82); she attested that her call came five years after her "sanctification" experience (*Sisters of the Spirit*, ed. William Andrews [Bloomington: Indiana University Press, 1986], p. 35).

Chapter 2: Back to Africa

[1]Richard Herrnstein and Charles Murray, *The Bell Curve* (New York: Free Press, 1994). For critical responses to *The Bell Curve*, including critiques on the basis of genetics, statistical methods and more, see Steven Fraser, ed., *The Bell Curve Wars* (New York: BasicBooks, 1995), including Stephen Jay Gould, "Curveball," pp. 11-22, and Henry Louis Gates, "Why Now?" pp. 94-96.

[2]Worse yet is the potential impact on teachers who may start with assumptions regarding which students will do well; research shows that such assumptions often can affect students' performance. On the positive or negative impact of teachers' role-expectations in many (though not all) cases, see, for example, E. Pedersen, T.-A. Faucher and W. W. Eaton, "A New Perspective on the Effects of First-Grade Teachers on Children's Subsequent Adult Status," *Harvard Educational Review* 48 (1978): 1-31; compare William Wilkins, "The Concept of a Self-Fulfilling Prophecy," *Sociology of Education* 49 (1976): 175-83. For similar examples in social work, see D. M. Jones, "The Mystique of Expertise in Social Services," *Journal of Sociology and Social Welfare* 3 (1976): 332-46; in sociology, for example, R. L. Henshel, "The Boundary of the Self-Fulfilling Prophecy and the Dilemma of Social Prediction," *British Journal of Sociology* 33 (1982): 511-28; in large-scale urban planning, perhaps Henrika Kuklick, "Chicago Ideology and Urban Planning Policy," *Theory and Society* 9 (1980): 321-45. British and Canadian data show that in many cases teachers form assumptions based on children's moral performance (James Murphy, "Teacher Expectations and Working Class Under-Achievement," *British Journal of Sociology* 25 [1974]: 326-44) or on observed academic performance (Trevor Williams, "Teacher Prophecies and the Inheritance of Inequality," *Sociology of Education* 49 [1976]: 223-36). This suggests that motivating students to learn must begin early, since assignment to a group often becomes self-perpetuating (see Walter Schafer, Carol Olera and Kenneth Polk, "Programmed for Social Class Tracking in High School," *Trans-Action* 12 [1970]: 39-46; Donna Eder, "Ability Grouping as a Self-Fulfilling Prophecy," *Sociology of Education* 54 [1981]: 151-62); compare, for example, M. B. Smith's story "Alfred the Great," *Ebony,* February 1992, pp. 154-62.

[3]Compare Sharon Begley, "Three Is Not Enough," *Newsweek,* February 13, 1995, p. 69, which compares the high incidence of hypertension in African-Americans with the fact that "black Africans have among the lowest rates of hypertension in the world." Race is clearly *not* the determinant factor.

[4]Marek Kohn, "Science and Race Matters," *World Press Review,* December 1995, p. 48.

[5]So, for example, Lowell Noble, retired sociology professor, in "Blacks and Whites: Who's Inferior?"

Urban Family, Winter 1995, p. 34, challenging Herrnstein and Murray's *Bell Curve.* Noble, who is White, also suggests that if we hang intelligence on racial genetics, we should do the same with morality—with Whites faring rather badly, given their history of oppressing others in recent centuries (Native Americans, the Nazi Holocaust and so on).

[6]Sribala Subramanian, "The Story in Our Genes," *Time,* January 16, 1995, p. 54, reviewing a work by population geneticists Luca Cavalli-Sforza, Paolo Menozzi and Alberto Piazza.

[7]Begley, "Three Is Not Enough," p. 67.

[8]Ibid., p. 69.

[9]Lisa Graham McMinn and Mark R. McMinn (professors at Wheaton College), "For Whom the Bell Curves," *Christianity Today,* December 12, 1994, p. 19, also challenging Herrnstein and Murray's *Bell Curve.* One may also note that those deprived of control over their lives (in situations like imprisonment) "suffer lower morale and worse health" (David Myers, "Who's Happy? Who's Not?" *Christianity Today,* November 23, 1992, p. 25), although African-Americans, despite the pressures we face, "are actually slightly *less* vulnerable to depression" than Whites (ibid., p. 23).

[10]William Pannell, *The Coming Race Wars?* (Grand Rapids, Mich.: Zondervan, 1993), p. 129.

[11]W. E. B. Du Bois, *The World and Africa,* rev. ed. (New York: International Publishers, 1965), p. 18.

[12]Raymond W. Mack, *Race, Class and Power,* 2nd ed. (New York: D. Van Nostrand, 1968), p. 59.

[13]Erskine Clarke, *Wrestlin' Jacob: A Portrait of Religion in the Old South* (Atlanta: John Knox, 1979), p. 109.

[14]Ibid., p. 111.

[15]Marcus Garvey, remarking that Egypt, Ethiopia and Timbuktu were greater empires than Europe in their day; quoted in Grant, ed., *Black Protest,* p. 202.

[16]As quoted on p. 78 in Lerone Bennett Jr., "Voices of the Past Speak to the Present," *Ebony,* February 1994, pp. 78-84. The concluding statement of the classic Yale symposium on Black studies in the 1960s declared that Black studies "are needed . . . to remove the scales of ignorance from the eyes of black and white America" (Armstead L. Robinson, "A Concluding Statement," in *Black Studies in the University,* ed. A. L. Robinson, C. C. Foster and D. H. Ogilvie [New York: Bantam, 1969], p. 217).

[17]The Eurocentric views of history are regularly challenged by Afrocentric writers who point out the racism inherent in Eurocentric historiography's roots (such as John G. Jackson, *Ethiopia and the Origin of Civilization* [Baltimore: Black Classic Press, n.d.], pp. 3-6). Thus, for example, "most historians writing about the subject have attributed the civilizations of East Africa to every known people except the East Africans" (John Henrik Clarke, introduction to John G. Jackson, *Introduction to African Civilizations* [New York: Carol Publishing Group, 1970], p. 25).

[18]Roland Oliver and J. D. Fage, *A Short History of Africa* (Oxford: Facts on File, 1989), pp. 1-2, contrasting this situation with European entry into parts of South America and Asia.

[19]For example, Quintilian *Institutio oratoria* 7.1.14 (LCL 3:12-13); Juvenal *Satires* 6.602-9 (LCL pp. 132-33); also references in Robert K. Sherk, ed., *The Roman Empire: Augustus to Hadrian* (New York: Cambridge University Press, 1988), p. 245, §188 (especially *Oxyrhynchus Papyri* 744; *BGU* 1210; *ILS* 1486); Jane F. Gardner, *Women in Roman Law and Society* (Bloomington: Indiana University Press, 1986), p. 6; Suzanne Dixon, *The Roman Mother* (Norman: Oklahoma University Press, 1988), pp. 19, 23, 95; Beryl Rawson, "Children in the Roman *Familia,*" in *The Family in Ancient Rome: New Perspectives,* ed. Beryl Rawson (Ithaca, N.Y.: Cornell University Press, 1986), p. 172.

[20]For killing in traditional African societies, see Mbiti, *African Religions and Philosophies,* pp. 146, 152-53, 240-41. Some cultures, such as the Temne (West Africa), burn or suffocate deformed children, associating them with devils (John Dawson, "Urbanization and Mental Health in a West African Community," in *Magic, Faith and Healing,* ed. Ari Kiev [New York: Free Press, 1964], p. 324), but the Romans likewise generally burned deformed infants (W. Den Boer, *Private Morality in Greece and Rome* [Leiden: Brill, 1979], pp. 98-99, 113, 116).

[21]Compare "Druid," in *The New Encyclopaedia Britannica Micropaedia,* 12 vols., 15th ed. (Chicago: Encyclopaedia Britannica, 1992), 4:233: "The Druids offered human sacrifices for those who were gravely sick or in danger of death in battle. Huge wickerwork images were filled with living men and then burned; although the Druids preferred to sacrifice criminals, they would choose innocent

victims if necessary." Caesar's account is confirmed by early Irish sources.

[22]Human sacrifice was admittedly once practiced by Ashanti and some other traditional African religions, though it was later universally rejected (Pobee, *Toward an African Theology,* p. 54). Sometimes a few African slaves were buried alive with the corpse of a chief (Murray Gordon, *Slavery in the Arab World* [New York: New Amsterdam Books, 1989], pp. 6-7). Archaeological evidence also suggests the sacrifice of women and children at the graves of important personages in a Katoto burial ground (F. Van Noten with D. Cahen and P. De Maret, "Central Africa," in *Ancient Civilizations of Africa,* vol. 2 of *General History of Africa,* ed. G. Mokhtar [Berkeley: University of California Press, 1981], p. 633).

[23]Bruce Britten, *We Don't Want Your White Religion,* 2nd ed. (Roodepoort, South Africa: Word of Life, 1996), chap. 2. Because the book was in press at the same time as ours, we cannot provide the page numbers, but we thank Bruce Britten for an advance copy of his manuscript.

[24]Du Bois, *World and Africa,* p. 25, citing the witness of William Howitt, *Colonization and Christianity* (London: Longman, Orme, Brown, Green & Longmans, 1838), pp. 280-81. This is not to deny some other positive influences, such as British opposition to the Indian tradition of bride-burning (see especially William Carey in *Classics of Christian Missions,* ed. Francis M. DuBose [Nashville: Broadman, 1979], p. 24) or suppression of some dangerous bandits who killed wayfarers (see examples in Richard Pierard, "Social Concern in Christian Missions," *Christianity Today,* June 18, 1976, p. 8); but Western readers in the 1990s still generally lack full information about European colonialism's moral abuses.

[25]Du Bois, *World and Africa,* pp. 38-39.

[26]For example, Gordon, *Slavery in the Arab World,* p. 6, noting documentation as early as the eleventh century. Sometimes Africans sold other Africans in exchange "for Arab wares" (ibid., p. 7).

[27]Du Bois, *World and Africa,* pp. 192-93; see also Joel A. Rogers, *World's Greatest Men and Women of African Descent,* small ed. (New York: J. A. Rogers, 1935), p. 36. The Mamelukes eventually gained their freedom; they existed in Egypt from 1193 to 1805. Chancellor Williams (*The Destruction of Black Civilization* [Chicago: Third World Press, 1987], pp. 77, 153) believes that their revolt against Arab rule spelled the beginning of the transition to the almost exclusive use of Black slaves; but compare Gordon, *Slavery in the Arab World,* p. 107.

[28]The universal applicability of Jesus' message is a primary thesis of Acts (see, for example, Craig S. Keener, *The IVP Bible Background Commentary: New Testament* [Downers Grove, Ill.: Inter-Varsity Press, 1993], p. 323; James M. Scott, "Luke's Geographical Horizon," in *Graeco-Roman Setting,* vol. 2 of *The Book of Acts in Its First-Century Setting,* ed. David W. J. Gill and Conrad Gempf [Grand Rapids, Mich.: Eerdmans, 1994], pp. 483-544; Jacques Dupont, *The Salvation of the Gentiles* [New York: Paulist, 1979]). For concrete examples of various proposals for contextualization today, see some evangelical studies translating Christian concepts into relevant African symbols and addressing African issues (such as Cyril Okorocha, "The Meaning of Salvation: An African Perspective," and Kwame Bediako, "Jesus in African Culture: A Ghanaian Perspective," in *Emerging Voices in Global Christian Theology* [Grand Rapids, Mich.: Zondervan, 1994], pp. 59-92 and 93-121 respectively) and one Catholic proposal for adapting symbols of Maasai culture (Eugene Hillman, *Toward an African Christianity* [New York: Paulist, 1993]).

[29]Claims regarding Christianity's antiquity in Africa are documented below. West Africans found Christianity attractive and relevant once they could separate it from the cultural wrapping in which Europeans had delivered it (Lamin Sanneh, *West African Christianity* [Maryknoll, N.Y.: Orbis, 1983], p. 83; also see the revival of Black nationalism alongside Christianity in ibid., pp. 97-102). For statistics on Christian commitment in various parts of the world, see the helpful work by Patrick Johnstone, *Operation World,* 5th ed. (Grand Rapids, Mich.: Zondervan, 1993), including pp. 20-61.

[30]See, for example, Sanneh, *West African Christianity,* pp. 36, 167; and examples in Ruth A. Tucker, *From Jerusalem to Irian Jaya* (Grand Rapids, Mich.: Zondervan, 1983), and Stephen Neill, *A History of Christian Missions* (Baltimore: Penguin, 1964).

[31]Sanneh, *West African Christianity,* pp. 181-83. His church later (1917) sought entry into the World Evangelical Alliance (ibid.).

[32]Elizabeth Isichei, *A History of Christianity in Africa* (Lawrenceville, N.J.: Africa World Press,

1995), p. 54. The ungodly lifestyles of clergy in the Congo hindered the spread of Christianity there (ibid., p. 66; compare p. 68).

[33]Noll, *History of Christianity,* p. 341.

[34]Isichei, *History of Christianity in Africa,* p. 233.

[35]Ibid.

[36]Ibid., p. 75. While they too often remain "foreigners," "missionaries are often the most socially integrated of any foreigners living in a given society" (Gene Smillie, "Adaptors to Foreign Cultures," *Mission Today,* 1995, p. 4).

[37]See Gordon, *Slavery in the Arab World,* pp. 10, 199, 203, 209; compare Pierard, "Social Concern in Christian Missions," p. 9, on Dr. John Philip's opposition to oppression in South Africa and on William Knibb in Jamaica. Missionaries often worked alongside antislavery advocates and gave presentations in their conventions (for example, *Proceedings of the General Anti-slavery Convention, June 13-20, 1843* [London: General Anti-slavery Convention, 1843], pp. 41-45).

[38]Isichei, *History of Christianity in Africa,* pp. 242-43.

[39]Du Bois, *World and Africa,* p. 20; compare his critiques of religious hypocrisy that undermined the true values of Christianity, pp. 17, 21, 50, 73. Even Darwinism apparently was not inherently racist and had to be perverted to serve racist ends; see David N. Livingstone, *Darwin's Forgotten Defenders* (Grand Rapids, Mich.: Eerdmans, 1987).

[40]Walter J. Hollenweger Jr., *The Pentecostals* (Peabody, Mass.: Hendrickson, 1988), p. 135.

[41]See Lerone Bennett Jr., *Before the "Mayflower,"* rev. ed. (Baltimore: Penguin, 1966; many of these essays were originally published in *Ebony* magazine), p. 13; for African kingdoms concurrent with medieval Europe, see Du Bois, *World and Africa,* pp. 204-25.

[42]See, for example, Cheikh Anta Diop, *The African Origin of Civilization,* trans. Mercer Cook (Westport, Conn.: Lawrence Hill, 1974), p. 230.

[43]Du Bois, *World and Africa,* pp. 217-19; compare O. D. Pelt and R. L. Smith, *The Story of the National Baptists* (New York: Vantage, 1960), p. 22.

[44]Charles B. Copher (*Black Biblical Studies* [Chicago: Black Light Fellowship, 1993], pp. 109-10) argues that the early medieval European view of Blacks was favorable, until it was influenced by the negative images in Jewish sources; on pp. 110-13 he contends that it was in the fifteenth century and following that Europeans began interpreting Noah's curse as justification for slavery (and confusing Cain and Canaan) as had the Muslims before them.

[45]Cain Hope Felder (*Troubling Biblical Waters* [Maryknoll, N.Y.: Orbis, 1989], pp. 8-9), Martin Bernal (*The Fabrication of Ancient Greece, 1785-1985,* vol. 1 of *Black Athena* [London: Free Association Books, 1987], p. 15) and John Henrik Clarke ("Africa in the Ancient World," in *Kemet and the African Worldview,* ed. Maulana Karenga and Jacob Carruthers [Los Angeles: University of Sankore, 1986], p. 45—citing Professor Bruce Williams of the University of Chicago) suggest that it is older than Egypt. John H. Taylor, *Egypt and Nubia* (Cambridge, Mass.: Harvard University Press, 1991), p. 9, argues from archaeological evidence that Nubia's first "widespread" culture dates to c. 3500-3000 B.C.E., and provides evidence for trade between Nubia and Egypt in this period. David O'Connor ("Nubia Before the New Kingdom," in *Africa in Antiquity I* [Brooklyn, N.Y.: Brooklyn Museum, 1978], p. 47) likewise finds evidences of civilization into the fourth millennium B.C.E. On ancient Nubian civilization, see also N. M. Sherif, "Nubia Before Napata (-3100 to -750)," and S. Adam with J. Vercoutter, "The Importance of Nubia," in *Ancient Civilizations of Africa,* ed. Mokhtar, pp. 245-74 and 226-43, respectively.

[46]Randall C. Bailey, "Beyond Identification: The Use of Africans in Old Testament Poetry and Narratives," in *Stony the Road We Trod,* ed. Cain Hope Felder (Minneapolis: Fortress, 1991), p. 180; Alfred G. Dunston Jr., *The Black Man in the Old Testament and Its World* (Philadelphia: Dorrance, 1974), pp. 45-49, 101-37; Copher, *Black Biblical Studies,* pp. 58-65; Frank M. Snowden Jr., *Before Color Prejudice* (Cambridge, Mass.: Harvard University Press, 1983), pp. 44-46; see evidence also in Du Bois, *World and Africa,* pp. 132-34. Dunston's caution is nevertheless apropros: in an era before color prejudice, Israel's prophets denounced the sins of Black peoples as well as lighter ones, for all peoples were guilty of wrongdoing (*Black Man in the Old Testament,* p. 147; compare similarly Felder, *Troubling Biblical Waters,* p. 20).

[47]On Romans in North Africa, see, for example, A. Mahjoubi, "The Roman Period," in *Ancient Civilizations of Africa,* ed. Mokhtar, pp. 465-99; T. R. S. Broughton, *The Romanization of Africa*

Proconsularis (Baltimore: Johns Hopkins University Press, 1929), pp. 13-46 (the Republic), 47-87 (the early Empire), 88-118 (the first century). The pre-Punic culture persisted through the Punic and Roman, including Christian, periods, until the coming of Islam (Mahjoubi, "Roman Period," p. 498); this cultural persistence manifested itself even in the indigenous Donatist schism in the period of Augustine (see L. R. Holme, *The Extinction of the Christian Churches in North Africa* [New York: Burt Franklin, 1969], pp. 48-51; Broughton, *Romanization of Africa*, p. 228; W. H. C. Frend, *The Donatist Church* [Oxford: Oxford University Press, 1952]). The North Africans continued worshiping ancestral gods (even if sometimes under Roman names) "until the coming of Christianity, another Semitic religion" (Broughton, *Romanization of Africa*, p. 228).

[48]G. W. B. Huntingford, "The Kingdom of Axum," in *The Dawn of African History*, ed. Roland Oliver (London: Oxford University Press, 1961), p. 28. Yet South Arabia itself probably includes a mixing of East African and northerly Arabian populations from an early period; see Runoko Rashidi, "Africans in Early Asian Civilizations: A Historical Overview," in *African Presence in Early Asia*, ed. Ivan Van Sertima and Runoko Rashidi (New Brunswick, N.J.: Transaction Books [Rutgers]/Journal of African Civilizations, 1988), pp. 22-29, especially pp. 22-23.

[49]Du Bois, *World and Africa*, p. 117.

[50]Bernard Lewis, *Race and Slavery in the Middle East* (New York: Oxford University Press, 1990), p. 23; compare F. E. Peters, *Muhammad and the Origins of Islam* (Albany: State University of New York, 1994), pp. 51-55.

[51]Lewis, *Race and Slavery in the Middle East*, p. 23.

[52]For this argument, see Rogers, *World's Greatest Men and Women*, pp. 18-20.

[53]See William Y. Adams, *Nubia: Corridor to Africa* (Princeton, N.J.: Princeton University Press, 1977), p. 386; compare Mbiti, *African Religions*, p. 243. The line that may rival Abyssinia's for longevity is that of the ruler of Japan (Adams, *Nubia*, p. 386); the Kanuri's ruling dynasty in Nigeria may have lasted a thousand years (till 1846). Rashidi contends that the Sabeans were a South Arabian people whose ancestry was largely though not wholly African (see Rashidi, "Africans in Early Asian Civilizations," pp. 23-24). On the Semitic element, see also Williams, *Destruction of Black Civilization*, p. 273; for arguments that the Sabeans may have been Ethiopian, see Felder, *Troubling Biblical Waters*, pp. 22-36, and David Tuesday Adamo, "The Place of Africa and Africans in the Old Testament and Its Environment," Ph.D. dissertation, Baylor University, 1986, pp. 137-44. The direction of influence between South Arabia and Ethiopia is disputed (Dunston, *Black Man in the Old Testament*, p. 15, derives the Ethiopians from Saba in South Arabia), but they may have traveled both ways. On the queen of Sheba in Ethiopian tradition (which probably derives from the early Christian era), see William Leo Hansberry, *Pillars in Ethiopian History* (Washington, D.C.: Howard University Press, 1981), pp. 33-59; on this queen as queen of Ethiopia in early Jewish tradition, see also Scott, "Luke's Geographical Horizon," p. 536; on the story's historicity, Adamo, "Place of Africa and Africans," pp. 131-37.

[54]On Hannibal's character, see in particular Polybius *Rise of Roman Republic* 9.22-26.

[55]Du Bois, *World and Africa*, pp. 141-42. Ancient sources indicate many Blacks in Carthage, including auxiliaries in the army (also a Roman practice—Snowden, *Before Color Prejudice*, p. 33), and racial intermixing (see J. Desanges, "The Proto-Berbers," in *Ancient Civilizations of Africa*, ed. Mokhtar, p. 427; Broughton, *Romanization of Africa*, pp. 8-9); the Black (Suetonius, *colore fusco*) poet Terence was from Carthage. The Carthaginians had many Black African (Numidian) mercenaries (see Polybius *Roman Republic* 3.113), and abandoning them may have cost them the war (15.13, 15). Most pre-Carthaginians were, however, apparently ancestors of the modern Berbers (A. A. Kwapong, "Carthage, Greece and Rome," in *Dawn of African History*, ed. Oliver, p. 14). Scholars dispute *how* dark most North Africans were in the early period; whereas some argue that the Arab conquests lightened the general population, others (like Gordon, *Slavery in the Arab World*, p. 43) emphasize the mixture of White Berbers and their Black slaves under Arab domination.

[56]Gordon, *Slavery in the Arab World*, p. 109.

[57]Du Bois, *World and Africa*, pp. 141-42. On Numidia, see B. H. Warmington, "The Carthaginian Period," in *Ancient Civilizations of Africa*, ed. Mokhtar, pp. 459-61; on ancient Mauritania, ibid., p. 462. On Mediterranean civilizations' links with West Africa, see Oliver and Fage, *Short History of Africa*, pp. 39-50.

[58]Bennett, *Before the "Mayflower,"* p. 16. According to Ghanian traditions of rulers, the kingdom extended forty-four kings before the Christian era (contemporary with the Nubian pharaohs of Egypt's seventh-century B.C. Twenty-fifth Dynasty); see Williams, *Destruction of Black Civilization,* p. 197. Extant evidence indicates that this Soninke empire existed at least by the fifth century A.D. (Gordon, *Slavery in the Arab World,* pp. 109-10).

[59]Bennett, *Before the "Mayflower,"* pp. 16-17; compare Williams, *Destruction of Black Civilization,* p. 197.

[60]Weakened further by the Berber Abu Bakr, it suffered at the hands of the Fulani, once subject to it, from the 1200s (see Basil Davidson with F. K. Buah, *A History of West Africa to the Nineteenth Century* [Garden City, N.Y.: Doubleday/Anchor, 1966], pp. 39-51; also see Williams, *Destruction of Black Civilization,* p. 199). Bennett (*Before the "Mayflower,"* p. 17) calls its oppressors "Moslem fanatics."

[61]Du Bois, *World and Africa,* pp. 211-12. As of 1493, its form of slavery focused on having various subject peoples provide specific goods (Basil Davidson, *Africa in History* [New York: Macmillan, 1968], p. 181).

[62]Bennett, *Before the "Mayflower,"* p. 18.

[63]Ibid., p. 22.

[64]Du Bois, *World and Africa,* pp. 211-12.

[65]Williams, *Destruction of Black Civilization,* p. 205.

[66]The university used Arabic because it was the main language of trade and main written language available, not to invite conversion to Islam (ibid., p. 206).

[67]Bennett, *Before the "Mayflower,"* pp. 18-19.

[68]Williams, *Destruction of Black Civilization,* p. 204.

[69]Sanneh, *West African Christianity,* p. 229.

[70]Ibid., p. 230.

[71]Gordon, *Slavery in the Arab World,* pp. 28-29. Likewise, against papal rules, some European lords hampered conversion of Muslim slaves taken in reprisal for slave raids against Europeans (ibid., p. 29).

[72]Sanneh, *West African Christianity,* pp. 212-13. Traditional Arabs claim "that since the language of their revelation is Arabic, allegedly the language of Adam and of God, it is the language of Islam. So, strictly speaking, 'anyone who becomes a Muslim becomes an Arab' (Al-Hariri, p. 23)" (Georges Houssney, "Unity: The Unfulfilled Dream of the Arabs," *Reach Out* 3 [June 1989]: 14). One may compare some ethnocentric Christian missionaries of the past, although Western colonial authorities and Protestant missionaries were often at odds (see, for example, Sanneh, *West African Christianity,* pp. 36, 167; examples in Tucker, *From Jerusalem to Irian Jaya,* and Neill, *History of Christian Missions*). Missionaries rarely resorted to force to create a "Christian state" analogous to the Islamic model. Most emphasized translating the Bible into indigenous languages; today they generally also emphasize partnership with indigenous church leadership. For a contrast between the Christian emphasis on translating the meaning and the Muslim emphasis on preserving the wording, see Bediako, "Jesus in African Culture," p. 120.

[73]Sanneh, *West African Christianity,* p. 213. Eyewitness accounts verify how Islam was mixed with traditional practices even in the kingdom of Mali, farther to the north, in the 1300s and 1400s (ibid., pp. 228-29).

[74]Ibid., p. 214.

[75]Gordon, *Slavery in the Arab World,* p. 31. Although Arabs make up under one-sixth of the world's Muslims, Islam has retained a strong Arab coloring focused on the Arabian sanctuary and Arabic Qur'an; "unlike Christianity, it did not break with the milieu in which it was born" (Michael Cook, *Muhammad* [New York: Oxford University Press, 1983], p. 88). Islam has nevertheless become more diverse today than in the past (ibid.)

[76]Z. Dramani-Issifou, "Islam as a Social System in Africa Since the Seventh Century," in *Africa from the Seventh to the Eleventh Century,* vol. 3 of *General History of Africa,* ed. M. El Fasi with I. Hrbek (Berkeley: University of California Press, 1988), p. 115.

[77]Williams, *Destruction of Black Civilization,* p. 209.

[78]Ibid.

[79]Ibid., p. 207. Jackson, *Introduction to African Civilizations,* p. 301, gives the date of Babo's

deportation as March 18, 1594. Appealing to Islamic law, Babo achieved his own freedom, although he argued only against enslaving Muslims, not other Africans (Gordon, *Slavery in the Arab World,* pp. 32-33). Whereas he insisted that the Ham myth did not justify the enslavement of Muslim Africans, many of his contemporaries disagreed (Lewis, *Race and Slavery in the Middle East,* pp. 57-58).

[80]Williams, *Destruction of Black Civilization,* p. 208.

[81]Gordon, *Slavery in the Arab World,* pp. 112-13, following sources from the 1500s; compare Lewis, *Race and Slavery in the Middle East,* pp. 58-59.

[82]Williams, *Destruction of Black Civilization,* p. 209.

[83]Du Bois, *World and Africa,* p. 212.

[84]Ibid.

[85]See ibid., pp. 164-75; on the powerful, enduring and often peaceful empires of Africa, see further ibid., pp. 148-63.

[86]For a beautifully illustrated survey of various West African kingdoms, both before and after the influence of Islam from the north, see Anthony Atmore, Gillian Stacey and Werner Forman, *Black Kingdoms, Black Peoples: The West African Heritage* (London: Orbis, 1979).

[87]*World Press Review,* April 1994, p. 41, summarizing David Keys's report on the findings of British archaeologist Patrick Darling in London's *Independent.*

[88]Sanneh, *West African Christianity,* pp. 228-29 (as noted above, citing eyewitness sources).

[89]Bennett, *Before the "Mayflower,"* p. 17.

[90]Gordon, *Slavery in the Arab World,* p. 135.

[91]Bennett, *Before the "Mayflower,"* p. 18; for more detail on Mali, see Davidson, *Africa in History,* pp. 53-63.

[92]Rogers, *World's Greatest Men and Women,* p. 62; compare also the Ashanti ruler who beat off the British (p. 63).

[93]Williams, *Destruction of Black Civilization,* pp. 209-19.

[94]Du Bois, *World and Africa,* p. 172; on this empire, see further Roland Oliver, "The Riddle of Zimbabwe" (including excavations, Arab reports and so on), in *Dawn of African History,* ed. Oliver, pp. 53-59.

[95]Jackson, *Introduction to African Civilizations,* p. 285.

[96]Williams, *Destruction of Black Civilization,* pp. 278-83.

[97]Ibid., p. 283.

[98]Ibid., pp. 284-85.

[99]Ibid., pp. 285-86.

[100]Ibid., pp. 286-89. On Portuguese tyranny and treachery against the Congolese, see ibid., pp. 245-72; on the political abuses of Portuguese Catholic missions (if not always by the missionaries themselves) in this period, see Sanneh, *West African Christianity,* pp. 35-52 (contrast the later growth toward more partnership and indigenous leadership models, more in line with the missions models of the New Testament, recorded later in the book). Whereas Islamic conquerors wiped out Christianity in Nubia, the Atlantic slave trade wiped it out in fifteenth- and sixteenth-century West Africa (Dunston, *Black Man in the Old Testament,* pp. 42-43). Many Congolese spoke, wrote and read Portuguese fluently, and when the Portuguese fought them in 1665, both sides "fought under the banner of the Cross"; yet by the late eighteenth century "few traces remained of Congo's former Christianity," and the kingdom declined rapidly (C. R. Boxer, "The Old Kingdom of the Congo," in *Dawn of African History,* ed. Oliver, p. 81).

[101]Rogers, *World's Greatest Men and Women,* pp. 51-56. His reported cruelty (such as executing fifteen virgins when his mother died, and slaughtering thousands when one person wounded him) eventually led to revolt and his death (p. 56).

[102]Ibid., p. 63.

[103]On a more popular level see also Craig Keener, "Early African Christianity," *A.M.E. Zion Missionary Seer,* July 1995, pp. 9, 37.

[104]Many later Protestant missionaries to regions of Africa also suffered; lacking immunity to local diseases, only one in four survived their first term of service in the Congo, and most survivors buried children or spouses there (Tucker, *From Jerusalem to Irian Jaya,* pp. 155-56). Rowland Bingham's work in East Africa followed the death of his companions and a serious threat to his own life, but

once the work was indigenous it quickly expanded from forty-eight to ten thousand—only to face severe repression from Western colonial powers (in this case Italy; ibid., pp. 295-300). Although many Western missionaries accepted colonialism, they fought its evils, including the slave trade, and faced the ridicule of their intellectual contemporaries in Europe who thought race theories had a scientific basis (ibid., p. 140).

[105]Ibid., p. 45.

[106]For example, Henry Wace, "Tertullianus," in *A Dictionary of Christian Biography and Literature to the End of the Sixth Century A.D.* (Peabody, Mass.: Hendrickson, 1994), p. 940. A. C. Coxe calls Tertullian the "founder" of Latin Christianity (*Ante-Nicene Fathers* [Peabody, Mass.: Hendrickson, 1994; reprint of 1885 ed.], 3:title page). For more on Tertullian, see, for example, Stuart Donaldson, *Church Life and Thought in North Africa A.D. 200* (Cambridge: Cambridge University Press, 1909), pp. 21-41; on the early Catholic North African church of his time, pp. 42-123; on Montanism (a reaction to worldliness and laxity in the church, marked by some Pentecostal phenomena), see pp. 166-72. Tertullian joined the Montanists by A.D. 213 but later broke with them because of differences (p. 171).

[107]*Apology* 37 (*Ante-Nicene Fathers* 3:45). Henry Chadwick (*The Early Church* [Baltimore: Penguin, 1967], p. 65), after commenting on this passage, also suggests that the massive African church may have supplied the first Latin translation for Roman Christians. The church grew while competing with the cults of Isis and Mithras and with the worship of the emperor (Donaldson, *Church Life and Thought*, pp. 139-65). Donaldson thinks it grew especially in North Africa because the polytheists there more than elsewhere "had firmly grasped the idea of a supreme Deity" (ibid., p. 11).

[108]Mahjoubi, "Roman Period," p. 497; also Holme, *Extinction of the Christian Churches*, pp. 2-3, following Mommsen and Milman. On the strength of the North African church to 398, see Holme, *Extinction of the Christian Churches*, pp. 22-53; and see A. H. M. Jones, *A History of Rome Through the Fifth Century* (New York: Walker, 1970), 2:339-40, on Constantine's benefactions to the church there.

[109]Mahjoubi, "Roman Period," p. 497. On Valerian's and Diocletian's persecutions there, see Jones, *History of Rome*, pp. 330-35. See, for example, the accounts of Felicitas and Perpetua (Donaldson, *Church Life and Thought*, pp. 128-37; also two sources noted by Catherine Clark Kroeger: Ake Jason Fridh, *Le problème de la passion des saintes Perpetue et Felicite* [Stockholm: Almqvist & Friskell, 1968]; Marie Louise von Franz, *The Passion of Perpetua* [Irving, Tex.: Spring, 1980]), whose tombs have also been recovered (for photo, see Donaldson, *Church Life and Thought*, frontispiece). On other North African martyrs, see Donaldson, *Church Life and Thought*, pp. 124-27.

[110]Du Bois, *World and Africa*, p. 144, quoting Theodor Mommsen, *The Provinces of the Roman Empire* (London: Bentley, 1886), 2:345.

[111]See Du Bois, *World and Africa*, p. 144. On the North African church, see also Sanneh, *West African Christianity*, pp. 6-13; Joseph Ezeigbo, "A History of Early Christianity in Africa," *Reach Out* 7, nos. 3-4 (1994): 23-25; on the "golden age" of the North African church (especially Augustine), see Holme, *Extinction of the Christian Churches*, pp. 54-75. Yosef A. A. ben-Jochannan (*African Origins of the Major "Western Religions"* [Baltimore: Black Classic Press, 1991], pp. 73-137) rightly emphasizes the African impact on early Christianity, including the persecutions Romans inflicted on African Christians; although ben-Jochannan disagrees with the premise, he finds it understandable that North African fathers affirmed Christian orthodoxy such as Jesus' being the only way (pp. 119-20).

[112]Ancient sources indicate many intermediate races in North Africa. Many Black Africans lived in Carthage (a Phoenician colony), especially serving in its army (Desanges, "Proto-Berbers," p. 427). Ancient texts identify many Blacks in North Africa (especially in Libya [Ezekiel *Exagoge* 60-65], but also in Egypt and to the West), although not all North Africans were considered Black (Frank M. Snowden Jr., *Blacks in Antiquity* [Cambridge, Mass.: Belknap/Harvard University Press, 1970], p. 112). Some of the North African church fathers wrote of "Ethiopians" as Black in distinction from themselves (Snowden, *Blacks in Antiquity*, pp. 207-211). But given the common racial mixing in North Africa (ibid., p. 112), many or perhaps most of these fathers had some Black African blood and thus would be Black by the historic *American* definition. Catherine Clark Kroeger has shown us photographs of paintings of many early North African Christians in Italy, in many of which the

Christians are both dark and "Negroid" in character (for example, Proclus, a clearly Black deacon); we hope that she will publish these.

[113]Isichei, *History of Christianity in Africa,* p. 43. For early Coptic churches, see Jill Kamil, *Coptic Egypt,* rev. ed. (Cairo: American University Press, 1990), pp. 76-92; for monasteries, see ibid., pp. 116-39.

[114]Although the government officially recognizes a Christian population of only 6 percent, about 15.7 percent claim to be Coptic Orthodox Christians, and a smaller number claim to be Protestant.

[115]On one occasion of rioting in 1990, five churches were damaged and forty Copts injured; the 1991 annual report of the Egyptian Organization for Human Rights blamed the government for not defending human rights more forcefully, and also noted that torture had become standard in Egyptian prisons. In September 1991 three churches were burned to the ground (although the fire station was within five hundred yards of two of them, firefighers arrived only two hours later), with one Protestant church thus losing a library of over forty thousand volumes; hundreds of Muslim extremists threatened Copts; one person was killed, and Jihad called for the death of a Muslim physician who treated a wounded Copt. In 1992 Islamic Jihad killed fifteen Protestant Copts and one Muslim; in another incident they killed three Christian workers and the Muslim who had hired them. Persecution also extends to more official repression at times: in 1986 ten Christian converts from Islam were jailed, though later released; in 1991 the torture (some with electric shock machines) in prison of three Muslim converts to Christianity aroused international notice (including that of Amnesty International, and letters in the possession of one of this book's authors from the U.S. State Department). Some scholars, however, date too late the period in which Christians "lost effective power in Egypt" (Mbiti [*African Religions,* p. 317] assigns this to the thirteenth or fourteenth century, probably too late unless by "power" he means a frequent right to relative autonomy).

[116]Isichei, *History of Christianity in Africa,* p. 43.

[117]Mbiti, *African Religions,* p. 300. Although it is not the point of this essay, we note that many forms of Islam, although beginning half a millennium after Christianity, can also claim to be indigenously African in this sense by now, having been established in North Africa within a century of Muhammad's death in 632 (see ibid., p. 317).

[118]On the weakening of North Africa, especially under the Vandals, see P. Salama, "From Rome to Islam," in *Ancient Civilizations of Africa,* ed. Mokhtar, pp. 500-501; see also Holme, *Extinction of the Christian Churches,* pp. 76-118.

[119]Oliver and Fage, *Short History of Africa,* p. 45.

[120]Because Carthage was more luxurious even than Rome, the Vandals grew dependent on those they conquered, and the high culture of the North Africans really tamed and shaped the Vandals over the next century (Holme, *Extinction of the Christian Churches,* pp. 91-92; compare how Greek culture shaped the Roman conquerors). Vandals removed influential clergy, appropriating church property for the Arians (ibid., pp. 101-2); this thoroughly demoralized the once powerful North African church, though some spoke out and were exiled (pp. 103-8). More persecutions and oppression continued at various times until the Arab invasion (pp. 119-242).

[121]One may note the persistence of magical spells (as in Naphtali Lewis, *Life in Egypt Under Roman Rule* [Oxford: Clarendon Press, 1983], p. 97) and the Gnostic thought in Egypt which reduced the Trinity to a dualism that accorded better with some popular trends in ancient thought (ibid., p. 100).

[122]Sanneh, *West African Christianity,* p. 15; Isichei, *History of Christianity in Africa,* p. 44; Kwapong, "Carthage, Greece and Rome," p. 20; see also C.-A. Julien, *History of North Africa* (New York: Praeger, 1970), p. xvi. On the expansion of Islam and gradual conquest of North Africa, see M. El Fasi and I. Hrbek, "The Coming of Islam and the Expansion of the Muslim Empire," M. El Fasi and I. Hrbek, "Stages in the Development of Islam and Its Dissemination in Africa," and H. Monès, "The Conquest of North Africa and the Berber Resistance," in *Africa from the Seventh to the Eleventh Century,* ed. El Fasi with Hrbek, pp. 31-55, 56-91 and 224-45, respectively.

[123]T. Bianquis, "Egypt from the Arab Conquest Until the End of the Fatimid State (1171)," in *Africa from the Seventh to the Eleventh Century,* ed. El Fasi with Hrbek, p. 164; Kamil, *Coptic Egypt,* p. 39; see also Julien, *History of North Africa,* p. xvi. The Monophysites differed from the Melchites on a christological issue that today is often recognized as semantic. The Arabs knew the Nubian Christians as "Jacobites" (Monophysites) as well (Yusuf Fadl Hasan, *The Arabs and the Sudan*

[Edinburgh: University of Edinburgh Press, 1967], p. 9).

[124]Kamil, *Coptic Egypt*, p. 40.

[125]Ibid., p. 41. As Egypt was reduced to a mere province after the Arab conquest, its various Arab rulers sought more prominence (Hasan, *Arabs and the Sudan*, p. 68). Economic rather than religious realities drove some situations, such as most of the Umayyid dynasty's requirement that recent converts pay the tribute just like non-Muslims (El Fasi and Hrbek, "Stages in Development," p. 57); this led to hostile Berber reaction further west (Julien, *History of North Africa*, pp. 21-22).

[126]Kamil, *Coptic Egypt*, p. 41.

[127]Ibid., p. 42, also noting evidence for the successive plunder and destruction, then rebuilding, of monasteries.

[128]Ibid., p. 43; on the Coptic church today, see ibid., pp. 44-60.

[129]See Oliver and Fage, *Short History of Africa*, p. 59.

[130]See the earlier note on the suppression of Copts in Egypt and some examples of repression in the beginning of chapter five.

[131]Du Bois, *World and Africa*, p. 185. The eleventh-century Islamic invasion settled matters much more permanently than the first; see Bernard Lewis, "The Invading Crescent," in *Dawn of African History*, ed. Oliver, pp. 30-36.

[132]Sanneh, *West African Christianity*, p. 15 (on the conversion of the Berbers to Islam, see pp. 15-16).

[133]Ibid., pp. 16-17.

[134]Holme, *Extinction of the Christian Churches*, pp. 241-42.

[135]Donaldson (*Church Life and Thought*, p. 8) suggests that most of North Africa today is Arab due to the Arab invasions.

[136]Both Ebedmelech (possibly a prominent officer; see Adamo, "Place of Africa and Africans," pp. 198-206) and another person with apparently African blood in the royal court, "Jehudi, son of Nethaniah . . . son of an African" (Jer 36:14, 21, 23), testify to the presence of Africans in the royal court of Judah (Adamo, "Place of Africa and Africans," pp. 190-97). That Zephaniah's ancestry seems to include an African in the household of Hezekiah (Zeph 1:1) may suggest that some Judean kings secured Nubian wives for members of their family, probably as royal alliances with members of the family of the then-Nubian pharaohs (Gene Rice, "The African Roots of the Prophet Zephaniah," *The Journal of Religious Thought* 36 [1979]: 21-31, adequately refuting objections; compare Adamo, "Place of Africa and Africans," pp. 209-15). The African courier in 2 Samuel 18:21-22, 31-32, may likewise have been a royal courtier (Adamo, "Place of Africa and Africans," p. 130).

[137]On Luke's point, see Scott, "Luke's Geographical Horizon," pp. 533-38, which contends that part of Luke's "ends of the earth" (Acts 1:8) is the mission to "Ham," inaugurated in 8:27-40.

[138]The Egyptian and Hebrew term *Kush* seems to reflect the indigenous African name for an African people south of Egypt (William Leo Hansberry, *Africa and Africans As Seen by Classical Writers* [Washington, D.C.: Howard University Press, 1981], pp. 8-9), whereas the Greek term *Aethiopia* is later. Once it had been applied more narrowly to a mixed East African population in the modern period, an A.M.E. Zion bishop has suggested, it behooved translators of the King James Version to frequently retain "Ethiopia" as their rendering of the more accurate Hebrew *Kush* (King James was profiting from the slave trade, and identifying Kushites as "Africans" might have "distracted" him; see Dunston, *Black Man in the Old Testament*, p. 20).

[139]Snowden, *Blacks in Antiquity*, pp. 110, 132-33, on an earlier period; see also Du Bois, *World and Africa*, p. 140; A. A. Hakem with I. Hrbek and J. Vercoutter, "The Civilization of Napata and Meroe," in *Ancient Civilizations of Africa*, ed. Mokhtar, pp. 302-4. Bion of Soli in the *Aethiopica* noted that Candace was a dynastic title (like Pharaoh) rather than a personal name, applied to the ruling queen mother (Kirsopp Lake and Henry J. Cadbury, *English Translation and Commentary*, vol. 4 of *The Beginnings of Christianity*, 5 vols., ed. F. J. Foakes Jackson and Kirsopp Lake [Grand Rapids, Mich.: Baker Book House, 1979], p. 96); but it may be "a corruption of a Meroitic title" for all Nubia's "royal consorts or queen mothers" (Adams, *Nubia*, p. 260). Queen mother was a prominent office in Nubia (Oliver and Fage, *Short History of Africa*, p. 32). Some have argued for a more widespread role of women in early African societies as well, though here the evidence often becomes scarcer (see Ife Jogunosimi, "The Role of Royal Women in Ancient Egypt," in *Kemet and the African Worldview*, ed. Karenga and Carruthers, pp. 31-42; Daima M. Clark, "Similarities

Between Egyptian and Dogon Perception of Man," in *Kemet and the African Worldview*, pp. 119-20).

[140]F. F. Bruce, *The Acts of the Apostles* (Grand Rapids, Mich.: Eerdmans, 1951), pp. 190-91. Meroe probably achieved its wealth by exporting "traditional African products—ivory, slaves, rare skins, ostrich feathers, ebony and possibly gold" (Oliver and Fage, *Short History of Africa*, pp. 27-28).

[141]On the Blackness of "Ethiopians," see, for example, Petronius *Satyricon* 102; Seneca *Dialogues* 5.27.3; Sextus Empiricus *Against the Ethicists* 3.43; Philo *Allegorical Laws* 2.17, §67; *Apocalypse of Moses* 35:4—36:3; *Genesis Rabbah* 73:10; 86:3.

[142]See P. T. Crocker, "The City of Meroe and the Ethiopian Eunuch," *Buried History* 22, no. 3 (1986): 53-72; Taylor, *Egypt and Nubia*, pp. 46-48; J. Leclant, "The Empire of Kush: Napata and Meroe" (700s B.C.E.-300s C.E.), in *Ancient Civilizations of Africa*, ed. Mokhtar, pp. 278-95; Hakem, Hrbek and Vercoutter, "Civilization of Napata and Meroe," pp. 298-321. Meroe's art betrays Egyptian, Greco-Roman and traditional African influences (Taylor, *Egypt and Nubia*, p. 54). Rome was not the first power Nubia forced to relinquish its aspiration to extend its empire south of Egypt; Alexander the Great seems to have acquiesced to the same challenge (see Williams, *Destruction of Black Civilization*, p. 118).

[143]Oliver and Fage, *Short History of Africa*, p. 28.

[144]Ibid., p. 29.

[145]Snowden, *Blacks in Antiquity*, pp. 212-14; see also K. Michalowski, "The Spreading of Christianity in Nubia," in *Ancient Civilizations of Africa*, ed. Mokhtar, pp. 326-40. As Isichei (*Christianity in Africa*, pp. 30-31) suggests, the rapid conversion of Nobatia in northern Nubia (543 C.E.) may indicate a considerable prior Christian presence.

[146]Taylor, *Egypt and Nubia*, p. 63, citing archaeological evidence as well as historical records. The same dates appear in Bruce G. Trigger, "The Ballana Culture and the Coming of Christianity," in *Africa in Antiquity I*, p. 117.

[147]Snowden, *Blacks in Antiquity*, pp. 209-11. Medieval saints in Egyptian art were also dark-skinned (Desmond Stewart, *The Pyramids and Sphinx* [New York: Newsweek, 1971], p. 93).

[148]Adams, *Nubia*, p. 435; Isichei, *History of Christianity in Africa*, p. 31.

[149]Isichei, *History of Christianity in Africa*, p. 31.

[150]Williams, *Destruction of Black Civilization*, p. 145; see also Hasan, *Arabs and the Sudan*, pp. 17-41.

[151]Isichei, *History of Christianity in Africa*, p. 31.

[152]Williams, *Destruction of Black Civilization*, pp. 145-46.

[153]Taylor, *Egypt and Nubia*, p. 64. Gordon, *Slavery in the Arab World*, p. 108, says that 442 slaves were to be sent to Cairo annually.

[154]Williams, *Destruction of Black Civilization*, p. 146.

[155]Ibid.

[156]Gordon, *Slavery in the Arab World*, p. 108.

[157]Du Bois, *World and Africa*, p. 186.

[158]Ibid.

[159]Sanneh, *West African Christianity*, p. 16.

[160]Williams, *Destruction of Black Civilization*, p. 148. To simplify the text we have here treated the various Nubian kingdoms under the general rubric of "Nubia" ("a common practice"—Snowden, *Before Color Prejudice*, p. 3).

[161]Hasan, *Arabs and the Sudan*, pp. 92-93.

[162]Ibid., p. 93.

[163]The earliest Arab sources knew only Ethiopians and some Nubians (Lewis, *Race and Slavery in the Middle East*, p. 23). The earliest Arabic texts know of Africans as either *Habash* (Ethiopians and their neighbors) or *Sudan* (an Arabic designation for "Black," covering Africans in general); see ibid., p. 50.

[164]Williams, *Destruction of Black Civilization*, p. 149.

[165]Hasan, *Arabs and the Sudan*, pp. 90-123, especially p. 90.

[166]Du Bois, *World and Africa*, p. 147; on the overthrow of Christian Nubia, see also Hasan, *Arabs and the Sudan*, pp. 124-27.

[167]Du Bois, *World and Africa*, p. 187.

[168]Taylor, *Egypt and Nubia*, p. 64. As long as possible, they also maintained contacts with Egypt's Copts, with Armenian, Syrian and Palestinian Christians, and very likely with Ethiopian Christians (S. Jakobielski, "Christian Nubia at the Height of Its Civilization," in *Africa from the Seventh Through the Eleventh Century*, ed. El Fasi with Hrbek, p. 223). Catherine Kroeger has provided us some additional references for Nubian Christianity, including A. J. Arkell, "The Influence of Christian Nubia in the Chad Area Between AD 800-1200," *Kush* 11 (1963): 315-19; Paul Bowers, "Nubian Christianity: The Neglected Heritage," *East African Journal of Evangelical Theology* 4, no. 1 (1985); Glenn W. Olsen, "Early Christian Nubia: Progress and Prospects of Research," *Proceedings of the PMR Conference* 6 (1981): 74-77.

[169]Davidson, *Africa in History*, p. 102; see more fully Adams, *Nubia*.

[170]Adams, *Nubia*, pp. 539-44; on Islam's role in Nubia's fall, see also Du Bois, *World and Africa*, p. 215.

[171]William Y. Adams, "Medieval Nubia," in *Africa in Antiquity 1*, p. 125.

[172]Hasan, *Arabs and the Sudan*, p. 125.

[173]Ibid., p. 127.

[174]Ibid., p. 131; four hundred churches in 1203 had declined to 150 by 1520. A local rather than hierarchical church structure might in this case have saved them.

[175]Hansberry, *Pillars in Ethiopian History*, pp. 60, 66-67, 71; Ephraim Isaac, *The Ethiopian Church* (Boston: Henry N. Sawyer, 1968), p. 20; H. R. Reynolds, "Edesius," in *Dictionary of Christian Biography*, p. 287; see also Sanneh, *West African Christianity*, pp. 5-6; Davidson, *Africa in History*, pp. 99-100. On Ezana, see R. K. P. Pankhurst, ed., *The Ethiopian Royal Chronicles* (Addis Ababa: Oxford University Press, 1967), pp. 1-7. The account is undoubtedly historical; the Ethiopian account and the European account of Rufinus (*Ecclesiastical History* bk. 1—from Edesius himself) agree (see A. H. M. Jones and Elizabeth Monroe, *A History of Ethiopia* [Oxford: Clarendon, 1955], pp. 26-31). Isaac is himself an Ethiopian, and our Ethiopian friends have confirmed this material. Contrast the earlier dating in ben-Jochannan, *African Origins*, p. 73.

[176]See, for example, R. L. Richard, "Trinity, Holy," in *New Catholic Encyclopedia*, 17 vols. (Washington, D.C.: Catholic University of America, 1967), 14:297. North African theologians like Tertullian and Athanasius were among the foremost defenders of the orthodox faith in early Christianity (though many Gnostics and Arians also taught them). Ethiopian Christians continued to praise Father, Son and Holy Spirit (for example, Emperor Amda Tseyon, in Pankhurst, ed., *Ethiopian Royal Chronicles*, pp. 20, 25). African-American Christians taught the Trinity from the start as well (for example, Richard Allen, in James Melvin Washington, ed., *Conversations with God* [New York: HarperCollins, 1994], p. 8).

[177]Isaac, *Ethiopian Church*, p. 28. The rejection of Chalcedon (A.D. 451), shared with many other Eastern churches, is no longer held to be a major issue (most historians today regard the Monophysite/two natures controversy as largely semantic); and despite Rome's opposition to its own Monophysites, it maintained strong alliances with Ethiopia (ibid., p. 22).

[178]Isichei, *History of Christianity in Africa*, pp. 18, 31.

[179]Hansberry, *Pillars in Ethiopian History*, p. 74; inscriptions support these fourth-century claims (pp. 80-82). On Ethiopia's emergence as a Christian state, see especially ibid., pp. 60-82; on its early development as a Christian state, see pp. 83-109 (the African church became the central cultural and unifying agent of Ethiopian society). On the ease with which Christianity took root in African soil, see also Williams, *Destruction of Black Civilization*, p. 135 (Williams contrasts the reception of later Western missionaries who too often had mixed Christianity with Western culture).

[180]Adams, *Nubia*, pp. 386, 388. On its power in general, including archaeological and literary data, see Jones and Monroe, *History of Ethiopia*, pp. 21-25; F. Anfray, "The Civilization of Aksum from the First to the Seventh Century," and Y. M. Kobishanov, "Aksum: Political System, Economics and Culture, First to Fourth Century," in *Ancient Civilizations of Africa*, ed. Mokhtar, pp. 362-80 and 381-400, respectively. For Axum's subjection of Nubia in the early fourth century, see also Dunston, *Black Man in the Old Testament*, p. 41.

[181]Rashidi, "Africans in Early Asian Civilizations," pp. 28-29. Through the Axumites, Christian influence grew in South Arabia until the Jewish community there massacred many Christians (Tekle T. Mekouria, "Christian Aksum," in *Ancient Civilizations of Africa*, ed. Mokhtar, pp. 412-13).

[182]Hansberry, *Pillars in Ethiopian History*, p. 131. For more on Amda Tseyon (1314-1344), see Pank-

hurst, ed., *Ethiopian Royal Chronicles*, pp. 13-28, which includes his use of biblical language and his prayer for victory in the name of Jesus Christ the Son of God as he defended Ethiopia against advancing Muslim armies.

[183]Hansberry, *Pillars in Ethiopian History*, p. 132; Sanneh, *West African Christianity*, p. 16.

[184]On its distinctly Christian literature, see, for example, T. T. Mekouria, "The Horn of Africa," in *Africa from the Seventh Through the Eleventh Century*, ed. El Fasi with Hrbek, pp. 568-69; in general, see T. T. Mekouria, "Christian Axum," in the same volume, pp. 401-22.

[185]See Du Bois, *World and Africa*, p. 203; Isaac, *Ethiopian Church*, p. 26, on Prester John; in more detail, see Hansberry, *Pillars in Ethiopian History*, pp. 110-50.

[186]See Isaac, *Ethiopian Church*, p. 24.

[187]Isichei, *History of Christianity in Africa*, p. 47. In general, see E. Cerulli, "Ethiopia's Relations with the Muslim World," in *Africa from the Seventh Through the Eleventh Century*, ed. El Fasi with Hrbek, pp. 575-85.

[188]Isichei, *History of Christianity in Africa*, pp. 46-47.

[189]Sanneh, *West African Christianity*, p. 16.

[190]Ibid.

[191]Isaac, *Ethiopian Church*, pp. 26-27. On Lebna Dengel's vivid conflict with invading Muslims, full of firsthand acquaintance with Islam, see Pankhurst, ed., *Ethiopian Royal Chronicles*, pp. 49-69 (including mention of a Muslim who became a Christian, p. 67). When the Portuguese discovered the legendary kingdom of "Prester John," they unsuccessfully tried to convert it to Catholicism (see Jones and Monroe, *History of Ethiopia*, pp. 59-107).

[192]Isaac, *Ethiopian Church*, p. 18.

[193]See, for example, Tamera Marko, "Amazing Faith," *World Vision*, August 1995, pp. 10-15, which incudes the account of Yezeshwall Mammo, whose back was broken during beatings and torture. This article examines especially the contemporary charismatic and evangelical churches which, revitalized by persecution, grew from less than 1 percent of Ethiopia's population to about 10 percent in less than two decades. The Kale Haywet Church alone has over two million members.

[194]Egyptian rather than Axumite (Ethiopian) missionaries birthed the church in Nubia (Davidson, *Africa in History*, pp. 100-101).

[195]Hasan, *Arabs and the Sudan*, p. 131, including an eyewitness report of an occasion when they virtually begged Ethiopia to send them more clergy, but Ethiopia had none to spare.

[196]Britten, *We Don't Want Your White Religion*, chap. 2. Because the book was in press concurrent with this one, we cannot supply the page numbers.

[197]Besides other material on Nubia above, see Oliver and Fage, *Short History of Africa*, pp. 24-26; A. Hamid Zayed, "Egypt's Relations with the Rest of Africa," in *Ancient Civilizations of Africa*, ed. Mokhtar, pp. 136-54, especially pp. 148 (on the need for African products) and 152 (suggesting some long-range Egyptian influence on more distant African cultures). A. J. Arkell, "The Valley of the Nile," in the same volume, pp. 7-12 also documents considerable Egyptian influence and trade (as far as West Africa) before 2000 B.C.E.

[198]In Egypt as in antiquity in general, household slaves (as opposed to other slaves) generally had a much better life than Egyptian peasants (John A. Wilson, *The Culture of Ancient Egypt* [Chicago: University of Chicago Press, 1951], p. 187).

[199]John Henrik Clarke (*Africans at the Crossroads* [Trenton, N.J.: Africa World Press, 1991], p. 323) critiques the myth that Europeans were civilizers: "Conquerors are never benevolent. In nearly all cases they spread their way of life at the expense of the conquered people."

[200]Arthur M. Schlesinger Jr., *The Disuniting of America* (New York: W. W. Norton, 1992), p. 127. This observation does not disparage Schlesinger's more accurate insights about non-White ethnocentric excesses; one may also note his approval of giving proper due to African-American history and redressing past Eurocentric scholarship (as on pp. 15, 19, 38, 53, 58-60).

[201]Ibid., pp. 77-78. Most of our own ancestors were from West Africa rather than East or North Africa, but if White Americans descended from north and west Europe claim Greece and Rome as part of their heritage, they surely ought not object to our claiming other parts of Africa!

[202]Taylor, *Egypt and Nubia*, pp. 28-33.

[203]Ibid., p. 37.

[204]Ibid., p. 39.

[205]For Egypt's subjugation under the Ptolemaic Greeks and under the Romans, see Lewis, *Egypt Under Roman Rule*, pp. 9-17.

[206]See, for example, Isichei, *History of Christianity in Africa*, p. 13.

[207]Molefi Kete Asante, *Kemet, Afrocentricity and Knowledge* (Trenton, N.J.: Africa World Press, 1990), p. 61.

[208]Bianquis, "Egypt from the Arab Conquest," p. 164.

[209]Kamil, *Coptic Egypt*, p. 40.

[210]One thinks here of both viticulture and papyrus, though the latter was replaced by a more efficient resource; see Lewis, *Egypt Under Roman Rule*, pp. 124-25, 128.

[211]See, for example, Dramani-Issifou, "Islam as a Social System," pp. 112-15; Hasan, *Arabs and the Sudan*, p. 177. North Africa as a whole has now become culturally Arabized and Islamized (Dale F. Eickelman, *The Middle East*, 2nd ed. [Englewood Cliffs, N.J.: Prentice-Hall, 1989], pp. 9-10); ben-Jochannan, *African Origins*, p. 127, speaks of "the Asian population that presently occupy and control Egypt."

[212]Asante, *Kemet, Afrocentricity and Knowledge*, p. 61.

[213]See note 115 on the torture and killing of some Coptic Christians. Not all Muslims interpret the Qur'an or Hadith in the same way, but some can point to teachings that one should slay polytheists who do not submit to Islamic conquest (Qur'an Sûrah 9.5; also see 5.33, 36; 9.14); one must fight even Christians and Jews till they offer tribute as the conquered (Sûrah 9.29-30); one should not be friends with Christians or Jews (Sûrah 51). As *Reach Out* recently pointed out, some predominantly Muslim nations like Jordan, Lebanon, Mali, Niger and Senegal are tolerant, but nations under or close to *Shari'a*, traditional Islamic law (such as Sudan, Saudi Arabia, Pakistan), are much stricter and restrict religious freedom of expression for non-Muslims with severe penalties. Under the stricter interpretation of Islamic law, a Muslim who rejects Islam is punished and, if he remains unrepentant, is to be executed (thus the Hadith Al-Bukhari cites Muhammad as saying, "Kill him if he changes his religion").

[214]See "Cupolas and Culture," *World Press Review*, September 1990, p. 50; introduction to *Africa in Antiquity 1*, p. 10. See William Y. Adams, "Geography and Population of the Nile Valley," in *Africa in Antiquity 1*, p. 22: with over half the land now uninhabitable and nearly half the Nubians gone, "the requirements of modern technology threaten what centuries of foreign invasion and cultural transformation could never achieve in the past: the ethnic extinction of the Nubians."

Chapter 3: Black Is Still Beautiful

[1]On the page of current quotes, *Newsweek*, May 22, 1995, p. 15.

[2]Timothy McVeigh's alleged bomb strategy—even to details like the amount of ammonium nitrate fertilizer and fuel oil in his truck bomb—followed a plan laid out in the neo-Nazi *Turner Diaries*, whose author he phoned the day before the bombing, and copies of which he had distributed ("Neo-Nazi Novel a Blueprint for Hate," *SPLC Report* [Southern Poverty Law Center], September 1995, pp. 1, 5). He also placed calls to a nearby "Identity" enclave—a group that teaches that people of color are "mud people," Jews are physical descendants of Satan and God will help the Whites overturn Satan's armies at Armageddon ("Racist Identity Sect Fuels Nationwide Extremist Movement," *Klanwatch Intelligence Report*, August 1995, p. 3). Some wish to infiltrate nonracist fundamentalism (ibid., p. 5).

[3]See *Klanwatch Intelligence Report*, March 1995, available from the Southern Poverty Law Center (400 Washington Ave., Montgomery, AL 36104). This report is eerily prescient in view of the Oklahoma City bombing which shortly followed its release.

[4]"Aryan World Congress Draws Two Hundred Supremacists," *SPLC Report* (Southern Poverty Law Center), September 1995, p. 4.

[5]For example, Du Bois, *World and Africa*, pp. 224, 226-27.

[6]Aristotle *Politics* 1.1.4, 1252b; 1.2.18, 1255a; 3.9.3, 1285a.

[7]Du Bois, *World and Africa*, p. 105; see also ben-Jochannan, *African Origins*, p. 151.

[8]For the Herodotus reference, see Snowden, *Blacks in Antiquity*, p. 105; for Homer, see ibid., pp. 144-50; for the general statement, see ibid., passim.

[9]See C. Eric Lincoln, *Race, Religion and the Continuing American Dilemma* (New York: Hill & Wang, 1984), pp. 38-39.

[10]Rogers, *World's Greatest Men and Women,* pp. 37-50; see also George A. P. Bridgewater in ibid., pp. 57-60.

[11]Some writers with an explicit anti-Christian bias have blamed Christianity for starting slavery (Jackson, *Introduction to African Civilizations,* p. 305), but this identifies Western values with Christianity, ignores the introduction of slavery into Europe through the Arab slave trade, ignores the abolitionist Christians, ignores a long history of nonracially based slavery—in short, ignores much of history. (Documentation appears at appropriate points subsequently in this book.)

[12]Leviticus 25:39-43; Deuteronomy 15:12-18; also see Craig S. Keener, *Paul, Women and Wives* (Peabody, Mass.: Hendrickson, 1992), pp. 188-91.

[13]Leonard L. Haynes Jr., *The Negro Community Within American Protestantism, 1619-1844* (Boston: Christopher, 1953), pp. 27-31; Bennett, *Before the "Mayflower,"* p. 36.

[14]Bennett, *Before the "Mayflower,"* pp. 29-30.

[15]Ibid., p. 36.

[16]See ibid., p. 37. On escaped slaves, see, for example, Peter H. Wood, *Black Majority* (New York: Alfred A. Knopf, 1974), pp. 239-68.

[17]Lincoln, *Race, Religion,* p. 35.

[18]Ellis Cose, "One Drop of Bloody History," *Newsweek,* February 13, 1995, p. 70. He notes that the United States also curtailed the immigration of southern and eastern Europeans in 1924. Though later this policy was reversed, prejudice against those of primarily African descent remains.

[19]Bennett, *Before the "Mayflower,"* p. 37; also noted by C. Eric Lincoln in a public lecture November 9, 1990; see also the passing allusion to interracial relations in colonial Jamestown in Tom Morganthau, "What Color Is Black?" *Newsweek,* February 13, 1995, pp. 62-65; compare Wood, *Black Majority,* p. 98. Just as some came to fear "polluting" the White race through miscegenation, later in the nineteenth century some apparently favored it to "purify" the Black race. See nineteenth-century writer William Laird Clowes ("Miscegenation and the Race Problem, 1890," in *Black Image: European Eyewitness Accounts of Afro-American Life* [Port Washington, N.Y.: Kennikat, 1978], pp. 95-100), who agrees with proponents that miscegenation may improve Black intelligence but nevertheless urges that it remains undesirable!

[20]Bennett, *Before the "Mayflower,"* pp. 43-44; also see p. 35. For a full discussion of miscegenation in the United States see ibid., pp. 242-73. Scientific evidence, like historical evidence, works against White racist views that interracial unions (involuntary examples of which lie in the heritage of many of us) produce inferior persons. The mixing of diverse gene pools seems to produce "hybrid vigor," genetically stronger rather than weaker (Edward G. Olsen, "What Shall We Teach About Race and Racism?" in *Teaching in the Inner City,* ed. James C. Stone and Frederick W. Schneider [New York: Thomas Y. Crowell, 1970], p. 359).

[21]See David R. Roediger, *The Wages of Whiteness* (New York: Verso, 1991), p. 156. In this period (1864) the Democrats were race-baiting, which is far less the case today; yet politically expedient propaganda at the expense of minority communities is hardly a new idea.

[22]Cose, "One Drop of Bloody History," p. 70.

[23]See Dorothy Sterling, *We Are Your Sisters* (New York: W. W. Norton, 1984), pp. 213-16.

[24]Compare the elation of northern Blacks who experienced the comparative lack of racism in France and Canada. See ibid., pp. 144-47, 165-68, especially p. 147, where Josephine Brown exclaims that she, less than fifteen years old, was permitted to teach White students in France who were older than she (in contrast to segregated schools in the northern United States).

[25]See examples below in this chapter, as well as some in chapters five and six.

[26]Sterling, *We Are Your Sisters,* p. 115.

[27]Bennett, *Before the "Mayflower,"* pp. 49, 52. Until influenced by other abolitionists in his later years, Benjamin Franklin evaluated slavery in purely economic terms (see Matthew Mellon, *Early American Views on Negro Slavery* [New York: Mentor, 1969], p. 10). Despite debate, the vested economic interests of the White gentry kept slavery in the Constitution; see, for example, Thornton Anderson, *Creating the Constitution* (University Park: Pennsylvania State University, 1993), pp. 91-94, 102-6. This was true despite a gallant abolitionist attempt to argue that the Constitution's framers would *not* have sanctioned slavery (Joel Tiffany, *A Treatise on the Unconstitutionality of American Slavery* [n.p.: Author, n.d.; reprinted from a copy in the Fisk University Library], pp. 8-23; the rest of the book more feasibly lays against slavery *other* principles more rightly espoused

by the founding fathers).

[28]Pannell, *Coming Race Wars?* p. 46; Stanley M. Elkins, *Slavery: A Problem in American Institutional and Intellectual Life* (New York: Grosset & Dunlap, 1963), p. 208. Like Franklin and some other founding fathers, Jefferson was hardly an orthodox Christian; he was closer to deism (Noll, *History of Christianity,* pp. 134-35). The views of Washington and others on slavery were a topic of much discussion in the years prior to the Civil War; see, for example, Ezra Chase, *Teachings of Patriots and Statesmen* (Philadelphia: Bradley, 1861). The irony of the Declaration's proclamation of equality by creation while ignoring slavery's injustice was not lost on African-Americans such as Peter Williams in 1808 (Washington, ed., *Conversations with God,* p. 16).

[29]For northern slavery—which remained viable "for several decades after independence" (p. vii)—and its gradual peaceable abolition, see Arthur Zilversmit, *The First Emancipation* (Chicago: University of Chicago Press, 1967); also see Edgar J. McManus, *Black Bondage in the North* (Syracuse, N.Y.: Syracuse University Press, 1973).

[30]See Noll, *History of Christianity,* p. 139, citing especially orthodox Calvinist "Samuel Hopkins and other followers of Jonathan Edwards."

[31]Bennett, *Before the "Mayflower,"* pp. 62-63, 68.

[32]Susie King Taylor, *Reminiscence of My Life in Camp with the Thirty-third U.S. Colored Troops* (Boston: Author, 1902), reprinted as *A Black Woman's Civil War Memoirs* (New York: Markus Wiener, 1988), p. 83.

[33]See, for example, Tom Skinner, *How Black Is the Gospel?* (Philadelphia: J. B. Lippincott, 1970), pp. 30-31. Probably the most thorough treatment of the Reconstruction Era itself is Eric Foner, *Reconstruction* (New York: Harper & Row, 1988). Yet the perseverance of our people when we had to "do for ourselves" did not end with Reconstruction; for instance, 268 African-Americans received professional degrees from northern White schools and 516 from Black schools between 1914 and 1936 (J. C. Smith Jr., *Emancipation: The Making of the Black Lawyer, 1844-1944* [Philadelphia: University of Pennsylvania Press, 1993], p. 7); we know of at least twenty-two Black *women* lawyers between 1872 and 1930 (Smith, *Emancipation,* pp. 611-13), although they were not permitted to vote until 1920 (and by 1890 only thirty Black women held bachelor's degrees, versus three hundred Black men and twenty-five hundred White women—Patricia Hill Collins, *Black Feminist Thought* [New York: Routledge, Chapman & Hall, 1991], p. 149). On Black nurses, see, for example, Darlene Clark Hine, *Black Women in White* (Bloomington: Indiana University Press, 1989).

[34]Bennett, *Before the "Mayflower,"* p. 218, followed by Skinner, *How Black Is the Gospel?* pp. 31-32; see also Julian Bond, *A Time to Speak, a Time to Act* (New York: Simon & Schuster, 1972), p. 26. The North needed to negotiate with the South for economic reasons and also maintained an unhealthy racial ideology (see Marcia Y. Riggs, *Awake, Arise and Act* [Cleveland, Ohio: Pilgrim, 1994], p. 33).

[35]See, for example, the documented accounts in Sterling, *We Are Your Sisters,* for this period; C. Vann Woodward, *The Strange Career of Jim Crow* (New York: Oxford University Press, 1957), pp. 70-71; Foner, *Reconstruction,* pp. 595, 611; Dolphus Weary with William Hendricks, *I Ain't Comin' Back* (Wheaton, Ill.: Tyndale House, 1990), pp. 36-37.

[36]See especially Woodward, *Jim Crow;* see also Bennett, *Before the "Mayflower,"* p. 222. For some perspectives on segregation in the U.S. South, see, for example, Mary Frances Berry, "Repression of Blacks in the South, 1890-1945," and Al-Tony Gilmore, "The Black Southerner's Response to the Southern System of Race Relations," in *The Age of Segregation,* ed. Robert Harris (Jackson: University Press of Mississippi, 1978), pp. 29-43 and 67-88, respectively.

[37]See evidence in Charles Joyner, *Down by the Riverside* (Urbana: University of Illinois Press, 1984); also examples from the Slave Narratives, such as in Belinda Hurmence, ed., *Before Freedom* (New York: Penguin, 1990).

[38]Woodward, *Jim Crow,* p. 68. For the history of voting restrictions against Black people in Mississippi, including graphs and charts, see *Voting in Mississippi* (Washington, D.C.: U.S. Commission on Civil Rights, 1965), pp. 1-11.

[39]Skinner, *How Black Is the Gospel?* pp. 32-33, following Bennett.

[40]See, for example, Booker T. Washington, *Up from Slavery* (Boston: Americanist Library, 1965), p. 124; for the sake of accommodation Washington was willing to accept voting restrictions for the poor, provided they be applied across racial lines. Even the Montgomery bus boycott started with moderate

demands (see Taylor Branch, *Parting the Waters* [New York: Simon & Schuster, 1988], p. 144).

[41]Bennett, *Before the "Mayflower,"* p. 301.

[42]I. R. Mukenge, *The Black Church in Urban America* (Lanham, Md.: University Press of America, 1983), pp. 51-53; for a California town, see p. 83.

[43]See Robert William Fogel and Stanley L. Engerman, *Time on the Cross* (Boston: Little, Brown, 1974), pp. 260-61. Federal troops sometimes looted Black as well as White property (Joyner, *Down by the Riverside,* p. 227).

[44]Ironically, Muslims like Malcolm X and radicals like James Forman have sometimes been more ready to admit the biblical principle than professedly Bible-believing White Christians. For some comments on the biblical principle (as in 2 Sam 21:1-9), see Craig S. Keener, . . . *And Marries Another* (Peabody, Mass.: Hendrickson, 1991), p. 138 n. 2; Craig S. Keener, "Exorcising Racism," *Crucible,* Winter 1992, pp. 23-24; for a discussion of Forman's more specific call for reparations from the perspective of various denominational and theological circles, see Robert S. Lecky and H. Elliott Wright, eds., *Black Manifesto* (New York: Sheed & Ward, 1969); the Black Manifesto is also available in Cone and Wilmore, eds., *Black Theology,* 1:27-36.

[45]Most White philanthropy came from northern White churches (Mukenge, *Black Church,* p. 54); continuing through the migration, "those white-based institutions, along with the independent black ones, provided the constituency for the rising [Black] bourgeoisie" (ibid.).

[46]In the race wars of the early decades of the twentieth century (see, for example, William M. Tuttle Jr., *Race Riot* [New York: Atheneum, 1977], pp. 12, 22-30), nearly half actually occurred in the northern and border states; see also Fred Powledge, *Black Power/White Resistance* (New York: Clarion/Simon & Schuster, 1967), pp. 128-81.

[47]The settlement movement (1890-1914) provided places to live for immigrants, but parts of the movement failed to embrace Black American neighbors; see most fully Elisabeth Lasch-Quinn, *Black Neighbors* (Chapel Hill: University of North Carolina Press, 1993).

[48]Riggs, *Awake, Arise and Act,* p. 53; Riggs also notes that the higher cost of living in northern cities offset the higher wages available, thereby *decreasing* living standards.

[49]Pannell, *Coming Race Wars?* pp. 93-94.

[50]See James, *Never Forget,* pp. 128-30, noting blatantly different responses to Black and White testers.

[51]Louis Lomax, "When 'Nonviolence' Meets 'Black Power,' " in *Martin Luther King Jr.,* rev. ed., ed. C. Eric Lincoln (New York: Hill & Wang, 1984), p. 168 (originally published in Louis Lomax, *To Kill a Black Man* [Los Angeles: Holloway House, 1968], pp. 113-22, 159-69, 189-97).

[52]As early as 1919 White writers could recognize that many southern problems, such as race-based poverty, were simply transplanted to the northern cities: Carl Sandburg, *The Chicago Race Riots, July 1919,* introduction by Walter Lippmann (New York: Harcourt, Brace & Howe, 1919; republished with preface by Ralph McGill, New York: Harcourt, Brace & World, 1969), p. 80.

[53]Cornel West, *Race Matters* (Boston: Beacon, 1993), p. 4.

[54]Lomax, "When 'Nonviolence' Meets 'Black Power,' " pp. 168-71.

[55]Pannell (*Coming Race Wars?* p. 97) observes that Los Angeles County is 40 percent Anglo, 37 percent Latino, 12 percent Black and 11 percent Asian, but the sheriff's department is 72.4 percent Anglo. He further remarks that of 382 "questionable shootings" by police reported to the district attorney's office, only one was prosecuted (p. 96), and that sixty-two "problem officers" against whom five hundred complaints have been filed are for the most part still on the street (p. 97).

[56]For instance, one of the relatively few Whites killed during the L.A. riots was Matthew Haines, a thirty-two-year-old auto mechanic who "was pulled off his motorcycle by a mob and shot in the head. He had been riding to help a black friend start her car" (*Newsweek,* May 18, 1992, p. 47).

[57]For example, *ILS* 7503, in *The Roman Empire,* ed. Sherk, p. 229, no. 173; Dale Martin, *Slavery as Salvation* (New Haven, Conn.: Yale University Press, 1990), p. 42.

[58]Albert J. Raboteau, *Slave Religion* (New York: Oxford University Press, 1978), p. 141; compare Wilmore, *Black Religion and Black Radicalism,* p. 86.

[59]Jawanza Kunjufu, *Black Economics* (Chicago: African American Images, 1991), p. 15.

[60]Loren Schweninger, *Black Property Owners in the South, 1790-1915* (Urbana: University of Illinois Press, 1990), p. 104. The size of the estates may account for the fact that whereas only 42 percent of Black slaveholders lived in the Deep South, they held 60 percent of the slaves held by Black

masters.

[61]Ibid., p. 104.

[62]Larry Koger, *Black Slaveowners* (Jefferson, N.C.: McFarland, 1985), pp. 20-21; for more statistics, see pp. 18-30.

[63]Ibid., p. 23.

[64]Schweninger, *Black Property Owners*, pp. 105-6. Slaves sometimes complained that Black slave drivers were more severe than the White ones (for example, 1864, in Washington, ed., *Conversations with God*, p. 47). Whites as well as Blacks recognized *some* limitations; from the 1820s on the laws of southern states regarded maliciously killing a slave as first-degree murder (Kenneth M. Stampp, *The Peculiar Institution* [New York: Alfred A. Knopf, 1978], pp. 218-19).

[65]Koger, *Black Slaveowners*, p. 22.

[66]Du Bois, *World and Africa*, p. 72.

[67]Williams, *Destruction of Black Civilization*, p. 208.

[68]Gordon, *Slavery in the Arab World*, p. 191.

[69]Daniel P. Mannix with Malcolm Cowley, *Black Cargoes* (New York: Viking, 1962), pp. 257-58.

[70]For example, Bennett, *Before the "Mayflower,"* pp. 38-39; one may gain a sense of the feeling betrayed Africans had toward these traitors in Alex Haley's depiction of Kunta Kinte's attitude in *Roots* (New York: Dell, 1976).

[71]As noted elsewhere in this essay, we use "Uncle Tom" in the traditional current sense, not as a reference to the character in Harriet Beecher Stowe's *Uncle Tom's Cabin*.

[72]Wilmore, *Black Religion and Black Radicalism*, p. 56.

[73]See documents in Peter Ripley, ed., *Witness for Freedom* (Chapel Hill, N.C.: University of North Carolina Press, 1993), pp. 201-10.

[74]See Wilmore, *Black Religion and Black Radicalism*, p. 31. For another example, see Clarke, *Africans at the Crossroads*, p. 46: "in 1663, a group of slaves joined white indentured servants to plan a rebellion." (A White deacon may have also helped George Liele found the Silver Bluff Baptist Church in Savannah, though Liele became the leader; see Mukenge, *Black Church*, p. 27.)

[75]See Wilmore, *Black Religion and Black Radicalism*, p. 32. For some other Whites who served the Black community, see West, *Race Matters*, p. 85.

[76]For example, Joseph Cephas Carroll, *Slave Insurrections in the United States, 1800-1865* (n.p.: Chapman & Grimes, 1938), pp. 63-64, cites a circular warning letter purportedly written by a slave girl on June 7, 1802, because she "dearly" loves her master and mistress.

[77]Williams, *Destruction of Black Civilization*, p. 19.

[78]Ibid., p. 304.

[79]Ibid.

[80]As noted above, we define "Uncle Tom" here according to its current standard usage, not by its original and more positive use (for its day) in Harriet Beecher Stowe's *Uncle Tom's Cabin*, a book that strengthened abolitionist sentiment.

[81]On the importance of cultural identity and corporate social values alongside economic and political ideas, see West, *Race Matters*, pp. 13-19.

[82]Carl A. Grant and Christine E. Sleeter, "Race, Class, Gender, Exceptionality and Educational Reform," in *Multicultural Education: Issues and Perspectives*, ed. James A. Banks and Cherry A. McGee Banks (Boston: Allyn & Bacon, 1989), p. 52. Cultural sensitivity may also prevent schoolteachers' prejudices that can adversely affect children's educational future (James A. Banks, "Multicultural Education: Characteristics and Goals," in *Multicultural Education: Issues and Perspectives*, p. 19). For an early discussion of the importance of Black studies, see Robinson, Foster and Ogilvie, eds., *Black Studies in the University*. The drive for multicultural education as a whole sprang from the Civil Rights struggle (Banks, "Multicultural Education," p. 5; Grant and Sleeter, "Race, Class, Gender," p. 47; Christine E. Sleeter and Carl A. Grant, "An Analysis of Multicultural Education in the United States," *Harvard Educational Review* 57 [November 1987]: 421). Women's studies also adopted the model pioneered by Afro-American studies (Vivian Gordon, *Black Women, Feminism and Black Liberation* [Chicago: Third World, 1985], p. 15).

[83]Carter, "Cultural Value Differences," pp. 74-76, shows that African-American students are more apt to believe themselves at the mercy of a hostile environment than are White American students, possibly because they experience their environment as more hostile.

[84]Schlesinger, *Disuniting of America*, pp. 90-92, quotes Du Bois, King, Ralph Ellison, Frederick Douglass and others to argue that non-Blacks can provide role models for Black children too. While his basic contention is correct, neglecting the importance of Black role models overlooks the overwhelming sense of alienation experienced by many children growing up in all-Black projects or other low-income segregated communities, for whom Black role models are important to prove that color cannot limit their place in society. More important than the pigment of the role models, however, is that they are firsthand role models and not just distant characters on television.

[85]Although the early preachers argued that slaves should be taught to read (Raboteau, *Slave Religion*, p. 115; see also p. 240), laws in time forbade it, and slaves who were caught could face severe punishments.

[86]Sixteen months after her arrival in Boston as a nearly naked seven- or eight-year-old slave, she could write fluent English. After absorbing literary influences from her reading of the Bible, Milton and especially Alexander Pope's translation of Homer, she wrote a eulogy of Harvard at fourteen. Her poetry was hailed internationally by the time she was twenty, in 1773 (Bennett, *Before the "Mayflower,"* pp. 64-65). The enormous social difference between southern agricultural slavery and a favored position in eighteenth-century Boston under a wealthy patron is the difference between stifling and nurturing creative genius. History cannot record how much genius was lost to humanity through slavery.

[87]"Grant me to live a life of gratitude to thee for the innumerable benefits." See her later prayer for the child she was to bear, "who shall be greatly instrumental in promoting thy [glory]" (Washington, ed., *Conversations with God*, p. 7).

[88]As quoted in Lerone Bennett Jr., "Voices of the Past Speak to the Present," *Ebony*, February 1994, p. 82, along with other important quotes (such as Malcolm X: "Education is our passport to the future, for tomorrow belongs to the people who prepare for it today").

[89]Harvard psychiatrist Robert Coles, "Children of the American Ghetto," in *Teaching in the Inner City*, ed. Stone and Schneider, pp. 135-36; Bell, *And We Are Not Saved*, p. 163.

[90]Psychological disempowerment has been a reality for a long time; see Carter G. Woodson (1875-1950), *The Mis-education of the Negro* (Washington, D.C.: Associated Publishers, 1933; reprint Trenton, N.J.: Africa World Press, 1990).

[91]See Collins, *Black Feminist Thought*, pp. 67-90.

[92]Ibid., p. 54.

[93]See Mitchell and Thomas, *Preaching for Black Self-Esteem*, chap. 4, "Self-Esteem and Black Characteristics," pp. 59-76, on emphasizing the beauty of Blackness for hearers. Gordon (*Black Women*, pp. 1-13) rightly notes that Black women have different agendas from those of the largely White feminist movement of today, in part because White but not Black men hold most of the power in society (pp. 31-33, 69). Nevertheless, on a scale of wages for year-round full-time workers on which 100 represents the earnings for White men, Black men score 76, White women 55 and Black women 50 (ibid., p. 41). Likewise, "the homicide rate for Black women is superseded only by the homicide rate for Black men" (ibid., p. 37). Black women can face discrimination for both gender and race, and while White society seems more afraid of Black men (compare Pharaoh's attitude toward male Israelite slaves in Ex 1:16), too many Black men take out their frustrations with society physically on women. "Black men who rape Black women are given lighter sentences . . . compared to sentences for the rape of White women" (ibid., p. 37), as if White society expects us to mistreat ourselves. We cannot speak of the needs of our race without including the special needs of our sisters as well as of our brothers. For some theological reflections focusing specifically on Black women's situation, see three essays in Cone and Wilmore, eds., *Black Theology:* Jacquelyn Grant, "Black Theology and the Black Woman," 1:323-38; Renita J. Weems, "Womanist Reflections on Biblical Hermeneutics," 2:216-24; Clarice J. Martin, "Womanist Interpretations of the New Testament," 2:225-44.

[94]Michelle Ingrassia, "The Body of the Beholder," *Newsweek*, April 24, 1995, pp. 66-67.

[95]See more fully Craig S. Keener, "Sexual Infidelity as Exploitation," *Priscilla Papers* 7 (Fall 1993): 15-18, including some relevant supporting documentation.

[96]West, *Race Matters*, p. 17. Crosscultural studies indicate that men who grow up in homes without fathers tend to compensate for feelings of masculine deficiency by demeaning women and anything

they feel is feminine (often including their own children; see Mary Stewart Van Leeuwen, *Gender & Grace* [Downers Grove, Ill.: InterVarsity Press, 1990], pp. 130-63). Whatever has been done to our families by the broader society, we are wrong to perpetuate it and wrong to take it out on Black women.

[97]For some examples among many, see Sterling, *We Are Your Sisters;* Andrews, ed., *Sisters of the Spirit,* including Jarena Lee; Toni Cade, *The Black Woman: An Anthology* (New York: New American Library, 1970); Joyce A. Ladner, *Tomorrow's Tomorrow* (Garden City, N.Y.: Doubleday, 1971). We borrow the phrase from Weary's description of his mother in *I Ain't Comin' Back,* p. 14.

[98]Snowden, *Blacks in Antiquity,* pp. 105, 154, 178-79. On interracial marriage being unobjectionable in antiquity, see the evidence in ibid., pp. 4, 6, 178-79, 184, 192, 195; Snowden, *Before Color Prejudice,* pp. 94-97; Du Bois, *World and Africa,* pp. 226-27. In contrast to taboos created in U.S. race-slavery, interracial marriage became so common in imperial Portugal from the mid-1400s on that the royal family included significant Black blood; Du Bois adds that Blacks came to outnumber Whites as far north as Lisbon (*World and Africa,* p. 47). Most African-Americans today regard this as a matter of personal taste (75.6 percent in the Ebony Reader's Poll, *Ebony,* April 1991, p. 18), though we *are* concerned to provide more "marriageable" men.

[99]Surat *Al-Imran* 3.106-7, cited in Carl F. Ellis Jr., *Malcolm: The Man Behind the X* (Chattanooga, Tenn.: Accord, 1993), p. 61. The image even here should not be pressed, since it is based on "white" being the color of light.

[100]Many Arab texts characterize Black people as ugly and stinky, and Black slaves as needing mistreatment to stay humble (see the sources in Bernard Lewis, *Race and Color in Islam* [New York: Octagon Books, 1979], pp. 96-97; Bernard Lewis, ed. and trans., *Islam: From the Prophet Muhammad to the Capture of Constantinople* [Athens: Ohio University Press, 1987], 2:209; both cited in Ellis, *Malcolm,* pp. 111-13). Others have suggested that ethnocentrism is implicit in the Islamic tradition that the Qur'an cannot truly be translated, Arabic being the only proper tongue for God's revelation (and the Arabic that allegedly originally belonged only to the Quraysh tribe at that). Ben-Jochannan complains that even the preeminent African Muslim Bilal "was discriminated against by the Arabs" on account of his color (*African Origins,* p. 223). We should, however, distinguish cultural Arabism from Islam's teaching proper.

[101]On Arabs and interracial marriage, see Du Bois, *World and Africa,* pp. 193-94, 205; also see further discussion in our chapter five.

[102]Song of Solomon 1:5. Many modern White translators have, perhaps unwittingly, adapted the verse to their own culture's traditional tastes: "black but beautiful," they say. The Hebrew word here usually means "and"; it can sometimes mean "but," as these translators assume (compare 1:6), but here the woman's blackness is surely part of her beauty, for even the other women of Jerusalem praise her as the most beautiful woman in the world (1:8). Until the Latin Vulgate came into vogue, Christian commentators read "black and beautiful," following the Greek translation of the Old Testament (Snowden, *Blacks in Antiquity,* pp. 198-99). The King James also translates the woman's Hebrew depiction of Solomon, whom she calls "bright," as "white," although the text conjoins this with "ruddy" or "red," a head like gold and bushy black hair (Song 5:10-11; see William Dwight McKissic Sr., *Beyond Roots* [Wenonah, N.J.: Renaissance Productions, 1990], pp. 42-43, and other translations, such as the NASB). Yosef A. A. ben-Jochannan (*Africa: Mother of Western Civilization* [Baltimore: Black Classic Press, 1988], pp. 233-34) is among those who correctly object to the KJV mistranslation here, though he wrongly assumes that the woman in this passage is the Queen of Sheba.

[103]Nannie Helen Burroughs condemned the Black community's frequent stratification based on skin tone, emphasizing that character matters more than color (see the summary of her case in Riggs, *Awake, Arise and Act,* p. 60).

[104]Winthrop D. Jordan, *The White Man's Burden* (New York: Oxford University Press, 1974), p. 84.

[105]Banks, "Multicultural Education," p. 17; he goes on to note how economic and social status also affect the description of one's "color" in Puerto Rico.

[106]Chaps. 111 and following in *Roots.* Compare also the fictitious Ben Goldrich (his last name is a pun) in Bell, *And We Are Not Saved,* pp. 123-300, who does not join the community but certainly is committed to it.

[107]As quoted in Noll, *History of Christianity,* p. 241. Protesting White racism, the Reverend Francis Grimké likewise called race prejudice damnable (*The Negro: His Rights and Wrongs, the Forces for Him and Against Him* [reprint Ann Arbor, Mich.: University Microfilms, 1973], p. 60). See also, for example, the emphasis on racial reconciliation in the 1925 prayer of African-American Robert C. Lawson in Washington, ed., *Conversations with God,* p. 143.

[108]See West, *Race Matters,* pp. 25, 31.

[109]Ibid., p. 25.

[110]Ibid., pp. 25-26; compare Riggs, *Awake, Arise and Act,* pp. 9-10. Contemporary anthropologists also generally recognize race as a social rather than biological construct (see, for example, Begley, "Three Is Not Enough," p. 68).

Chapter 4: Was Egypt or Israel Black?

[1]See Cain Hope Felder, "Cultural Ideology, Afrocentrism and Biblical Interpretation," in *Black Theology,* ed. Cone and Wilmore, 2:189. Felder notes that whereas Ethiopia appears more than forty times and northern Europe never does, Eurocentric Bible maps have traditionally been more apt to include Europe than Ethiopia.

[2]Despite his thesis, Bernal concedes the title to Mesopotamia (*Fabrication of Ancient Greece,* p. 12).

[3]Some writers, such as George G. M. James (*Stolen Legacy* [New York: Philosophical Library, 1954; reprint n.p.: United Brothers Communications Systems, 1989]) and ben-Jochannan (*Africa,* pp. 375-452), go considerably beyond the evidence. For instance, James's evidence for Egyptian mystery systems is largely based on texts in Greek by writers half a millennium after Greeks had begun to control Alexandria, whereas archaeological evidence supports Greek mysteries three centuries before the conquest of Egypt. The ancient Eleusis sanctuary (see Epictetus *Discourses* 3.21.14: *palaiois* rites) was in continuous use from the sixth century B.C.E. or earlier (Walter Burkert, *Ancient Mystery Cults* [Cambridge, Mass.: Harvard University Press, 1987], p. 2), and its propaganda reached Russia, Italy and Egypt by the fourth century B.C.E. (Burkert, *Ancient Mystery Cults,* p. 37). Dionysiac festivals, an import from the East, seem to be featured in sixth-century Attic vase paintings (Walter Burkert, *Greek Religion,* trans. John Raffan [Cambridge, Mass.: Harvard University Press, 1985], p. 166), most of the myth's components being as early as the *Iliad* (Walter F. Otto, *Dionysus: Myth and Cult* [Bloomington: Indiana University Press, 1965], pp. 54-55). The Asiatic Cybele cult had origins in the Neolithic or Bronze Age (Burkert, *Ancient Mystery Cults,* pp. 5-6; *Greek Religion,* p. 177) and appeared in the Greek world by the third century B.C.E. (Giulia Sfameni Gasparro, *Soteriology and Mystic Aspects in the Cult of Cybele and Attis* [Leiden: Brill, 1985], p. 49).

Egyptian myths used in the mysteries (such as Osiris and Isis) plainly originated before that conquest, but Greek and Mesopotamian sources have parallels to these Egyptian stories, suggesting a shared continuum of ideas throughout Egypt and the ancient Near East. Few objective scholars, Black or White, who are genuinely conversant in ancient history will find much of James's argument persuasive; even the goal of the argument may not be helpful, though his motivation is commendable. Having read Greek philosophy, are we sure we *want* to claim it as our own? African philosophies (as described by John S. Mbiti, among many others) may address practical reality more closely. Arguments like the idea that Aristotle simply stole Egyptian books from Alexandria's library and claimed authorship (for example, Yosef A. A. ben-Jochannan, *Africa,* p. 379, and *African Origins,* p. 111; Paul C. Boyd, *The African Origin of Christianity* [London: Karia, 1991], p. 28) will not persuade any classicist conversant with Aristotle and his literary style. For that matter, Alexandria was not built before Aristotle's pupil Alexander arrived there, and its library was constructed only after both of them had died!

But even if we disagree with James's reason (Greek philosophy is "stolen") and if some think he goes too far in calling for the abolition of all Greek fraternities and sororities on Black campuses ("because they have been a source of the promotion of inferiority complex and of educating the Black people against themselves," *Stolen Legacy,* pp. 160-61), some of his warnings merit more consideration: Black intellectuals should "discontinue the practice of quoting Socrates, Plato and Aristotle in their speeches as intellectual models" (James, *Stolen Legacy,* p. 160).

[4]Martin Bernal, *The Archaeological and Documentary Evidence,* vol. 2 of *Black Athena* (New Brunswick, N.J.: Rutgers University Press, 1991); see especially pp. 409-94.

[5]Egyptian influence on Greece is easier to document than purported conquests (for which too much of the documentary evidence is too late). The eruption of Thera as an explanation for the plagues, pillar of fire and so on in the Bible (ibid., pp. 292-93) is sheer parallelomania (to borrow Sandmel's now-standard term).

[6]Bernal, *Fabrication of Ancient Greece*. Note that Christian apologists in early centuries contested Greek culture, emphasizing the antiquity of Egyptian and Israelite cultures; only in the Renaissance period did opposition to Egypt become fashionable in European Christian apologetics (p. 193).

[7]Michael Grant, *A Social History of Greece and Rome* (New York: Scribner's, 1992), p. 123.

[8]Jackson (*Introduction to African Civilizations*, p. 73) concedes that the fierce Assyrians were pure Semites, but cites a picture of an Elamite king at Susa who appears Black to argue that the Babylonians had Cushite blood.

[9]Bernal, *Fabrication of Ancient Greece*, p. 241. For some examples of racism in European scholarship, see, for example, pp. 201-4, 239-40.

[10]Sir Flinders W. M. Petrie, as quoted in Williams, *Destruction of Black Civilization*, p. 69. Petrie's seven classifications of Egyptian racial subtypes based on nose and beard shapes (Diop, *African Origin of Civilization*, p. 131; Cheikh Anta Diop, "Origin of the Ancient Egyptians," in *Great African Thinkers: Cheikh Anta Diop*, ed. Ivan Van Sertima [New Brunswick, N.J.: Journal of African Civilizations, 1986], p. 37) are unwarranted in view of current knowledge of genetics: such variations occur within the same families!

[11]As cited in Copher, *Black Biblical Studies*, p. 20; see his survey of the "new Hamite hypothesis," which makes Egyptians and Nubians White (p. 35). Anthropologists in different periods have classified them differently, but the Nubians were clearly what we would call Black and would have suffered discrimination in later prejudicial eras (Snowden, *Before Color Prejudice*, p. 17).

[12]Diop, *African Origin*, p. 22.

[13]Ibid., pp. 85-98; thus the civilization as a whole was not of Asian origin (pp. 100-128).

[14]As examples he lists their similar totemism (ibid., pp. 134-35), circumcision (pp. 135-38; see also Dunston, *Black Man in the Old Testament*, pp. 54-55), kingship (Diop, *African Origin*, pp. 138-39), cosmogony (pp. 139-41), social organization (p. 141) and matriarchy (pp. 142-45).

[15]Diop, *African Origin*, pp. 145-51.

[16]Ibid., pp. 153-55. See the column comparisons of Egyptian, Coptic and the Senegalese language Walaf in Diop, "Origin of the Ancient Egyptians," pp. 49-52; also Cheikh Anta Diop, "Origin of the Ancient Egyptians," in *Ancient Civilizations of Africa*, ed. Mokhtar, p. 28. For detailed comparisons between ancient Egyptians and the old Niger Congo group of languages, see Rekhety Wimby, "The Unity of African Languages," in *Kemet and the African Worldview*, ed. Karenga and Carruthers, pp. 151-66; when the essay was published in 1986 she was working on her master's degree in Egyptology at the University of Chicago. Obenga finds a close ancestral relationship as in Indo-European languages ("Report of the Symposium on 'The Peopling of Ancient Egypt,' " in *Ancient Civilizations of Africa*, pp. 64-65), whereas Abdelgadir M. Abdalla contends that the Egyptian language is related to proto-Semitic, "as could be abundantly demonstrated by supporting examples," though Egyptian may have influenced other African languages ("Report of the Symposium," p. 63). Perhaps ancient Egyptian represents an overlap of traditional African and proto-Semitic origins, all being part of a larger "Afroasiatic" linguistic system.

[17]Diop, *African Origin*, p. 1; "Origin of the Ancient Egyptians," in *Great African Thinkers*, pp. 42-46.

[18]Diop, "Origin of the Ancient Egyptians," in *Great African Thinkers*, pp. 41-42. On evidence for the melanin in mummies, see "Report on the Symposium," p. 61. Diop's conclusions are often followed by Afrocentric scholars such as Asante, for example in *Kemet, Afrocentricity and Knowledge*, p. 121; they have also been *expanded* in some more popular biblical works on Blacks in the Bible; see below.

[19]Some Afrocentric authors, especially those less conversant with the original sources than Diop is, cite part of the evidence and depend on other writers who do the same, without giving full attention to the scholarly works of Egyptologists whose lives have been devoted to the field.

[20]In asserting the Blackness of the Egyptian people, Diop himself does not define "Black" as monolithically as do some of those he critiques. He claims that "there are two variants of the black race: (a) straight-haired, represented in Asia by the Dravidians and in Africa by the Nubians . . . with

jet-black skins; (b) the kinky-haired blacks of the Equatorial regions. Both types entered into the composition of the Egyptian population" ("Origin of the Ancient Egyptians," in *Great African Thinkers*, p. 41).

[21]Jackson, *Introduction to African Civilizations*, p. 150. Diop's parallels are much stronger and probably reflect some degree of relationship.

[22]For one example of the contrast, see Pliny *Natural History* 2.80.189 in Snowden, *Before Color Prejudice*, p. 87; compare Sextus Empiricus *Outlines of Pyrrhonism* 1.79-80. A. T. Olmstead, *History of the Persian Empire* (Chicago: University of Chicago Press, 1959), p. 148, describes them from Persian accounts as fierce horse-riding nomads who drank fermented mare's milk "from bowls made of human skulls" and drank the blood of the first enemy killed in any battle. Although some Greeks viewed Scythians as "noble" barbarians (see, for example, Anacharsis to Croesus *Epistolae* 9; Diogenes Laertius *Lives* 1.101-5), sedentary peoples often commented on their savagery (for example, 2 Maccabees 4:47; 3 Maccabees 7:5; 4 Maccabees 10:7; Plutarch *Fortune of Alexander* 1.5, *Moralia* 328C; Chariton *Chaereas and Callirhoe* 2.9.3; Horace *Ode* 4.5.25; Diogenes Laertius *Lives* 1.102; Sextus Empiricus *Outlines of Pyrrhonism* 3.208, 210, compare 1.149). Ancients also remarked on their distance (Cicero *De Nat. Deorum* 2.34.88) and nomadic lifestyle (Horace *Ode* 1.35.9-10; 3.8.23-24; 4.14.42).

[23]See Snowden, *Blacks in Antiquity*.

[24]Lewis, *Race and Slavery in the Middle East*, p. 22.

[25]See ibid., plates 1-10, 16, 19. All plates appear between pp. 22 and 23.

[26]See ibid., plates 11-15. The Ethiopian king appears in plate 17. Yet Bilal (Muhammad's companion) is also clearly Black, in accord with tradition (plate 18).

[27]Ibid., p. 50. *Zanj* referred to Bantus in East Africa, sometimes loosely applied to Black Africans in general.

[28]Diop is more open to the use of skeletal measurements (which he believes makes most Egyptians African) but is skeptical of craniometry; by traditional craniometric criteria, at least five-sevenths of Black Africans would be classified as White ("Origin of the Ancient Egyptians," in *Ancient Civilizations of Africa*, p. 29).

[29]Du Bois, *World and Africa*, p. 107.

[30]The undocumented claim of Williams (*Destruction of Black Civilization*, p. 74) that Asians and mulattos, whom he restricts primarily to the upper class, never constituted more than a quarter of the population is not much more helpful. Where did southwest Asia leave off and northeast Africa begin?

[31]W. S. LaSor, "Egypt," in *The International Standard Bible Encyclopedia*, ed. Geoffrey W. Bromiley, 4 vols. (Grand Rapids, Mich.: Eerdmans, 1979-1988), 2:29; see likewise Paul Jordan, *Egypt the Black Land* (Oxford: Phaidon/New York: E. P. Dutton, 1976), p. 33. Abdalla argues that *KM (Kem)* does not mean "black," nor does it refer to individuals' color ("Report of the Symposium," p. 63).

[32]On a more conscious scale this occurred when remnants of Egyptian garrisons remained in Nubia after troops were withdrawn in the late seventeenth century B.C.E., intermarrying and settling there, and transferring their loyalty to Nubian rulers (Taylor, *Egypt and Nubia*, p. 25). There was no hostility toward "miscegenation" in terms of intermarriage.

[33]Du Bois, *World and Africa*, p. 114; see pp. 92, 94, 100-102, 105-6.

[34]Second Kings 19:9; Isaiah 37:9—although this may have been while Tirhakah (Taharqa, c. 690-664 B.C.E.) was a general, not yet king (see the work of Egyptologist Kenneth A. Kitchen, *Ancient Orient and the Old Testament* [Downers Grove, Ill.: InterVarsity Press, 1966], pp. 82-84; see also Old Testament scholar John Bright, *A History of Israel*, 3rd ed. [Philadelphia: Westminster Press, 1981], pp. 299-306; and Snowden, *Before Color Prejudice*, pp. 25-26, following Kitchen at points).

[35]Writers have suggested among explicitly "Black" Pharaohs various names, including Narmer, Menthoteps and (as mulatto) Thutmose III (for example, Felder, *Troubling Biblical Waters*, p. 11; compare Copher, *Black Biblical Studies*, pp. 24-28).

[36]Irmgard Woldering, *The Art of Egypt: The Time of the Pharaohs* (New York: Greystone, 1963), p. 27.

[37]See, for example, LaSor, "Egypt," p. 32.

[38]Ibid., p. 33; Woldering, *Art of Egypt*, p. 27.

[39]Wilson, *Culture of Ancient Egypt*, pp. 16-17, 27, 145, stressing both Egypt's autonomy and the influences from Africa and Asia. Jordan, *Egypt the Black Land*, p. 40, compares Egyptian and traditional African divine kings, but a survey of peoples will show that not all African peoples divinize their kings (Mbiti, *African Religions and Philosophies*, pp. 213-14). Claude L. Clark, "Parallels Between Egyptian Art and Southwestern Nigerian Art," in *Kemet and the African Worldview*, ed. Karenga and Carruthers, pp. 173-81, cites artistic cultural parallels, though one should examine broader samples of milieu to determine the likelihood and antiquity of direct contacts.

[40]Some darkening also occurred throughout Arab-controlled regions through Arabs' and Berbers' mixing with Black slaves (see Gordon, *Slavery in the Arab World*, p. 43); but this may have occurred less than one might expect, if we may generalize from evidence for infanticide of mulatto offspring in the Ottoman aristocracy (ibid., pp. 16-17).

[41]Including Bernal, *Archaeological and Documentary Evidence*, p. 40 (although he identifies the Hyksos too closely with Israel, pp. 335-58; Williams [*Destruction of Black Civilization*, pp. 84-85] goes even further on the basis of the garbled report of Josephus writing one and a half millennia after the fact; ben-Jochannan [*Africa*, p. 323] and especially Dunston [*Black Man in the Old Testament*, p. 70] are more careful here).

[42]Taylor, *Egypt and Nubia*, p. 7; see the comments on Nubian dialects' relationship to African languages, especially west of the Nile, in Adams, "Geography and Population of the Nile Valley," p. 20.

[43]For example, John Ruffle, *The Egyptians* (Ithaca, N.Y.: Cornell University Press, 1977), pp. 120-21, 147, 202-3; see the very dark brown people, including a Nubian princess, in W. Stevenson Smith, *The Art and Architecture of Ancient Egypt*, vol. 14 of *The Pelican History of Art*, ed. Nikolaus Pevsner (Baltimore: Penguin, 1958), plates 57, 59, 73, 77B, 144; Stephen Quirke and Jeffrey Spencer, eds., *The British Museum Book of Ancient Egypt* (London: Thames & Hudson, 1992), p. 12; Cyril Aldred, *Egypt to the End of the Old Kingdom* (New York: McGraw-Hill/London: Thames & Hudson, 1965), p. 131; T. G. H. James, *Ancient Egypt* (Austin: University of Texas, 1988), p. 186 (but the whole picture is dark).

[44]One may survey any book containing Egyptian art, such as Woldering, *Art of Egypt*, pp. 24, 26, 90, 110, 112, 139, 205; Ruffle, *Egyptians*, pp. 40-41, 129, 140-41, 144; Quirke and Spencer, *British Museum Book*, pp. 12, 19, 20-21, 25, 26, 27, 55, 75, 87, 91, 142-43; Jordan, *Egypt the Black Land*, pp. 136, 153; Leonard Cottrell, *Egypt* (London: Nicholas Vane, 1965), plates 66, 109, 110, 112, 113-17, 126, 129; Stewart, *Pyramids and Sphinx*, pp. 32, 43, 70, 112-13, 115-17, 121, 130; Aldred, *Egypt to the End*, pp. 39, 105, 108, 128-29, 132; James, *Ancient Egypt*, pp. 90-91, 118-19, 163; Smith, *Art and Architecture*, plates 58A, 64, 94, 107, 109, 141, 162-63; Werner Forman and Bedrich Forman, *Egyptian Art* (London: Peter Nevill, 1962), plates 18, 21, 27-28, 32, 45, 48, 58, 62, 69, 74, 77, 85-86. We are not citing evidence selectively; perusal of these books will offer no support to one arguing that the Egyptians were "White" by contemporary standards (though some were light brown, as evident in Smith, *Art and Architecture*, plate 58B). Although we consider especially complexion here, sometimes the artwork also includes clearly African features, including the lips (as in Ruffle, *Egyptians*, p. 184). Strongly "Africoid" or "Negroid" features apply especially to Nubians (see Ramses II's captives in Forman and Forman, *Egyptian Art*, plates 85-86; many prisoners in ibid., plate 94; an official of the Twenty-fifth Dynasty Nubian Pharaoh Taharka in ibid., plate 117; Nubians are both red and black—see Taylor, *Egypt and Nubia*, pp. 1, 33, from the time of Ramses II). But this is less significant for our purposes, since many Africans and African-Americans do not conform to these strictly defined features, and some members of other racial groups do. The issue for those whose complexion has been counted a mark of social inferiority is not where on the continuum between races someone appears, but in what racial category that person would appear in the twentieth-century United States (Asiatic features also appear). Note also that a large percentage of the paintings we cite derive from *after* the Hyksos period—when the Egyptians may have been, if anything, lighter than previously.

[45]Aldred, *Egypt to the End*, p. 108, though the only explicit evidence he provides, a pair of statues from c. 2620 B.C.E. (p. 109; he claims they represent the best surviving examples of painted statuary from this period), is also representative of the only period in which I have found a dark husband with a light wife among the paintings in books surveyed (it appears also in Smith, *Art and Architecture*, plate 29; H. A. Groenewegen-Frankfort and Bernard Ashmole, *The Ancient World* [New

York: New American Library, 1967], plate 6; etc.); see comments below. This artistic convention was probably limited to this period; where it occurs later (see Cottrell, *Egypt,* plate facing p. 174), it must be balanced against darker women with lighter men, and does not seem to represent a mere convention (consider the realism of the Amarna period).

[46]Ruffle, *Egyptians,* pp. 156-57; Forman and Forman, *Egyptian Art,* pp. 16-17; Colin Renfrew and Paul Bahn, *Archaeology* (London: Thames & Hudson, 1991), pp. 366-67.

[47]J. R. Harris, *Egyptian Art* (London: Spring Books/Drury House, 1966), p. 19.

[48]The women and girls who were professional mourners in a late Eighteenth Dynasty painting have light brown skin (Ruffle, *Egyptians,* p. 94; compare the nearly olive complexion in Quirke and Spencer, *British Museum Book,* p. 149; and James, *Ancient Egypt,* p. 151, at c. 1300 B.C.; see Woldering, *Art of Egypt,* p. 65, in the Twelfth Dynasty). These occasional illustrations may be of Greeks or other northerners; their complexion, however, appears to us not much different from the dull or pale brown of light-skinned Black persons secluded from much sunlight; their hair is braided as is that of darker Egyptian women in other artwork, and they could pass for "Black" (probably mulatto) in the United States (for example, Harris, *Egyptian Art,* plate 21a, c. 1400 B.C.E.). All the colors in the portrait from the Twenty-second Dynasty (945-715 B.C.) which includes an apparently light-skinned woman are faded (see Quirke and Spencer, *British Museum Book,* p. 59); an 1150 B.C. portrayal improbably leaves all characters light (ibid., p. 61). Both women (despite Negroid features) and men appeared light on alabaster carvings (Woldering, *Art of Egypt,* pp. 85, 159).

[49]For another very light brown woman from the Fourth Dynasty (c. 2590-2470 B.C.E.), see Harris, *Egyptian Art,* plate 5. The wife and daughter of Seneb the dwarf are also light (even pale, except for her black hair; her robe lacks color equally), in contrast to Seneb and his son, both painted reddish-brown (Forman and Forman, *Egyptian Art,* plate 35; Stewart, *Pyramids and Sphinx,* p. 66); but these too are from the Fourth Dynasty (Forman and Forman, *Egyptian Art,* p. 49).

[50]The yellowish wife alongside the brown husband cited in Aldred, *Egypt to the End,* could have been Asiatic (Forman and Forman [*Egyptian Art,* pp. 21, 43] think Nefert's yellow tinge is a personal detail); but contemporary parallels suggest conventions.

[51]For example (with some overlap of paintings among different books), Ruffle, *Egyptians,* pp. 184, 185; Woldering, *Art of Egypt,* pp. 87, 91, 93, 111, 112, 113, 132, 133, 162 (all from the 1300-1400s); Quirke and Spencer, *British Museum Book,* pp. 140-41; Cottrell, *Egypt,* p. 204; Stewart, *Pyramids and Sphinx,* pp. 116, 131; James, *Ancient Egypt,* p. 154; Jordan, *Egypt the Black Land,* pp. 105 (Middle Kingdom, before 1600 B.C.E.), 148-49, 193 (New Kingdom); Smith, *Art and Architecture,* plates 74 (daughters of Djehuty-hetep, Twelfth Dynasty; also in Forman and Forman, *Egyptian Art,* plate 41), 141, 151, 164; Harris, *Egyptian Art,* plates 21B, 24AB, 33-35. Some women are fully Negroid, as in Ruffle, *Egyptians,* p. 147; Woldering, *Art of Egypt,* p. 94; Smith, *Art and Architecture,* plate 144 (a Nubian princess during the Eighteenth Dynasty); Groenewegen-Frankfort and Ashmole, *Ancient World,* plates 13, 15. Queen Nefertari, still renowned for her beauty today, was clearly dark (for example, in *Wall Paintings of the Tomb of Nefertari* [Cairo: Egyptian Antiquities Organization, 1987], pp. 8, 27 and elsewhere; Smith, *Art and Architecture,* plate 159B; light brown in Woldering, *Art of Egypt,* p. 134; see also Du Bois, *World and Africa,* pp. 126-27; Rogers, *World's Greatest Men and Women,* p. 12); the wife of Ramses II, she may well have been a contemporary of Moses.

[52]For example, Quirke and Spencer, *British Museum Book,* pp. 152-53 (Eighteenth Dynasty); Harris, *Egyptian Art,* plate 22A (mid-Eighteenth Dynasty).

[53]See the beautiful dark brown wife of Nebamun in James, *Ancient Egypt,* p. 23; Quirke and Spencer, *British Museum Book,* pp. 152-53.

[54]Woldering, *Art of Egypt,* p. 99 (surviving Middle Kingdom sculptures were not painted; ibid., p. 129). The Old Kingdom stretched from the Third to the Eighth Dynasty (c. 2660-2134 B.C.E.). Convention was especially abandoned for individuality in the Amarna period, but this was short-lived (Forman and Forman, *Egyptian Art,* pp. 33-37; Groenewegen-Frankfort and Ashmole, *Ancient World,* p. 62). Nevertheless, paintings from later periods, most abundant in the masterpieces of the Eighteenth Dynasty, portray women as well as men as dark.

[55]A white woman and brown man appear together among deities at the judgment (Harris, *Egyptian Art,* plate 45, Nineteenth Dynasty). All characters in a portrayal in the Book of the Dead are fairly light brown (Forman and Forman, *Egyptian Art,* plates 106, 114), or, in the case of a deceased

woman, white (Forman and Forman, *Egyptian Art*, plate 116); perhaps the papyrus is faded, but the pallor might express the recognition that some color fades from lighter corpses after death or reflect a belief about the less colorful existence of the netherworld.

[56]Ruffle, *Egyptians*, p. 129; Harris, *Egyptian Art*, plate 22A.

[57]See Ruffle, *Egyptians*, p. 159. One may also compare the consistent colorations of deities, such as dark green for Osiris (Quirke and Spencer, *British Museum Book*, pp. 29, 220; Woldering, *Art of Egypt*, p. 139; Stewart, *Pyramids and Sphinx*, pp. 24-25, 70; see Ruffle, *Egyptians*, pp. 181, 192; green probably associates resurrection with the annual revivification of nature) and blue for the Nile god (Quirke and Spencer, *British Museum Book*, p. 16).

[58]Quirke and Spencer, *British Museum Book*, pp. 109, 111; James, *Ancient Egypt*, pp. 58, 79—though see the retention of brown even for Ptolemy I in Woldering, *Art of Egypt*, p. 205.

[59]The coloring remains on a second-century A.D. sarcophagus with Greek writing, and the man is clearly brown (see Quirke and Spencer, *British Museum Book*, p. 57; James, *Ancient Egypt*, p. 74). Greeks are clearly much lighter in their own artwork (Groenewegen-Frankfort and Ashmole, *Ancient World*, plates 38, 43, 71; we omit scenes where the whole figures were black, such as plate 45, or white, such as plate 46).

[60]See Quirke and Spencer, *British Museum Book*, p. 199; Smith, *Art and Architecture*, plates 105, 106, 160A; compare Woldering, *Art of Egypt*, p. 166; Du Bois, *World and Africa*, p. 105.

[61]Quirke and Spencer, *British Museum Book*, p. 209; the same photo appears in James, *Ancient Egypt*, p. 199. Note products from tropical Africa, including leopard skins.

[62]Especially the Amarna period, for which we have considerable evidence.

[63]See Du Bois, *World and Africa*, p. 105, explaining the "yellow" wives as "either signifying less exposure to the sun or intermarriage with Mongoloids and whites" (by noble men).

[64]Bruce G. Trigger, "Nubian, Negro, Black, Nilotic?" in *Africa in Antiquity I*, p. 27; see similarly Du Bois, *World and Africa*, p. 103.

[65]Taylor, *Egypt and Nubia*, p. 7; also see Trigger, "Nubian," p. 33.

[66]See, for example, Snowden, *Before Color Prejudice*, pp. 8, 17.

[67]The Ptolemies, including Cleopatra, were thus not fully "Black Egyptian," as some popular writers have affirmed; Cleopatra was part of the oppressor class, which descended from Macedonian-Greek colonialists installed after Alexander's conquest (Du Bois, *World and Africa*, p. 140, and John L. Johnson, *The Black Biblical Heritage* [Nashville: Winston-Derek, 1993], p. 219, do, however, cite evidence for some Black Egyptian blood in Cleopatra's own immediate line, through intermarriage).

[68]Felder, *Troubling Biblical Waters*, p. 37: "sophisticated theories about race and the phenomenon of racism are by-products of the post-biblical era."

[69]Du Bois, *World and Africa*, p. 145; Diop, *African Origin*, p. 48; Dunston, *Black Man in the Old Testament*, pp. 7-8.

[70]Bernal, *Fabrication of Ancient Greece*, pp. 241-42.

[71]See also Diop, *African Origin*, pp. 43, 48: "dark red" is simply part of the Black race, which rarely exists as purely black in color.

[72]Dunston, *Black Man in the Old Testament*, p. 32, on book 2 of Herodotus's *Histories*.

[73]Bennett, *Before the "Mayflower,"* p. 7.

[74]Copher, *Black Biblical Studies*, p. 36. A measure of the fondness Dr. Copher earned from his students and colleagues may be gathered from the festschrift in his honor, Randall C. Bailey and Jacquelyn Grant, eds., *The Recovery of Black Presence* (Nashville: Abingdon, 1995).

[75]Hollenweger, *Pentecostals*, p. 294; Wilmore, *Black Religion and Black Radicalism*, pp. 153-54, on the Church of the Living God. See the accurate assessment of Robert C. Lawson (in Washington, ed., *Conversations with God*, p. 143): God's Son was born of Mary, "who had the blood of many nations in her veins"; or the words of Frederick Buechner as quoted in Ben Witherington III, *The Christology of Jesus* (Minneapolis: Fortress, 1990), p. v: the biblical writers do not describe Jesus physically "because it was his life inside of them that was the news they hawked rather than the color of his eyes."

[76]Copher (*Black Biblical Studies*, p. 119) calls this line of interpretation (which he attributes to the Black Hebrews) "aberrant."

[77]Ancient writers *did* describe Ethiopians' hair as "woolly," but referred thus to the texture (see Snowden, *Blacks in Antiquity*, pp. 6, 264 notes 50-52), whereas John refers explicitly to its *color*.

[78]Other ancient writers also specified the shade of white with "like wool" (*1 Enoch* 46:1-2; 71:10) or "like snow" (*Joseph and Asenath* 5:4; 16:18/13; 22:7).

[79]Compare C. Rowland, "The Vision of the Risen Christ in Rev. 1.13ff.," *Journal of Theological Studies* 31 (1980): 1-11; C. Rowland, "A Man Clothed in Linen," *Journal for the Study of the New Testament* 24 (1985): 99-110; *Apocalypse of Zephaniah* 6:11-15; *3 Enoch* 22:4-9; 26:2-7.

[80]Compare similar language, for example, in 1Qp Genesis Apocryphon column 2; *1 Enoch* 14:18; 106:2, 10; 4 Ezra 10:25; *3 Enoch* 18:25; 28:7; 35:2; *Testament of Abraham* 2, 12A; *Joseph and Asenath* 14:9; *2 Enoch* 1:5; *b. Baba Batra* 75a; even *Paris Great Magical Papyrus* 4.635-38, 696-99, 703-4; Achilles Tatius 1.4.2.

[81]In Mediterranean antiquity, white often symbolized purity, but because of its association with sunlight, not skin color (compare the deity Helios/Mithras in *Paris Great Magical Papyrus* 4.637-38, 698-99; the righteous dead in *Pseudo-Philo* 64:6; angels in 2 Maccabees 11:8; 3 Maccabees 6:18; *Ethiopic Enoch* 71:1; 87:2; also the apparel of Egyptian priests in Plutarch *Isis* 3, *Moralia* 352C; Apuleius *Metamorphoses* 11.23; Lewis, *Life in Egypt Under Roman Rule,* p. 92). Thus the West African Yoruba, unaffected by Mediterranean or Middle Eastern religions, speak of God as the "One clothed in white," who is the "Essentially white Object, white Object, white Material without pattern (entirely white)" (Mbiti, *African Religions,* p. 277); various societies positively associate white with the spirit world (Elizabeth Isichei, *A History of Christianity in Africa* [Lawrenceville, N.J.: Africa World Press, 1995], p. 64).

[82]See Ethelbert Stauffer, *Jesus and His Story,* trans. Richard Winston and Clara Winston (New York: Alfred A. Knopf, 1960), pp. 59-60; Du Bois, *World and Africa,* p. 143; Keener, *IVP Bible Background Commentary: New Testament,* p. 281. Although physical description figured in some ancient literature (John Drury, *Tradition and Design in Luke's Gospel* [London: Darton, Longman & Todd, 1976], p. 29, on the *Life of Aesop; Acts of Paul* and *Thecla* 3; and Abraham J. Malherbe, "A Physical Description of Paul," *Harvard Theological* 79, nos. 1-3 [1986]: 170-75), it was not an essential ingredient of ancient biography (Graham N. Stanton, *Jesus of Nazareth in New Testament Preaching* [Cambridge: Cambridge University Press, 1974], p. 124).

[83]For arguments about Black Israelites pro and con, but especially evidence demonstrating that ancient Israelites were *not* Black and that contemporary Israelis rejected the Hebrew Israelites' claim to Jewishness, see Israel J. Gerber, *The Heritage Seekers* (Middle Village, N.Y.: Jonathan David, 1977), pp. 64-101, especially 64-92. Gerber was a Jewish rabbi who long taught at a Black institution. Valid political agendas do not justify intentional distortion of history.

[84]Clarke, *Africans at the Crossroads,* p. 356.

[85]See, for example, the documentation in Edward H. Flannery, *The Anguish of the Jews* (New York: Macmillan, 1965). Flannery is a priest, often documenting atrocities committed by Catholic clergy and laity. See also Adriaan H. Bredero, *Christendom and Christianity in the Middle Ages* (Grand Rapids, Mich.: Eerdmans, 1994), pp. 274-318; for the earlier period, see James Parkes, *The Conflict of the Church and the Synagogue* (New York: Atheneum, 1969).

[86]See Felder, "Cultural Ideology," p. 188. Diop (*African Origin,* p. xv) contends that Semitic peoples derive from a "mixture of white-skinned and black-skinned people in western Asia" and that Black realities thus underlie much of the Old Testament. Whether or not one accepts this sort of mixed ancestry for all Semites, their ancestry is not identical with the European ancestry of most White Americans.

[87]Marcus Garvey, *The Philosophy and Opinions of Marcus Garvey,* ed. Amy Jacques-Garvey, 2 vols. (New York: Universal Publishing, 1923-1925), 1:33-34, as quoted in ben-Jochannan, *African Origins,* p. 276. Garvey especially stirred U.S. Black interest in Ethiopia (Kenneth King, "Some Notes on Arnold J. Ford and New World Black Attitudes to Ethiopia," in *Black Apostles,* ed. Burkett and Newman, pp. 49-55). He sometimes elevated symbol over history, however, as in proclaiming the Father, Son and Spirit he invoked as the God of Ethiopia *rather* than (not just in addition to) the Whites' God of Isaac and Jacob.

[88]For instance, Josef Ben-Levi regards the Canaanites and Sumerians as Black ("The First and Second Intermediate Periods in Kemetic History," in *Kemet and the African Worldview,* ed. Karenga and Carruthers, pp. 57-58; see some other support for this position below). Compare some arguments in Walter Arthur McCray, *The Black Presence in the Bible: Teacher's Guide* (Chicago: Black Light Fellowship, 1990); Johnson, *Black Biblical Heritage,* pp. 18-145. Both McCray and Johnson are,

however, theologically sound and in most respects helpful (most of what follows agrees with them, especially with McCray, whose focus is intentionally more academic than Johnson's).

[89]Even Runoko Rashidi ("More Light on Sumer, Elam and India," in *African Presence in Early Asia,* ed. Van Sertima and Rashidi, pp. 164-65) concurs that the "blackheads of Sumer," whom he regards as from Africa, were a minority in the region of Sumer. Arguing only for Sumerians and Elamites ("Africans in Early Asian Civilizations: A Historical Overview," in *African Presence in Early Asia,* pp. 15-22), he does not regard the Assyrians, for instance, as Black (ibid., pp. 21-22). A wall painting from the late Minoan period (before 1400 B.C.E.) suggests that Cretans were "White" (Groenewegen-Frankfort and Ashmole, *Ancient World,* plate 28, between pp. 96 and 97); but for Near Eastern and especially Egyptian influences in Crete, see Bernal, *Archaeological and Documentary Evidence,* pp. 63-77, 154-86; Hansberry, *Africa and Africans As Seen by Classical Writers,* pp. 37-39.

[90]McCray (*Black Presence in the Bible,* p. 62) is nuanced in his position, allowing for *degrees* of Blackness (again, part of the question returns to where "Black" pigmentation and features leave off and "White" begin, if such a point objectively exists). He also recognizes that Genesis 10 does not emphasize individuals or races but peoples (p. 49). Although nearly all writers agree that Genesis 10 positively teaches the common humanity of all peoples, opinions vary as to the list's historical value (as noted by Arthur C. Custance, *Noah's Three Sons* [Grand Rapids, Mich.: Zondervan, 1975], p. 57). Many Afrocentric writers, including George Alexander McGuire, who led the African Orthodox Church in conjunction with Garvey, have assumed Ham's own blackness (see Washington, ed., *Conversations with God,* p. 134). While we question some features of this "old Hamite hypothesis," however, it undoubtedly has more truth to it than what Copher (*Black Biblical Studies,* p. 35) calls the "new Hamite hypothesis," which excluded some Blacks from being "Negroid" and made both Egyptians and Nubians White!

[91]See, for example, Katie Geneva Cannon, "Slave Ideology and Biblical Interpretation," in *Recovery of Black Presence,* ed. Bailey and Grant, p. 121. By contrast, the contention that both Africans and Asians are "Hamites" in the sense of Genesis 10 places even more people under the rubric of Ham (Custance, *Noah's Three Sons*) and probably goes too far, despite its main proponent's generous contention that all ancient civilization and technology comes from the Hamite—that is, African and Asian—peoples (Custance, *Noah's Three Sons,* pp. 13-14, 26, 38-42, 153-216). Probably Israelite geography assigned to Ham the peoples south of Israel's homeland, to Japheth those to the north and west, and to Shem those to the east, regarding Palestine as the focus (Scott, "Luke's Geographical Horizon," p. 501, following Yohanan Aharoni, *The Land of the Bible* [London: Burns & Oates, 1979], pp. 6, 8).

[92]"Racist Identity Sect Fuels Nationwide Extremist Movement," *Klanwatch Intelligence Report,* August 1995, p. 3.

[93]Palestinian Talmud, Taanit 1:6, §8; Babylonian Talmud, Sanhedrin 108b; *Genesis Rabbah* 36:7. Copher, *Black Biblical Studies,* p. 100, also cites two of these sources plus two others.

[94]By Wahb ibn Munabbih in Ibn Qutayba, *Kitab Al-Ma'arif,* p. 26, as translated in Lewis, ed. and trans., *Islam,* 2:210 (from Ellis, *Malcolm,* pp. 109-10); see also Y. Talib with F. Samir, "The African Diaspora in Asia," in *Africa from the Seventh to the Eleventh Century,* ed. El Fasi with Hrbek, p. 721, though the authors express doubt that this was the majority view. The view that a people was "cursed" with blackness actually inheres in a sacred book of the Mormon religion: in the Book of Mormon, 2 Nephi 5:21 (white skin being delightful but black being loathsome). For this reason among others, Mormonism has historically held little appeal to most African-Americans.

[95]Gordon, *Slavery in the Arab World,* p. 32. We say "even" because this action contravened Islamic law; see further chapter five.

[96]Lewis, *Race and Slavery in the Middle East,* p. 55; although some Arab writers rejected the idea, it was widespread.

[97]Against slaveholders' myth that the mark on Cain or the curse on Ham (actually Canaan) turned them Black, antislavery ministers in the nineteenth century pointed out that the Bible itself said no such thing (for example, John Rankin, a Presbyterian pastor in Ohio, *Letters on American Slavery Addressed to Mr. Thomas Rankin,* 5th ed. [Boston: Isaac Knapp, 1838; reprint New York: Arno/New York Times, 1969], pp. 6-7, though some of his responses are biblically and scientifically inaccurate). Copher, *Black Biblical Studies,* p. 100, notes that one manuscript of the Septuagint has "cursed be Ham"; but given Ham's role in the story, it is not surprising that a copyist would

introduce this error (either intending to correct what he assumed to be an error or, more likely, simply inadvertently).

[98]Clarke, *Africans at the Crossroads,* p. 342.

[99]Copher, *Black Biblical Studies,* pp. 110-13, notes its use to support slavery (as well as the confusion between Canaan and Cain) in the fifteenth century and later, following the same usage known in Islam.

[100]For a particularly disgusting White supremacist application of the myth, see the 1860 account in Thomas Virgil Peterson, *Ham and Japheth* (Metuchen, N.J.: Scarecrow, 1978), pp. 141-58.

[101]Boers believed God appointed all Africans as "descendants of Ham" to be their slaves, a practice that led to conflict with the British, who were by this period firmly antislavery (Basil Davidson, *Africa in History* [New York: Macmillan, 1968], pp. 228-29; note also Livingstone's eyewitness complaint against Boer practice in the 1840s, p. 229).

[102]So, for example, Dunston, *Black Man in the Old Testament,* p. 53; among non-Afrocentric writers, for example, A. F. Walls, "Africa," in *New Bible Dictionary,* ed. J. D. Douglas et al., 2nd ed. (Downers Grove, Ill.: InterVarsity Press, 1982), p. 18. Custance's speculation that the curse was explicitly applied only to Canaan lest Noah curse himself by cursing his own son (see *Noah's Three Sons,* p. 25), while plausible on the level of the story itself, and Diop's suggestion that Noah meant to curse Ham and thereby not Canaan but Israel's oppressors in Egypt (*African Origin,* p. 7) both neglect the book's intention of equipping the Israelites to seize the Promised Land from Canaan (assuming a date in the Mosaic period; the majority of scholars who date the book later can nevertheless still recognize the function of this *tradition* in the conquest). This latter point also diminishes the force of Custance's suggestion that the curse was not severe (*Noah's Three Sons,* p. 149).

[103]For example, Johnson, *Black Biblical Heritage,* p. 222; Boyd, *African Origin,* p. 114.

[104]As suggested by Johnson, *Black Biblical Heritage,* p. 222. Contrast the much more accurate appraisal by Bernal, *Fabrication of Ancient Greece,* p. xiii, that Canaanite, Hebrew and Phoenician are related dialects (on p. xxiv he correctly regards Semitic languages in general as "Afroasiatic," a broader language category now widely employed by linguists).

[105]See, for example, M. Liverani, "Ugarit; Ugaritic," in *International Standard Bible Encyclopedia,* ed. Bromiley, 4:939.

[106]Copher (*Black Biblical Studies,* p. 99) argues that "Ham" probably did not mean "black" when the Noah story was first written; though modern scholars often follow the rabbinic etymology (by which Ham is turned black due to sin), Copher notes (p. 101) that Philo and Josephus associate the term with "heat" instead. The Egyptian *KM (Kem)* also may not mean "black" with reference to individuals' color ("Report of the Symposium," p. 63).

[107]In the wake of deconstruction some identify an argument that is well argued with truth. But some arguments are more probable—and more plausible—than others, a factor of which deconstruction and its successors often take too little account. The positive insight of this approach, however, is its refusal to sanction any particular ethnocentric bias over any other.

[108]Schlesinger, *Disuniting of America,* pp. 94-96; compare pp. 69-78. Schlesinger seems especially put off by one professor who, Schlesinger says, "describes Europeans as cold, individualistic, materialistic, and aggressive 'ice people' who grew up in caves ... whereas Africans who grew up in sunlight, with the intellectual and physical superiority provided by melanin, are warm, humanistic and communitarian 'sun people' "; that professor also claims that " 'rich Jews' financed the slave trade" (pp. 67-68; also see p. 71). Some Afrocentrists have merely turned nineteenth-century anthropological racism on its head, but in so doing they unwittingly capitulate to the tools and values of their oppressors. The radical feminist reconstruction of mythical matriarchal prehistory has likewise discredited some who have embraced it (see, for example, Grant, *Social History of Greece and Rome,* p. 6, on Engels).

[109]Johnson, *Black Biblical Heritage,* p. 209; McKissic, *Beyond Roots,* p. 37, also cites Alonzo Holly as holding this position. Scholars must evaluate their sources, however; thus, for instance, Josephus should not be cited to prove a point over one thousand years earlier that would be known only by speculation in his day (as in Johnson, *Black Biblical Heritage,* p. 3); similarly, a writer citing E. G. White should probably know that the "E." stands for "Ellen" and not refer to "his" book (Johnson, *Black Biblical Heritage,* p. 191).

[110]Oscar Cullmann, *The State in the New Testament* (New York: Charles Scribner's Sons, 1956), p. 15; Oscar Cullmann, *Peter: Disciple, Apostle, Martyr* (Philadelphia: Westminster Press, 1953), p. 22 n. 24; F. F. Bruce, *New Testament History* (Garden City, N.Y.: Doubleday, 1977), p. 93; Floyd V. Filson, *A New Testament History* (Philadelphia: Westminster Press, 1964), p. 52; Joseph Klausner, *Jesus: His Life, Times and Teaching* (New York: Menorah, 1979), p. 284 n. 11. "Zealot" in this period may mean "zealous for God's law" rather than "revolutionary" (W. J. Heard, "Revolutionary Movements," in *Dictionary of Jesus and the Gospels*, ed. Joel B. Green, Scot McKnight and I. Howard Marshall [Downers Grove, Ill.: InterVarsity Press, 1992], p. 696; Witherington, *Christology of Jesus*, p. 97), but would hardly apply specifically to a Canaanite in any case.

[111]For example, Johnson, *Black Biblical Heritage*, p. 199. For a plausible defense of the "south" reading (since Arabia can appear as "east" in biblical tradition), see W. D. Davies and Dale C. Allison, *Introduction and Commentary on Matthew I-VII*, vol. 1 of *A Critical and Exegetical Commentary on the Gospel According to Saint Matthew*, International Critical Commentaries, 3 vols. (Edinburgh: T & T Clark, 1988), p. 228; but for the reasons given below we think it unlikely.

[112]Cicero *De Legibus* 2.10.26 (Loeb Classical Library 16:402-3); Chariton *Chaereas and Callirhoe* 5.9.4 (trans., p. 80; Greek text, p. 81); Diogenes Laertius *Lives* 8.1.3 (LCL 2:322-23); Philostratus *Life of Apollonus of Tyana* 1, §24 (LCL 1:84-85); Dio Chrysostom *Oration* 36.38-48; Lucian *The Runaways* par. 8 (LCL 5:64-65); Josephus *Jewish Antiquities* 10.10.3-4, §§195-203 (LCL 6:270-71); Philo *De Specialibus Legibus* 3.18, §100 (LCL 7:538-39); Philo *Quod omnis Probus Liber sit* 11, §74 (LCL 9:52-53); compare Herodotus *History* 3, §§79-80 (LCL 2:104-5). Compare related comments about Chaldeans and "men of the East" in Juvenal *Satires* 6.553-64 (LCL pp. 128-29); Marcus Aurelius *Meditations* 3.3.1; Apuleius *Metamorphoses* 2.12; *Sibylline Oracles* 3:227 (second century B.C.E.); *Pesiqta Rabbati* 14:8. Magi had long functioned as a priestly caste in Persia; see, for example, Olmstead, *History of the Persian Empire*, pp. 28-29, 196, 251, 372, 449, 477-78, 496. Babylonian Magi chanted hymns while "frankincense and other costly perfumes burned on the silver altars" (Olmstead, *History of the Persian Empire*, p. 517).

[113]McKissic, *Beyond Roots*, p. 29.

[114]See O. R. Gurney, *The Hittites*, 2nd ed. (Baltimore: Penguin, 1954), pp. 9, 18, 117-18 (including recognizable parallels with Greek and Latin syntax). Gurney does concede, however, that most of the vocabulary in one form of Hittite is not Indo-European (p. 119).

[115]For example, McKissic, *Beyond Roots*, pp. 27-28. Roland Kenneth Harrison, *Introduction to the Old Testament* (Grand Rapids, Mich.: Eerdmans, 1969), p. 98, calls them "swarthy," as McKissic notes. The Sumerians were certainly dark (calling themselves the "Black-headed people"), possibly from what is now southern Iraq (though some contend for a more northerly origin); see F. R. Steele, "Sumer," 4:653-62 in *International Standard Bible Encyclopedia*, ed. Bromiley, 4:654. Runoko Rashidi ("Africans in Early Asian Civilizations," in *African Presence in Early Asia*, ed. Van Sertima and Rashidi, pp. 15-19) argues that the Sumerians were of African origin (though the evidence he cites does not appear to be conclusive).

[116]Rashidi, "More Light on Sumer, Elam and India," pp. 164-65.

[117]Harrison, *Introduction to the Old Testament*, p..101.

[118]Most likely Joseph arrived in the Hyksos period (see Nahum M. Sarna, *Understanding Genesis* [New York: Schocken, 1970], pp. 211-27). "On" was in the Delta region controlled by the Hyksos, so while Asenath was *geographically* African and in any case relatively dark by U.S. standards, we must for the present leave the precise character of her Egyptian ancestry open to debate. Still, some evidence suggests that she may not have belonged to the Hyksos elite. First, Asenath's name (if not a later redaction) is of a type documented only in the post-Hyksos period (thus the name appears to be solely native Egyptian; her father's name is also indigenously Egyptian, but could more easily have been adopted by Hyksos masters). Second, the Hyksos adopted existing customs and "appointed Egyptian bureaucrats to administer the land" (Rosalie David, *Discovering Ancient Egypt* [London: O'Mara, 1993], pp. 145-46). Third, the Hyksos adopted Seth (originally an evil deity) but also restored the worship of Re (the deity worshiped at On), which was indigenously Egyptian (David, *Discovering Ancient Egypt*, p. 146). Especially in the latter case, one might have expected them to have employed Egyptian priests most schooled in ancient lore. Finally, no one objected to interracial marriages, and the Hyksos probably also intermarried with native Egyptians. But the matter is not beyond doubt.

[119]For a womanist reading of Hagar's relationship with Sarah, see Renita J. Weems, *Just a Sister Away* (San Diego: LuraMedia, 1988), pp. 1-21.

[120]See the picture in Quirke and Spencer, *British Museum Book,* p. 12, from Egypt's Twelfth Dynasty (c. 1900 B.C.E.); compare Catherine Clark Kroeger, "Black Is Blessed: A Study of Black and/or African Women in the Bible" (Minneapolis: Christians for Biblical Equality, n.d.), p. 1; Taylor, *Egypt and Nubia,* also portrays some Nubians as Egyptian slaves (as well as military workers in Palestine) in the mid-second millennium B.C.E. Egyptians enslaved Black Africans, "Semites," Asians and others; the basis was economic and political, however, not racial (see Du Bois, *World and Africa,* p. 106). But Sneferu of the Sixth Dynasty (c. 2345-2181) took many African prisoners, and there were numerous wars with Nubia under the Middle Kingdom (2133-1786), including the conquest of part of Nubia under Sesostris III (1878-1843; Snowden, *Before Color Prejudice,* pp. 21-22).

[121]In Abraham's day fifty men would have been sufficient to constitute a garrison (Charles F. Pfeiffer, *Tell el Amarna and the Bible* [Grand Rapids, Mich.: Baker Book House, 1963], pp. 69-70). Abraham, in other words, was a quite wealthy nomadic prince. A princess of the ancient kingdom of Mitanni had 317 servant girls (see in Cyrus H. Gordon, *The Ancient Near East* [New York: W. W. Norton, 1965], p. 87 n. 1, although he tries to apply this to companies of troops).

[122]One need not appeal to the Israelites' adoption of some Egyptian names (see Sarna, *Understanding Genesis,* p. 214, which cites Egyptian texts documenting that children of Semitic slaves in Egypt usually took Egyptian names), any more than the imposition of Babylonian names on them during that exile or the much more forceful change of our names (such as Kunta Kinte to Toby) here; the evidence for intermarriage is sufficient by itself.

[123]Compare similarly Dunston, *Black Man in the Old Testament,* p. 69, on Israel's heterogeneity. But Dunston's suggestion of much intermarriage among Egyptians *during* the sojourn in Egypt (pp. 58-74, especially pp. 62-69; compare ben-Jochannan, *African Origins,* p. 155) is more questionable, since the Israelites would have dealt mainly with the Semitic Hyksos in the Delta region until reduced to slavery, and afterward remained generally segregated from Egyptians in Goshen (group slavery rather than household slavery: "state slavery, the organized imposition of forced labor upon the male population"—Nahum H. Sarna, *Exploring Exodus* [New York: Schocken, 1986], p. 21). Dunston's declaration that no more than "fourteen thousand people in the Exodus population . . . had any Hebrew blood (genes) at all" (*Black Man in the Old Testament,* p. 69) is thus exaggerated. To illustrate that a rapid numerical expansion of Israelites was possible genetically, one may compare the rapid multiplication of Iran's population under Khomeini's policies.

[124]Felder, *Troubling Biblical Waters,* p. 12.

[125]Also, for example, McCray, *Black Presence in the Bible,* p. 17.

[126]See Felder, *Troubling Biblical Waters,* p. 42 (likewise observed by others, such as Du Bois, *World and Africa,* p. 131; Keener, *And Marries Another,* p. 167 n. 30). Bell (*And We Are Not Saved,* p. 134), speaking through the reliable character Geneva Crenshaw, critiques Bob Jones University's policy thus: "To take seriously the church school's claim that its opposition to intermarriage—based on the inferiority of blacks—is a part of its religious belief, one must assume, as much of the country does, that the deity is white" (a questionable assumption indeed!).

[127]See, for example, Copher, *Black Biblical Studies,* p. 38. For an insightful womanist reading of Num 12:1-16, see Weems, *Just a Sister Away,* pp. 71-83.

[128]Much of Rome's hostility toward Jewish people grew from Judaism's success in converting Romans, especially Roman women; see John G. Gager, *The Origins of Anti-Semitism* (New York: Oxford University Press, 1983); Bernard J. Bamberger, *Proselytism in the Talmudic Period* (New York: KTAV, 1968; 1st ed. Hebrew Union College, 1939). The idea that European Jewry intermarried with Gentiles in medieval times is, however, untenable; European anti-Semitism segregated the Jews in ghettos. Dunston's similar suggestion that Black Jews died or were converted by Muslims whereas White Jews arose in Europe through intermarriage could explain some current data, but not enough to support the idea of an original predominantly Black Israelite stock (especially given his undocumented suggestion that Paul had European as well as Israelite ancestry; *Black Man in the Old Testament,* p. 73).

[129]Diop, *African Origin,* p. 69; Diop also cites a few Germanic as well as Latin parallels in Berber grammar.

[130]See, for example, McKissic, *Beyond Roots,* p. 40.

[131]Ibid., p. 48; compare Copher, *Black Biblical Studies,* pp. 45-65.

[132]A.M.E. bishop Henry McNeal Turner, around the turn of the twentieth century, proposed that White Christians could make restitution for past oppression by providing financial support for Black missionary endeavors—a call that unfortunately was little heeded (Wilmore, *Black Religion and Black Radicalism,* pp. 123-24).

[133]For the likelihood of greater Black sensitivity, see, for example, Walter L. Yates, "The God-Consciousness of the Black Church in Historical Perspective," in *Quest for a Black Theology,* ed. James Gardiner and J. Deotis Roberts Sr. (Philadelphia: Pilgrim, 1971), pp. 57-61.

[134]On the Black church's commitment to missions, influenced both by evangelical missions thought and by a feeling of kinship with Africa, see African-American writer Monroe Fordham, *Major Themes in Northern Black Religious Thought, 1800-1860* (Hicksville, N.Y.: Exposition, 1975), pp. 85-109. Note the centrality of missions in "What the National Baptist Convention Stands For" (Pelt and Smith, *Story of the National Baptists,* pp. 209-21; originally published by Lewis G. Jordan in *Negro Baptist History, USA),* especially principles 13 and 14 (pp. 211-12).

[135]Compare conflicts with the East India Company (the colonial period equivalent of a multinational corporation, but with less restraints), for example, in Neill, *History of Christian Missions,* pp. 262-65, and Tucker, *From Jerusalem to Irian Jaya,* p. 117; also see Kellsye Finnie, *William Carey* (Fort Washington, Penn.: Christian Literature Crusade, 1986), pp. 88, 92-95.

[136]As noted, for example, by Tucker, *From Jerusalem to Irian Jaya,* p. 114 (though she noted many missionaries before him).

[137]Noll, *History of Christianity,* pp. 136-37. On Liele, see further his letter in Milton C. Sernett, ed., *Afro-American History: A Documentary Witness* (Durham, N.C.: Duke University Press, 1985), pp. 43-48; compare Edward Holmes, "George Liele," *Foundations* 9 (1966): 333-45 (cited in Sernett); on Black Baptists and missions in general, especially in the late nineteenth and early twentieth centuries, see S. D. Martin, *Black Baptists and African Missions* (Macon, Ga.: Mercer University Press, 1992).

[138]See Wilmore, *Black Religion and Black Radicalism,* pp. 77, 79, and especially p. 106; Raboteau, *Slave Religion,* pp. 140-41.

[139]Sanneh, *West African Christianity,* p. 76; Noll, *History of Christianity,* p. 136. See more fully Grant Gordon, *From Slavery to Freedom: The Life of David George, Pioneer Black Baptist Minister* (Hantsport, Nova Scotia: Lancelot, 1993), which also recounts George's intense spiritual experience and Calvinistic theology. For many African-American missionaries (Presbyterian, Baptist and others) in the Congo, see Isichei, *History of Christianity in Africa,* pp. 189-90.

[140]Noll, *History of Christianity,* p. 340.

[141]Britten, *We Don't Want Your White Religion,* chap. 1, on the Black missionaries Exupersantius, Felix and his sister Regula, citing *World Christian,* September 1989, p. 15, and today's official seal of Switzerland. See especially chap. 4, citing B. Kato, the late former general secretary of the Association of Evangelicals of Africa; S. O. Odunaike; and Festo Kivengere. Many African nations are currently sending missionaries, including some to the West.

[142]Jordan, *White Man's Burden,* pp. 99-110.

[143]Trigger, "Nubian," p. 27; he gives clear examples of earlier racist thinking on p. 28. Pobee, *Toward an African Theology,* pp. 60-61, points to late-nineteenth-century anthropologists who declared that Africans were closer to apes than to civilized Europeans. Some Afrocentric writers like Jackson (*Introduction to African Civilizations,* pp. 90-91) also comment on the subjective development of modern racial categories.

[144]Clarke, *Wrestlin' Jacob,* p. 108; Livingstone, *Darwin's Forgotten Defenders,* pp. 59-60. Agassiz adopted Harvard's prevailing Unitarianism (Livingstone, *Darwin's Defenders,* pp. 58, 60).

[145]Clarke, *Wrestlin' Jacob,* p. 108.

[146]Livingstone, *Darwin's Defenders,* p. 60.

[147]Clarke, *Wrestlin' Jacob,* pp. 110-12.

[148]Livingstone, *Darwin's Defenders,* pp. 60-64.

[149]Ibid., p. 63. His Sundays were taken up with church and teaching African-American boys (ibid., p. 62), who at the time before integrated public schools had limited access to formal education.

[150]Du Bois, *World and Africa,* pp. 115-16. Compare Begley, "Three Is Not Enough," pp. 67-69: the

three primary racial categories derive from the "standard types" at the goals of European trade routes in China and Africa.

[151]Ben-Jochannan, *Africa*, p. 23.

[152]Du Bois, *World and Africa*, p. 97, concluding the discussion on pp. 92-97; compare similarly Dunston, *Black Man in the Old Testament*, pp. 7-8.

[153]Trigger, "Nubian," p. 27.

[154]Ibid., p. 27.

[155]Begley, "Three Is Not Enough," pp. 67-68.

[156]Ibid., p. 68.

[157]Diop, "Origin of the Ancient Egyptians," in *Ancient Civilizations of Africa*, p. 28.

[158]Begley, "Three Is Not Enough," p. 67.

[159]Renfrew and Bahn, *Archaeology*, p. 371.

[160]Ibid. Genetically Africans are the most distinct from other peoples. Some genetic evidence may indicate that all humans ultimately descended from Black African ancestry, but other strands of evidence have been used to argue that either an African or an Asian provenance is possible, and the matter remains in dispute. No one, however, makes this claim for Europeans (see Renfrew and Bahn, *Archaeology*, pp. 401-3).

[161]Ibid., p. 168.

[162]Mack, *Race, Class and Power*, p. 58.

[163]Ibid., p. 57.

[164]Many modern anthropologists recognize race as a social rather than biological construct, viewing ideological racism as humanity's "most dangerous myth" (Olsen, "What Shall We Teach," p. 360).

[165]Mack, *Race, Class and Power*, p. 57. Compare Glenda Valentine, "Shades of Gray: The Conundrum of Color Categories," *Teaching Tolerance*, Spring 1995, p. 47.

[166]West, *Race Matters*, pp. 99-100.

[167]Ibid., p. 4.

[168]See, for example, Oliver and Fage, *Short History of Africa*, pp. 2-4.

[169]See McKissic, *Beyond Roots*, pp. 16-17. Diop, "Origin of the Ancient Egyptians," in *Ancient Civilizations of Africa*, p. 27, notes the biological principle that warm-blooded animals from warm humid areas tend to secrete black pigment.

[170]Sribala Subramanian, "The Story in Our Genes," *Time*, January 16, 1995, p. 55.

Chapter 5: God of Our Weary Years

[1]W. E. B. Du Bois, *Prayers for Dark People*, ed. Herbert Aptheker (Amherst: University of Massachusetts, 1980), pp. 22, 26.

[2]As McCray (*Black Presence in the Bible*, p. 33) points out, *nigger* is used as a class as well as a race distinction; compare p. 160 n. 72. White racism helped create and maintain Black solidarity (see, for example, James, *Never Forget*, p. 50). Although Christians need not agree among themselves on every detail, we can surely agree that the gospel is relevant to every human situation and that it therefore challenges a racist society. This is the basic goal of Black theology: "It seeks to plumb the black condition in the light of God's revelation in Jesus Christ. . . . It is the affirmation of black humanity that emancipates black people from white racism, thus providing authentic freedom for both white and black people" (Statement by the National Committee of Black Churchmen, June 13, 1969, in *Black Theology*, ed. Cone and Wilmore, 1:38). For a sample of early Black evangelical theology see William H. Bentley, "Factors in the Origin and Focus of the National Black Evangelical Association," in *Black Theology*, 1:233-44; compare Calvin Bruce, "Black Evangelical Christianity and Black Theology, in *Black Theology II*, ed. Bruce and Jones, pp. 163-87.

[3]Identification with the oppressed is a major theme in Black theology; see, for example, James H. Cone, *God of the Oppressed* (New York: Seabury, 1975); *For My People: Black Theology and the Black Church* (Maryknoll, N.Y.: Orbis, 1984). For a summary of views to 1989, see Dwight N. Hopkins, *Black Theology—USA and South Africa: Politics, Culture and Liberation* (Maryknoll, N.Y.: Orbis, 1989). As John S. Mbiti notes (*New Testament Eschatology in an African Background* [London: Oxford University Press, 1971], p. 189), African theology must first be biblical if it is Christian theology (see also and more fully, for example, Tite Tiénou, "The Church in African

Theology," in *Biblical Interpretation and the Church* [Nashville: Thomas Nelson, 1984], pp. 151-65, on some contrasts between Christianity and the traditional worldview), but to be truly African it must also "reflect the African situation and understanding"—the biblical message applied in an African context (contrast Maulana Karenga, "Restoration of the Husia," in *Kemet and the African Worldview*, ed. Karenga and Carruthers, pp. 83-99; Karenga rejects Christian and Jewish theology in favor of ancient Egyptian religion). James King attributes the Black community's solidarity to the struggle against oppression (though Janice Hale-Benson attributes it to a survival of tribal unity; Breckenridge and Breckenridge, *What Color Is Your God?* p. 222).

[4]*Contending Ideologies in South Africa*, ed. James Leatt, Theo Kneifel and Klaus Nürnburger (Cape Town: David Phelp, 1986), p. 117; compare Pobee, *Toward an African Theology*, pp. 34-35 (including comments on the meaning of Cone's "blackness" of God). This may be one reason Bantu Stephen Biko, a major leader in the movement, and Donald Woods, a White journalist, were able to forge a close friendship, in contrast to the expectations of anyone persuaded by the apartheid regime's propaganda (see Donald Woods, *Biko* [New York: Random House, 1978]). The philosophy of Negritude also depended not on skin color but on advancing "African cultural values" (Mbiti, *African Religions*, p. 350). While respecting Black theology's usefulness in the United States, Mbiti doubts that either color issues or a thoroughgoing emphasis on liberation is intrinsic to African theology ("An African Views American Black Theology," in *Black Theology*, ed. Cone and Wilmore, 1:383-84); Desmond Tutu counters that Black theology *is* essential for *South* African theology ("Black Theology/African Theology," in *Black Theology*, 1:391).

[5]Riggs, *Awake, Arise and Act*, p. 32.

[6]Bell, *And We Are Not Saved*, p. 254.

[7]A more recent book by Bell (*Confronting Authority* [Boston: Beacon, 1994]) describes how he was fired from Harvard Law School in 1992 for continuing his protests concerning the school's failure to tenure Black women.

[8]Julian Bond, *A Time to Speak, a Time to Act* (New York: Simon & Schuster, 1972), p. 13.

[9]Multiculturalism's proponents define it in a variety of ways, some positive and others negative (compare James A. Banks, "Multicultural Education: Characteristics and Goals," in *Multicultural Education: Issues and Perspectives*, ed. Banks and Banks, pp. 6, 23; Sleeter and Grant, "Analysis of Multicultural Education," pp. 421-22, 430). Although some wrongly subordinate all moral questions to their cultural settings (see B. M. Bullivant, "Culture: Its Nature and Meaning for Educators," in *Multicultural Education: Issues and Perspectives*, p. 41—a generally helpful article), we do affirm with others that an appropriate appreciation for cultural diversity need not obscure some moral absolutes inherent in our common humanity (Ricardo L. García, "Educating for Human Rights: A Curricular Blueprint," *Multicultural Education for the Twenty-first Century*, ed. Carlos Díaz [Washington, D.C.: National Education Association, 1992], pp. 167-78; on the history of this approach, see pp. 171-74; also see Stephen A. Grunlan and Marvin K. Mayers, *Cultural Anthropology: A Christian Perspective* [Grand Rapids, Mich.: Zondervan: 1979], pp. 12-13).

[10]One may consider, for example, the unpopular stances of A. Philip Randolph, who favored women's right to vote, Ireland's freedom from Britain and (like many other African-American spokespersons, including C. H. Mason, founding leader of the Church of God in Christ, but unlike the NAACP) opposed World War I "at a time when thousands of people who opposed the war were being arrested. Anybody who spoke against the war could be called a traitor or a German spy" (Sarah E. Wright, *A. Philip Randolph* [Englewood Cliffs, N.J.: Silver Burdett/Simon & Schuster, 1990], p. 51). A judge released him, declaring that White socialists must really be behind Randolph's writings because he doubted that Blacks could write so intelligently (ibid., p. 53)! Although Randolph accepted World War II as a war over racism, he rejected the Vietnam War (ibid., pp. 89, 120).

[11]Compare, for example, White settlers' attempts to keep African slaves and Native Americans antagonistic to each other, lest they join forces against the White settlers (Daniel H. Usner Jr., *Indians, Settlers and Slaves in a Frontier Exchange Economy* [Chapel Hill: University of North Carolina Press, 1992], pp. 72-74).

[12]Lewis, *Race and Slavery in the Middle East*, p. 3, mentions pre-Columbian American and other civilizations; more detailed documentation may be found in works on those areas.

13Ibid., p. 79 (Yemen and then Saudi Arabia a few weeks later); Fogel and Engerman, *Time on the Cross*, p. 13.

14Gordon, *Slavery in the Arab World*, p. 233, also citing the assessment of journalist Eric Rouleau.

15Jorge I. Domínguez, "Assessing Human Rights Conditions," in *Enhancing Global Human Rights*, by Jorge I. Domínguez et al. (New York: McGraw-Hill, 1979), p. 91; Gordon, *Slavery in the Arab World*, p. 233. Mannix with Cowley (*Black Cargoes*, p. 257) complained that "the great powers are too much concerned with oil diplomacy to investigate the situation."

16"Captive Workers," *World Press Review*, May 1991, p. 50, following Denis MacShane in Hong Kong's *Far Eastern Economic Review*. In Roman and even many cases of U.S. slavery, slaves were paid small bonuses or wages (for the United States, see Fogel and Engerman, *Time on the Cross*, pp. 148-49)—but it was slavery nonetheless.

17"The Maid's Tale," *World Press Review*, December 1995, p. 25. She had lost forty-four pounds as well.

18Lewis, *Race and Slavery in the Middle East*, p. 99; see also John Wesley's claim in La Roy Sunderland, *The Testimony of God Against Slavery: Or, A Collection of Passages from the Bible Which Show the Sin of Holding Property in Man, with Notes* (Boston: Webster & Southard, 1835), p. 91.

19Gordon, *Slavery in the Arab World*, pp. 14, 19, 39; Lewis, *Race and Slavery in the Middle East*, p. 78. In this section we depend especially on research by Gordon and Lewis, who both provide full documentation which we have not chosen to duplicate here. Lewis's work is especially impressive, given his work as a historian of the Islamic world and his direct dependence on medieval Arabic sources in most cases. See the more popular and derivative treatments by Shirley W. Madany, "Arabs and Slave Trade," *Reach Out* 7, nos. 3-4 (1994): 17-19, and—somewhat less relevant—Craig S. Keener, "Christianity, Islam and Slavery," *Reach Out* 7, nos. 3-4 (1994): 20-22.

20Gordon, *Slavery in the Arab World*, p. 40.

21Lewis, *Race and Slavery in the Middle East*, p. 6. Islamic law requires a master who beats his slave to the point of serious bodily injuries to either sell or free the slave (Talib with Samir, "The African Diaspora in Asia," p. 720).

22Indeed, the enslavement of Africans was as early as the Pharaonic Egyptian enslavement of Nubians (Talib and Samir, "African Diaspora," p. 714).

23Bredero, *Christendom and Christianity in the Middle Ages*, p. 9.

24Gordon, *Slavery in the Arab World*, p. 105.

25Ibid., p. 19; he affirms that the Qur'an itself sanctioned slavery (ibid., p. x) and assumes the same for the Bible (ibid., p. 20).

26Lewis (*Race and Slavery in the Middle East*, p. 5) assumes that regulating it entails implicit acceptance of its validity. We would respond, however, that one may provisionally begin by improving an unjust situation without acquiescing that this situation represents the ideal against which other principles may militate. Whether Muhammad would have approved of slavery's abolition (had he conceived of it) is a more appropriate question, but one with which history may have left us no certain answer—apart, perhaps, from his own slaveholding.

27This was also the practice of "those of his companions who could afford it," some of whom "acquired more by conquest" (Lewis, *Race and Slavery in the Middle East*, p. 5, citing further W. Montgomery Watt, *Muhammad at Medina* [Oxford: Oxford University Press, 1965], pp. 293-96, 344, and *Encyclopedia of Islam*, 2nd ed., on the Banu Qurayza, in which men were beheaded while women and children were enslaved). Many of the first African slaves converted were manumitted, though this was not the later practice (Talib and Samir, "African Diaspora," pp. 709-10, 720).

28See, for example, Gordon, *Slavery in the Arab World*, p. xi.

29Lewis, *Race and Slavery in the Middle East*, p. 78, citing Qur'an 5.87 and Muslim comments on it. This principle contrasts with Jesus' way of interpreting some Old Testament laws as concessions to human sinfulness rather than the ideal standard (Mt 19:3-8; Mk 10:2-9).

30Nation of Islam is distinct from historic forms of Islam, having originated in the 1930s with W. D. Fard, who (according to Elijah Muhammad) claimed that Black people were gods and that he himself was Messiah, God in person (Malcolm X with Alex Haley, *The Autobiography of Malcolm X* [New York: Grove, 1965], pp. 207-8). Differences between Nation of Islam and historic Islam will be examined briefly in the authors' next book, which will complement *Black Man's Religion*, but see more fully Mustafa El-Amin, *The Religion of Islam and the Nation of Islam: What Is the Difference?* (Newark, N.J.: El-Amin Productions, 1991). See also Adib Rashad, *The History of Islam and Black Nationalism in the Americas*, 2nd ed. (Beltsville, Md: Writers', 1991); Glenn J. Usry, "Street Questions: Questions Concerning Christianity and Islam in Urban Areas," M.R.E. thesis, Hood Theological Seminary, 1995.

[31]Norman Robert Bennett, *Mirambo of Tanzania, ca. 1840-1884* (New York: Oxford University Press, 1971), p. 16; Mannix and Cowley, *Black Cargoes*, p. 257. There were more Christians in East than in West Africa at this time, though due to the areas involved probably only a minority of those enslaved in East Africa would have been Christians. On British impounding of slave ships and returning former slaves to the coast of West Africa (in Freetown, Sierra Leone), see, for example, Sanneh, *West African Christianity*, p. 75.

[32]This is commonly noted—for example, by Bennett, *Before the "Mayflower,"* pp. 34-35; Lewis, *Race and Slavery in the Middle East*, p. 12, and in many sources cited throughout this book. Because of Nation of Islam propaganda, McKissic (*Beyond Roots*, p. 52) notes his astonishment to learn that "Arab Muslims" were the first "to target Blacks . . . for slavery" and that many Black Africans in earlier periods converted to Islam only to gain better treatment from their masters. Nevertheless, the Europeans certainly did their best to make up for lost time!

[33]Bethwell Ogot, "The Muslim Trade," in *Daily Nation* (Nairobi, Kenya), responding to Ali Mazrui and citing substantial historical data (reprinted in *World Press Review*, August 1993, p. 23). On the duration, see also Lewis, *Race and Slavery in the Middle East*, p. 59.

[34]Gordon, *Slavery in the Arab World*, p. ix. Whereas the transatlantic trade involved an estimated eleven million slaves, the Arab trade across the Sahara, Red Sea and Indian Ocean had already involved over seven million before the transatlantic trade began, and grew still more afterward (ibid., pp. 147-49).

[35]Ibid., pp. 116-18.

[36]Ibid., p. 24.

[37]Lewis, *Race and Slavery in the Middle East*, p. 59.

[38]Gordon, *Slavery in the Arab World*, p. 25. Europeans later retaliated against Barbary pirates' slave raiding attacks on European ships (ibid., p. 27).

[39]Lewis, *Race and Slavery in the Middle East*, pp. 11-12.

[40]Ibid., p. 12. For East and West African slaves throughout the Middle Ages, see ibid., pp. 51-52.

[41]Gordon, *Slavery in the Arab World*, p. 149.

[42]Ibid., pp. 149-50.

[43]Ibid., p. 150.

[44]Lewis, *Race and Slavery in the Middle East*, pp. 56-57.

[45]Gordon, *Slavery in the Arab World*, pp. 57, 150; also ibid., p. 43. On higher prices, see also Lewis, *Race and Slavery in the Middle East*, p. 13. Talib and Samir ("African Diaspora," p. 720) point out that Islam borrowed its practice of slave concubines (recognized by the Qur'an) from pre-Islamic Arab custom.

[46]Gordon, *Slavery in the Arab World*, pp. 92-93. By the nineteenth century the sultan had four hundred Black eunuchs, thirty to forty White ones and a harem of fifteen hundred women.

[47]Ibid., p. 86.

[48]Lewis, *Race and Slavery in the Middle East*, pp. 94, 97. For Arab artistic depictions associating Black slaves with sexual evil, see ibid., plates 21-23 (all plates are between pp. 22 and 23).

[49]On the sexual use of slaves of a variety of races in Mediterranean antiquity, see Keener, *Paul, Women and Wives*, pp. 197, 217; more fully, Keener, *And Marries Another*, pp. 79, 185 n. 133. Even some cultures in precolonial Africa employed slaves in this manner; see J. K. Henn, "Women in the Rural Economy," in *African Women South of the Sahara* (New York: Longman, 1984), pp. 5-6.

[50]Gordon, *Slavery in the Arab World*, p. 83. Gordon opens chap. 4 ("Sex and Slavery in the Arab World," pp. 79-104) by observing, "The most common and enduring purpose for acquiring slaves in the Arab world was to exploit them for sexual purposes. Islamic law conferred upon the owner of slaves full control over their sexual and reproductive functions as well as the fruits of their labor" (p. 79).

[51]Lewis, *Race and Slavery in the Middle East,* p. 91.

[52]Gordon, *Slavery in the Arab World,* p. 43.

[53]Ibid.

[54]Ibid., pp. 16-17. Gordon here follows a report from the British Anti-slavery Society, the generalization value of which we may question unless corroborating evidence is available.

[55]Lewis, *Race and Slavery in the Middle East,* pp. 101-2. On racial prejudice in Islam, see also Gordon, *Slavery in the Arab World,* pp. 98-104.

[56]Lewis, *Race and Slavery in the Middle East,* pp. 18-20.

[57]See Snowden, *Blacks in Antiquity;* also Snowden, *Before Color Prejudice,* pp. 46-59, 63-108. "The very striking similarities in the total picture that emerge from an examination of the basic sources— Egyptian, Greek, Roman, and early Christian—point to a highly favorable image of blacks and to white-black relationships differing markedly from those that have developed in more color-conscious societies" (*Before Color Prejudice,* p. vii).

[58]See Lewis, *Race and Slavery in the Middle East,* pp. 17-20.

[59]Snowden, *Before Color Prejudice,* pp. 99-108, especially pp. 99-101. The darkness/light symbolism of the church fathers reflects the symbolism of the day (common throughout history among both Black and White peoples—pp. 82-83), and while we would see it as somewhat less benign than Snowden does (pp. 107-8), in context its intention was surely as nonracial as its origin. It apparently rarely if ever (Snowden documents no instances, but unrecorded exceptions may have occurred) affected practical matters (such as slavery) as the much more derogatory, anti-African language of some later Arab writers did.

[60]See Lewis, *Race and Slavery in the Middle East,* pp. 21-25. "Much of early Arab historiography, at least until the mid-ninth century," focuses on tribal rivalries among the Arabs themselves (ibid., p. 44).

[61]Gordon, *Slavery in the Arab World,* p. 100. Early Arabs viewed lighter peoples (Persians, Spaniards and Greeks) as "red," connoting inferiority (Lewis, *Race and Slavery in the Middle East,* p. 21).

[62]Gordon, *Slavery in the Arab World,* pp. 27-28. By contrast, Islamic law permitted non-Muslim monotheistic subjects to hold slaves, but the non-Muslims had to release them immediately if they converted to Islam (Lewis, *Race and Slavery in the Middle East,* p. 8)—which most slaves naturally would (compare the same practice in medieval Europe with regard to Christians and Jews—Bredero, *Christendom and Christianity,* p. 274).

[63]Gordon, *Slavery in the Arab World,* p. 98; Lewis, *Race and Slavery in the Middle East,* p. 56. Because Arabs took so many Nubian slaves, *al-Nuba* in time became nearly synonymous with "black slaves" (Hasan, *Arabs and the Sudan,* p. 8).

[64]Gordon, *Slavery in the Arab World,* p. 107.

[65]Arabs were especially impressed with the slaves the *Baqt* got them from Nubia, and they sought pretty Nubian girls as concubines (Hasan, *Arabs and the Sudan,* p. 43); on the slave trade and their advancement into Nubia, see ibid., pp. 42-50.

[66]Gordon, *Slavery in the Arab World,* p. 104.

[67]Lewis, *Race and Slavery in the Middle East,* pp. 54-55.

[68]Ibid., p. 53.

[69]Ibid., pp. 82-83.

[70]Gordon, *Slavery in the Arab World,* p. 102. White slaves became "increasingly rare" in the later period (Lewis, *Race and Slavery in the Middle East,* pp. 55-56).

[71]Gordon, *Slavery in the Arab World,* p. 81; Lewis, *Race and Slavery in the Middle East,* p. 56. In medieval Egypt, White slaves sometimes sold for only double the price of Black ones (five hundred versus one thousand or more dirhams; Lewis, *Race and Slavery in the Middle East,* p. 13); by contrast, eyewitness reports from the 1830s indicate Abyssinian slave girls being sold for one and a half to two times the price of Black girls, but as little as one-tenth that of White girls (ibid., p. 75).

[72]Gordon, *Slavery in the Arab World,* p. 81. By the end of the nineteenth century White slavery had nearly ended in the Arabian peninsula, but the Black slave trade, though reduced, continued into the mid-twentieth century (Lewis, *Race and Slavery in the Middle East,* p. 82).

[73]Lewis, *Race and Slavery in the Middle East,* pp. 72-73.

[74]Ibid., p. 59. One Black eunuch who did rise to power in Egypt thereby drew the satirical abuse of

an Arab poet (ibid.)

[75]Ibid., pp. 56, 77.

[76]For conquest and enslavement, which produced attitudes of conqueror versus conquered, see ibid., pp. 37-42.

[77]Gordon, *Slavery in the Arab World*, pp. 102-3; Lewis, *Race and Slavery in the Middle East*, p. 92. See also Talib and Samir, "African Diaspora," pp. 721-22, noting the data and their Greco-Roman origin.

[78]Lewis, *Race and Slavery in the Middle East*, p. 92. He provides abundant examples of negative views in medieval Arab literature (pp. 92-93), although noting some positive views as well (they were sometimes stereotyped as cheerful, brave, generous and strong in rhythm—p. 93).

[79]See the Roman writer Pliny *Natural History* 2.80.189 in Snowden, *Before Color Prejudice*, pp. 86-87.

[80]Ibn Qutayba, *Al-Ma'arif,* ed. Tharwat 'Ukasha, 2nd ed. (Cairo, 1969), p. 26, as cited in Lewis, *Race and Slavery in the Middle East*, p. 46.

[81]In *Tabaqat al-Umam,* ed. L. Cheiko (Beirut, 1912), p. 9, as cited in Lewis, *Race and Slavery in the Middle East*, pp. 47-48.

[82]In *Mukhtasar Kitab al-Buldan,* ed. M. J. de Goeje (Leiden, 1885), 5:162, as cited in Lewis, *Race and Slavery in the Middle East*, pp. 45-46.

[83]Lewis, *Race and Slavery in the Middle East*, pp. 89-90.

[84]For example, though proselytes were theoretically equal in ancient Judaism, their social status generally remained inferior. See *m. Horayot* 3:8; *Numbers Rabbah* 6:1; perhaps CD 14.4; also see Joachim Jeremias, *Jerusalem in the Time of Jesus* (Philadelphia: Fortress, 1975), pp. 272, 323; J. M. Baumgarten, "The Exclusion of 'Netinim' and Proselytes in 4QFlorilegium," *Revue de Qumrân* 8 (June 1972): 87-96; Gerald Blidstein, "4Q Florilegium and Rabbinic Sources on Bastard and Proselyte," *Revue de Qumrân* 8 (March 1974): 431-35.

[85]Lewis, *Race and Slavery in the Middle East*, p. 37. Ibid., pp. 28-36, provides substantial evidence for the insults and discrimination against Blacks and dark Arabs in Islamic sources by the eighth century.

[86]Ibid., p. 20, citing the 467th-468th nights (omitted in Lane's version); Lewis points out that the rulers in *The Thousand and One Nights* are basically White supremacists and Blacks hold menial roles. We believe that analogous language appears in such earlier writers as the North African theologian Augustine, who, despite the fact that he was emphasizing spiritual equality, allegorically took darkness of skin negatively (*Enarrationes in Psalmos* 73.16/ *Corpus Christianorum, Series Latina* 39.1014, in Snowden, *Blacks in Antiquity*, p. 204).

[87]Lewis, *Race and Slavery in the Middle East*, pp. 85-86.

[88]Ibid., p. 91. Compare Hasan, *Arabs and the Sudan,* p. 43, for appreciation for Nubian girls as concubines.

[89]Gordon, *Slavery in the Arab World*, p. 69. Mamelukes, White military slaves, became politically dominant under the Ayyubid dynasty, although Black military slaves became more prominent again in the late eighteenth century (ibid., pp. 72, 75).

[90]Ibid., pp. 161-62. These popular sentiments sometimes contrasted with the pragmatism of the actual British officials in charge of pursuing the empire's trade interests, but ultimately prevailed (see ibid., p. 8).

[91]Lewis, *Race and Slavery in the Middle East*, p. 79. It should be noted that by this period access to new African slaves had been cut off to the United States as well; but U.S. slaveholders produced more slaves on their own plantations and hence had little need of a continuing supply of Africans as did the Caribbean.

[92]Gordon, *Slavery in the Arab World*, pp. 162-63.

[93]Lewis, *Race and Slavery in the Middle East*, pp. 78-79.

[94]The first concessions concerning Black slaves came in 1847; the Ottoman authorities banned the Black slave trade, except in the Hijaz, in 1857 (ibid., p. 80).

[95]Ibid., p. 80.

[96]Ibid., p. 81.

[97]The nature of colonialism varied from region to region, but for examples of forced labor and other exploitation, see Davidson, *Africa in History*, pp. 257-60. The British South Africa Company forced

Shona natives to labor for them whenever they needed them, using their wives as hostages to guarantee compliance (Robin Hallett, *Africa Since 1875* [Ann Arbor: University of Michigan Press, 1974], p. 507).

[98]See, for example, Robert William Fogel, *Without Consent or Contract* (New York: W. W. Norton, 1989), pp. 236-37.

[99]Gordon, *Slavery in the Arab World,* pp. 162-63.

[100]Ibid., pp. 164-65. The sultan appealed to considerable historical precedent for continuing slavery (Lewis, *Race and Slavery in the Middle East,* p. 3). The nineteenth-century Moroccan writer Ahmad ibn Khalid al-Nasiri (1834-1897) noted the continued "unlimited enslavement of the blacks," complaining that "men traffic in them like beasts, or worse" (ibid., p. 58).

[101]Gordon, *Slavery in the Arab World,* p. 171.

[102]Lewis, *Race and Slavery on the Middle East,* p. 79.

[103]Gordon, *Slavery in Arab World,* pp. 46-47.

[104]Ibid., pp. 177-82.

[105]Hallett, *Africa Since 1875,* p. 111.

[106]Gordon, *Slavery in the Arab World,* pp. 51-52. This agricultural use of slaves, however, had been rare in the Arab world (ibid., pp. 50-51, 54), perhaps in part due to the nature of the land the Arabs controlled, hence the base of their economy.

[107]Ibid., p. 51.

[108]Ibid., pp. 141-43.

[109]Hallett, *Africa Since 1875,* pp. 560-61.

[110]Gordon, *Slavery in the Arab World,* pp. 191-92.

[111]Ibid., pp. 192-207.

[112]Hallett, *Africa Since 1875,* p. 580. On British force ending Zanzibar slavery, see also Oliver and Fage, *Short History of Africa,* p. 153.

[113]Mannix with Cowley, *Black Cargoes,* p. 258. Until this period the numbers may have been closer to twenty to twenty-five thousand (see Gordon, *Slavery in the Arab World,* p. 53, following Abdulaziz Y. Lodhi), although all numbers are at best estimates.

[114]Mannix with Cowley, *Black Cargoes,* p. 259, citing an eyewitness report (although we may doubt if the witnesses actually *counted* the victims). Even if the numbers were half this, the vessel was transporting a heavy cargo; most slavers packed ten to twenty-five slaves into each ship, and rarely more than seventy-five to one hundred (Gordon, *Slavery in the Arab World,* p. 11).

[115]Mannix with Cowley, *Black Cargoes,* p. 259; for a fuller discussion of the East African trade, see chap. 11, "Slave Catching in the Indian Ocean," pp. 241-62.

[116]Williams, *Destruction of Black Civilization,* p. 23. Arabs may have been darkened through mulatto blood (ibid.); this rarely appeared in the White U.S. population, given the White American prohibition of interracial marriage and the enslavement of all products of interracial unions.

[117]Williams, *Destruction of Black Civilization,* p. 47. This is not to diminish European shame; for one serious reaction to recent European colonialism (in this case the bitter French colonialism in Algeria), see Frantz Fanon, *The Wretched of the Earth* (New York: Grove, 1963).

[118]Williams, *Destruction of Black Civilization,* p. 56.

[119]Ibid., p. 208.

[120]Ibid., p. 155; he says he also confirmed this by his field studies in the Sudan.

[121]Ibid., p. 158.

[122]Ibid., p. 159.

[123]Ibid., p. 47.

[124]Sanneh, *West African Christianity,* p. 74; see further Isichei, *History of Christianity in Africa,* pp. 219, 233, including discrimination against African Christians.

[125]Sanneh, *West African Christianity,* pp. 214-16; on collaboration in education (at Western initiative), see pp. 219-20; compare Isichei, *History of Christianity in Africa,* p. 233.

[126]Mbiti, *African Religions,* p. 330.

[127]Tom Masland et al., "Slavery," *Newsweek,* May 4, 1992, p. 37.

[128]"A School for Iqbal," *Amnesty Action,* Summer 1995, pp. 5, 10.

[129]Ibid., pp. 38-39.

[130]The newspaper was cited in *Mercy Magazine,* January 1994, p. 3

[131]See many reports, such as those in *Africa News*, July 6-19, 1992, p. 16; *Newsweek*, October 12, 1992, p. 49; *ESA Advocate*, October 1992, p. 6; *World Press Review*, March 1989, pp. 28-29, and June 1991, p. 36; *Amnesty Action*, Fall 1993, p. 2.

[132]*World Press Review*, March 1994, p. 31, based on a report in the *Herald* of Harare, Zimbabwe. "Sudan: Caught in a Vicious Cycle of Human Rights Abuses, Poverty and Political Turmoil," *Amnesty Action*, Winter 1995, pp. 1, 3, estimates instead one million deaths and three million displacements.

[133]See "Sudan—the Ravages of War: Political Killings and Humanitarian Disaster" (New York: Amnesty International, September 29, 1993), pp. 6-9. This is available for $3.00 from Amnesty International U.S.A., 322 Eighth Ave., New York, NY 10001. See also "Civil War Brings Suffering to Sudan," *Christianity Today*, May 17, 1993, p. 82. Since the fundamentalist regime in Khartoum announced jihad against the Nuba people in 1992, under a quarter of the original 1.5 million Nuba remain in the region (Julie Flint, "On the Wrong Side of a 'Jihad,' " *World Press Review*, November 1995, pp. 37-38).

[134]"Forgotten Slaves," *World Press Review*, January 1991, p. 57; Masland et al., "Slavery," p. 32.

[135]Gordon, *Slavery in the Arab World*, p. xi. A U.S. scholar visiting that region also told us that he personally was shown sales receipts for "Christian slaves."

[136]"Sudan: Caught," p. 1.

[137]Ibid., p. 3.

[138]Shyam Bhatia, "A War's Human Booty," *World Press Review*, August 1995, p. 40 (from London's *Observer*, April 9, 1995). For releasing his findings Mahmoud was rewarded with two years in a Sudanese jail.

[139]Ibid., p. 40.

[140]Masland et al., "Slavery," p. 30. This is despite the *official* emancipation of slaves there on July 5, 1980 (Gordon, *Slavery in the Arab World*, p. x; compare Lewis, *Race and Slavery in the Middle East*, p. 79).

[141]"Slavery," p. 32. Gordon (*Slavery in the Arab World*, p. x) places the estimate at two hundred thousand men, women and children.

[142]Masland et al., "Slavery," p. 32. On Arab beatings and brandings of African slaves in the Sudan, see Bhatia, "Booty," p. 40.

[143]Masland et al., "Slavery," p. 30.

[144]Larry Pierce, "Where There's Faith, There's Hope for Boys," *Christianity Today*, September 13, 1993, p. 80; the research includes interviews with Abdul Momen, born in Bangladesh and now professor at Merrimack College in North Andover, Massachusetts, and Faith Willard, the Christian with whom he works.

[145]*Amnesty Action*, Fall 1993, p. 4; "Saudi Arabia—Religious Intolerance: The Arrest, Detention and Torture of Christian Worshippers and Shi'a Muslims" (New York: Amnesty International, September 14, 1993; available for $3.00 from Amnesty International U.S.A., 322 Eighth Ave., New York, NY 10001).

[146]Gordon, *Slavery in the Arab World*, p. 231; the quotation is excerpted from a letter by M. Morillon, French ambassador to Saudi Arabia, dated November 7, 1953.

[147]Also pointed out by others, including Williams (*Destruction of Black Civilization*, p. 23), whose criticisms address imperialism in general and are not theological critiques of Islamic religion. Under Shari'a, Islamic law, only Muslims are qualified to testify in court. A Muslim who renounces Islam and cannot be persuaded to recant is executed, in accord with the citation of Muhammad in the *Hadith Al-Bukhari:* "Kill him if he changes his religion" (compare, for example, the Fatwa on apostasy enacted in Lebanon, November 13, 1989). Even in freer states like Egypt, "charges of blasphemy against writers, printers and publishers have drawn eight-year prison sentences" (Laura Shapiro with Daniel Pedersen and Marcus Mabry, "The Fundamentals of Freedom," *Newsweek*, November 15, 1993, p. 87). At the same time, Islamic fundamentalists are also being repressed (in March 1993 "police killed 29 alleged Islamic militants," and eight people died as police stormed a mosque in Aswan the same month; see *Amnesty Action*, Summer 1993, p. 4; "Egypt—Grave Human Rights Abuses Amid Political Violence" [New York: Amnesty International, May 1993], available from Amnesty International U.S.A. for $2.00; compare Christopher Dickey and Carol Berger, "A Message from Mubarak," *Newsweek*, July 19, 1993, p. 28). Those Muslims who favor

the imposition of Islamic law would not understand this law as negating human rights. Even the "Universal Declaration of Human Rights in Islam" (1981) bases human rights not in human dignity (as the United Nations does) but on divine law. While this provides a more absolute foundation for rights, it also suggests that different rights may obtain for different groups—women's rights may be different from men's; non-Muslims in a Muslim state and especially Muslim converts to other religions (versus others converted to Islam) fare quite differently from Muslims under Islamic law. See more fully Samuel Shahid, " 'Rights' of Non-Muslims in an Islamic State," *Reach Out* 5, nos. 3-4 (April 1992), pp. 5-11, as well as other articles in that issue.

[148]Williams, *Destruction of Black Civilization*, p. 56. Portuguese priests (of whom generally only the basest were sent to Africa) participated in the slave trade and (priestly vows of celibacy notwithstanding) had harems of African girls in the Congo (ibid., p. 253; on the power of the bishops, see p. 248).

[149]For one contrast between Jesus and the exploitation of Christianity (as well as other instruments) by Whites, see Skinner, *How Black Is the Gospel?* pp. 11-13.

[150]"Fence of Death," *World Press Review*, July 1992, p. 31, quoting Hugh McCullum in *Horizon*, a monthly from Harare; Masland et al., "Slavery," pp. 32-33.

[151]"The Case of the Vanished Russian Gold," *Newsweek*, October 14, 1991, p. 49.

[152]For example, Ulrich Völklein, "German Business Reveals Its Sins," *World Press Review*, July 1995, pp. 17-18. For the minority of Christians and others who opposed the Nazi regime (as opposed to the vast majority of citizens who did not), see, for example, David P. Gushee, *The Righteous Gentiles of the Holocaust* (Minneapolis: Fortress, 1994).

[153]"Child Laborers," *World Press Review*, October 1992, p. 33, following studies by journalists in the Philippines. One may also compare the child soldiers recruited for the rebel Mon Tai Army in eastern Myanmar, whose government opponents more forcibly exploit the labor of local populations (see Thierry Falise and Christophe Loviny, "Child Soldiers of Myanmar," *World Press Review*, October 1994, p. 25, from Hong Kong's *Eastern Express*).

[154]"Young 'Slaves,' " *World Press Review*, January 1992, p. 33, citing the Portuguese report from Lisbon's *O Público*. On child labor see also *World Vision*, December 1995; *World Press Review*, January 1996.

[155]*Newsweek*, September 30, 1991, p. 17. The Latin American nation where the most slave exploitation occurs is currently Brazil: "Recruited workers for private sugar-cane plantations, gold mines, ranches, and charcoal plants arrive at work locations to discover that they owe unpayable bills for transportation, food, lodging, and tool rental," whereupon they are enslaved. A Brazilian priest has labored to expose the racket, but "numbers of documented cases have increased from 597 in 1989 to 16,442 cases" by the end of 1992 (*The Other Side*, November 1993, p. 13).

[156]Walter Pinpong, Ghana executive director of International Needs, reporting the information to *Christianity Today*, August 16, 1993, p. 54 ("Ministry Breaks Slave Bonds").

[157]"The Lord's Army," *World Press Review*, October 1995, p. 26; this article also reports that the revolutionaries hack off the feet of those caught riding bicycles, because bicycles violate their law!

[158]In turning to other forms of injustice besides slavery, we may recall the warnings of Vernon Johns, Martin Luther King Jr.'s predecessor in the Dexter Avenue Church: he accused his congregation "of persisting in the white man's view of slavery—that labor was demeaning—when Negroes should know that it was oppression, not labor, that demeaned them. On the contrary, the desire to avoid labor had enticed Whites into the corruption of slavery" (Branch, *Parting the Waters*, p. 17).

[159]*Amnesty Action*, January 1991, p. 7.

[160]*Amnesty Action*, November 1991, p. 4.

[161]*Reach Out*, April 1992, p. 29.

[162]For this reason some Kurds have become dissatisfied with Islam, which suppressed the Christian Kurdish majority in the twelfth century; see *Reach Out* 6 (Spring 1993; the whole issue, published by Horizons International, addresses "The Plight of the Kurds"). For the imprisonment without trial and torture (such as splitting open feet, wounding testicles, being forced to ask Allah to bless the Turkish army or be beaten and starved) of Kurds in Turkey, see Mehdi Zana, "A Kurd's Tale of Turkish Prison," *World Press Review*, July 1995, pp. 13-15.

[163]Thierry Lalevée, "Tehran's New Allies in Africa: Exporting the Islamic Revolution," in the Arab-oriented French monthly *Arabies*, translated in *World Press Review*, September 1993, pp. 20-21,

noting, for example, the guerrilla movement in Uganda; when Idi Amin held power in Uganda, he may have murdered as many as half a million people.

[164]For example, "Mass Murder," *Newsweek,* May 9, 1994, pp. 40-41, photographs by Patrick Robert; Scott Harrison, "Goma: Life and Death Among Rwanda's Displaced," *Amnesty Action,* Winter 1995, p. 9. For political and ethnic repression, rape and murder elsewhere in Africa, see also "Zaire—Violence Against Democracy" (New York: Amnesty International, September 16, 1993; available for $3.00 from Amnesty International U.S.A., 322 Eighth Ave., New York, NY 10001).

[165]See, for example, the collections of Hammurabi, Lipit-Ishtar and Eshnunna in *Ancient Near Eastern Texts Relating to the Old Testament,* ed. James B. Pritchard, 2nd ed. (Princeton, N.J.: Princeton University, 1955), and Roman codes such as Gaius's *Institutes.* On the issue of slavery in Old Testament law, see Keener, *Paul, Women and Wives,* pp. 188-91.

[166]For example, Sunderland, *Testimony of God Against Slavery,* pp. 12-79. "Evangelicalism" was the dominant form of public Christianity in the nineteenth-century United States (see, for example, Noll, *History of Christianity,* pp. 163-64 and elsewhere). Against some modern critics, biblical "liberation theology" is neither new nor originally a product of liberal theology. Evangelicals often remained leaders in social concern after the Civil War and into the early twentieth century (see Norris Magnuson, *Salvation in the Slums* (Metuchen, N.J.: Scarecrow, 1977). During the fundamentalist-modernist controversy of the early twentieth century, some Christians unfortunately abandoned the evangelical heritage of social justice while others abandoned the evangelical heritage of personal salvation and biblical authority (see, for example, Ronald J. Sider, *One-Sided Christianity?* [Grand Rapids, Mich.: Zondervan/San Francisco: HarperSanFrancisco, 1993]).

[167]Noll, *History of Christianity,* p. 199.

[168]Raboteau, *Slave Religion,* pp. 101-3; Haynes, *Negro Community Within American Protestantism,* p. 51. Raboteau's work is extremely well documented, so where we cite him the reader may find other sources (which we have not duplicated here) by consulting his work. Charles C. Jones (*The Religious Instruction of the Negroes in the United States* [Savannah, Ga.: Thomas Purse, 1842], pp. 44-45) complained how little religious instruction had initially targeted African slaves in the colonies.

[169]Raboteau, *Slave Religion,* p. 102.

[170]Ibid., p. 103; Noll, *History of Christianity,* p. 79.

[171]See Raboteau, *Slave Religion,* pp. 123-125; compare also Clarke, *Africans at the Crossroads,* p. 46: "Some slaves took the Christian version of the Bible literally and believed that God meant all men to be free." J. M. Washington (*Frustrated Fellowship* [Macon, Ga.: Mercer University Press, 1986], p. ix) correctly observes that the evangelical message of the Great Awakening "helped . . . slaves to gain a new sense of self-worth."

[172]Isichei, *History of Christianity in Africa,* p. 71.

[173]Noll, *History of Christianity,* pp. 101-2, 226. For example, "when a small Baptist congregation tried to organize in Tidewater, Virginia," the local parson beat the Baptist minister, repeatedly slamming his head against the ground; the sheriff then gave him twenty lashes with the whip—after which the beaten man returned and preached. The wealthy planters viewed "Baptists and other dissenters" as undermining "order by refusing to defer to their social betters and by insisting on the rights of absolutely everyone to act on the gospel message" (pp. 101-2). In the early 1700s church membership ranged as low as 5 percent in the South, much lower than in the North.

[174]Raboteau, *Slave Religion,* p. 126. Following Aristotle's view that Greeks should not enslave Greeks, Europeans felt that Christians should not enslave Christians. Slaveholders thus came up with a simple solution: do not allow Black people to become Christians (Pelt and Smith, *Story of the National Baptists,* pp. 22-23). Christians in the Roman Empire, however, had undercut Aristotle's ideological basis for slavery altogether (ibid., p. 22).

[175]On which see, for example, material in Sernett, ed., *Afro-American History,* pp. 135-59. For early reports and historical surveys of these churches, see, for example, Bishop Daniel Alexander Payne (A.M.E.), *Recollections of Seventy Years,* introduction by Francis J. Grimké, new preface by Benjamin Quarles (reprint ed., New York: Arno/New York Times, 1969); David Henry Bradley Sr., *A History of the A.M.E. Zion Church,* 2 vols. (Nashville: Parthenon, 1956-1970); Richard Allen, *The Life Experience and Gospel Labors of the Rt. Rev. Richard Allen, to Which Is Annexed The Rise and Progress of the African Methodist Episcopal Church in the United States of America* (New York: Abingdon, 1960); James A. Handy, *Scraps of African Methodist Episcopal History* (Phil-

adelphia: A.M.E. Book Concern, probably shortly after 1900; reprint Ann Arbor, Mich.: University Microfilms, 1973); William Jacob Walls, *The African Methodist Episcopal Zion Church, Reality of the Black Church* (Charlotte, N.C.: A.M.E. Zion Publishing House, 1974).

[176]Raboteau, *Slave Religion*, p. 132; compare p. 148; John Brown Childs, *The Political Black Minister* (Boston: G. K. Hall, 1980), pp. 29-30. Methodist Gilbert Haven trusted that as eschatological redemption approached, humanity must overcome racial divisions and be united in Christ (Timothy Smith, *Revivalism and Social Reform* [Baltimore: Johns Hopkins University Press, 1980], p. 221).

[177]Raboteau, *Slave Religion*, pp. 133-41.

[178]Noll, *History of Christianity*, p. 109, emphasizing that the Great Awakening bridged "the chasm between white and black cultures."

[179]Bennett, *Before the "Mayflower,"* p. 63.

[180]Raboteau, *Slave Religion*, pp. 133-41.

[181]Noll, *History of Christianity*, p. 138. On Liele and David George, see also Washington, *Frustrated Fellowship*, pp. 8-9; Pelt and Smith, *Story of the National Baptists*, pp. 29-41; on Bryan, see Pelt and Smith, *Story of the National Baptists*, pp. 41-45; Sernett, *Afro-American History*, pp. 48-50.

[182]Noll, *History of Christianity*, pp. 138-39.

[183]Washington, *Frustrated Fellowship*, p. 11.

[184]Ibid., p. 12.

[185]Raboteau, *Slave Religion*, p. 147; Pelt and Smith, *Story of the National Baptists*, pp. 59-65 (though many Whites disagreed with these policies—p. 65-66); see William Goodell, *The American Slave Code in Theory and Practice* (n.p.: American and Foreign Anti-slavery Society, 1853), pp. 326-27 (Goodell protests that slaves were thus unrecognized as thinking and religious beings, pp. 251-57). In most other periods slaves could assemble more openly on many plantations, but prayers for freedom nevertheless had to be conducted in secret (Raboteau, *Slave Religion*, p. 219). Even in freer times, slaves were sometimes forbidden to attend churches, depending on the slaveholders' views (Cheryl J. Sanders, *Slavery and Conversion* [Ann Arbor, Mich.: University Microfilms, 1987], p. 85). French slaveholders in Louisiana restricted slaves' religious practices, perhaps because slaves' religious *advocates* had become too zealous (see V. Alton Moody, *Slavery on Louisiana Sugar Plantations* [New York: AMS, 1976], p. 91).

[186]Raboteau, *Slave Religion*, pp. 196-207. On Black churches in the South before Emancipation, see Edward D. Smith, *Climbing Jacob's Ladder* (Washington, D.C.: Smithsonian Institution, 1988), pp. 75-100. But free urban Blacks had always been able to accomplish the most; see Washington, *Frustrated Fellowship*, p. x.

[187]On Richard Allen, Absalom Jones and the movement founded by them and others, see especially Wilmore, *Black Religion and Black Radicalism*, pp. 80-89; compare Noll, *History of Christianity*, pp. 201-3; Lerone Bennett Jr., "The First Generation," *Ebony*, February 1995, p. 80. For Black congregations in the North from 1740 to 1800, see Smith, *Climbing Jacob's Ladder*, pp. 29-40; for 1800-1860, see pp. 41-74 (Philadelphia, pp. 42-46; New York, pp. 47-48, 58; Boston, pp. 48-56; Providence and Newport, pp. 56-57; Wilmington, p. 57).

[188]Raboteau, *Slave Religion*, pp. 209-10. Many Black Baptist ministers traveled south with the Union armies as volunteer teachers and ministers for the freed slaves (Pelt and Smith, *Story of the National Baptists*, p. 70).

[189]See Mukenge, *Black Church*, pp. 36-38. Thus the C.M.E. grew from 67,888 in 1873 to 120,000 in 1880; the Baptists from 25,000 (recorded) in 1850 to 500,000 in 1870; the A.M.E. from 20,000 in 1856 to 400,000 in 1880; and the A.M.E. Zion from 4,600 in 1856 to 120,000 in 1880 (ibid., p. 39).

[190]For example, Wilmore, *Black Religion and Black Radicalism*, pp. 36-44; compare L. V. Stennis, *The Black Church* (Seattle: Chi-Mik, 1981), pp. 15-21 (although he elsewhere feels the C.M.E. Church, in which he is a minister, should have remained part of the Methodist Episcopal Church South). The Black church remained radical against slavery before the Civil War (Cone, *Black Theology and Black Power*, pp. 94-103), though they later often compromised under segregation due to insurmountable pressures from White power structures (ibid., p. 105).

[191]See also Grimké, *The Negro*, pp. 59-60.

[192]Wilmore, *Black Religion and Black Radicalism*, p. 40. He was soon followed by Henry Highland Garnet (1843); see "Address to the Slaves of the United States of America," in *Witness for Freedom*, ed. Ripley, p. 169.

[193]Wilmore, *Black Religion and Black Radicalism,* p. 42.

[194]See note 175, above, on A.M.E. and A.M.E. Zion history.

[195]Noll, *History of Christianity,* p. 203, on the National Negro Convention.

[196]Fordham, *Major Themes in Northern Black Religious Thought,* pp. 111-37.

[197]Ibid., p. 111.

[198]See Wilbert E. Moore, *American Negro Slavery and Abolition* (New York: Third Press, 1971), p. 149, though John Eliot and Cotton Mather were upset especially by the *way* slavery was practiced.

[199]See Herbert S. Klein, "Anglicanism, Catholicism and the Negro Slave," in *The Debate over Slavery,* ed. Ann Lane (Urbana: University of Illinois Press, 1971), pp. 172-73. Nevertheless, in contrast to other bodies developing in different ways in different colonies, the South generally shaped Anglicanism to bolster the slave system and stifle dissent (Noll, *History of Christianity,* p. 90).

[200]John Woolman, *Some Considerations on the Keeping of Negroes 1754; Considerations on Keeping Negroes 1762* (Philadelphia: James Chattin, 1754; reprint New York: Viking, 1976).

[201]See the later collection of his preaching in Samuel Hopkins, *Timely Articles on Slavery* (1854; reprint Miami: Mnemosyne, 1969).

[202]Raboteau, *Slave Religion,* p. 143; Childs, *Political Black Minister,* pp. 27-28 (noting that Wesley also prophesied slavery's destruction).

[203]Alice Dana Adams, *The Neglected Period of Anti-slavery in America (1808-1831)* (Gloucester, Mass.: Peter Smith, 1964), p. 97.

[204]Wilmore, *Black Religion and Black Radicalism,* p. 34.

[205]Adams, *Neglected Period,* p. 97.

[206]Ibid.

[207]Although Baptists by their polity had no central organization from which to make pronouncements, some ministers even in the South and as early as 1808 were working against slavery (ibid., pp. 100-101; Haynes, *Negro Community,* pp. 111-12). Although others believed slavery was sinful, they felt that the Baptist doctrine of "individual liberty of conscience" prohibited them from *interfering* with the slaveholders (Washington, *Frustrated Fellowship,* pp. 16-17; Washington notes the prevailing White American ideal that "religious liberty" allowed White Americans to do as they pleased—p. 25). For Baptist antislavery work, see Washington, *Frustrated Fellowship,* pp. 27-38; these abolitionists especially used Acts 10:34: "God is no respecter of persons" (ibid., p. 27). Methodists probably outnumbered Baptists in the antislavery cause; it is worth noting (whether as a cause or effect) that Baptists grew especially in rural and southern areas (where slaveholding predominated), whereas Methodists flourished in urban and northern areas (see Smith, *Revivalism and Social Reform,* pp. 22-23).

[208]Adams, *Neglected Period,* pp. 98-100.

[209]Ibid., p. 97; cf. Raboteau, *Slave Religion,* pp. 144-45. While churches in the earliest period did not promote slavery and some actively opposed it, most failed to address the issue (see Lester B. Scherer, *Slavery and the Churches in Early America, 1619-1819* [Grand Rapids, Mich.: Eerdmans, 1975])—just as most people today, Christian and non-Christian, remain silent on most of the injustices we enumerated earlier in this chapter. Adams declares that Episcopalians and Catholics appeared to remain neutral (*Neglected Period,* p. 101); the arguments for Catholic support of U.S. slavery in Richard Roscoe Miller, *Slavery and Catholicism* (Durham, N.C.: North State University Press, 1957), are marred by the book's anti-Catholicism. Catholic work among U.S. Blacks mainly began in 1929; see Charles S. Johnson with Elizabeth L. Allen et al., *Into the Main Stream* (Chapel Hill: University of North Carolina Press, 1947), p. 283. Friends (Quakers) were strongly antislavery (Johnson et al., *Into the Main Stream,* pp. 101-3; Mannix with Cowley, *Black Cargoes,* pp. 171-90). Samuel J. May (*Some Recollections of Our Antislavery Conflict* [Boston: Fields, Osgood, 1869]), a Unitarian clergyman, sadly reports how few Unitarians supported abolitionism as late as the 1840s (pp. 333-45). The Fugitive Slave Act raised many more outcries from about 1850 on (pp. 366-67), although May remained unsatisfied with the response (pp. 372-73). Some like William Ellery Channing, however, retained their evangelical abolitionist convictions when they became Unitarian (compare Noll, *History of Christianity,* pp. 234-35), and in time more Unitarians embraced the cause. For Congregationalist antislavery, see Calvin Montague Clark, *American Slavery and Maine Congregationalists* (Bangor, Maine: Author, 1940).

[210]Pelt and Smith, *Story of the National Baptists,* p. 27.

211Ibid., pp. 27-28.

212For such a comparison and historical retrospect, see Tim Stafford, "In Reluctant Praise of Extremism," *Christianity Today*, October 26, 1992, pp. 18-22. Probably most looked on the most radical abolitionists like John Brown, who would not stop short of violence, somewhat as mainstream prolifers and prochoicers alike view extremists who kill abortionists today—quite unfavorably.

213Milton C. Sernett, *Black Religion and American Evangelicalism* (Metuchen, N.J.: Scarecrow, 1975), pp. 37-41, noting that the Methodists' compromises failed to mitigate the mistrust based on their reputation for opposing slavery. See more fully Haynes, *Negro Community*, pp. 108-11; Donald G. Matthews, *Slavery and Methodism* (Princeton, N.J.: Princeton University Press, 1965), pp. 62-87, addressing the period up until abolitionism's rise in the North from 1832 on.

214Noll, *History of Christianity*, p. 174.

215Childs, *Political Black Minister*, p. 29.

216Stampp, *Peculiar Institution*, pp. 157-58. On divided denominations, beginning with the Presbyterians, see also Sernett, *Black Religion and American Evangelicalism*, pp. 47-51; for the Methodists in particular, see Matthews, *Slavery and Methodism*, pp. 113-282; on the Baptists, see Pelt and Smith, *Story of the National Baptists*, p. 67 (1845). On differing Methodist responses to slavery and post-Civil War racial questions, see the work of African-American minister L. M. Hagood, *The Colored Man in the Methodist Episcopal Church* (Cincinnati: Cranston & Stowe, 1890). For a later period, see, for example, James M. Shopshire, "Black Methodist Protestants, 1877-1939," in *Recovery of Black Presence*, ed. Bailey and Grant, pp. 177-91.

217See especially H. Shelton Smith, *In His Image, But . . .* (Durham, N.C.: Duke University Press, 1972)—for example, pp. vii-viii, 73.

218Adams, *Neglected Period*, p. 96; also see ibid., pp. 58-62. For southern antislavery voices, see, for example, Hinton Rowan Helper (from North Carolina), *The Impending Crisis of the South* (New York: Author, 1857); John Spencer Bassett (a professor at Trinity College), *Anti-slavery Leaders of North Carolina* (Baltimore: Johns Hopkins University Press, 1898).

219W. Sherman Savage, *The Controversy over the Distribution of Abolition Literature, 1830-1860* (n.p.: Association for the Study of Negro Life and History, 1938), p. 34, from the *Ohio Archaeological and Historical Society* 20, nos. 1-2: 281. The minister, a theological student, was named Amos Dresser.

220Stampp, *Peculiar Institution*, pp. 159-60.

221For example, George S. Sawyer (*Southern Institutes: Or, An Inquiry into the Origin and Early Prevalence of Slavery and the Slave-Trade* [Philadelphia: J. B. Lippincott, 1858]), argued from the Bible (essays 2, 5), Greek and Roman culture (3-4) and other societies that slavery has always been practiced—without responding to biblical antislavery arguments. Compare similarly Fred A. Ross (pastor of a Presbyterian church in Huntsville, Alabama), *Slavery Ordained of God* (n.p.: J. B. Lippincott, 1857), who endeavored to be eloquent and often invoked God's name, but used little Scripture and supplied no context for the Scripture he did use. He resorted instead to moral arguments for why slavery is necessary for everyone's good and abolition hurtful, and claimed that the Bible nowhere calls slavery a sin (contrast Sunderland and others).

222See fully La Roy Sunderland, *Anti Slavery Manual, Containing a Collection of Facts and Arguments on American Slavery* (New York: S. W. Benedict, 1837).

223Raboteau, *Slave Religion*, pp. 152-80; also see Wilmore, *Black Religion and Black Radicalism*, pp. 32-33; Stampp, *Peculiar Institution*, p. 160; David Brian Davis, *The Problem of Slavery in the Age of Revolution, 1770-1823* (Ithaca, N.Y.: Cornell University Press, 1975), pp. 523-56. For a fuller treatment of the repressive biblical hermeneutic practiced by Whites who favored slavery, see Katie Geneva Cannon, "Slave Ideology and Biblical Interpretation," in *Recovery of Black Presence*, ed. Bailey and Grant, pp. 119-28; for a treatment of how oppressors have abused Jesus, see Jacquelyn Grant, "Womanist Jesus and the Mutual Struggle for Liberation." in *Recovery of Black Presence*, especially pp. 133-36.

224Modern commentators not infrequently remark that those who favored slavery took verses out of context or simply appealed to the institutions that existed in biblical times without taking into account whether the Bible supported or resisted such institutions; the abolitionists, by contrast, took into account Scripture's historical situation (Smith, *Revivalism and Social Reform*, pp. 217-18) and looked for broader principles in Scripture (see, for example, Rebecca Merrill Groothuis, *Women*

Caught in the Conflict [Grand Rapids, Mich.: Baker Book House, 1994], pp. 35-37). Slaveholders' abuse of Scripture remains a textbook example of culturally insensitive hermeneutics even to this day (see, for example, W. W. Klein, C. L. Blomberg and R. L. Hubbard, *Introduction to Biblical Interpretation* [Dallas: Word, 1993], p. 12).

[225]Those who thought that slavery was "against nature" believed that it was immoral (Aristotle *Politics* 1.2.3, 1253b; see Keener, *Paul, Women and Wives*, p. 205). In the nineteenth century, slavery's defenders still insisted on the *natural* character of slavery, against those who decried it as unbiblical (for example, Samuel Seabury, *American Slavery Distinguished from the Slavery of the English Theorists and Justified by the Law of Nature* [New York: Mason Brothers, 1861], p. iii: northerners agitate unrest by considering slavery a moral evil, but the Constitution proves otherwise). Abolitionists contended, as Paul evidently believed, that it was *against* nature (for example, Rankin, *Letters on American Slavery Addressed to Mr. Thomas Rankin*, p. 60).

[226]On the context and cultural background of this passage, as well as Paul's request for one slave's freedom so he could join Paul in ministry, see especially Keener, *Paul, Women and Wives*, pp. 184-224; Keener, "Slaves, Obey Your Masters: Ephesians 6:5," *A.M.E. Zion Quarterly Review* 107 (October 1995): 32-54; on Paul's particular mission strategy, see also Keener, "Subversive Conservative," *Christian History* 14 (August 1995): 35-37. We have summarized our response only briefly here because it is argued in detail there with extensive documentation.

[227]Any person in one generation can criticize anyone in other generations for not matching up to later cultural standards. Such critiques will spare *no one* in history (including Martin, Malcolm, Farrakhan and ourselves). But unless a modern reader starts with the most blatant ethnocentrism (cultural bigotry), one must take into account the contemporary situation a historical person was addressing when evaluating that person's commitments. Direct challenges to the slave system would have confirmed the Roman stereotype of Christians as subversive and brought swift retribution. If we today think that Paul should have spoken more strongly, we need to notice which issues of justice we ourselves do not regularly address. We often fail to address them regularly either because we might appear so radical as to undermine our cause in the long run or because those issues are not directly relevant to the point we are addressing in a particular letter or essay (especially when they are very involved and would require lengthy digression). That Paul's words were used out of context against his intent produced other circumstances contrary to his intent besides slavery; many slaves rejected Christianity (at least in its White form) because masters had linked it with obedience and social control (William L. Van Deburg, *The Slave Drivers* [Westport, Conn.: Greenwood, 1979], pp. 21-23).

[228]Tom Skinner, *Words of Revolution* (Grand Rapids, Mich.: Zondervan, 1970), pp. 20-21; see also Pobee, *Toward an African Theology*, p. 35.

[229]That something can be used contrary to its original purpose may also be illustrated by an opposite sort of example to the one above: the "natural rights" philosophy of John Locke later proved helpful in combating slavery (influencing even the evangelicals—see David W. Bebbington, *Evangelicalism in Modern Britain* [Grand Rapids, Mich.: Baker Book House/London: Unwin Hyman, 1994], pp. 52, 71-72), even though Locke *himself* justified slavery "as a continuation of a state of war in which a captive was enslaved rather than killed" (Scherer, *Slavery and the Churches*, pp. 106-7).

[230]Noll, *History of Christianity*, p. 79.

[231]David W. Bebbington, "William Wilberforce," in *Eerdmans Handbook to the History of Christianity*, ed. Tim Dowley (Grand Rapids, Mich.: Eerdmans, 1977), p. 561; compare *The New Encyclopedia Britannica*, 15th ed. (Chicago: University of Chicago, 1992), 12:654.

[232]Theodore Jennings Jr., *Good News to the Poor* (Nashville: Abingdon, 1990), pp. 80-88.

[233]Ibid., p. 86.

[234]Ibid., pp. 87-92. Eventually the equivalent of 95 percent of the members of the growing Wesleyan "connection," or fellowship, "signed Wesleyan anti-slavery parliamentary petitions" (Bebbington, *Evangelicalism in Modern Britain*, p. 72).

[235]Bebbington, "William Wilberforce," p. 556. John Newton, composer of "Amazing Grace," was a slave trader who repented (albeit much too gradually for our taste!) and later as a mature Christian became an active abolitionist.

[236]Bebbington, *Evangelicalism in Modern Britain*, p. 72.

[237]Gilbert Hobbs Barnes, *The Antislavery Impulse, 1830-1844* (1933; reprint New York: Harcourt,

Brace & World, 1964), p. 53. Unfortunately, Garrison's reputation—generated by polemical out-of-context quotations in southern editorials—sometimes hurt the fledgling cause as much as helped it (ibid., p. 57). Further, despite support from many Christians, Garrison eventually came to attack church and state and the Bible as much as the slave traffic, and his anarchism alienated many of his Christian supporters (Smith, *Revivalism and Social Reform,* pp. 182-83; Nancy A. Hardesty, *Women Called to Witness* [Nashville: Abingdon, 1984], p. 123). Some felt forced to choose between proslavery Christianity and an anti-Christian abolitionism (Smith, *Revivalism and Social Reform,* p. 187).

238Compare, for example, the debate between the Reverend W. G. Brownlow and the abolitionist Congregational minister Reverend A. Pryne, *Ought American Slavery to Be Perpetuated?* (Philadelphia: J. B. Lippincott, 1858).

239See Weld's *The Bible Against Slavery* (1837), which Hardesty (*Women Called to Witness,* p. 76) calls "the epitome of the Finneyites' argument for immediate abolition." See also the Reverend Dr. Willis, "The Bible vs. Slavery," in *Autographs for Freedom* (Auburn, N.Y.: Alden, Beardsley, 1854), 2:151-55; see also, for example, Antoinette L. Brown, "The Size of Souls," pp. 41-43, William Marsh, "The Law of Liberty," pp. 61-62, and William Brock, "Slaveholding Not a Misfortune but a Crime," p. 158, in the same volume. See the long collection in Leonard Bacon (pastor of the First Church in New Haven), *Slavery Discussed in Occasional Essays, from 1833 to 1846* (New York: Baker and Scribner, 1846).

240Sunderland, *Testimony Against Slavery.*

241George B. Cheever, *God Against Slavery: And the Freedom and Duty of the Pulpit to Rebuke It as a Sin Against God* (New York: Joseph H. Ladd, 1857), a fierce denunciation of slavery. For other abolitionist literature complaining of slavery's sins, see, for example, *Interesting Memoirs and Documents Relating to American Slavery and the Glorious Struggle Now Making for Complete Emancipation* (London: Chapman, 1846; reprint Miami: Mnemosyne, 1969).

242Lewis Tappan, "Disfellowshipping the Slaveholder," in *Autographs for Freedom,* 2:164. Smith (*Revivalism and Social Reform,* p. 85) emphasizes that revivalism was transdenominational and the opponents of revivalism were the primary voices of dogmatic narrowness. This evangelical ecumenicity did not, however, easily cross *issues* like slavery.

243Barnes, *Antislavery Impulse,* pp. 3-11; Hardesty, *Women Called to Witness,* 49-51. Princeton's Old School Calvinists "joined Southern preachers in working out a maddeningly ingenious defense of slavery," namely, that God chose some to be free and others for enslavement, just as he chose some to be saved and others to be damned (Smith, *Revivalism and Social Reform,* p. 186). Meanwhile, New School Calvinists moved closer to Wesley, while Arminianism and revivalism appeared to go "hand in hand" (ibid. pp. 27-28).

244Hollenweger, *The Pentecostals,* p. 21. After 1865 social crusades (challenging racism, alcoholism, slum housing and so on) characterized American religion, springing from evangelicalism's holiness emphasis (Smith, *Revivalism and Social Reform,* pp. 148-62; on churches helping the poor, see pp. 163-77).

245Barnes, *Antislavery Impulse,* pp. 12-13. This thesis is argued in substantially greater detail by Hardesty, *Women Called to Witness.*

246Barnes, *Antislavery Impulse,* p. 12.

247Ibid., pp. 14-15.

248Ibid., pp. 19-21.

249Smith, *Revivalism and Social Reform,* p. 180.

250Barnes, *Antislavery Impulse,* p. 16.

251Ibid., pp. 71-72; Louis Filler, *The Crusade Against Slavery, 1830-1860* (New York: Harper & Row, 1960), pp. 68-69; compare Hardesty, *Women Called to Witness,* p. 46.

252Barnes, *Antislavery Impulse,* p. 73. The hero allows himself to suffer so that Cassy and Emmeline can flee to freedom; although in modern usage his name often symbolizes compromise, when Stowe wrote the work in 1852 Uncle Tom "was a Christ figure meant to encourage others in the spiritual struggle against human bondage" (Noll, *History of Christianity,* p. 410).

253Filler, *Crusade Against Slavery,* pp. 69-70; Hardesty, *Women Called to Witness,* pp. 46-47.

254See Hardesty, *Women Called to Witness,* p. 118 (public reaction was so strong in some quarters that arsonists burned the New York church). Compare Smith, *Revivalism and Social Reform,* p.

252: "If Finney, the Tappans, and abolitionists like Theodore Dwight Weld and Wesleyan Methodist Orange Scott were not radical enough for some of the young historians of the late 1960s, they seemed revolutionary firebrands indeed to their own generation." Oberlin and Finney denounced racist Ohio laws, exploitation of women, expansionist imperialism and so forth. On Oberlin radicalism, see also Robert W. Cruver, "The Pillar of Fire: Yesterday, Today and Tomorrow, with an Introduction to Biblical Holiness and the Holiness Movement," M.T.S. thesis, Asbury Theological Seminary, 1992, p. 31.

[255]Barnes, *Antislavery Impulse,* pp. 74-78. For evangelical influence in northern abolitionist politics before the Civil War, see Richard J. Carwardine, *Evangelicals and Politics in Antebellum America* (New Haven, Conn.: Yale University Press, 1993).

[256]See "David Walker's *Appeal,*" the text of which is printed in *Witness for Freedom,* ed. Ripley, pp. 42-46.

[257]For example, Charles L. Blockson, *The Underground Railroad in Pennsylvania* (Jacksonville, N.C.: Flame International, 1981), pp. 13-14, 35-36, 41, 46, 60, 64, 87, 105.

[258]Ibid., p. 12.

[259]Noll, *History of Christianity,* pp. 314-18.

[260]Ibid., p. 318.

[261]Wilmore, *Black Religion and Black Radicalism,* p. 4. Noll (*History of Christianity,* p. 551) regards it as one of the greatest signs of Christianity's authentic power that African-Americans embraced the true, biblical gospel despite the ungodly, unbiblical means by which it was often conveyed to them.

[262]Sanders, *Slavery and Conversion,* p. 231.

[263]James Curry, whose holder's oldest son taught him how to read. See John W. Blassingame, ed., *Slave Testimony* (Baton Rouge: Louisiana State University Press, 1977), pp. 130-31.

[264]This spiritual is recorded in Bennett, *Before the "Mayflower,"* p. 80.

[265]Blockson, *Underground Railroad,* pp. 180-84.

[266]See the whole work of African-American writer J. Garfield Owens, *All God's Chillun: Meditations on Negro Spirituals* (Nashville: Abingdon, 1971); also Cone, *Black Theology and Black Power,* pp. 93-94. The spirituals reflected confidence that God would liberate; see, for example, Janice E. Hale, "The Transmission of Faith to Young African American Children," in *Recovery of Black Presence,* ed. Bailey and Grant, pp. 198-201.

[267]Bennett, *Before the "Mayflower,"* p. 111; Wilmore, *Black Religion and Black Radicalism,* pp. 53-57. The Scriptures played a critical role in the revolt (Noll, *History of Christianity,* p. 161).

[268]Sernett, *Black Religion and American Evangelicalism,* pp. 59-81.

[269]Joyner, *Down by the Riverside,* pp. 156-57. The Anglican ministers to the slaves usually worked hard not to offend the plantation owners (Wood, *Black Majority,* pp. 137-38).

[270]Joyner, *Down by the Riverside,* p. 158.

[271]Ibid., p. 158; compare Raboteau, *Slave Religion,* pp. 101-2.

[272]Sernett, *Black Religion and American Evangelicalism,* p. 68.

[273]Despite objections to many aspects of Garvey's message in the Black church, many sermons from leading Baptist and Methodist churchmen appeared in his *Negro World,* opposing his imprisonment and reflecting favorably on his organization's work. See Randall K. Burkett, ed., *Black Redemption: Churchmen Speak for the Garvey Movement* (Philadelphia: Temple University Press, 1978).

[274]Garvey, *Philosophy,* 1:22, as quoted in ben-Jochannan, *African Origins of the Major "Western Religions,"* p. 277. Some Black nationalists were also churchmen; see, for example, David M. Dean, *Defender of the Race: James Theodore Holly* (Boston: Lambeth, 1979). Garvey's UNIA had a religious ethos, and Garvey effectively acted as a "Black theologian," seeking to revise theology to help Black morale (Randall K. Burkett, *Garveyism as a Religious Movement* [Metuchen, N.J.: Scarecrow, 1978], pp. 15-70; the values are obvious, but the danger comes when divine truth is modified in the cause of self-esteem). Many clergy (Baptist, A.M.E. and others) participated (Burkett, *Garveyism,* pp. 111-94). Garvey accepted followers regardless of their religion as long as they were Black nationalists. Noble Drew Ali (Timothy Drew) was the first to create an Islamic religious nationalism (Rashad, *History of Islam and Black Nationalism,* p. 64).

[275]"Discouragements: Hostility of the Press, Silence and Cowardice of the Pulpit," delivered November 20, 1900; in *The Works of Francis J. Grimké,* ed. Carter G. Woodson, 4 vols. (Washington, D.C.:

Associated Publishers, 1942), 1:247. Grimké openly condemned White ministers who allowed segregation in their congregations or denominations; he thereby alienated many fellow Presbyterian clergy (Presbyterian schools even in the North usually rejected Black students). See Woodson's introduction to Grimké's *Works*, pp. xiv-xvi. Grimké argued that segregation contradicted Scripture.

[276]Du Bois, *Prayers for Dark People*, p. 63.

[277]Noll (*History of Christianity*, p. 545), a White evangelical, complains that most White evangelicals are too secure in society to confront the pain of the cross and embrace the gospel's power for liberation the way the African-American community has experienced it.

Chapter 6: Militant Christianity

[1]See also Cheryl Sanders, *Empowerment Ethics for a Liberated People* (Minneapolis: Fortress, 1995), chap. 4, "Cooperation"; compare Letty Russell, "A Feminist Looks at Black Theology," in *Black Theology II*, ed. Bruce and Jones: "no one is free until all are free" (p. 263).

[2]Grimké, *The Negro*, pp. 39-40. See also his other sermons against prejudice: Francis J. Grimké, "Christianity and Race Prejudice: Two Discourses Delivered in the Fifteenth Street Presbyterian Church, Washington, D.C., May 29th and June 5th, 1910" (reprint Ann Arbor, Mich.: University Microfilms, 1973). The Bible offers plenty of perspective on human oppression for those with sensitivity to hear it; among recent exegetical studies one might sample David Rensberger, "Oppression and Identity in the Gospel of John," in *Recovery of Black Presence*, ed. Bailey and Grant, pp. 77-94; Koala Jones-Warsaw, "Toward a Womanist Hermeneutic: A Reading of Judges 19-21," *The Journal of the Interdenominational Theological Center* 22 (Fall 1994): 18-35. The Black church has traditionally found relevant application of historic principles in the Bible (for example, the call for moral renewal in John W. Waters, "When the Vultures Are Finished, Can There Be Life?" in *Recovery of Black Presence*, pp. 95-106).

[3]Because women rarely could make enough money to live on in that society, widows were poor and often easily oppressed legally if no one stood up for them. Today we might think of single mothers or others who are in vulnerable positions in society. (This was one reason Jesus opposed divorce in Mark 10:1-12, a passage that occurs in the context of identifying with the oppressed, as we point out below. In that culture, husbands could divorce their wives without the wife's consent; see Keener, *And Marries Another*, pp. 38-49).

[4]See, for example, the evaluations of two African-American psychiatrists, William H. Grier and Price M. Cobbs, *The Jesus Bag* (New York: McGraw-Hill, 1971), p. 167.

[5]See, for example, Wilmore, *Black Religion and Black Radicalism*, pp. 62-73. For more on this revolt, see, for example, Willie Lee Rose, ed., *A Documentary History of Slavery in North America* (New York: Oxford University Press, 1976), pp. 122-34.

[6]See ibid., pp. 57-62; Carroll, *Slave Insurrections*, pp. 86-87 (the latter also complaining because Vesey took the Bible as God's literal Word). One of his counselors was the Reverend Morris Brown, who later became a protégé of the founding A.M.E. bishop Richard Allen, who may have supported his role in the conspiracy; ultimately Morris became an A.M.E. bishop himself (Wilmore, *Black Religion and Black Radicalism*, p. 60). Other religious elements (such as Gullah Jack, an African conjurer) also played roles (see Wilmore, *Black Religion and Black Radicalism*, p. 59; Bennett, *Before the "Mayflower,"* p. 115), but the exodus and conquest story of the Bible remained central (Wilmore, *Black Religion and Black Radicalism*, pp. 58-59; Bennett, *Before the "Mayflower,"* p. 113). For more on this revolt, see, for example, Rose, *Documentary History of Slavery*, pp. 115-21.

[7]See, for example, Wilmore, *Black Religion and Black Radicalism*, pp. 53-57. For more on this revolt, see Rose, *Documentary History of Slavery*, pp. 107-14.

[8]In Africa, compare John Chilembwe, who joined the National Baptist Convention and worked with African-American missionaries for schools, agriculture, health needs and the abolition of liquor in Nyasaland until he and some followers died in an aborted revolt against colonial authorities in 1915 (Isichei, *History of Christianity in Africa*, pp. 249-50). Many White North American Christians believe slave revolts unjust, yet accept the Revolutionary War—a rebellion against a considerably lesser form of oppression—as just. By contrast, the Bible's one positive example of warfare conducted neither in self-defense nor explicitly at God's command is Abram's expedition to rescue Lot

and others from a captivity that would entail enslavement (Gen 14:12-16). If a just war can exist, battling unjust enslavement would surely constitute just cause (though whether Christians should seek to abolish this by war or by other means is debated).

[9]Sernett, *Black Religion and American Evangelicalism*, pp. 37-41, 47. From 1788 to 1831 Black Baptists grew quickly as White Americans in general began to emphasize freedom of worship, but after Nat Turner's revolt southern slaveholders began to repress Black Baptists (Washington, *Frustrated Fellowship*, p. 23).

[10]Sernett, *Black Religion and American Evangelicalism*, p. 101.

[11]For example, Noll, *History of Christianity*, p. 205.

[12]Douglass both appealed to Christian conviction (*Frederick Douglass*, ed. B. Quarles [Englewood Cliffs, N.J.: Prentice-Hall, 1968], p. 97) and professed growing alienation from the segregated White churches and the nonabolitionist Black churches influenced by them (ibid., pp. 15, 47; W. L. Van Deburg, "The Tragedy of Frederick Douglass," *Christianity Today*, January 31, 1975, pp. 7-8).

[13]See Sarah H. Bradford, *Scenes in the Life of Harriet Tubman* (Auburn, N.Y.: W. J. Moses, 1869); for example, p. 1: "well has she been called 'Moses,' for she has been a leader and deliverer unto hundreds of her people." Tubman's biblically informed faith is widely reported (on both Tubman and Sojourner Truth here, see, for example, Cheryl J. Sanders, "Black Women in Biblical Perspective," in *Living the Intersection*, ed. Sanders, pp. 122-23).

[14]Cone, *For My People*, pp. 123-25. Wilmore, in *Black Religion and Black Radicalism*, thoroughly treats the religious roots of most historic Black resistance. With the exception of a few, like Jupiter Hammon, most Black preachers were involved in the struggle against slavery, but their particular positions varied from Richard Allen (who "condemned slavery but counseled the slaves to love and obey their masters" till it was abolished—p. 68) to Nat Turner; also see Charles V. Hamilton, *The Black Preacher in America* (New York: William Morrow, 1972), pp. 37-69.

[15]For examples of the Christian commitment of many Black leaders in this period, one may peruse the Charles N. Hunter Papers, 1818-1931 (Raleigh, N.C.; now in the Duke University manuscripts collection), including a letter from Emma Hunter dated February 1900 from Washington, D.C.

[16]J. Deotis Roberts, *A Black Political Theology* (Philadelphia: Westminster Press, 1974), p. 88, as cited in Sider, *One-Sided Christianity?* p. 116.

[17]Sterling, *We Are Your Sisters*, p. 493.

[18]Bennett, *Before the "Mayflower,"* p. 313.

[19]In Africa one may compare Albert Luthuli (1898-1967), long the head of the African National Congress, who was the first South African to win the Nobel Peace Prize (1960) and a noted Christian leader. See the theologically insightful postscript to his "Let My People Go," conveniently available in *Classics of Christian Missions*, ed. Francis M. DuBose (Nashville: Broadman, 1979), pp. 409-26; and more recently, Caesar Molebatsi, whose moving story appears in *A Flame for Justice*, written with David Virtue (Batavia, Ill.: Lion, 1991). Nelson Mandela, Oliver Tambo and Alan Paton, all of whom worked for racial justice in South Africa, were active Christians (Mandela a Wesleyan); see Mark Noll, "Midwives of South Africa's Rebirth," *Christianity Today*, July 17, 1995, pp. 33-34.

[20]PACWA stands for the Pan African Christian Women Assembly, which is part of the Association of Evangelicals of Africa and Madagascar.

[21]"PACWA Covenant," appendix 1, in *Our Time Has Come*, ed. Judy Mbugua (Grand Rapids, Mich.: Baker Book House/Carlisle, U.K.: Paternoster/World Evangelical Fellowship, 1994), pp. 145-48.

[22]This is what many Black theologians mean when they say, "God is Black." Because God identifies with the oppressed, he identifies with our people in lands where we are especially oppressed (employing a social rather than melanin-based definition of Blackness).

[23]While one may not agree with all of Marcus Garvey's teaching, he rightly noted that though a better day was coming, "whilst we are hoping by our Christian virtues to have an entry into Paradise we also realize that we are living on earth, and that the things that are practised in Paradise are not practiced here" (in Grant, ed., *Black Protest*, p. 201, an excerpt from A. J. Garvey's 1923 collection of Marcus Garvey's work).

[24]Howard Thurman also contends that Jesus was one of the oppressed, making his case clearly from the historical evidence (*Jesus and the Disinherited* [Richmond, Ind.: Friends United, 1981], pp. 15-

18). For historical explanation of the nature and likelihood of Jesus' suffering, see, for example, Josef Blinzler, *The Trial of Jesus* (Westminster, Md.: Newman, 1959); and material on the passion narrative in Craig Keener's forthcoming academic commentary on Matthew (Eerdmans); see also that commentary for more detailed treatment and surveys of positions for the Synoptic Gospel pericopes whose point we have summarized below.

[25]Marx viewed religion as a way the poor coped with capitalism's bondage; by abolishing religion, he maintained, one could force the proletariat to seek true happiness (Bud Bultmann, *Revolution by Candlelight* [Portland, Ore.: Multnomah Press, 1991], pp. 11-12, citing Karl Marx, "Contribution to the Critique of Hegel's *Philosophy of Right: Introduction,*" from *The Marx-Engels Reader,* ed. Robert C. Tucker [New York: W. W. Norton, 1972], p. 12). In all societies where atheism was enforced under Marxism, religion revived when Marxism died (even in Albania, where atheism was enforced most strictly); it is also questionable whether atheistic Marxism ever successfully delivered on its promise of corporate happiness (see Bultmann, *Revolution*).

[26]See Hart M. Nelsen and Anne Kusener Nelsen, *Black Church in the Sixties* (Lexington: University Press of Kentucky, 1975), depending on a considerable survey of data (although some sectors of the Black church resisted as well as supported social protest; see Mukenge, *Black Church*, pp. 2-3). Some White opponents of the Black church criticized it for its social emphasis, accusing it of concern for solely social issues and of being a separate religion from historic Christianity; they were convinced (quite wrongly!) that the Black church would disappear once the Civil Rights Movement accomplished its objectives (following the Black scholar J. R. Washington Jr., *Black Religion* [Boston: Beacon, 1964], pp. 27-29, 234-35, who in his day was reviewed favorably by the normally perceptive White liberal scholar Martin Marty; J. M. Washington [*Frustrated Fellowship*, p. 8] critiques the ethnocentrism of the earlier Washington). But the gospels of social justice and personal salvation were united in American evangelical religion in the nineteenth century; they separated only in the early twentieth century as fundamentalists reacted against modernists' "social gospel" (see, for example, Sider, *One-Sided Christianity?*).

[27]Cone, *God of the Oppressed*, p. 192; also compare p. 194: the cross "makes it possible to struggle for freedom because we know that God is struggling too." See also the comments of Tom Skinner, *If Christ Is the Answer, What Are the Questions?* (Grand Rapids, Mich.: Zondervan, 1974), pp. 109-18.

[28]We mean that Jesus "turned him away" through radical demands, not that he did not wish the man to become a disciple; compare, for example, Diogenes Laertius *Lives* 7.1.22.

[29]First Timothy 1:10, for example, condemns "kidnappers," which in ancient parlance meant slave traders (so also NIV and NRSV); compare, for example, Exodus 21:16; Deuteronomy 24:7; *Hammurabi* 14; Robin Scroggs, *The New Testament and Homosexuality* (Philadelphia: Fortress, 1983), p. 120; Martin Goodman, *State and Society in Roman Galilee, A.D. 132-212* (Totowa, N.J.: Rowman & Allanheld, 1983), p. 38.

[30]For example, Weary with Hendricks, *I Ain't Comin' Back*, p. 94. This was long after the Supreme Court denied the feasibility of the "separate but equal" doctrine.

[31]See William Lane, *Hebrews,* Word Biblical Commentary 47B (Dallas: Word, 1991), pp. 371-73. Ben-Jochannan complains that the Moses who later would say "Thou shalt not kill" *murdered* his Egyptian brother (*African Origins*, p. 153). But Moses was acting for justice "by any means necessary," violently defending an oppressed slave being beaten by a taskmaster; here he was a revolutionary like Nat Turner or John Brown. To oppose this act would be to oppose slave revolts and the Civil War (and certainly the *Revolutionary* War, which fought a much tamer form of oppression). While one of us authors is a pacifist and feels that Moses acted on his own without God's blessing, he concurs that the action was nevertheless *just* (see Genesis 14:14-16).

[32]Branch, *Parting the Waters*, p. 19. It was Johns's niece Barbara who precipitated the school strike that led to *Brown* v. *Board of Education* (ibid., pp. 20-21).

[33]Ibid., pp. 12, 16.

[34]King, *Where Do We Go from Here?* (New York: Harper & Row, 1967), p. 132, as cited in Lincoln and Mamiya, *Black Church,* p. 269. Distinct classes in the African-American community began forming during freedom (Mukenge, *Black Church*, pp. 45-73), although it was only after World War II that the class structure "began to objectively resemble the white class structure" (ibid., p. 66). Contemporary studies must take into account class as well as ethnicity (for example, Leon F.

Williams, "Revisiting the Mission of Social Work at the End of the Century: A Critique," in *Perspectives on Equity and Justice in Social Work,* ed. Pearson, p. 62).

[35]Grace Bustill Douglass (1782-1842), wife of the Reverend Robert Douglass; Sterling, *We Are Your Sisters,* pp. 103-4.

[36]Maria Stewart, 1833, in ibid., p. 157. On Black women's clubs and other means of nineteenth- and twentieth-century urban "uplift" (including holiness churches), see Sanders, *Empowerment Ethics,* chap. 3; and especially Riggs, *Awake, Arise and Act* (the whole book), for a model of achievement. On African-American women's education, see Sanders, *Empowerment Ethics,* chap. 5.

[37]Jacquelyn Grant, "Womanist Jesus and the Mutual Struggle for Liberation," in *Recovery of Black Presence,* ed. Bailey and Grant, pp. 129-30.

[38]Weary with Hendricks, *I Ain't Comin' Back,* p. 126.

[39]European colonialists also used upward mobility in the form of educational elitism to alienate African leaders from their roots in the colonial period (Williams, *Destruction of Black Civilization,* p. 25). We need as much education as we can get (see Du Bois, *Prayers for Dark People,* pp. 28, 37, 53 on education; pp. 3, 42, 50, 75 on hard work; pp. 17, 18, 27, 39, 71 on persevering in what one has begun), but we dare not in the process forget our people, with whom any of us rises or falls.

[40]Du Bois, *Prayers for Dark People,* p. 23.

[41]Bell (*And We Are Not Saved,* p. 250) warns against seeking to become exploiters ourselves. See Thurman, *Jesus and the Disinherited,* p. 88: "Jesus rejected hatred because he saw that hatred meant death to the mind, death to the spirit, death to communion with his Father. He affirmed life; and hatred was the great denial." And see Pobee, *Toward an African Theology,* "hate is ultimately self-defeating because it sooner or later reduces one to the very wicked acts which one condemned in his oppressors. For another thing, hate is difficult to sustain forever, even if it may be useful at one point or other. . . . In this connection it is not without significance that both Elijah Muhammad and Malcolm X modified their positions with time. Yet another reason is that no group, not even the oppressed, is flawlessly righteous and without its share of inhumanity, injustice, and arrogance."

[42]See African-American writer Harold A. Carter, *The Prayer Tradition of Black People* (Valley Forge, Penn.: Judson, 1976), p. 62: "The single most remarkable trait of Black prayers was the total absence of the spirit of hate, revenge, and malice, especially to the White power structure. There was a positive affirmation of life, expressed in praise." Compare Stephen Hays's report of a slave woman's prayer: "O Lord, bless my master. When he calls upon thee to damn his soul, do not hear him, do not hear him, but hear me—save him—make him know he is wicked, and he will pray to thee" (1816; in Washington, ed., *Conversations with God,* p. 19).

[43]For continuing injustices, see, for example, judicial injustice in Nigeria ("Nigeria: Can Oil and Democracy Mix?" *Amnesty Action,* Fall 1995, pp. 1, 3). One African scholar notes, "In Africa there has been uneasiness between member states of the Organisation of the African Unity resulting in much carnage and wastage of badly needed resources, both human and material: Ethiopia versus Somalia, Uganda versus Tanzania, Uganda versus Kenya, Ghana versus Guinea, Ghana versus Togoland, and so on. Nigeria saw much carnage and wanton destruction of her resources as a result of a cruel and bloody civil war lasting from 1967 to 1970. Bribery and corruption are front-page news in Africa as in America, in Asia as in Europe" (Pobee, *Toward an African Theology,* p. 107). Another adds that Africans are capable of evils as well as of good, just like all peoples (Mbiti, *African Religions,* p. 274). The first complains that some advocates for liberation further advocate an oppression of the former oppressors—which brings the liberated down to the oppressors' moral level (Pobee, *Toward an African Theology,* p. 141)—that is, it allows the oppressors to define us and to define the terms of "success."

[44]This is an international problem—for example, boys raiding a boarding school in Kenya, raping seventy-one schoolgirls and causing the deaths of nineteen others in the process (*Newsweek,* August 12, 1991, p. 15); or police forcing Cameroonian women escaped from harems to return there (Jorge I. Domínguez, "Assessing Human Rights Conditions," in *Enhancing Global Human Rights,* by Domínguez et al., p. 92); or a Turkish judge upholding a husband's right to beat his wife (Rosemary Mumbi, "Battered Women," in *Our Time Has Come,* ed. Mbugua, p. 67); see further examples in "Against Their Will: Rape and Sexual Abuse in Custody," *Amnesty Action,* January 1992, p. 6. The history of most cultures is unfortunately replete with examples of men repressing women

instead of honoring them, and many cultures continue to practice such customs today (see, for example, Keener, *Paul, Women and Wives,* pp. 7-8; G. G. Hull, "Under the Yoke: Facing the Challenge of Global Oppression," in *World Christian Summer Reader 1990* [Pasadena, Calif.: World Christian]: 16-19; and the following essays in *Our Time Has Come:* Mary Dija Ogebe, "Social Injustice," pp. 61-66; F. N. Chola, "Child Abuse in Africa," pp. 71-74; Maureen Mnkandla, "Sexual Abuse," pp. 88-93). Womanist authors in particular, writing from the special vantage point of being both women and African-American, critique the multidimensional character of oppression (see, for example, Jacquelyn Grant, *White Women's Christ and Black Women's Jesus* [Atlanta: Scholars, 1989], pp. 195-201; Kelly Brown Douglas, "To Reflect the Image of God," in *Living the Intersection,* ed. Sanders, pp. 67-77).

[45]This is not to deny that Whites can be oppressed; Bell (*And We Are Not Saved,* p. 254) observes that they too are often "exploited, deceived, and betrayed by those in power." But they are not oppressed as a *race* in this country (race-baiting political rhetoric aside), and therefore we must address their oppression in other than racial terms.

[46]Wright, *A. Philip Randolph,* pp. 58-59.

[47]Thomas F. Pettigrew, *Racially Separate or Together?* (New York: McGraw-Hill, 1971), pp. 303-7.

[48]Ibid., p. 307.

[49]Spencer Perkins and Chris Rice, *More Than Equals* (Downers Grove, Ill.: InterVarsity Press, 1993), pp. 140-42.

[50]Katz, *White Awareness,* p. vi.

[51]See, for example, Kenneth Scott Latourette, *Three Centuries of Advance, A.D. 1500-A.D. 1800,* vo 3 of *A History of the Expansion of Christianity* (New York: Harper & Brothers, 1939), pp. 232-39, especially pp. 236-37. Others report that some Moravians went so far as to become slaves themselves.

[52]Bernard Asbell, "Not like Other Children," in *Teaching in the Inner City,* ed. Stone and Schneider, p. 21, quoting the superintendent of a nearly all-Black school district in 1970: "If the white world could understand . . . how the nonwhite has had hostility trampled into him for a hundred years, then the white world would begin to understand the problem they have given us to unravel in the lives of these children. Maybe they'd understand how hard it is to convince a kid, in the face of all his home and community influences, that he really belongs in the same world a white man belongs in."

[53]Also acknowledged by White writers on the subject, such as Katz, *White Awareness,* p. 4; compare Schlesinger, *Disuniting of America,* pp. 15, 19, 38, 53, 58, 60 (though he especially warns against pressing culture-specific education as far as separatism, pp. 16-17).

[54]At the beginning of the Union the colonies needed assurances of states' rights. Attempts to adjust geographical districts to accommodate racial differences (admittedly not the intention of those who designed geographical districts) have currently been reversed; more radical suggestions of representation have met with stiffer resistance (Lani Guinier's proposals may have cost her a Supreme Court seat). The framers of the Constitution favored geographical representation, an issue in their day; still, one wonders if they *might* not have arranged matters differently had they confronted our current social situation of racial division and held contemporary views on racial equality.

[55]Sterling, *We Are Your Sisters,* pp. 274-75.

[56]Edward G. Olsen, "What Shall We Teach About Race and Racism?" in *Teaching in the Inner City,* ed. Stone and Schneider, p. 357.

[57]See Carlos F. Díaz, "Resistance to Multicultural Education," in *Multicultural Education for the Twenty-first Century,* ed. Díaz, p. 195.

[58]See B. M. Bullivant, "Culture: Its Nature and Meaning for Educators," in *Multicultural Education: Issues and Perspectives,* ed. Banks and Banks, pp. 39-40. In the Bible, members of a minority within a larger society should seek its good for their own sake (Jeremiah 29:7) and for others' (2 Kings 7:8-10), even if that society has marginalized them.

[59]Olsen, "What Shall We Teach?" p. 360.

[60]Bennett, *Before the "Mayflower,"* p. 196.

[61]See Perkins and Rice, *More Than Equals,* p. 142 and elsewhere. The African-American psychiatrists Grier and Cobbs (*Jesus Bag,* pp. 166-80) contended in 1971 (when religion was admittedly more

pervasive in the Black community) that the solution that could surmount the Black-White impasse flows from the moral strength in Black Americans' religious experience.

[62]Skinner, *How Black Is the Gospel?* p. 35. Even many churches within the same denomination are often segregated from one another by race and culture (see, for example, Johnson et al., *Into the Main Stream,* p. 281); but some degree of basic separation remains inevitable as long as each holds to its own cultural traditions. Nevertheless, Black Christians have historically favored reconciliation because they recognized the problem (for example, Benjamin E. Mays, then president of Morehouse College, in *Seeking to Be Christian in Race Relations* [New York: Friendship, 1946]).

[63]Pannell, *Coming Race Wars?* pp. 106-7. West (*Race Matters,* p. 58) also recognizes the role of religious institutions as some of the few forces really working for the Black community. Mukenge (*Black Church,* p. 204) contends that the church has "a special ability to maintain mental health and psychological stability" in the current crisis situation.

[64]Thurman, *Jesus the Disinherited,* pp. 11-12.

[65]George H. Gallup Jr. and Timothy Jones, "Uncovering America's Hidden Saints," *Christianity Today,* August 17, 1992, p. 28. Awareness of the need to address such issues is also increasing (see Billy Graham, "Racism and the Evangelical Church," *Christianity Today,* October 4, 1993, p. 27: "Racial and ethnic hostility is the foremost social problem facing our world today"). Like many Christian publications, *Christianity Today* fairly regularly includes articles by both Black and White authors on the importance of racial reconciliation in the Christian community: for example, Robin McDonald, "Stretch Your Racial Comfort Zone," June 22, 1992, p. 14; Ken Sidey, "What's in a Word?" February 5, 1990, pp. 40-41; Glandion Carney, "Amen, Brother!" March 19, 1990, pp. 21-23.

[66]Sara Bullard, *Free at Last: A History of the Civil Rights Movement and Those Who Died in the Struggle* (New York: Southern Poverty Law Center, 1993), pp. 66-67. See also, for example, William Hanson, a White worker in SNCC, jailed and then beaten by other White inmates (Branch, *Parting the Waters,* p. 622).

[67]African-American journalist Edward Gilbreath, in "Billy Graham Had a Dream," *Christian History* 14 (August 1995): 44-46. On Graham's opposition to segregation and inclusion of Black staffers, see also Branch, *Parting the Waters,* p. 227.

[68]Branch, *Parting the Waters,* p. 314. Contrast even Adam Clayton Powell, who created serious problems for King (ibid.).

[69]Ibid., pp. 227-28, 594-95, 602. They mutually agreed that it was tactically wiser to keep their cooperation especially private. Graham *was* on the right side, despite the unpopularity of such a position among many of his southern White supporters. He could have said more, a deficiency he seems to be making up more today.

[70]Perkins and Rice, *More Than Equals* (see above).

[71]As Pobee notes in his demand for reconciliation (*African Theology,* p. 37), "Neither can we accept false detente, collusion-detente, and capitulation-detente, because these are bogeys and devilish parodies of true reconciliation."

[72]The story of John Perkins, a Black evangelical minister active in the Civil Rights Movement, community development and social activism, is told in John Perkins, *Let Justice Roll Down* (Ventura, Calif.: Regal, 1976), and *With Justice for All* (Ventura, Calif.: Regal, 1982); Gordon D. Aeschliman, *John Perkins: Land Where My Father Died* (Ventura, Calif.: Regal, 1987).

[73]For a White Harvard psychiatrist's analysis and critique of the way White liberals have traditionally sought to bring Black ghetto children "up" to their own cultural level, assuming their social supe-riority and demeaning Black culture in the process, see Robert Coles, "Children of the American Ghetto," in *Teaching in the Inner City,* ed. Stone and Schneider, pp. 136-37.

[74]See also, for example, McKissic, *Beyond Roots,* p. 55.

[75]Lincoln, *Race, Religion,* p. 12.

[76]Woodward, *Strange Career of Jim Crow,* p. 51.

[77]Josephus *Against Apion* 2.210 (LCL 1:376-79).

[78]News reports include Gayle White, "Colorblind Calling," *The Atlanta Journal & Constitution,* November 3, 1991, pp. M1, 4 (the fullest account); Flo Johnston, "Ordination Will Cross Racial Lines," *Chicago Tribune,* August 9, 1991, NS 2, p. 9; see also *Canton [Ohio] Repository,* January 25, 1992, p. A6; *Raleigh News & Observer,* September 1, 1991, p. C1; *Durham Herald-Sun,* July

20, 1991, p. A5. See a related story in *Urbana Update* 6 (Winter 1991): 3, 5; testimonies in "A White Convert to the Black Church," *The Reconciler* 2 (Spring 1995): 1, 8; "White Minister Converts to Black Christianity," *Spirit of Truth,* August 1992, pp. 42-43. Northern churches dually aligned with the National and American Baptist conventions have traditionally included more multiracial ministries.

[79]Cited in White, "Colorblind Calling," p. 4.

[80]On Luke 7:1-10, see Craig S. Keener, "Encounter with Truth: The Centurion's Servant," *A.M.E. Zion Missionary Seer,* November 1994, p. 9.

[81]We stress "temporarily" because racism apparently appeared even at Azusa Street. In one account Charles Parham, who advocated British Israelism, unsuccessfully tried to seize the Azusa Street Mission from William Seymour. See especially Cecil Robeck, "William J. Seymour and 'the Bible Evidence,' " in *Initial Evidence: Historical and Biblical Perspectives on the Pentecostal Doctrine of Spirit Baptism,* ed. Gary B. McGee (Peabody, Mass.: Hendrickson, 1991), pp. 72-95.

[82]See, for example, James S. Tinney, "William J. Seymour: Father of Modern-Day Pentecostalism," in *Black Apostles,* ed. Burkett and Newman, pp. 213-25; see also Breckenridge and Breckenridge, *What Color Is Your God?* p. 220, and White Pentecostal literature: Edith Blumhofer, *The Assemblies of God* (Springfield, Mo.: Gospel Publishing House, 1985), pp. 28-30; William J. Menzies, *Anointed to Serve* (Springfield, Mo.: Gospel Publishing House, 1971), pp. 48-49.

[83]Hollenweger, *The Pentecostals,* p. xxviii. Even some indigenous movements not currently associated with mainstream Pentecostalism have roots in movements related to Pentecostalism; for example, the vast Zionist wing of South Africa's independent churches derives from John Alexander Dowie and the Apostolic Faith Mission (ibid., p. 65). The movement especially encourages the marginalized (ibid., pp. 457-63).

[84]For example, Jarena Lee (c. 1808), describing her "sanctification" experience and ecstatic joy that accompanied it (see Washington, ed., *Conversations with God,* pp. 14-15), and probably also David Alexander Payne (1837; ibid., pp. 34-35). For faith in the efficacy of prayer, consider Sojourner Truth (1878; ibid., p. 55) and Amanda Smith (1893, p. 72); for intimate communion with God, an example is Elizabeth Dabney (1945; ibid., pp. 176-77). See especially the description of hearing God's voice at Azusa Street by C. H. Mason (1907; ibid., pp. 112-13).

[85]The prayer of James Alexander Forbes Jr. in Washington, ed., *Conversations with God,* pp. 231-2.

[86]See Lincoln and Mamiya, *Black Church,* pp. 76, 79, 81; also Frank Robinson, "C. H. Mason and the White COGIC" (West Angeles Church of God in Christ tape ministry, 3045 Crenshaw Blvd., Los Angeles, CA 90016); Breckenridge and Breckenridge, *What Color Is Your God?* p. 219. The predominantly White Assemblies of God ordained Black ministers as early as 1915, but by the midcentury had capitulated to the racism of the nation and deferred, their statement claimed, to COGIC, until the late 1950s (see fully Howard N. Kenyon, "Black Ministers in the Assemblies of God," *A/G Heritage,* Spring 1987, pp. 10-20; this helpful article was forwarded to us by Gary McGee of the Assemblies of God Seminary).

[87]*The Ku Klux Klan,* ed. Sara Bullard, 4th ed. (Montgomery, Ala.: Klanwatch, 1991), p. 47. Readers may secure this very important booklet from Klanwatch, a project of the Southern Poverty Law Center, 400 Washington Ave., Montgomery, Alabama 36104.

[88]Edith Blumhofer, *Aimee Semple McPherson* (Grand Rapids, Mich.: Eerdmans, 1993), p. 276.

[89]See, for example, Rev. and Mrs. Willie Spencer, *Church of God: Black Women in the Church, Historical Highlights and Profiles* (Pittsburgh: Magna Graphics, 1986), p. iii (addressing especially the Cleveland, Tennessee, Church of God), and especially Cheryl J. Sanders, *Saints in Exile: The Holiness-Pentecostal Experience in African American Religion and Culture* (New York: Oxford University Press, 1996), chap. 1, "The Sanctified Churches and Christian Reform: Confronting the Barriers of Race, Sex and Class," pp. 17-34 (in our prepublication copy of the manuscript, which Professor Sanders graciously provided), especially on William Seymour and Azusa Street, pp. 27-34. On sentiments of racial equality in postbellum evangelicalism, see also Magnuson, *Salvation in the Slums,* pp. 118-26.

[90]See especially David Edwin Harrell Jr., *White Sects and Black Men in the Recent South* (Nashville: Vanderbilt University Press, 1971), chap. 4, "Integration and the Sects," pp. 78-106. A. A. Allen broke racial barriers in Atlanta, Little Rock and Winston-Salem in the 1950s and had an interracial

ministry team by the early 1960s (ibid., pp. 104-5), despite his reported theological and behavioral problems (compare David Edwin Harrell Jr., *All Things Are Possible* [Bloomington: Indiana University Press, 1975], pp. 66-75).

[91]See J. Lee Grady, "Pentecostals Renounce Racism," *Christianity Today*, December 12, 1994, p. 58. See COGIC bishop Ithiel Clemmons in "Racial and Spiritual Unity in the Body of Christ," *A/G Advance/Enrichment* 34 (Fall 1995): 66-68.

[92]Jesus' teachings do not square well with racism, as one Black preacher pointed out in a story about a Black man who asked a White man for some food. The White man told him to come around to the back door, then determined to lead him in a prayer when he brought out the food. "Repeat after me," he began. "Our Father . . ." The Black man started, "Your Father." The White man asked why the Black man said "*your* Father," to which the Black man responded, "Well, boss, if I say 'Our Father,' that would make you and me brothers, and I'm 'fraid the Lord wouldn't like it, you makin' your brother come to the back porch to get a piece of bread" (James W. English, *Handyman of the Lord: The Life and Ministry of the Reverend William Holmes Borders* [New York: Meredith, 1967], pp. 33-34).

[93]Compare, for example, Sirach 50:25-26; Josephus *Antiquities of the Jews* 11.84, 114; 12.156; 20.125; *Jewish Wars* 2.232-46; 4 Baruch 8; *m. Giṭṭin* 1:5; *b. Baba Qamma* 38b; *p. Ta'anit* 4:5, §10; *Lamentations Rabbah* 1:1, §§14-15; *Koheleth Rabbah* 10:8, §1; Ferdinand Dexinger, "Limits of Tolerance in Judaism," in *Jewish and Christian Self-Definition*, ed. Ben F. Meyer and E. P. Sanders, 3 vols. (Philadelphia: Fortress, 1980-1982), 2:88-114. More schismatics than full transgressors (see Isaiah Sonne, "The Use of Rabbinic Literature as Historical Sources," *Jewish Quarterly Review* 36 [1945-1946]: 154-62), Samaritans essentially ranked halfway between Israelites and Gentiles, sometimes making classification problematic (see *m. Terumot* 3:9; *t. 'Aboda Zara* 2:8; 3:1, 3, 5; *Terumot* 4:14; *b. Bekorot* 11b; *Megilla* 25b; *Sanhedrin* 57a; *p. Ketubot* 3:1, §3; *Deuteronomy Rabbah* 2:33; compare also Justin *Apology I* 53 with *Dialogus cum Tryphone Judaeo* 41; 120). Some later sources regard them as pseudoproselytes (*b. Qiddušin* 75b; *Numbers Rabbah* 8:9). Samaritan sources also polemicize against Judaism (for example, John Bowman, ed., *Samaritan Documents Relating to Their History, Religion and Life*, Pittsburgh Original Texts and Translations Series 2 [Pittsburgh: Pickwick, 1977], p. 299).

[94]Spencer Perkins also points this out in his article "Can Blacks and Whites Be Neighbors?" *Urban Family*, Winter 1992, pp. 21-23, and in *More Than Equals*. That a Samaritan (in this case probably a trader) is found outside Samaria is not surprising; see, for example, *Corpus Papyrorum Judaicarum* 3:102-4, §513; 3:105, §514; A. T. Kraabel, "New Evidence of the Samaritan Diaspora Has Been Found on Delos," *Biblical Archaeologist* 47 (1984): 44-46.

[95]On the proverbial impurity of Samaritan women, see, for example, *m. Niddah* 4:1; 5:1; *Toharot* 5:8; *b. Šabbat* 17a; compare *b. Yebamot* 68a; for the possible antiquity of the ruling, see David Daube, *The New Testament and Rabbinic Judaism* (New York: Arno, 1973), p. 373. Much Samaritan food (Jn 4:8) was unclean (see *m. Demai* 2:3; *Šebi'it* 8:10; *p. 'Aboda Zara* 5:11, §2; compare *p. 'Aboda Zara* 5:4, §3) or at least needed to be tithed first (*t. Demai* 1:11; 5:24). And the woman's vessel would have been unclean for drinking, since she was unclean (Jn 4:7; compare Gentile vessels in *b. 'Aboda Zara* 67b; 75b, bar.; *Pesaḥim* 44b), though in an early period one could buy wine from Samaritans (*b. 'Erubin* 36b-37a).

[96]Merely prophesying the temple's destruction invited scourging and the threat of death (Jer 26:11; Josephus *Jewish Wars* 6.300-9; E. P. Sanders, *Jesus and Judaism* [Philadelphia: Fortress, 1985], p. 302; see R. E. Winkle, "The Jeremiah Model for Jesus in the Temple," *Andrews University Seminary Studies* 24 [1986]: 155-72). The Sadducees, whose positions depended on keeping peace between the Romans and the people, were permitted to punish violations of the sanctity of the temple—and only this offense—with death (Josephus *Jewish Wars* 6.124-26; *Antiquities of the Jews* 15.417; compare John J. O'Rourke, "Roman Law and the Early Church," in *The Catacombs and the Colosseum* [Valley Forge, Penn.: Judson, 1971], p. 174). Jesus' act in the outer court did not technically qualify, but they undoubtedly regarded it as close enough.

[97]Whatever the possible religious motivations behind the charge against Jesus, it is certainly also political: by claiming to be a king, Jesus implied a worldly kingdom that would challenge Rome (see, for example, Bruce, *New Testament History*, p. 199). The political charge in Luke 23:2 accurately summarizes the gist of the charge in Mark and Matthew: Jesus was a revolutionary

(Gerhard Schneider, "The Political Charge Against Jesus (Luke 23:2)," in *Jesus and the Politics of His Day* [Cambridge: Cambridge University Press, 1984], pp. 403-14; compare similarly the Johannine charges—J. A. T. Robinson, " 'His Witness Is True': A Test of the Johannine Claim," in *Jesus and the Politics*, pp. 453-76). This is easily the charge of *lese majesty* (Blinzler, *Trial of Jesus*, p. 213, citing *Digest* 48.4.1, 3-4; compare Ernst Bammel, "The *Titulus,*" in *Jesus and the Politics*, p. 357), for which the normal punishment in the provinces was crucifixion (Blinzler, *Trial of Jesus*, p. 238).

[98]These words echo the title of chap. 2 in Skinner's *Words of Revolution*. For background on the text in its own historical context (without the present application), see Craig S. Keener's forthcoming academic commentary on Matthew.

[99]For background on this and other passages, see the appropriate passages in Keener, *IVP Bible Background Commentary*. Cyrene is in North Africa, which included a large Jewish population (see Shim'on Applebaum, *Jews and Greeks in Ancient Cyrene* [Leiden: Brill, 1979]) and, like most Jewish communities in the Empire, probably boasted local converts as well (Lucius is a Greek name, typical in eastern Mediterranean cities regardless of ancestry). "Niger" was a common name, among Egyptian Jews and others (for example, *Corpus Papyrorum Judaicarum* 2:139, §243; 2:140, §§248-49; 2:141-42, §254; 2:143, §261; 2:145, §§269-70; 2:146, §274; 2:147, §§275-76), Jews elsewhere (Josephus *Jewish Wars* 3.11; 4.359-63) and Romans (Tacitus *Annals* 3.66; inscription in A. Deissmann, *Light from the Ancient East* [Grand Rapids, Mich.: Baker Book House, 1978], p. 443; compare E. A. Judge, *Rank and Status in the World of the Caesars and St. Paul* [Canterbury, U.K.: University of Canterbury, 1982], p. 36 n. 20). Although names like "Niger" normally did *not* convey significance regarding complexion (Snowden, *Blacks in Antiquity*, p. 12), the use of a popular *nick*name here may convey a dark complexion (see Felder, *Troubling Biblical Waters*, pp. 47-48; also acknowledged by other writers, such as Michael Green, *I Believe in the Holy Spirit*, 2nd rev. ed. [Grand Rapids, Mich.: Eerdmans, 1989], p. 123).

[100]That Manaen was "brought up" with Herod Antipas may mean as a slave in his household, freed on reaching adulthood as was common (Rawson, "Children in the Roman *Familia,*" pp. 12-13; compare *Joseph and Asenath* 10:4/6; 17:4). He might have been the son of Herod's nursemaid (see Dixon, *Roman Mother*, p. 128; though compare F. F. Bruce, *Commentary on Acts*, New International Commentary on the New Testament [Grand Rapids, Mich.: Eerdmans, 1977], pp. 260-61, who presupposes a higher social status, as in *SIG* 2.798). Some scholars have also proposed that Paul's citizenship came from his parents' being freed slaves; one of the synagogues mentioned in Acts 6:9 consisted of former slaves and their families (*Inscriptions Reveal* [Jerusalem: Israel Museum, 1973], pp. 83, 182-83, §182), and Paul probably belonged either to this one (see Bruce, *Acts of the Apostles*, p. 156; but compare Deissmann, *Light from the Ancient East*, p. 441) or—perhaps more likely (based on what Luke tells us)—to the synagogue of the Cilicians (immigrants from the vicinity of Tarsus) before he became a follower of Jesus. Freedmen achieved citizenship (J. E. Stambaugh and D. L. Balch, *The Social Environment of the New Testament* [Philadelphia: Westminster Press, 1986], p. 31) and often achieved greater wealth than the freeborn (for example, Petronius *Satyricon* 57). Being freeborn, however, afforded higher status (Martial *Epigrams* 1.81; Gaius *Institutes* 1.10); and whatever his ancestry, Paul was freeborn (Acts 22:28).

[101]Paul's activity, if understood, would have appeared virtuous within Judaism; compare Acts 18:18 and 21:24 with Josephus *Antiquities of the Jews* 19.293-94; *Jewish Wars* 2.313-14.

[102]Josephus *Antiquities of the Jews* 15.417; *Jewish Wars* 6.124-26.

[103]Other Roman prefects in Judea before the war also left cases pending (see A. N. Sherwin-White, *Roman Society and Roman Law in the New Testament* [Oxford: Oxford University Press, 1963], p. 53), and bribery was rampant (Josephus *Jewish Wars* 2.273; compare *Koheleth Rabbah* 11:1, §1); for Felix's corruption, see also Josephus *Antiquities of the Jews* 20.182.

[104]See the exploratory paper by Oliver Trimiew, "Paul as Prisoner," presented at the 1993 Society of Biblical Literature meeting in Washington, D.C.

[105]Various interpretations of the dividing wall exist, but it seems best to interpret it with the following context, in which God's people appear as a temple (2:19-22), as in some contemporary Jewish documents (for example, 1QS 8.5-9; Bertril Gärtner, *The Temple and the Community in Qumran and the New Testament* [Cambridge: Cambridge University Press, 1965], pp. 16-46). This works well on the assumption that Paul wrote Ephesians (compare 1 Corinthians 3:16), an assumption

often, however, disputed.

[106]Josephus *Jewish Wars* 2.266-70. Paul's whole letter to the Romans is also significant as a summons to ethnic reconciliation (in that case, the salvation-historically significant Jewish-Gentile barrier); compare Keener, *IVP Bible Background Commentary*, p. 412-13; Craig S. Keener, "Missions and Racial Reconciliation in Romans," *A.M.E. Zion Missionary Seer*, January 1995, p. 7; Craig S. Keener, "Exorcising Racism," *The Crucible*, Winter 1992, p. 24.

[107]See, for example, Keener, *Paul, Women and Wives*, p. 204, and sources cited there. On the cultural context of exhortations to submission, see further Alan Padgett, "The Pauline Rationale for Submission," *Evangelical Quarterly* 59 (1987): 39-52.

[108]The message of Christ, once truly understood, has brought even former Klansmen to repentance, leading them to humble themselves and devote themselves to work for the Black community: for example, Tom Tarrants, now director of a School of Urban Mission in Washington, D.C. (see Tom Tarrants, "The Conversion of a Klansman," *Urban Family*, Spring 1992, pp. 22-23). But that development also places a demand on us that requires special grace: we must accept their repentance and their desire to make restitution for their sin against us.

[109]It could be argued that El-Hajj Malik El-Shabazz, earlier known as Malcolm X, paid a price for it too, if the Nation of Islam itself wished to silence him for moving away from their ranks and for a more mainstream attitude toward Christians, Whites and other groups from which he had previously been alienated.

[110]Bennett, *Before the "Mayflower,"* pp. 107-10.

[111]Williams, *Destruction of Black Civilization*, pp. 311-12.

[112]Ibid., p. 327.

[113]Skinner, *How Black Is the Gospel?* p. 34.

[114]Olsen, "What Shall We Teach?" p. 359.

[115]Robert Coles, "White Pieties and Black Reality," in *Teaching in the Inner City*, ed. Stone and Schneider, pp. 80-85; the quotes are from p. 83.

[116]See Pannell, *Coming Race Wars?* p. 117: nearly 40 percent "of the work force commutes from suburb to suburb because manufacturing and related industries have moved there. Nearly 60 percent of all the office space in the country is located in the suburbs."

[117]*Voting* rights do empower the individual, but economic power, which remains highly influential in our society, is not equitably distributed, nor is access to it equitably distributed (see also Black evangelical John Perkins, *With Justice for All*, p. 169). Offering that observation is, of course, much easier for us than proposing a solution; but see John Perkins, *Beyond Charity* (Grand Rapids, Mich.: Baker Book House, 1993).

[118]Bell, *And We Are Not Saved*, p. 47. Others present the inequities in still starker terms; West (*Race Matters*, p. 6) declares that in 1989 1 percent of the population owned 37 percent of the wealth, and the 9 percent directly below it owned about 50 percent. The decline of industrial jobs in the North and the mechanization of southern agriculture (which employed 50 percent of Black teenagers four decades ago) have contributed materially to Black unemployment; new immigrants and White women also now compete for jobs in the same marketplace (West, *Race Matters*, p. 54). In such a climate, prejudice, inferior educational opportunities in early childhood and the despair that often accompanies such problems will naturally produce high unemployment.

[119]Williams, *Destruction of Black Civilization*, p. 326.

[120]See also Francis J. Grimké, "Sources from Which No Help May Be Expected: The General Government, Political Parties," delivered November 27, 1900; in *Works*, 1:247-60.

[121]Lomax, "When 'Nonviolence' Meets 'Black Power,'" p. 173. African-Americans are more apt to recognize that human nature is intrinsically evil (or at least largely evil) than are White Americans, possibly due to our "experience of oppression and discrimination by American society" (Robert T. Carter, "Cultural Value Differences Between African Americans and White Americans," *Journal of College Student Development* 31 [January 1990]: 76).

[122]Bishop Wellington Boone, at a New Generation student conference. Or as Derrick Bell describes the ideal motivation for African-Americans, "If revenge was a component of their drive, it was not the retaliatory 'we will get them' but the competitive 'we will *show* them' " (*And We Are Not Saved*, p. 217).

[123]History has made trust difficult even within the church; compare some responses from within the

Black church toward the Southern Baptist Convention's attempts to repudiate racism (Timothy Morgan, "Racist No More?" *Christianity Today,* August 14, 1995, p. 53). The conflict seems to center on the question, Should one accept fellow Christians' attempts and help them to move further, or fear being betrayed again since it has often happened before?

[124]Rajmohan Gandhi, "African Americans, What Will You Offer to the World?" *Urban Family,* Fall 1993, p. 15.

[125]Louis Farrakhan, *A Torchlight for America* (Chicago: FCN, 1993), p. 82: "our suffering uniquely prepares us not as slaves . . . or second-class citizens, but to be examples and leaders for humanity." This is not to agree with nineteenth-century U.S. apologists for slavery that any measure of positive outcome justified the evil perpetrated (on these apologists, see Cannon, "Slave Ideology and Biblical Interpretation," pp. 122-23).

[126]This is not, however, to claim that one should do evil that good might come; see especially Mignon R. Jacobs and Gloria A. Johnson, "The Conceptual Dynamics of Good and Evil in the Joseph Story," paper presented at the 1994 Society of Biblical Literature meeting in Chicago.

[127]Many of the perspectives in this paragraph derive from a lecture given by Zanna Towns, of Kenya, at Christian Stronghold Baptist Church in Philadelphia on March 7, 1993. The tape of the lecture, "Breaking Barriers," providing a positive African perspective on our African-American heritage, was graciously forwarded to us by Adele Brooks of Carver Foreign Missions (an African-American missions agency) in Atlanta.

[128]For example, William Douglass, *Sermons Preached in the African Protestant Episcopal Church of St. Thomas, Philadelphia* (Philadelphia: King & Baird, 1854), pp. 221-26; Lemuel Haynes (1776) in Washington, ed., *Conversations with God,* p. 6. This was also the historic view of salvation among Black Baptists, before the advent of White liberal theology; see the eloquent essays in Edward M. Brawley, ed., *The Negro Baptist Pulpit* (Philadelphia: American Baptist Publication Society, 1890), especially chaps. 5-9. Black Methodists held a similar conviction; for example, M. C. B. Mason, *The Gospel Message* (Cincinnati: Jennings and Graham, 1905). Mason was corresponding secretary of the Freedmen's Aid and Southern Education Society. See p. 22: the gospel requires that one be "born again," and other proposed ways or religions are inadequate.

[129]See Sanders, *Slavery and Conversion,* pp. 34-63 (noting the same characteristics in biblical conversion stories, pp. 59-63); for supernatural visions or hearing, see pp. 44-45.

Bibliography

This bibliography includes only sources cited directly in *Black Man's Religion* or in the second, follow-up volume, which will address more specific biblical and theological objections to Christianity. (The most helpful contributions are asterisked.) Brief news reports without titles or authors are listed under the periodicals in which they appeared.

Abogunrin, S. O. "The Modern Search of the Historical Jesus in Relation to Christianity in Africa." *Africa Theological Journal* 9, no. 3 (1980): 18-29.

Achilles Tatius. *Clitophon and Leucippe.* Translated by S. Gaselee. Loeb Classical Libary. London: Wm. Heinemann/New York: G. P. Putnam's Sons, 1917.

Adam, S., with J. Vercoutter. "The Importance of Nubia: A Link Between Central Africa and the Mediterranean." In *Ancient Civilizations of Africa,* pp. 226-43. Edited by G. Mokhtar. Vol. 2 of *General History of Africa.* Berkeley: University of California Press/London: Heinemann Educational Books/Paris: United Nations Educational, Scientific and Cultural Organizations, 1981.

**Adamo, David Tuesday. "The Place of Africa and Africans in the Old Testament and Its Environment." Ph.D. dissertation, Baylor University, 1986.

Adams, Alice Dana. *The Neglected Period of Anti-slavery in America (1808-1831).* Radcliffe College Monographs 14. Gloucester, Mass.: Peter Smith, 1964.

Adams, William Y. "Geography and Population of the Nile Valley." In *Africa in Antiquity 1: The Arts of Ancient Nubia and the Sudan—the Essays,* pp. 16-25. Brooklyn, N.Y.: Brooklyn Museum, 1978.

———. "Medieval Nubia." In *Africa in Antiquity 1: The Arts of Ancient Nubia and the Sudan—the Essays,* pp. 120-25. Brooklyn, N.Y.: Brooklyn Museum, 1978.

*———. *Nubia: Corridor to Africa.* Princeton, N.J.: Princeton University Press, 1977.

Aeschliman, Gordon D. *John Perkins: Land Where My Father Died.* Ventura, Calif.: Regal, 1987.

Africa News, July 6-19, 1992, p. 16.

"Against Their Will: Rape and Sexual Abuse in Custody." *Amnesty Action,* January 1992, p. 6.

Aharoni, Yohanan. *The Archaeology of the Land of Israel.* Translated by Anson F. Rainey. Philadelphia: Westminster Press, 1982.

———. *The Land of the Bible: A Historical Geography.* London: Burns & Oates, 1979.

———. "The Negeb." In *Archaeology and Old Testament Study.* Edited by D. Winton Thomas. Oxford: Clarendon, 1967.

Albright, William Foxwell. *The Biblical Period from Abraham to Ezra.* New York: Harper & Row, 1963.

———. *From the Stone Age to Christianity: Monotheism and the Historical Process.* Baltimore: Johns Hopkins University Press, 1946.

———. "The Furniture of El in Canaanite Mythology." *Bulletin of the American Schools of Oriental Research* 91 (October 1943): 42-43.

———. "What Were the Cherubim?" In *The Biblical Archaeologist Reader,* pp. 95-97. Edited by G. Ernest Wright and David Noel Freedman. Garden City, N.Y.: Doubleday, 1961.

———. *Yahweh and the Gods of Canaan.* Garden City, N.Y.: Doubleday, 1968.

Aldred, Cyril. *Egypt to the End of the Old Kingdom.* New York: McGraw-Hill/London: Thames & Hudson, 1965.

Allen, Richard. *The Life Experience and Gospel Labors of the Rt. Rev. Richard Allen, to Which Is Annexed The Rise and Progress of the African Methodist Episcopal Church in the United States of America.* Introduction by George A. Singleton. New York: Abingdon, 1960.

Allen, Willoughby C. *A Critical and Exegetical Commentary on the Gospel According to St. Matthew.* 3rd ed. International Critical Commentaries. Edinburgh: T & T Clark, 1977.

"Amazing Grace: Fifty Years of the Black Church." *Ebony,* April 1995, pp. 87-96.

Amnesty Action, January 1991, p. 7; November 1991, p. 4; Summer 1993, p. 4; Fall 1993, pp. 2, 4.

Anderson, Thornton. *Creating the Constitution: The Convention of 1787 and the First Congress.* University Park: Pennsylvania State University Press, 1993.

Andrews, S. J. "The Worship of the Tabernacle Compared with That of the Second Temple." *Journal of Biblical Literature* 6 (June 1886): 56-68.

Andrews, William L., ed. *Sisters of the Spirit: Three Black Women's Autobiographies of the Nineteenth Century.* Bloomington: Indiana University Press, 1986.

Anfray, F. "The Civilization of Aksum from the First to the Seventh Century." In *Ancient Civilizations of Africa,* pp. 362-80. Edited by G. Mokhtar. Vol. 2 of *General History of Africa.* Berkeley: University of California Press/London: Heinemann Educational Books/Paris: United Nations Educational, Scientific and Cultural Organizations, 1981.

Ante-Nicene Fathers: The Writings of the Fathers down to A.D. 325. Vol. 3. Edited by Alexander Roberts and James Donaldson. Peabody, Mass.: Hendrickson, 1994.

Apocalypse of Moses. In *The Old Testament Pseudepigrapha.* 2 vols. Edited by James H. Charlesworth. Garden City, N.Y.: Doubleday, 1983-1985.

Applebaum, Shim'on. "Economic Life in Palestine." In *The Jewish People in the First Century: Historical Geography, Political History, Social, Cultural and Religious Life and Institutions,* pp. 631-700. Edited by S. Safrai and M. Stern with D. Flusser and W. C. van Unnik. 2 vols. Assen: Van Gorcum, 1974 (vol. 1); Philadelphia: Fortress, 1976 (vol. 2).

_____. *Jews and Greeks in Ancient Cyrene.* Studies in Judaism in Late Antiquity 28. Leiden: Brill, 1979.

Apuleius. *Metamorphoses (The Golden Ass).* Translated by W. Adlington. Rev. ed. by S. Gaselee. Loeb Classical Library. Cambridge, Mass.: Harvard University Press, 1915.

Aristotle. *Politics.* Translated by H. Rackham. Loeb Classical Library. Cambridge, Mass.: Harvard University Press/London: Heinemann, 1932.

Arkell, A. J. "The Influence of Christian Nubia in the Chad Area Between A.D. 800-1200." *Kush* 11 (1963): 315-19.

_____. "The Valley of the Nile." In *The Dawn of African History,* pp. 7-12. Edited by Roland Oliver. London: Oxford University Press, 1961.

Aronson, David. "The Inside Story." *Teaching Tolerance,* Spring 1995, pp. 23-29.

Arowele, P. J. "This Generation Seeks Signs: The Miracles of Jesus with Reference to the African Situation." *African Theological Journal* 10, no. 3 (1981): 17-28.

"Aryan World Congress Draws Two Hundred Supremacists." *SPLC Report* (Southern Poverty Law Center) 25 (September 1995): 4.

*Asante, Molefi Kete. *Kemet, Afrocentricity and Knowledge.* Trenton, N.J.: Africa World Press, 1990.

Asbell, Bernard. "Not like Other Children." In *Teaching in the Inner City: A Book of Readings,* pp. 7-23. Edited by James C. Stone and Frederick W. Schneider. Commitment to Teaching 3. New York: Thomas Y. Crowell, 1970.

Atmore, Anthony, Gillian Stacey and Werner Forman, *Black Kingdoms, Black Peoples: The West African Heritage.* London: Orbis, 1979.

Aune, David E. "Greco-Roman Biography." In *Greco-Roman Literature and the New Testament: Selected Forms and Genres,* pp. 107-26. Edited by David E. Aune. SBL Sources for Biblical Study 21. Atlanta: Scholars Press, 1988.

_____. *The New Testament in Its Literary Environment.* Library of Early Christianity 8. Philadelphia: Westminster Press, 1987.

_____. *Prophecy in Early Christianity and the Ancient Mediterranean World.* Grand Rapids, Mich.:

Eerdmans, 1983.

The Babylonian Talmud. Edited by Isidore Epstein. London: Soncino, 1948.

Bacon, Leonard. *Slavery Discussed in Occasional Essays, from 1833 to 1846.* New York: Baker & Scribner, 1846. Reprint New York: Arno/New York Times, 1969.

Badawy, Alexander. *A History of Egyptian Architecture: The Empire (1580-1085 B.C.).* Berkeley: University of California Press, 1968.

Baer, Hans A. *The Black Spiritual Movement: A Religious Response to Racism.* Knoxville: University of Tennessee Press, 1984.

Bailey, Randall C. "Beyond Identification: The Use of Africans in Old Testament Poetry and Narratives." In *Stony the Road We Trod: African American Biblical Interpretation,* pp. 165-84. Edited by Cain Hope Felder. Minneapolis: Fortress, 1991.

Bailey, Randall C., and Jacquelyn Grant, eds. *The Recovery of Black Presence: An Interdisciplinary Exploration.* Nashville: Abingdon, 1995.

Bamberger, Bernard J. *Proselytism in the Talmudic Period.* New York: KTAV Publishing House, 1968. (The first edition was published by Hebrew Union College Press, 1939.)

Bammel, Ernst. "The *Titulus.*" In *Jesus and the Politics of His Day,* pp. 353-64. Edited by Ernst Bammel and C. F. D. Moule. Cambridge: Cambridge University Press, 1984.

Banks, James A. "Multicultural Education: Characteristics and Goals." In *Multicultural Education: Issues and Perspectives,* pp. 2-26. Edited by James A. Banks and Cherry A. McGee Banks. Boston: Allyn & Bacon, 1989.

*Barnes, Gilbert Hobbs. *The Antislavery Impulse, 1830-1844.* N.p.: American Historical Associations, 1933. Reprint New York: Harcourt, Brace & World, 1964.

Barnett, Paul. *Is the New Testament Reliable? A Look at the Historical Evidence.* Downers Grove, Ill.: InterVarsity Press, 1986.

Barrett, C. K. *The Gospel According to St. John: An Introduction with Commentary and Notes on the Greek Text.* 2nd ed. Philadelphia: Westminster Press, 1978.

─────. *The Holy Spirit and the Gospel Tradition.* London: S.P.C.K., 1966.

Barry, Mary Franes. "Repression of Blacks in the South, 1890-1945: Enforcing the System of Segregation." In *The Age of Segregation: Race Relations in the South, 1890-1945,* pp. 29-43. Edited by Robert Haws. Jackson: University Press of Mississippi, 1978.

Bassett, John Spencer. *Anti-slavery Leaders of North Carolina.* John Hopkins University Studies in Historical and Political Science 6. Baltimore: Johns Hopkins University Press, 1898.

Baumgarten, J. M. "The Exclusion of 'Netinim' and Proselytes in 4QFlorilegium." *Revue de Qumrân* 8 (June 1972): 87-96.

Bebbington, David W. *Evangelicalism in Modern Britain: A History from the 1730s to the 1980s.* London: Unwin Hyman/Routledge/Grand Rapids, Mich.: Baker Book House, 1989.

─────. "William Wilberforce." In *Eerdmans Handbook to the History of Christianity,* p. 561. Edited by Tim Dowley. Grand Rapids, Mich.: Eerdmans, 1977.

Bediako, Kwame. "Jesus in African Culture: A Ghanaian Perspective." In *Emerging Voices in Global Christian Theology,* pp. 93-121. Edited by William A. Dyrness. Grand Rapids, Mich.: Zondervan, 1994.

Begley, Sharon. "Three Is Not Enough: Surprising New Lessons from the Controversial Science of Race." *Newsweek,* February 13, 1995, pp. 67-69.

Bell, Derrick. *And We Are Not Saved: The Elusive Quest for Racial Justice.* New York: BasicBooks/HarperCollins, 1987.

─────. *Confronting Authority: Reflections of an Ardent Protester.* Boston: Beacon, 1994.

Ben-Jochannan, Yosef A. A. *Africa: Mother of Western Civilization.* N.p.: Alkebu-lan Books Associates, 1971. Reprint Baltimore: Black Classic Press, 1988.

─────. *African Origins of the Major "Western Religions."* N.p.: Alkebu-lan Books Associates, 1970. Reprint Baltimore: Black Classic Press, 1991.

Ben-Levi, Josef. "The First and Second Intermediate Periods in Kemetic History." In *Kemet and the African Worldview: Research, Rescue and Restoration,* pp. 55-69. Edited by Maulana Karenga and Jacob H. Carruthers. Los Angeles: University of Sankore Press, 1986.

**Bennett, Lerone, Jr. *Before the Mayflower: A History of the Negro in America, 1619-1964.* Rev. ed. Baltimore: Penguin, 1966.

_____. "The First Generation." *Ebony,* February 1995, pp. 75-82, 186.

_____. "Martin or Malcolm? The Hero in Black History." *Ebony,* February 1994, pp. 68-76.

_____. "Voices of the Past Speak to the Present." *Ebony,* February 1994, pp. 78-84.

Bennett, Norman Robert. *Mirambo of Tanzania, ca. 1840-1884.* New York: Oxford University Press, 1971.

Benoit, Pierre. *Jesus and the Gospels.* Translated by Benet Weatherhead. 2 vols. New York: Herder & Herder/London: Darton, Longman & Todd, 1973 (vol. 1). New York: Seabury/Crossroad/London: Darton, Longman & Todd, 1974 (vol. 2).

Bentley, William H. "Factors in the Origin and Focus of the National Black Evangelical Association." In *Black Theology: A Documentary History,* 1:233-44. Edited by James H. Cone and Gayraud S. Wilmore. 2 vols. Maryknoll, N.Y.: Orbis Books, 1993.

*Bernal, Martin. *Black Athena: The Afroasiatic Roots of Classical Civilization.* Vol. 1: *The Fabrication of Ancient Greece, 1785-1985.* London: Free Association Books, 1987. Vol. 2: *The Archaeological and Documentary Evidence.* New Brunswick, N.J.: Rutgers University Press, 1991.

Bhatia, Shyam. "A War's Human Booty." *World Press Review,* August 1995, 40. Reprinted from *The Observer,* April 9, 1995.

Bianquis, T. "Egypt from the Arab Conquest Until the End of the Fatimid State (1171)." In *Africa from the Seventh to the Eleventh Century,* pp. 163-93. Edited by M. El Fasi with I. Hrbek. Vol. 3 of *General History of Africa.* Berkeley: University of California Press/London: Heinemann Educational Books/Paris: United Nations Educational, Scientific and Cultural Organization, 1988.

Blassingame, John W. *The Slave Community: Plantation Life in the Antebellum South.* Rev. ed. New York: Oxford University Press, 1979.

_____, ed. *Slave Testimony: Two Centuries of Letters, Speeches, Interviews and Autobiographies.* Baton Rouge: Louisiana State University Press, 1977.

Blidstein, Gerald. "4Q Florilegium and Rabbinic Sources on Bastard and Proselyte." *Revue de Qumrân* 8 (March 1974): 431-35.

Blinzler, Josef. *The Trial of Jesus: The Jewish and Roman Proceedings Against Jesus Christ Described and Assessed from the Oldest Accounts.* Translated by Isabel McHugh and Florence McHugh. Westminster, Md.: Newman, 1959.

Blockson, Charles L. *The Underground Railroad in Pennsylvania.* Jacksonville, N.C.: Flame International, 1981.

Blomberg, Craig. *The Historical Reliability of the Gospels.* Downers Grove, Ill.: InterVarsity Press, 1987.

Blumhofer, Edith L. W. *Aimee Semple McPherson: Everybody's Sister.* Grand Rapids, Mich.: Eerdmans, 1993.

_____. *The Assemblies of God: A Popular History.* Springfield, Mo.: Gospel Publishing House, 1985.

Bockmuehl, Klaus. *The Unreal God of Modern Theology: Bultmann, Barth and the Theology of Atheism: A Call to Recovering the Truth of God's Reality.* Translated by Geoffrey W. Bromiley. Colorado Springs: Helmers & Howard, 1988.

Bond, Julian. *A Time to Speak, a Time to Act: The Movement in Politics.* New York: Simon & Schuster, 1972.

The Book of Mormon. Salt Lake City: Church of Jesus Christ of Latter-day Saints, 1981. (1st ed. 1830.)

The Book of the Dead, or Going Forth by Day: Ideas of the Ancient Egyptians Concerning the Hereafter As Expressed in Their Own Terms. Translated by Thomas George Allen. Oriental Institute of the University of Chicago Studies in Ancient Oriental Civilization 37. Chicago: University of Chicago Press, 1974.

Bowers, Paul. "Nubian Christianity: The Neglected Heritage." *East African Journal of Evangelical Theology* 4, no. 1 (1985).

Bowling, A. "Tell el Amarna." In *Zondervan Pictorial Encyclopedia of the Bible,* 5:617. Edited by Merrill C. Tenney. Grand Rapids, Mich.: Zondervan, 1976.

Bowman, John. *The Fourth Gospel and the Jews: A Study in R. Akiba, Esther and the Gospel of John.* Pittsburgh Theological Monograph 8. Pittsburgh: Pickwick, 1975.

Bowman, John, ed. *Samaritan Documents Relating to Their History, Religion and Life.* Pittsburgh

Original Texts and Translations Series 2. Pittsburgh: Pickwick, 1977.

Boxer, C. R. "The Old Kingdom of the Congo." In *The Dawn of African History,* pp. 75-81. Edited by Roland Oliver. London: Oxford University Press, 1961.

Boyd, Gregory A. *Cynic, Sage or Son of God? Recovering the Real Jesus in an Age of Revisionist Replies.* Wheaton, Ill.: BridgePoint/Victor, 1995.

Boyd, Paul C. *A Biblical and Historical Account.* Vol. 1 of *The African Origin of Christianity.* London: Karia, 1991.

Bradford, Sarah H. *Scenes in the Life of Harriet Tubman.* Auburn, N.Y.: W. J. Moses, 1869. Reprint Freeport, N.Y.: Books for Libraries, 1971.

Bradley, David Henry, Sr. *A History of the A.M.E. Zion Church.* 2 vols. Nashville: Parthenon, 1956-1970.

*Branch, Taylor. *Parting the Waters: America in the King Years, 1954-1963.* New York: Simon & Schuster, 1988.

Brawley, Edward M., ed. *The Negro Baptist Pulpit: A Collection of Sermons and Papers on Baptist Doctrine and Missionary and Educational Work by Colored Baptist Ministers.* Philadelphia: American Baptist Publication Society, 1890. Reprint Freeport, N.Y.: Books for Libraries/Black Heritage Library Collection, 1971.

Breasted, James Henry. *Ancient Records of Egypt.* New York: Russell and Russell, 1906.

*Breckenridge, James, and Lillian Breckenridge. *What Color Is Your God? Multicultural Education in the Church.* Wheaton, Ill.: BridgePoint/Victor, 1995.

Bredero, Adriaan H. *Christendom and Christianity in the Middle Ages: The Relations Between Religion, Church and Society.* Translated by Reinder Bruinsma. Grand Rapids, Mich.: Eerdmans, 1994.

Bright, John. *A History of Israel.* 3rd ed. Philadelphia: Westminster Press, 1981.

Britten, Bruce. *We Don't Want Your White Religion.* 2nd ed. Roodepoort, South Africa: Word of Life, 1996.

Brock, William. "Slavery Not a Misfortune but a Crime." In *Autographs for Freedom,* 2:158. Edited by Julia Griffiths. Auburn, N.Y.: Alden, Beardsley, 1854.

Brown, Antoinette L. "The Size of Souls." In *Autographs for Freedom,* 2:41-43. Edited by Julia Griffiths. Auburn, N.Y.: Alden, Beardsley, 1854.

Brown, Raymond E. *The Death of the Messiah: From Gethsemane to the Grave—a Commentary on the Passion Narratives in the Four Gospels.* 2 vols. New York: Doubleday, 1994.

──────. *The Gospel According to John.* 2 vols. Anchor Bible Commentary 29-29A. Garden City, N.Y.: Doubleday, 1966-1970.

Brownlow, W. G., and A. Pryne. *Ought American Slavery to Be Perpetuated? A Debate Between Rev. W. G. Bronwlow and Rev. A. Pryne Held at Philadelphia, September 1958.* Philadelphia: J. B. Lippincott, 1858. Reprint Miami: Mnemosyne, 1969.

Bruce, Calvin E. "Black Evangelical Christianity and Black Theology." In *Black Theology II: Essays on the Formation and Outreach of Contemporary Black Theology,* pp. 163-87. Edited by Calvin E. Bruce and William R. Jones. Lewisburg, Va.: Bucknell University Press/Cranbury, N.J.: Associated University Presses, 1978.

Bruce, F. F. *The Acts of the Apostles: The Greek Text with Introduction and Commentary.* Grand Rapids, Mich.: Eerdmans, 1951.

──────. *The Books and the Parchments: Some Chapters on the Transmission of the Bible.* 3rd rev. ed. Old Tappan, N.J.: Fleming H. Revell, 1963.

──────. *Commentary on the Book of the Acts: The English Text with Introduction, Exposition and Notes.* New International Commentary on the New Testament. Grand Rapids, Mich.: Eerdmans, 1977.

──────. *History of the Bible in English.* 3rd ed. New York: Oxford University Press, 1978.

──────. *Jesus and Christian Origins Outside the New Testament.* Grand Rapids, Mich.: Eerdmans, 1974.

*──────. *The New Testament Documents: Are They Reliable?* 5th ed. Grand Rapids, Mich.: Eerdmans, 1980.

──────. *New Testament History.* Garden City, N.Y.: Doubleday, 1977.

Bullard, Sara. *Free at Last: A History of the Civil Rights Movement and Those Who Died in the

Struggle. New York: Oxford University Press/Southern Poverty Law Center, 1993.

*Bullard, Sara, ed. *The Ku Klux Klan: A History of Racism and Violence.* 4th ed. Compiled by the staff of the Southern Poverty Law Center. Montgomery, Ala.: Klanwatch/Southern Poverty Law Center, 1991.

Bullivant, Brian M. "Culture: Its Nature and Meaning for Educators." In *Multicultural Education: Issues and Perspectives,* pp. 27-45. Edited by James A. Banks and Cherry A. McGee Banks. Boston: Allyn & Bacon, 1989.

Bultmann, Bud. *Revolution by Candlelight: The Real Story Behind the Changes in Eastern Europe.* Portland, Ore.: Multnomah Press, 1991.

Burkert, Walter. *Ancient Mystery Cults.* Carl Newell Jackson Lectures. Cambridge, Mass.: Harvard University Press, 1987.

──────. *Greek Religion.* Translated by John Raffan. Cambridge, Mass.: Harvard University Press, 1985.

Burkett, Randall K., ed. *Black Redemption: Churchmen Speak for the Garvey Movement.* Philadelphia: Temple University Press, 1978.

──────. *Garveyism as a Religious Movement: The Institutionalization of a Black Civil Religion.* American Theological Library Association Monograph 13. Metuchen, N.J.: Scarecrow/London: American Theological Library Association, 1978.

Burnham, Kenneth E. "Father Divine and the Peace Mission Movement." In *Black Apostles: Afro-American Clergy Confront the Twentieth Century,* pp. 25-47. Edited by Randall K. Burkett and Richard Newman. Boston: G. K. Hall, 1978.

Burridge, Richard A. *What Are the Gospels? A Comparison with Graeco-Roman Biography.* Society for New Testament Studies Monograph Series 70. Cambridge: Cambridge University Press, 1992.

Cadbury, Henry J. *The Making of Luke-Acts.* London: S.P.C.K., 1968.

Cade, Toni. *The Black Woman: An Anthology.* New York: New American Library, 1970.

Campbell, William. *The Qur'an and the Bible in the Light of History and Science.* N.p.: Middle East Resources, n.d. Available from Reasons to Believe, P.O. Box 5978, Pasadena, CA 91117-0978.

Cannon, Katie Geneva. "Slave Ideology and Biblical Interpretation." In *The Recovery of Black Presence: An Interdisciplinary Exploration—Essays in Honor of Dr. Charles B. Copher,* pp. 119-28. Edited by Randall C. Bailey and Jacquelyn Grant. Nashville: Abingdon, 1995.

Canton Repository (Canton, Ohio), January 25, 1992, p. A6.

"Captive Workers." *World Press Review,* May 1991, p. 50, following Denis MacShane in Hong Kong's *Far Eastern Economic Review.*

Carney, Glandion. "Amen, Brother!" *Christianity Today,* March 19, 1990, pp. 21-23.

Carpenter, J. Estlin. *The Composition of the Hexateuch.* London: Longmans, Green, 1902. Appendices by George Harford, pp. 379-523.

Carroll, Joseph Cephas. *Slave Insurrections in the United States, 1800-1865.* N.p.: Chapman & Grimes, 1938. Reprint New York: New American Library, 1969.

Carson, D. A. *The King James Version Debate: A Plea for Realism.* Grand Rapids, Mich.: Baker Book House, 1979.

Carson, D. A., Douglas J. Moo and Leon Morris. *An Introduction to the New Testament.* Grand Rapids, Mich.: Zondervan, 1992.

Carter, Harold A. *The Prayer Tradition of Black People.* Valley Forge, Penn.: Judson, 1976.

Carter, Robert T. "Cultural Value Differences Between African Americans and White Americans." *Journal of College Student Development* 31 (January 1990): 71-79.

Carwardine, Richard J. *Evangelicals and Politics in Antebellum America.* New Haven, Conn.: Yale University Press, 1993.

"The Case of the Vanished Russian Gold." *Newsweek,* October 14, 1991, p. 49.

Cassuto, Umberto. *A Commentary on the Book of Exodus.* Translated by Israel Abrahams. Jerusalem: Magnes, 1967.

──────. "The Palace of Baal." *Journal of Biblical Literature* 61 (1942): 51-56.

Cerulli, E. "Ethiopia's Relations with the Muslim World." In *Africa from the Seventh to the Eleventh Century,* pp. 575-85. Edited by M. El Fasi with I. Hrbek. Vol. 3 of *General History of Africa.* Berkeley: University of California Press/London: Heinemann Educational Books/Paris: United Nations Educational, Scientific and Cultural Organization, 1988.

Chadwick, Henry. *The Early Church*. Baltimore: Penguin, 1967.

Chariton. *Chaereas and Callirhoe*. Translated by Warren E. Blake. Ann Arbor: University of Michigan Press/London: Oxford University Press, 1939. Greek text: Oxford: Clarendon, 1938.

Chase, Ezra B. *Teachings of Patriots and Statements: Or, The "Founders of the Republic" on Slavery*. Philadelphia: J. W. Bradley, 1861. Reprint Miami: Mnemosyne, 1969.

Cheever, George B. *God Against Slavery: And the Freedom and Duty of the Pulpit to Rebuke It as a Sin Against God*. New York: Joseph H. Ladd, 1857. Reprint Miami: Mnemosyne, 1969.

"Child Laborers." *World Press Review*, October 1992, p. 33.

Childs, John Brown. *The Political Black Minister: A Study in Afro-American Politics and Religion*. Reference Publications in Afro-American Studies. Boston: G. K. Hall, 1980.

Chola, F. N. "Child Abuse in Africa." *In Our Time Has Come: African Christian Women Address the Issues of Today*, pp. 71-74. Edited by Judy Mbugua. Grand Rapids, Mich.: Baker Book House/Carlisle, U.K.: Paternoster/World Evangelical Fellowship, 1994.

Cicero. *Works*. Translated by Harry Caplan et al. 28 vols. Loeb Classical Library. Cambridge, Mass.: Harvard University Press.

"Civil War Brings Suffering to Sudan: Militants Single Out Christians for Persecution." *Christianity Today*, May 17, 1993, p. 82.

Clark, Calvin Montague. *American Slavery and Maine Congregationalists: A Chapter in the History of the Development of Anti-slavery Sentiment in the Protestant Churches of the North*. Bangor, Maine: Author, 1940.

Clark, Claude L. "Parallels Between Egyptian Art and Southwestern Nigerian Art." In *Kemet and the African Worldview: Research, Rescue and Restoration*, pp. 173-81. Edited by Maulana Karenga and Jacob H. Carruthers. Los Angeles: University of Sankore Press, 1986.

Clark, Daima M. "Similarities Between Egyptian and Dogon Perception of Man, God and Nature." In *Kemet and the African Worldview: Research, Rescue and Restoration*, pp. 119-30. Edited by Maulana Karenga and Jacob H. Carruthers. Los Angeles: University of Sankore Press, 1986.

Clarke, Erskine. *Wrestlin' Jacob: A Portrait of Religion in the Old South*. Atlanta: John Knox, 1979.

Clarke, John Henrik. "Africa in the Ancient World." In *Kemet and the African Worldview: Research, Rescue and Restoration*, pp. 45-54. Edited by Maulana Karenga and Jacob H. Carruthers. Los Angeles: University of Sankore Press, 1986.

———. *Africans at the Crossroads: Notes for an African World Revolution*. Trenton, N.J.: Africa World Press, 1991.

———. Introduction to John G. Jackson, *Introduction to African Civilizations*, pp. 3-35. New York: Carol, 1970.

Clemmons, Ithiel. "Racial and Spiritual Unity in the Body of Christ." *A/G Advance/Enrichment* 31, no. 8 (Fall 1995): 66-68.

Clifford, Richard J. "Tent of El and Israelite Tent of Meeting." *Catholic Biblical Quarterly* 33 (April 1971): 221-27.

Clines, David J. A. *The Theme of the Pentateuch. Journal for the Study of the Old Testament* Supplement Series 10. Sheffield, U.K.: Department of Biblical Studies, 1978.

Clowes, William Laird. "Miscegenation and the Race Problem, 1890." In *Black Image: European Eyewitness Accounts of Afro-American Life*, pp. 95-100. Port Washington, N.Y.: Kennikat/National University Publications, 1978.

*Coles, Robert. "Children of the American Ghetto." In *Teaching in the Inner City: A Book of Readings*, pp. 132-37. Edited by James C. Stone and Frederick W. Schneider. Commitment to Teaching 3. New York: Thomas Y. Crowell, 1970.

*———. "White Pieties and Black Reality." In *Teaching in the Inner City: A Book of Readings*, pp. 80-85. Edited by James C. Stone and Frederick W. Schneider. Commitment to Teaching 3. New York: Thomas Y. Crowell, 1970.

*Collins, Patricia Hill. *Black Feminist Thought: Knowledge, Consciousness and the Politics of Empowerment*. Perspectives on Gender 2. New York: Routledge, Chapman & Hall, 1991.

*Cone, James H. *Black Theology and Black Power*. 20th anniversary ed. San Francisco: HarperSanFrancisco, 1989.

*———. *For My People: Black Theology and the Black Church*. Maryknoll, N.Y.: Orbis, 1984.

———. *God of the Oppressed*. New York: Seabury, 1975.

*Cone, James H., and Gayraud S. Wilmore, eds. *Black Theology: A Documentary History*. 2 vols. Maryknoll, N.Y.: Orbis, 1993.

Cone, Joan Kernan. "The Urgency of Choice in the Untracked Classroom." *Teaching Tolerance*, Fall 1993, pp. 57-63.

Cook, Michael. *Muhammad*. Past Masters Series. New York: Oxford University Press, 1983.

*Copher, Charles B. *Black Biblical Studies: An Anthology—Biblical and Theological Issues on the Black Presence in the Bible*. Chicago: Black Light Fellowship, 1993.

Corpus Inscriptionum Iudaicarum: Recueil des inscriptions juives qui vont du IIIe siècle avant Jesus-Christ au VIIe siècle de notre ere. Edited by P. Jean-Baptiste Frey. 2 vols. Rome: Pontificio Istituto di Archeologia Cristiana, 1936-1952.

Corpus Papyrorum Judaicarum. Edited by Victor A. Tcherikover with Alexander Fuks. 3 vols. Vol. 3 edited by Victor A. Tcherikover, Alexander Fuks and Menahem Stern with David M. Lewis. Cambridge, Mass.: Harvard University Press/Magnes/Hebrew University, 1957-1964.

Cose, Ellis. "One Drop of Bloody History." *Newsweek*, February 13, 1995, p. 70.

"Counting Up the Human Cost." *Newsweek*, May 18, 1992, p. 47.

Craig, William Lane. "The Bodily Resurrection of Jesus." In *Studies of History and Tradition in the Four Gospels*, pp. 47-74. Edited by R. T. France and David Wenham. Vol. 1/2 of *Gospel Perspectives*. 6 vols. Sheffield, U.K.: JSOT Press, 1980-1986.

————. "The Problem of Miracles: A Historical and Philosophical Perspective." In *The Miracles of Jesus*, pp. 9-48. Edited by David Wenham and Craig Blomberg. Vol. 6 of *Gospel Perspectives*. 6 vols. Sheffield, U.K.: JSOT Press, 1980-1986.

Craigie, Peter C. *The Book of Deuteronomy*. New International Commentary on the Old Testament. Grand Rapids, Mich.: Eerdmans, 1976.

Crocker, P. T. "The City of Meroe and the Ethiopian Eunuch." *Buried History* 22, no. 3 (1986): 53-72.

Cross, Frank Moore, Jr. "The Priestly Tabernacle." in *The Biblical Archaeologist Reader*, pp. 201-28. Edited by David Noel Freedman and G. Ernest Wright. Garden City, N.Y.: Doubleday, 1961.

————. "The Tabernacle: A Study from an Archaeological and Historical Approach." *Biblical Archaeologist* 10 (September 1947): 45-68.

Cruver, Robert W. "The Pillar of Fire: Yesterday, Today and Tomorrow, with an Introduction to Biblical Holiness and the Holiness Movement." M.T.S. thesis, Asbury Theological Seminary, 1992.

Cullmann, Oscar. *Peter: Disciple, Apostle, Martyr*. Philadelphia: Westminster Press, 1953.

————. *The State in the New Testament*. New York: Charles Scribner's Sons, 1956.

Culpepper, R. Alan. *The Johannine School: An Evaluation of the Johannine-School Hypothesis Based on an Investigation of the Nature of Ancient Schools*. SBL Dissertation Series 26. Missoula, Mont.: Scholars Press, 1975.

Cummings, Lorine L. "A Womanist Response to the Afrocentric Idea: Jarena Lee, Womanist Preacher." In *Living the Intersection: Womanism and Afrocentrism in Theology*, pp. 57-66. Edited by Cheryl J. Sanders. Minneapolis: Fortress, 1995.

"Cupolas and Culture." *World Press Review*, September 1990, p. 50.

Custance, Arthur C. *Noah's Three Sons: Human History in Three Dimensions*. Doorway Papers 1. Grand Rapids, Mich.: Zondervan, 1975.

The Cynic Epistles: A Study Edition. Edited by Abraham J. Malherbe. Society of Biblical Literature Sources for Biblical Study 12. Missoula, Mont.: Scholars Press, 1977.

Daube, David. *The New Testament and Rabbinic Judaism*. London: University of London, 1956. Reprint New York: Arno, 1973.

Davidson, Basil. *Africa in History: Themes and Outlines*. New York: Macmillan, 1968.

*Davidson, Basil, with F. K. Buah. *A History of West Africa to the Nineteenth Century*. Garden City, N.Y.: Doubleday/Anchor, 1966.

Davies, G. Henton. "Tabernacle." In *Interpreter's Dictionary of the Bible*, 4:498-506. New York: Abingdon, 1962.

Davies, W. D. "Reflexions on Tradition: The Aboth Revisited." In *Christian History and Interpretation: Studies Presented to John Knox*, pp. 129-37. Edited by W. R. Farmer, C. F. D. Moule and Richard R. Niebuhr. Cambridge: Cambridge University Press, 1967.

Davies, W. D., and Dale C. Allison. *A Critical and Exegetical Commentary on the Gospel According to Saint Matthew.* International Critical Commentaries. 3 vols. Vol. 1: *Introduction and Commentary on Matthew I-VII.* Edinburgh: T & T Clark, 1988. Vol. 2: *Introduction and Commentary on Matthew VIII-XVIII.* Edinburgh: T & T Clark, 1991.

Davis, David Brian. *The Problem of Slavery in the Age of Revolution, 1770-1823.* Ithaca, N.Y.: Cornell University Press, 1975.

Dean, David M. *Defender of the Race: James Theodore Holly, Black Nationalist Bishop.* Boston: Lambeth, 1979.

Deedat, Ahmed. *Is the Bible God's Word?* Chicago: Kazi, n.d.

Deere, Jack. *Surprised by the Power of the Spirit: A Former Dallas Seminary Professor Discovers That God Speaks and Heals Today.* Grand Rapids, Mich.: Zondervan, 1993.

Deissmann, Adolf. *Light from the Ancient East.* Grand Rapids, Mich.: Baker Book House, 1978.

De Kruijf, Th. C. "The Glory of the Only Son (John i 14)." In *Studies in John: Presented to Professor Dr. J. N. Sevenster on the Occasion of his Seventieth Birthday,* pp. 111-23. Edited by W. C. van Unnik. Supplements to *Novum Testamentum* 24. Leiden: Brill, 1970.

Delaporte, L. *Mesopotamia: The Babylonian and Assyrian Civilization.* New York: Barnes & Noble, 1970.

Desanges, J. "The Proto-Berbers." In *Ancient Civilizations of Africa,* pp. 423-40. Edited by G. Mokhtar. Vol. 2 of *General History of Africa.* Berkeley: University of California Press/London: Heinemann Educational Books/Paris: United Nations Educational, Scientific and Cultural Organization, 1981.

De Vaux, Roland. *Ancient Israel: Its Life and Institutions.* New York: McGraw-Hill, 1961.

Dever, William G. "The MB IIC Stratifications in the Northwest Gate Area at Shechem." *Bulletin of the American Schools of Oriental Research* 216 (December 1974): 43.

Dexinger, Ferdinand. "Limits of Tolerance in Judaism: The Samaritan Example." In *Jewish and Christian Self-Definition,* 2:88-114. Edited by Ben F. Meyer and E. P. Sanders. 3 vols. Philadelphia: Fortress, 1980-1982.

Díaz, Carlos F. "Resistance to Multicultural Education: Concerns and Responses." In *Multicultural Education for the Twenty-first Century,* pp. 193-203. Edited by Carlos Díaz. Washington, D.C.: National Education Association, 1992.

Dibelius, Martin. *Studies in the Acts of the Apostles.* London: SCM Press, 1956.

Dickey, Christopher, and Carol Berger. "A Message from Mubarak." *Newsweek,* July 19, 1993, p. 28.

Dio Chrysostom. *Orations.* Translated by J. W. Cohoon and H. Lamar Crosby. 5 vols. Loeb Classical Library. Cambridge, Mass.: Harvard University Press, 1932-1951.

Diogenes Laertius. *Lives of Eminent Philosophers.* Translated by R. D. Hicks. 2 vols. Loeb Classical Library. Cambridge, Mass.: Harvard University Press, 1925.

Diop, Cheikh Anta. *The African Origin of Civilization.* Translated by Mercer Cook. Westport, Conn.: Lawrence Hill, 1974.

*_____. "Origin of the Ancient Egyptians." In *Ancient Civilizations of Africa,* pp. 27-57. Edited by G. Mokhtar. Vol. 2 of *General History of Africa.* Berkeley: University of California Press/London: Heinemann Educational Books;/Paris: United Nations Educational, Scientific and Cultural Organization, 1981.

*_____. "Origin of the Ancient Egyptians." In *Great African Thinkers: Cheikh Anta Diop,* pp. 35-63. Edited by Ivan Van Sertima. New Brunswick, N.J.: Journal of African Civilizations, 1986.

Dixon, Suzanne. *The Roman Mother.* Norman: Oklahoma University Press, 1988.

Domínguez, Jorge I. "Assessing Human Rights Conditions." In Jorge I. Domínguez et al., *Enhancing Global Human Rights,* pp. 21-116. 1980s Project/Council on Foreign Relations. New York: McGraw-Hill, 1979.

Douglas, Kelly Brown. "To Reflect the Image of God: A Womanist Perspective on Right Relationship." In *Living the Intersection: Womanism and Afrocentrism in Theology,* pp. 67-77. Edited by Cheryl J. Sanders. Minneapolis: Fortress, 1995.

Douglass, William. *Sermons Preached in the African Protestant Episcopal Church of St. Thomas, Philadelphia.* Philadelphia: King & Baird, 1854. Reprint Freeport, N.Y.: Books for Libraries/Black Heritage Library Collection, 1971.

Dowley, Tim, ed. *Eerdmans Handbook to the History of Christianity.* Grand Rapids, Mich.: Eerdmans, 1977.

Dramani-Issifou, Z. "Islam as a Social System in Africa Since the Seventh Century." In *Africa from the Seventh to the Eleventh Century*, pp. 92-118. Edited by M. El Fasi with I. Hrbek. Vol. 3 of *General History of Africa*. Berkeley: University of California Press/London: Heinemann Educational Books/Paris: United Nations Educational, Scientific and Cultural Organization, 1988.

Draper, Jonathan. "The Jesus Tradition in the Didache." In *The Jesus Tradition Outside the Gospels*, 5:269-87. Edited by David Wenham. Vol. 5 of *Gospel Perspectives*. 6 vols. Sheffield, U.K.: JSOT Press, 1980-1986.

"Druid." In *The New Encyclopaedia Britannica Micropaedia*, 4:233. 15th ed. 12 vols. Chicago: Encyclopaedia Britannica, 1992.

Drury, John. *Tradition and Design in Luke's Gospel: A Study in Early Christian Historiography*. London: Darton, Longman & Todd, 1976.

Du Bois, W. E. B. *Prayers for Dark People*. Edited by Herbert Aptheker. Amherst: University of Massachusetts Press, 1980.

**_____. *The World and Africa: An Inquiry into the Part Which Africa Has Played in History*. Rev. ed., including new writings of W. E. B. Du Bois, 1955-1961. New York: International Publishers, 1965.

*Dunston, Bishop Alfred G., Jr. *The Black Man in the Old Testament and Its World*. Philadelphia: Dorrance, 1974.

Du Plessis, I. J. "Christ as the 'Only Begotten.' " *Neotestamentica* 2 (1968): 22-31.

Dupont, Jacques. *The Salvation of the Gentiles: Essays on the Acts of the Apostles*. Translated by John R. Keating. New York: Paulist, 1979.

_____. *The Sources of Acts: The Present Position*. London: Darton, Longman & Todd, 1964.

Durham Herald-Sun, July 20, 1991, p. A5.

"Ebony Readers' Poll." *Ebony*, April 1991, 18.

Eder, Donna. "Ability Grouping as a Self-Fulfilling Prophecy: A Micro-analysis of Teacher-Student Interaction." *Sociology of Education* 54 (July 1981): 151-62.

Edgerly, Adam, and Carl F. Ellis Jr. "Emergence of Islam in the African-American Community." *Reach Out* 7, nos. 3-4 (1994): 8-16.

Edwards, I. E. S., et al., eds. *Cambridge Ancient History*. 3rd ed. Cambridge: Cambridge University Press, 1975.

"Egypt—Grave Human Rights Abuses Amid Political Violence." New York: Amnesty International, 1993.

Eickelman, Dale F. *The Middle East: An Anthropological Approach*. 2nd ed. Englewood Cliffs, N.J.: Prentice-Hall, 1989.

*El-Amin, Mustafa. *The Religion of Islam and the Nation of Islam: What Is the Difference?* Newark, N.J.: El-Amin Productions, 1991.

El Fasi, M., and I. Hrbek. "The Coming of Islam and the Expansion of the Muslim Empire." In *Africa from the Seventh to the Eleventh Century*, pp. 31-55. Edited by M. El Fasi with I. Hrbek. Vol. 3 of *General History of Africa*. Berkeley: University of California Press/London: Heinemann Educational Books/Paris: United Nations Educational, Scientific and Cultural Organization, 1988.

_____. "Stages in the Development of Islam and Its Dissemination in Africa." In *Africa from the Seventh to the Eleventh Century*, pp. 56-91. Edited by M. El Fasi with I. Hrbek. Vol. 3 of *General History of Africa*. Berkeley: University of California Press;/London: Heinemann Educational Books/Paris: United Nations Educational, Scientific and Cultural Organization, 1988.

Eliade, Mircea. *Birth and Rebirth: The Religious Meanings of Initiation in Human Culture*. New York: Harper & Brothers, 1958.

Elkins, Stanley M. *Slavery: A Problem in American Institutional and Intellectual Life*. New York: Grosset & Dunlap, 1963.

*Ellis, Carl F., Jr. "Afrocentrism and Christianity: Complement or Conflict?" *Urban Family*, Summer 1995, pp. 15-16.

_____. *Malcolm: The Man Behind the X*. Chattanooga, Tenn.: Accord, 1993.

English, James W. *Handyman of the Lord: The Life and Ministry of the Reverend William Holmes Borders*. New York: Meredith, 1967.

ESA Advocate (Evangelicals for Social Action), October 1992, p. 6.

The Ethiopic Book of Enoch: A New Edition in the Light of the Aramaic Dead Sea Scrolls. Translated by Michael A. Knibb in consultation with Edward Ullendorff. 2 vols. Oxford: Clarendon, 1978.

Ezeigbo, Joseph. "A History of Early Christianity in Africa." *Reach Out* 7, nos. 3-4 (1994): 23-25.

Ezekiel's Exagoge. In *The Old Testament Pseudepigrapha.* Edited by James H. Charlesworth. 2 vols. Garden City, N.Y.: Doubleday, 1983-1985.

Falise, Thierry, and Christophe Loviny. "Child Soldiers of Myanmar." *World Press Review,* October 1994, p. 25; from Hong Kong's *Eastern Express.*

Fanon, Frantz. *The Wretched of the Earth.* Translated by Constance Farrington. New York: Grove, 1963.

Farrakhan, Louis. *A Torchlight for America.* Chicago: FCN, 1993.

The Fathers According to Rabbi Nathan. Translated by Judah Goldin. Yale Judaica Series 10. New Haven, Conn.: Yale University Press, 1955.

The Fathers According to Rabbi Nathan ('Abot de Rabbi Nathan), Version B. Translation and commentary by Anthony J. Saldarini. Studies in Judaism in Late Antiquity 11. Leiden: Brill, 1975.

Fauset, Arthur Huff. *Black Gods of the Metropolis.* Publications of the Philadelphia Anthropological Society 3. Philadelphia: University of Pennsylvania Press/London: Oxford University Press, 1944.

Fee, Gordon D. *The First Epistle to the Corinthians.* New International Commentary on the New Testament. Grand Rapids, Mich.: Eerdmans, 1987.

Felder, Cain Hope. "Cultural Ideology, Afrocentrism and Biblical Interpretation." In *Black Theology: A Documentary History,* 2:184-95. Edited by James H. Cone and Gayraud S. Wilmore. 2 vols. Maryknoll, N.Y.: Orbis, 1993.

**_____. *Troubling Biblical Waters: Race, Class and Family.* Bishop Henry McNeal Turner Studies in North American Black Religion 3. Maryknoll, N.Y.: Orbis, 1989.

_____, ed. *The Original African Heritage Study Bible: King James Version.* Nashville: James C. Winston/Winston-Derek, 1993.

Feldman, Susan, ed. *African Myths and Tales.* New York: Dell, 1963.

"Fence of Death." *World Press Review,* July 1992, p. 31. Following Hugh McCullum in *Horizon,* a monthly from Harare, Zimbabwe.

Ferguson, Everett. *Backgrounds of Early Christianity.* Grand Rapids, Mich.: Eerdmans, 1987.

Filler, Louis. *The Crusade Against Slavery, 1830-1860.* New York: Harper & Row, 1960.

Filson, Floyd V. *A New Testament History.* Philadelphia: Westminster Press, 1964.

Finnie, Kelsye M. *William Carey: Missionary Pioneer.* Fort Washington, Penn.: Christian Literature Crusade, 1986.

Flannery, Edward H. *The Anguish of the Jews: Twenty-three Centuries of Anti-Semitism.* New York: Macmillan, 1965.

Flint, Julie. "On the Wrong Side of a 'Jihad.' " *World Press Review,* November 1995, pp. 37-38.

Foakes Jackson, F. J., and Kirsopp Lake. "The Internal Evidence of Acts." In *The Beginnings of Christianity,* 2:121-204. Edited by F. J. Foakes Jackson and Kirsopp Lake. 5 vols. Grand Rapids, Mich.: Baker Book House, 1979.

Fogel, Robert William. *Without Consent or Contract: The Rise and Fall of American Slavery.* New York: W. W. Norton, 1989.

Fogel, Robert William, and Stanley L. Engerman. *Time on the Cross: The Economics of American Negro Slavery.* Boston: Little, Brown, 1974.

Foner, Eric. *Reconstruction: America's Unfinished Revolution, 1863-1877.* New York: Harper & Row, 1988.

Forbes, R. J. *Studies in Ancient Technology.* 9 vols. Leiden: Brill, 1966.

Fordham, Monroe. *Major Themes in Northern Black Religious Thought, 1800-1860.* Hicksville, N.Y.: Exposition, 1975.

"Forgotten Slaves." *World Press Review,* January 1991, p. 57.

Forman, Werner, and Bedrich Forman. *Egyptian Art.* Text by Milada Vilimkova. Translated by Till Gottheimer. London: Peter Nevill, 1962.

France, R. T. "The Authenticity of the Sayings of Jesus." In *History, Criticism and Faith,* pp. 101-43. Edited by Colin Brown. Downers Grove, Ill.: InterVarsity Press, 1976.

_____. *The Evidence for Jesus.* Downers Grove, Ill.: InterVarsity Press, 1986.

Franz, Marie Louise von. *The Passion of Perpetua.* Irving, Tex.: Spring, 1980.

Frend, W. H. C. *The Donatist Church: A Movement of Protest in Roman North Africa.* Oxford: Oxford University Press, 1952.

Freyne, Sean. *Galilee, Jesus and the Gospels: Literary Approaches and Historical Investigations.* Philadelphia: Fortress, 1988.

Fridh, Ake Jason. *Le problème de la passion des saintes Perpetue et Felicite.* Stockholm: Almqvist & Friskell, 1968.

Friedman, Richard E. "The Tabernacle in the Temple." *Biblical Archaeologist* 43 (Fall 1980): 241-48.

Fusco, V. "Le sezioni-noi degli Atti nella discussione recente." *Biblia e Oriente* 25, no. 2 (1983): 73-86.

Gager, John G. *The Origins of Anti-Semitism: Attitudes Toward Judaism in Pagan and Christian Antiquity.* New York: Oxford University Press, 1983.

Gaius. *The Institutes.* Translation and introduction by W. M. Gordon and O. F. Robinson, with the Latin text of Seckel and Kuebler. Texts in Roman Law. Ithaca, N.Y.: Cornell University Press, 1988.

Gallup, George H., Jr., and Timothy Jones. "Uncovering America's Hidden Saints." *Christianity Today,* August 17, 1992, pp. 26-29.

García, Ricardo L. "Educating for Human Rights: A Curricular Blueprint." In *Multicultural Education for the Twenty-first Century,* pp. 167-78. Edited by Carlos Díaz. Washington, D.C.: National Education Association, 1992.

Gardner, Jane F. *Women in Roman Law and Society.* Bloomington: Indiana University Press, 1986.

Garnet, Henry Highland. "Address to the Slaves of the United States of America." In *Witness for Freedom: African American Voices on Race, Slavery and Emancipation,* pp. 165-69. Edited by Peter Ripley. Chapel Hill: University of North Carolina Press, 1993.

Garrett, Duane. *Rethinking Genesis: The Sources and Authorship of the First Book of the Pentateuch.* Grand Rapids, Mich.: Baker Book House, 1991.

Gärtner, Bertril. *The Temple and the Community in Qumran and the New Testament: A Comparative Study in the Temple Symbolism of the Qumran Texts and the New Testament.* Cambridge: Cambridge University Press, 1965.

Garvey, Marcus. *The Philosophy and Opinions of Marcus Garvey.* Edited by Amy Jacques-Garvey. Vols. 1-2. New York: Universal Publishing House, 1923-1925.

Gasparro, Giulia Sfameni. *Soteriology and Mystic Aspects in the Cult of Cybele and Attis.* Études Préliminaires aux Religions Orientales dans l'Empire Romain 103. Leiden: Brill, 1985.

Gates, Henry Louis. "Why Now?" In *The Bell Curve Wars: Race, Intelligence and the Future of America,* pp. 94-96. Edited by Steven Fraser. New York: BasicBooks/HarperCollins, 1995.

The Genesis Apocryphon of Qumran Cave I: A Commentary. Commentary by Joseph A. Fitzmyer. 2nd rev. ed. Biblical et Orientalia 18A. Rome: Biblical Institute Press, 1971.

Genesis Rabbah. In *The Midrash Rabbah.* Edited by Harry Freedman and Maurice Simon. 5 vols. London: Soncino, 1977.

Gerber, Israel J. *The Heritage Seekers: American Blacks in Search of Jewish Identity.* Middle Village, N.Y.: Jonathan David, 1977.

Gerhardsson, Birger. *Memory and Manuscript: Oral Tradition and Written Transmission in Rabbinic Judaism and Early Christianity.* Acta Seminarii Neotestamentici Upsaliensis 22. Uppsala: C. W. K. Gleerup, 1961.

Gibson, J. C. L. *Canaanite Myths and Legends.* Edinburgh: T and T Clark, 1977.

Gilbreath, Edward. "Billy Graham Had a Dream." *Christian History* 14 (August 1995): 44-46.

Gilkes, Cheryl Townsend. "We Have a Beautiful Mother: Womanist Musings on the Afrocentric Idea." In *Living the Intersection: Womanism and Afrocentrism in Theology,* pp. 21-42. Edited by Cheryl J. Sanders. Minneapolis: Fortress, 1995.

Gilmore, Al-Tony. "The Black Southerner's Response to the Southern System of Race Relations: 1900 to Post-World War II." In *The Age of Segregation: Race Relations in the South, 1890-1945,* pp. 67-88. Edited by Robert Haws. Jackson: University Press of Mississippi, 1978.

Goodell, William. *The American Slave Code in Theory and Practice: Its Distinctive Features Shown by Its Statutes, Judicial Decisions and Illustrative Facts.* N.p.: American & Foreign Anti-slavery Society, 1853. Reprint New York: Negro Universities Press/New American Library, 1969.

Goodman, Martin. *State and Society in Roman Galilee, A.D. 132-212*. Oxford Centre for Postgraduate Hebrew Studies. Totowa, N.J.: Rowman & Allanheld, 1983.

Goppelt, Leonhard. *Theology of the New Testament*. Edited by Jürgen Roloff. Translated by John E. Alsup. 2 vols. Grand Rapids, Mich.: Eerdmans, 1981-1982.

Gordon, Cyrus H. *The Ancient Near East*. New York: W. W. Norton, 1965.

──────. *The Common Background of Greek and Hebrew Civilizations*. New York: W. W. Norton, 1965.

Gordon, Grant. *From Slavery to Freedom: The Life of David George, Pioneer Black Baptist Minister*. Hantsport, Novia Scotia: Lancelot, 1993.

*Gordon, Murray. *Slavery in the Arab World*. New York: New Amsterdam Books, 1989. Originally published as *L'Esclavage dans le monde arabe*. Paris: Editions Robert Laffont, 1987.

Gordon, Vivian G. *Black Women, Feminism and Black Liberation: Which Way?* Chicago: Third World Press, 1985.

Gould, Stephen Jay. "Curveball." In *The Bell Curve Wars: Race, Intelligence and the Future of America*, pp. 11-22. Edited by Steven Fraser. New York: BasicBooks/HarperCollins, 1995.

Grady, J. Lee. "Pentecostals Renounce Racism." *Christianity Today*, December 12, 1994, p. 58.

Graham, Billy. "Racism and the Evangelical Church." *Christianity Today*, October 4, 1993, p. 27.

Graham, Lloyd. *Deceptions and Myths of the Bible*. New York: Citadel/Carol, 1991.

Grant, Carl A., and Christine E. Sleeter. "Race, Class, Gender, Exceptionality and Educational Reform." In *Multicultural Education: Issues and Perspectives*, pp. 46-65. Edited by James A. Banks and Cherry A. McGee Banks. Boston: Allyn & Bacon, 1989.

Grant, Jacquelyn. "Black Theology and the Black Woman." In *Black Theology: A Documentary History*, 1:323-38. Edited by James H. Cone and Gayraud S. Wilmore. 2 vols. Maryknoll, N.Y.: Orbis, 1993.

*──────. *White Women's Christ and Black Women's Jesus: Feminist Christology and Womanist Response*. American Academy of Religion Series 64. Atlanta: Scholars Press, 1989.

──────. "Womanist Jesus and the Mutual Struggle for Liberation." In *The Recovery of Black Presence: An Interdisciplinary Exploration—Essays in Honor of Dr. Charles B. Copher*, pp. 129-42. Edited by Randall C. Bailey and Jacquelyn Grant. Nashville: Abingdon, 1995.

Grant, Joanne, ed. *Black Protest: History, Documents and Analyses, 1619 to the Present*. Greenwich, Conn.: Fawcett, 1968.

Grant, Michael. *A Social History of Greece and Rome*. New York: Charles Scribner's Sons/Oxford: Maxwell Macmillan International, 1992.

Grant, Robert M. *Gods and the One God*. Library of Early Christianity 1. Philadelphia: Westminster Press, 1986.

Gray, J. "Ugarit." In *Archaeology and Old Testament Study*. Edited by D. Winton Thomas. Oxford: Clarendon, 1967.

The Greek Magical Papyri in Translation (including the Demotic Spells). Edited by Hans Dieter Betz. 2nd ed. Chicago: University of Chicago Press, 1992.

Green, Michael. *I Believe in the Holy Spirit*. 2nd rev. ed. Grand Rapids, Mich.: Eerdmans, 1989.

Grier, William H., and Price M. Cobbs. *The Jesus Bag*. New York: McGraw-Hill, 1971.

Grimké, Francis J. "Christianity and Race Prejudice: Two Discourses Delivered in the Fifteenth Street Presbyterian Church, Washington, D.C., May 29th and June 5th, 1910." Reprint Ann Arbor, Mich.: University Microfilms, 1973.

──────. "Discouragements: Hostility of the Press, Silence and Cowardice of the Pulpit." Sermon delivered November 20, 1900. In *Addresses Mainly Personal and Racial*, pp. 234-47, vol. 1 of *The Works of Francis J. Grimké*. Edited by Carter G. Woodson. 4 vols. Washington, D.C. Associated Publishers, 1942.

──────. *The Negro: His Rights and Wrongs, the Forces For Him and Against Him (Collected Sermons Delivered in Washington, D.C., at Fifteenth Street Presbyterian Church, November 20, 27, December 4, 11)*. Reprint Ann Arbor, Mich.: University Microfilms, 1973.

──────. "Sources from Which No Help May Be Expected: The General Government, Political Parties." Sermon delivered November 27, 1900. In *Addresses Mainly Personal and Racial*, pp. 247-60, vol. 1 of *The Works of Francis J. Grimké*. Edited by Carter G. Woodson. 4 vols. Washington, D.C. Associated Publishers, 1942.

Groenewegen-Frankfort, H. A., and Bernard Ashmole. *The Ancient World*. Library of Art History 1. New York: New American Library/Mentor, 1967.

Groothuis, Rebecca Merrill. *Women Caught in the Conflict: The Culture War Between Traditionalism and Feminism*. Grand Rapids, Mich.: Baker Book House, 1994.

Grunlan, Stephen A., and Marvin K. Mayers. *Cultural Anthropology: A Christian Perspective*. Grand Rapids, Mich.: Zondervan, 1979.

Guillaume, Alfred. *Islam*. 2nd rev. ed. New York: Penguin, 1956.

Gurney, O. R. *The Hittites*. 2nd ed. Baltimore: Penguin, 1954.

———. *Some Aspects of Hittite Religion*. Oxford: Oxford University Press/British Academy, 1977.

Gushee, David P. *The Righteous Gentiles of the Holocaust: A Christian Interpretation*. Minneapolis: Augsburg Fortress, 1994.

Guthrie, Donald. *New Testament Introduction*. Downers Grove, Ill.: InterVarsity Press, 1970.

Guthrie, W. K. C. *Orpheus and Greek Religion: A Study of the Orphic Movement*. 2nd ed. New York: W. W. Norton, 1966.

Hagood, L. M. *The Colored Man in the Methodist Episcopal Church*. Cincinnati: Cranston & Stowe, 1890. Reprint Westport, Conn.: Negro Universities Press/Greenwood, 1970.

Hakem, A. A., with I. Hrbek and J. Vercoutter. "The Civilization of Napata and Meroe." In *Ancient Civilizations of Africa*, pp. 298-321. Edited by G. Mokhtar. Vol. 2 of *General History of Africa*. Berkeley: University of California Press/London: Heinemann Educational Books/Paris: United Nations Educational, Scientific and Cultural Organization, 1981.

"The Haldeman Diaries." *Newsweek*, May 30, 1994, p. 6.

Hale, Janice E. "The Transmission of Faith to Young African American Children." In *The Recovery of Black Presence: An Interdisciplinary Exploration—Essays in Honor of Dr. Charles B. Copher*, pp. 193-207. Edited by Randall C. Bailey and Jacquelyn Grant. Nashville: Abingdon, 1995.

Haley, Alex. *Roots*. New York: Dell, 1976.

Hallett, Robin. *Africa Since 1875: A Modern History*. University of Michigan History of the Modern World. Ann Arbor: University of Michigan Press, 1974.

Hamilton, Charles V. *The Black Preacher in America*. New York: William Morrow, 1972.

Handy, James A. *Scraps of African Methodist Episcopal History*. Philadelphia: A. M. E. Book Concern, n.d. (probably shortly after 1900). Reprint Ann Arbor, Mich.: University Microfilms, 1973.

Haney, Marsha S. "African American Muslims." *Reach Out* 7, nos. 3-4 (1994): 3-5; reprinted from *Theology, News and Notes*, March 1992.

Hansberry, William Leo. *Africa and Africans As Seen by Classical Writers*. Edited by Joseph E. Harris. William Leo Hansberry African History Notebook 2. Washington, D.C.: Howard University Press, 1981.

———. Pillars in Ethiopian History. Edited by Joseph E. Harris. William Leo Hansberry African History Notebook 1. Washington, D.C.: Howard University Press, 1981.

Haran, Menahem. "The Priestly Image of the Tabernacle." *Hebrew Union College Annual* 36 (1965): 191-226.

———. *Temples and Temple-Service in Ancient Israel*. Oxford: Clarendon, 1978.

Hardesty, Nancy A. *Women Called to Witness: Evangelical Feminism in the Nineteenth Century*. Nashville: Abingdon, 1984.

Harding, Vincent. "The Religion of Black Power." In *Black Theology: A Documentary History*, 1:40-65. Edited by James H. Cone and Gayraud S. Wilmore. 2 vols. Maryknoll, N.Y.: Orbis, 1993.

Harrell, David Edwin, Jr. *All Things Are Possible: The Healing and Charismatic Revivals in Modern America*. Bloomington: Indiana University Press, 1975.

———. *White Sects and Black Men in the Recent South*. Nashville: Vanderbilt University Press, 1971.

Harris, J. R. *Egyptian Art*. London: Spring Books/Drury House, 1966.

Harrison, Roland Kenneth. *Introduction to the Old Testament*. Grand Rapids, Mich.: Eerdmans, 1969.

Harrison, Scott. "Goma: Life and Death Among Rwanda's Displaced." *Amnesty Action*, Winter 1995, p. 9.

Hasan, Yusuf Fadl. *The Arabs and the Sudan: From the Seventh to the Early Sixteenth Century*. Edinburgh: University of Edinburgh, 1967.

Haynes, Leonard L., Jr. *The Negro Community Within American Protestantism, 1619-1844.* Boston: Christopher, 1953.

Heard, W. J. "Revolutionary Movements." In *Dictionary of Jesus and the Gospels,* pp. 688-98. Edited by Joel B. Green, Scot McKnight and I. Howard Marshall. Downers Grove, Ill.: InterVarsity Press, 1992.

Helper, Hinton Rowan. *The Impending Crisis of the South: How to Meet It.* New York: Author, 1857. Reprint Miami: Mnemosyne, 1969.

Hengel, Martin. *Studies in the Gospel of Mark.* Translated by John Bowden. Philadelphia: Fortress, 1985.

Henn, Jeanne K. "Women in the Rural Economy: Past, Present and Future." In *African Women South of the Sahara,* pp. 1-18. Edited by Margaret Jean Hay and Sharon Stichter. New York: Longman, 1984.

Henshel, Richard L. "The Boundary of the Self-Fulfilling Prophecy and the Dilemma of Social Prediction." *British Journal of Sociology* 33 (December 1982): 511-28.

Herodotus. *History.* Translated by A. D. Godley. 4 vols. Loeb Classical Library. Cambridge, Mass.: Harvard University Press, 1920-1925.

Herrnstein, Richard, and Charles Murray. *The Bell Curve.* New York: Free Press, 1994.

Herskovits, Melville J. *The Myth of the Negro Past.* Boston: Beacon, 1990 (original edition 1941).

Heschel, Abraham J. *The Prophets.* New York: Harper & Row, 1962.

Hill, David. *New Testament Prophecy.* Atlanta: John Knox, 1979.

Hilliard, Donald, Jr. "Does Race Matter?" Sermon preached at the Cathedral, Second Baptist Church, Perth Amboy, N.J., November 12, 1994.

Hillman, Eugene. *Toward an African Christianity: Inculturation Applied.* New York: Paulist, 1993.

Hine, Darlene Clark. *Black Women in White: Racial Conflict and Cooperation in the Nursing Profession, 1890-1950.* Bloomington: Indiana University Press, 1989.

Holladay, Carl R. *"Theios Anēr" in Hellenistic Judaism: A Critique of the Use of This Category in New Testament Christology.* SBL Dissertation Series 40. Missoula, Mont.: Scholars Press, 1977.

Hollenweger, Walter J. *The Pentecostals.* Translated by R. A. Wilson. London: SCM Press, 1972/ Peabody, Mass.: Hendrickson, 1988.

Holme, L. R. *The Extinction of the Christian Churches in North Africa.* 1898; reprint New York: Burt Franklin, 1969.

Holmes, Edward A. "George Liele: Negro Slavery's Prophet of Deliverance." *Foundations* 9 (October 1966): 333-45.

Hopkins, Dwight N. *Black Theology—USA and South Africa: Politics, Culture and Liberation.* Maryknoll, N.Y.: Orbis, 1989.

Hopkins, Samuel. *Timely Articles on Slavery.* 1854; reprint Miami: Mnemosyne, 1969.

Houssney, Georges. "Unity: The Unfulfilled Dream of the Arabs." *Reach Out* 3 (June 1989): 14-15.

Hull, Gretchen Gaebelein. "Under the Yoke: Facing the Challenge of Global Oppression." In *World Christian Summer Reader 1990,* pp. 16-19. Pasadena, Calif.: World Christian.

Hunter, Emma. Letter dated February 1900, from Washington, D.C. Charles N. Hunter Papers, 1818-1931. Durham, N.C.: Duke University Manuscripts Collection.

Huntingford, G. W. B. "The Kingdom of Axum." In *The Dawn of African History,* pp. 22-29. Edited by Roland Oliver. London: Oxford University Press, 1961.

Hurmence, Belinda, ed. *Before Freedom: Forty-eight Oral Histories of Former North and South Carolina Slaves.* New York: Penguin, 1990.

Ingrassia, Michelle. "The Body of the Beholder." *Newsweek,* April 24, 1995, pp. 66-67.

Inscriptions Reveal: Documents from the Time of the Bible, the Mishna and the Talmud. Edited by Efrat Carmon. Translated by R. Grafman. Jerusalem: Israel Museum, 1973.

Interesting Memoirs and Documents Relating to American Slavery and the Glorious Struggle Now Making for Complete Emancipation. London: Chapman, Brothers, 1846. Reprint Miami: Mnemosyne, 1969.

*Isaac, Ephraim. *The Ethiopian Church.* Boston: Henry N. Sawyer, 1968. Includes a chapter on the traditional art of Ethiopia by Marjorie LeMay.

**Isichei, Elizabeth. *A History of Christianity in Africa from Antiquity to the Present.* Lawrenceville, N.J.: Africa World Press/Grand Rapids, Mich.: Eerdmans, 1995.

Isocrates. *Orations.* Translated by George Norlin and Larue van Hook. 3 vols. Loeb Classical Library. London: Heinemann/New York: G. P. Putnam's Sons, 1928-1961.

Jackson, John G. *Ethiopia and the Origin of Civilization: A Critical Review of the Evidence of Archaeology, Anthropology, History and Comparative Religion According to the Most Reliable Sources and Authorities.* Baltimore: Black Classic Press, n.d. (first published 1939).

———. *Introduction to African Civilizations.* New York: Carol, 1970.

Jacobs, Mignon R., and Gloria A. Johnson. "The Conceptual Dynamics of Good and Evil in the Joseph Story: An Exegetical and Hermeneutical Inquiry." Paper presented at the African-American Theology and Biblical Hermeneutics Group, Society of Biblical Literature annual meeting, 1994.

Jakobielski, S. "Christian Nubia at the Height of Its Civilization." In *Africa from the Seventh to the Eleventh Century,* pp. 194-223. Edited by M. El Fasi with I. Hrbek. Vol. 3 in *General History of Africa.* Berkeley: University of California Press/London: Heinemann Educational Books/Paris: United Nations Educational, Scientific and Cultural Organization, 1988.

James, George G. M. *Stolen Legacy: Greek Philosophy Is Stolen Egyptian Philosophy.* New York: Philosophical Library, 1954; reprint African Publication Society, 1980; United Brothers Communications Systems, 1989.

James, Kay Coles, with Jacqulline Cobb Fuller. *Never Forget: The Riveting Story of One Woman's Journey from Public Housing to the Corridors of Power.* Grand Rapids, Mich.: Zondervan/HarperCollins, 1992.

James, T. G. H. *Ancient Egypt: The Land and Its Legacy.* Austin: University of Texas Press, 1988.

Jennings, Theodore W., Jr. *Good News to the Poor: John Wesley's Evangelical Economics.* Nashville: Abingdon, 1990.

Jeremias, Joachim. *Jerusalem in the Time of Jesus.* London: SCM Press, 1969/Philadelphia: Fortress, 1975.

Jogunosimi, Ife. "The Role of Royal Women in Ancient Egypt." In *Kemet and the African Worldview: Research, Rescue and Restoration,* pp. 31-42. Edited by Maulana Karenga and Jacob H. Carruthers. Los Angeles: University of Sankore Press, 1986.

Johnson, Charles S., with Elizabeth L. Allen et al. *Into the Main Stream: A Survey of Best Practices in Race Relations in the South.* Chapel Hill: University of North Carolina Press, 1947.

Johnson, John L. *The Black Biblical Heritage.* Nashville: Winston-Derek, 1993.

Johnson, Luke T. *The Writings of the New Testament: An Introduction.* Philadelphia: Fortress, 1986.

Johnston, Flo. "Ordination Will Cross Racial Lines." *Chicago Tribune,* August 9, 1991, sec. 2, p. 9.

Johnstone, Patrick, *Operation World.* 5th ed. Grand Rapids, Mich.: Zondervan, 1993.

Jones, A. M. H. *A History of Rome Through the Fifth Century.* Vol. 2, *The Empire.* New York: Walker, 1970.

Jones, A. H. M., and Elizabeth Monroe. *A History of Ethiopia.* Oxford: Clarendon, 1955 (first printed in 1935 as *A History of Abyssinia*).

Jones, Charles C. *The Religious Instruction of the Negroes in the United States.* Savannah: Thomas Purse, 1842. Reprint Freeport, N.Y.: Books for Libraries/Black Heritage Library Collection, 1971.

Jones, Dorothy M. "The Mystique of Expertise in Social Services: An Alaska Example." *Journal of Sociology and Social Welfare* 3 (January 1976): 332-46.

Jones-Warsaw, Koala. "Toward a Womanist Hermeneutic: A Reading of Judges 19-21." *The Journal of the Interdenominational Theological Center* 22 (Fall 1994): 18-35.

Jordan, Paul. *Egypt the Black Land.* Oxford: Phaidon/New York: E. P. Dutton, 1976.

Jordan, Winthrop D. *The White Man's Burden: Historical Origins of Racism in the United States.* New York: Oxford University Press, 1974.

Joseph and Asenath. Translated by C. Burchard. In *The Old Testament Pseudepigrapha,* 2:177-247. Edited by James H. Charlesworth. 2 vols. Garden City, N.Y.: Doubleday, 1983-1985.

Joseph et Asèneth: Introduction, texte critique, traduction et notes. Edited by Marc Philonenko. Studia Post-Biblica tertium decimum. Leiden: Brill, 1968.

Josephus. *Works.* Translated by H. St. J. Thackeray et al. 10 vols. Loeb Classical Library. Cambridge, Mass.: Harvard University Press, 1926-1965.

*Joyner, Charles. *Down by the Riverside: A South Carolina Slave Community.* Urbana: University of Illinois Press, 1984.

Judge, E. A. *Rank and Status in the World of the Caesars and St. Paul.* Broadhead Memorial Lecture 1981. University of Canterbury Publications 29. Canterbury, U.K.: University of Canterbury, 1982.

Julien, Charles-André. *History of North Africa: Tunisia, Algeria, Morocco—from the Arab Conquest to 1830.* Edited and revised by C. C. Stewart and R. Le Tourneau. Translated by John Petrie. New York: Praeger, 1970.

Juvenal. *Satires.* Rev. ed. Translated by G. G. Ramsay. Loeb Classical Library. Cambridge, Mass.: Harvard University Press, 1940.

Kamil, Jill. *Coptic Egypt: History and Guide.* Plans and maps by Hassan Ibrahim. Rev. ed. Cairo: American University in Cairo Press, 1990.

Karenga, Maulana. "Restoration of the Husia: Reviving a Sacred Legacy." In *Kemet and the African Worldview: Research, Rescue and Restoration,* pp. 83-99. Edited by Maulana Karenga and Jacob H. Carruthers. Los Angeles: University of Sankore Press, 1986.

Katz, Judith H. *White Awareness: Handbook for Anti-racism Training.* Norman: University of Oklahoma Press, 1978.

Katz, Phyllis A. "The Acquisition of Racial Attitudes in Children." In *Towards the Elimination of Racism,* pp. 125-54. Edited by Phyllis A. Katz. New York: Pergamon, 1976.

Kee, Howard Clark. *Miracle in the Early Christian World: A Study in Sociohistorical Method.* New Haven, Conn.: Yale University Press, 1983.

Keener, Craig S. . . . *And Marries Another: Divorce and Remarriage in the Teaching of the New Testament.* Peabody, Mass.: Hendrickson, 1991.

———. "Christianity, Islam and Slavery." *Reach Out* 7, nos. 3-4 (1994): 20-22.

———. "Encounter with Truth: Early African Christianity." *A.M.E. Zion Missionary Seer,* July 1995, pp. 9, 37.

———. "Encounter with Truth: Missions and Racial Reconciliation in Romans." *A.M.E. Zion Missionary Seer,* January 1995, p. 7.

———. "Encounter with Truth: The Centurion's Servant." *A.M.E. Zion Missionary Seer,* November 1994, p. 9.

———. "Exorcising Racism." *The Crucible* 2 (Winter 1992): 21-26.

———. "The Function of Johannine Pneumatology in the Context of Late First-Century Judaism." Ann Arbor, Mich.: University Microfilms International, 1991 (from Duke University Ph.D. dissertation).

———. "The Gospels as Historically Reliable Biography." *A.M.E. Zion Quarterly Review* 105 (October 1993): 12-23.

———. *The IVP Bible Background Commentary: New Testament.* Downers Grove, Ill.: InterVarsity Press, 1993.

———. *Paul, Women and Wives: Marriage and Women's Ministry in the Letters of Paul.* Peabody, Mass.: Hendrickson, 1992.

———. "Sexual Infidelity as Exploitation." *Priscilla Papers* 7 (Fall 1993): 15-18.

———. "Slaves, Obey Your Masters: Ephesians 6:5." *The A.M.E. Zion Quarterly Review* 107, no. 4 (October 1995): 32-54.

———. *The Spirit in the Gospels and Acts: Rebirth and Prophetic Empowerment.* Peabody, Mass.: Hendrickson, 1996.

———. "Subversive Conservative." *Christian History* 14 (August 1995): 35-37.

———. *Three Crucial Questions About the Holy Spirit.* Grand Rapids, Mich.: Baker Book House, 1996.

———. "A White Convert to the Black Church." *The Reconciler* 2 (Spring 1995): 1, 8.

———. "White Minister Converts to Black Christianity." *Spirit of Truth,* August 1992, 42-43.

Kennedy, George A. *Classical Rhetoric and Its Christian and Secular Tradition from Ancient to Modern Times.* Chapel Hill: University of North Carolina Press, 1980.

Kenyon, Howard N. "Black Ministers in the Assemblies of God." *A/G Heritage,* Spring 1987, pp. 10-20.

King, Kenneth J. "Some Notes on Arnold J. Ford and New World Black Attitudes to Ethiopia." In *Black Apostles: Afro-American Clergy Confront the Twentieth Century,* pp. 49-55. Edited by Randall K. Burkett and Richard Newman. Boston: G. K. Hall, 1978.

Kitchen, Kenneth A. *Ancient Orient and the Old Testament.* Downers Grove, Ill.: InterVarsity Press, 1966.

————. *The Bible in Its World: The Bible and Archaeology Today.* Downers Grove, Ill.: InterVarsity Press, 1978.

————. "Some Egyptian Background to the Old Testament." *Tyndale Bulletin* 516 (1960): 8-9.

Klausner, Joseph. *Jesus: His Life, Times and Teaching.* Translated by Herbert Danby. 1925; reprint New York: Menorah, 1979.

Klein, Herbert S. "Anglicanism, Catholicism and the Negro Slave." In *The Debate over Slavery: Stanley Elkins and His Critics,* pp. 137-90. Edited by Ann J. Lane. Urbana: University of Illinois Press, 1971.

Klein, William W., Craig L. Blomberg and Robert L. Hubbard Jr. *Introduction to Biblical Interpretation.* Dallas: Word, 1993.

Kobishanov, Y. M. "Aksum: Political System, Economics and Culture, First to Fourth Century." In *Ancient Civilizations of Africa,* pp. 381-400. Edited by G. Mokhtar. Vol. 2 of *General History of Africa.* Berkeley: University of California Press;/London: Heinemann Educational Books/Paris: United Nations Educational, Scientific and Cultural Organization, 1981.

Koester, Helmut. *Introduction to the New Testament.* 2 vols. Hermeneia Foundations and Facets Series. Vol. 1: *History, Culture and Religion of the Hellenistic Age.* Vol. 2: *History and Literature of Early Christianity.* Philadelphia: Fortress, 1982.

*Koger, Larry. *Black Slaveowners: Free Black Slave Masters in South Carolina, 1790-1860.* Jefferson, N.C.: McFarland, 1985.

Kohn, Marek. "Science and Race Matters." *World Press Review,* December 1995, p. 48.

Kraabel, A. T. "New Evidence of the Samaritan Diaspora Has Been Found on Delos." *Biblical Archaeologist* 47, no. 1 (1984): 44-46.

Kroeger, Catherine Clark. "Black Is Blessed: A Study of Black and/or African Women in the Bible." Minneapolis: Christians for Biblical Equality, n.d.

Kuklick, Henrika. "Chicago Sociology and Urban Planning Policy: Sociological Theory as Occupational Ideology." *Theory and Society* 9 (November 1980): 321-45.

*Kunjufu, Jawanza. *Black Economics: Solutions for Economic and Community Empowerment.* Chicago: African American Images, 1991.

Kwapong, A. A. "Carthage, Greece and Rome." In *The Dawn of African History,* pp. 13-21. Edited by Roland Oliver. London: Oxford University Press, 1961.

Ladd, George Eldon. *A Theology of the New Testament.* Grand Rapids, Mich.: Eerdmans, 1974.

Ladner, Joyce A. *Tomorrow's Tomorrow: The Black Woman.* Garden City, N.Y.: Doubleday, 1971.

Lake, Kirsopp, and Henry J. Cadbury. *English Translation and Commentary.* Vol. 4 of *The Beginnings of Christianity.* 5 vols. Edited by F. J. Foakes Jackson and Kirsopp Lake. Grand Rapids, Mich.: Baker Book House, 1979.

Lalevée, Thierry. "Tehran's New Allies in Africa: Exporting the Islamic Revolution." *World Press Review,* September 1993, pp. 20-21, from the Arab-oriented French monthly *Arabies.*

Lane, William L. *Hebrews 9-13.* Word Biblical Commentary 47B. Dallas: Word, 1991.

Larsen, David B., and Christopher A. Hall, "Holy Health," *Christianity Today,* November 23, 1992, pp. 18-22.

Lasch-Quinn, Elisabeth. *Black Neighbors: Race and the Limits of Reform in the American Settlement House Movement, 1890-1945.* Chapel Hill: University of North Carolina Press, 1993.

LaSor, William Sanford. "Egypt." In *The International Standard Bible Encyclopedia,* 2:29-47. Edited by Geoffrey W. Bromiley. 4 vols. Grand Rapids, Mich.: Eerdmans, 1979-1988.

LaSor, William Sanford, David Allen Hubbard and Frederick William Bush. *Old Testament Survey: The Message, Form and Background of the Old Testament.* Grand Rapids, Mich.: Eerdmans, 1982.

Latourette, Kenneth Scott. *Three Centuries of Advance, A.D. 1500-A.D. 1800.* Vol. 3 of *A History of the Expansion of Christianity.* New York: Harper & Brothers, 1939.

Leatt, James, Theo Kneifel and Klaus Nürnburger, eds. *Contending Ideologies in South Africa.* Cape Town: David Phelp, 1986.

Lecky, Robert S., and H. Elliott Wright, eds. *Black Manifesto: Religion, Racism and Reparations.* New York: Sheed & Ward, 1969.

Leclant, J. "The Empire of Kush: Napata and Meroe." In *Ancient Civilizations of Africa,* pp. 278-

95. Edited by G. Mokhtar. Vol. 2 of *General History of Africa.* Berkeley: University of California Press/London: Heinemann Educational Books/Paris: United Nations Educational, Scientific and Cultural Organization, 1981.

Lee, Jarena. "The Life and Religious Experience of Jarena Lee, a Coloured Lady, Giving an Account of Her Call to Preach the Gospel." Rev. ed. Philadelphia: Author, 1836. Reprinted in *Sisters of the Spirit: Three Black Women's Autobiographies of the Nineteenth Century,* pp. 25-48. Edited by William L. Andrews. Bloomington: Indiana University Press, 1986.

Lewis, Bernard. *History Remembered, Recovered, Invented.* New York: Simon & Schuster, 1975.

———. "The Invading Crescent." In *The Dawn of African History,* pp. 30-36. Edited by Roland Oliver. London: Oxford University Press, 1961.

**———. *Race and Slavery in the Middle East: An Historical Enquiry.* New York: Oxford University Press, 1990.

Lewis, Naphtali. *Life in Egypt Under Roman Rule.* Oxford: Clarendon, 1983.

*Lincoln, C. Eric. *The Black Muslims in America.* 3rd ed. Trenton, N.J.: Africa World Press/Grand Rapids, Mich.: Eerdmans, 1994 (revised from the author's Ph.D. thesis at Boston University).

*———. *Race, Religion and the Continuing American Dilemma.* New York: Hill & Wang, 1984.

*Lincoln, C. Eric, and Lawrence H. Mamiya. *The Black Church in the African American Experience.* Durham, N.C.: Duke University Press, 1990.

Liverani, M. "Ugarit; Ugaritic." In *The International Standard Bible Encyclopedia,* 4:937-41. Edited by Geoffrey W. Bromiley. 4 vols. Grand Rapids, Mich.: Eerdmans, 1979-1988.

Livingstone, David N. *Darwin's Forgotten Defenders: The Encounter Between Evangelical Theology and Evolutionary Thought.* Grand Rapids, Mich.: Eerdmans/Edinburgh: Scottish Academic Press, 1987.

Lloyd, Seton. *The Archaeology of Mesopotamia.* London: Thames & Hudson, 1978.

Lohse, Eduard. *Die Texte Aus Qumran.* Munich: Kösel-Verlag, 1971.

Lomax, Louis. "When 'Nonviolence' Meets 'Black Power.'" In *Martin Luther King Jr.: A Profile,* pp. 157-80. Rev. ed. Edited by C. Eric Lincoln. New York: Hill & Wang, 1984. (Originally published in Louis Lomax, *To Kill a Black Man* [Los Angeles: Holloway House, 1968], pp. 113-22, 159-69, 189-97.)

"The Lord's Army." *World Press Review,* October 1995, p. 26.

Lucas, A. *Ancient Egyptian Materials and Industries.* 4th ed. London: Edward Arnold, 1962.

Lucian. *Works.* Translated by A. M. Harmon, K. Kilburn and M. D. Macleod. 8 vols. Loeb Classical Library. Cambridge, Mass.: Harvard University Press, 1913-1961.

Lurker, Manfred. *The Gods and Symbols of Ancient Egypt: An Illustrated Dictionary.* London: Thames & Hudson, 1980.

Luthuli, Albert. Postscript to "Let My People Go." In *Classics of Christian Missions,* pp. 409-26. Edited by Francis M. DuBose. Nashville: Broadman, 1979.

Mack, Raymond W., ed. *Race, Class and Power.* 2nd ed. New York: D. Van Nostrand, 1968.

Madany, Shirley W. "Arabs and Slave Trade." *Reach Out* 7, nos. 3-4 (1994): 17-19.

Maddox, Robert. *The Purpose of Luke-Acts.* Edinburgh: T & T Clark, 1982.

Magnuson, Norris. *Salvation in the Slums: Evangelical Social Work, 1865-1920.* American Theological Library Association Monograph 10. Metuchen, N.J.: Scarecrow, 1977. Reprint Grand Rapids, Mich.: Baker Book House, 1990.

Mahjoubi, A. "The Roman Period." In *Ancient Civilizations of Africa,* pp. 465-99. Edited by G. Mokhtar. Vol. 2 of *General History of Africa.* Berkeley: University of California Press/London: Heinemann Educational Books/Paris: United Nations Educational, Scientific and Cultural Organization, 1981.

Maillot, A. "Quelques remarques sur la Naissance Virginale du Christ." *Foi et Vie* 77 (1978): 30-44.

Malcolm X (El-Hajj Malik El-Shabazz), with Alex Haley. *The Autobiography of Malcolm X.* New York: Grove, 1965.

Malherbe, Abraham J. "A Physical Description of Paul." *Harvard Theological Review* 79, nos. 1-3 (1986): 170-75.

*Mannix, Daniel P., with Malcolm Cowley. *Black Cargoes: A History of the Atlantic Slave Trade, 1518-1865.* New York: Viking, 1962.

Marcus Aurelius. *Meditations.* Translated by C. R. Haines. Loeb Classical Library. Cambridge,

Mass.: Harvard University Press, 1916.

Marko, Tamera. "Amazing Faith: Evangelical Churches Grow in Ethiopia." *World Vision,* August 1995, pp. 10-15.

Marsh, William. "The Law of Liberty." In *Autographs for Freedom,* 2:61-62. Edited by Julia Griffiths. Auburn, N.Y.: Alden, Beardsley, 1854.

Marshall, I. Howard. *The Origins of New Testament Christology.* Rev. ed. Downers Grove, Ill.: InterVarsity Press, 1990.

Martial. *Epigrams.* Translated by Walter C. A. Ker. 2 vols. Loeb Classical Library. New York: G. P. Putnam's Sons/London: Heinemann, 1920.

Martin, Clarice J. "Womanist Interpretations of the New Testament: The Quest for Holistic and Inclusive Translation and Interpretation." In *Black Theology: A Documentary History,* 2:225-44. Edited by James H. Cone and Gayraud S. Wilmore. 2 vols. Maryknoll, N.Y.: Orbis, 1993.

Martin, Dale B. *Slavery as Salvation: The Metaphor of Slavery in Pauline Christianity.* New Haven, Conn.: Yale University Press, 1990.

Martin, Sandy D. *Black Baptists and African Missions: The Origins of a Movement, 1880-1915.* Macon, Ga.: Mercer University Press, 1992.

Martin, Walter R. *The Kingdom of the Cults: An Analysis of the Major Cult Systems in the Present Christian Era.* 3rd rev. ed. Minneapolis: Bethany Fellowship, 1977.

**Masland, Tom, et al. "Slavery." *Newsweek,* May 4, 1992, pp. 30-39.

Mason, M. C. B. *The Gospel Message.* Cincinnati: Jennings and Graham, 1905.

"Mass Murder." *Newsweek,* May 9, 1994, pp. 40-41.

Matthews, Donald G. *Slavery and Methodism: A Chapter in American Morality, 1780-1845.* Princeton, N.J.: Princeton University Press, 1965.

May, Samuel J. *Some Recollections of Our Antislavery Conflict.* Boston: Fields, Osgood, 1869. Reprint New York: Arno/New York Times, 1968.

Mays, Benjamin E. *Seeking to Be Christian in Race Relations.* Study and Action Pamphlets on Race Relations. New York: Friendship, 1946.

Mazar, Amihay. "Excavations at Tell Qasile, 1971-72: Preliminary Report." *Israel Exploration Journal* 23, no. 2 (1973): 65-67.

———. "A Philistine Temple at Tell Qasile." *Biblical Archaeologist* 36 (May 1973): 42-48.

Mazar, Benjamin, ed. *Views of the Biblical World.* 5 vols. New York: Arco, 1959.

*Mbiti, John S. *African Religions and Philosophies.* Garden City, N.Y.: Doubleday, 1970.

———. "An African Views American Black Theology." In *Black Theology: A Documentary History,* 1:379-84. Edited by James H. Cone and Gayraud S. Wilmore. 2 vols. Maryknoll, N.Y.: Orbis, 1993. Vol. 1: 1966-1979.

———. *New Testament Eschatology in an African Background: A Study of the Encounter Between New Testament Theology and African Traditional Concepts.* London: Oxford University Press, 1971.

*McCray, Walter Arthur. *The Black Presence in the Bible: Teacher's Guide.* Chicago: Black Light Fellowship, 1990.

McDonald, Robin. "Stretch Your Racial Comfort Zone." *Christianity Today,* June 22, 1992, p. 14.

McDowell, Deborah E. "Slavery as a Sacred Text: Witnessing in *Dessa Rose.*" In *Living the Intersection: Womanism and Afrocentrism in Theology,* pp. 81-103. Edited by Cheryl J. Sanders. Minneapolis: Fortress, 1995.

*McKissic, William Dwight, Sr. *Beyond Roots.* Wenonah, N.J.: Renaissance Productions, 1990.

McManus, Edgar J. *Black Bondage in the North.* Syracuse, N.Y.: Syracuse University Press, 1973.

McMinn, Lisa Graham, and Mark R. McMinn. "For Whom the Bell Curves." *Christianity Today,* December 12, 1994, p. 19 (challenging Hernnstein and Murray's *The Bell Curve*).

Meier, John P. *A Marginal Jew: Rethinking the Historical Jesus.* 2 vols. Anchor Bible Reference Library. New York: Doubleday, 1991-1994.

Mekilta de-Rabbi Ishmael. Translated by Jacob Z. Lauterbach. 3 vols. Philadelphia: Jewish Publication Society of America, 1933-1935.

*Mekouria, Tekle Tsadik. "Christian Aksum." In *Ancient Civilizations of Africa,* pp. 401-22. Edited by G. Mokhtar. Vol. 2 of *General History of Africa.* Berkeley: University of California Press/ London: Heinemann Educational Books/Paris: United Nations Educational, Scientific and Cultural Organization, 1981.

———. "The Horn of Africa." In *Africa from the Seventh to the Eleventh Century*, pp. 558-74. Edited by M. El Fasi with I. Hrbek. Vol. 3 of *General History of Africa*. Berkeley: University of California Press/London: Heinemann Educational Books/Paris: United Nations Educational, Scientific and Cultural Organization, 1988.

Mellon, Matthew T. *Early American Views on Negro Slavery: From the Letters and Papers of the Founders of the Republic*. 2nd ed. New York: Mentor/New American Library, 1969.

Menzies, William J. *Anointed to Serve: The Story of the Assemblies of God*. Springfield, Mo.: Gospel Publishing House, 1971.

Mercy Magazine, January 1994, p. 3.

Metzger, Bruce M. "Considerations of Methodology in the Study of the Mystery Religions and Early Christianity." *Harvard Theological Review* 48 (January 1955): 1-20.

———. *The Text of the New Testament: Its Transmission, Corruption and Restoration*. 2nd ed. New York: Oxford University Press, 1968.

Michalowski, Kazimierz. *Art of Ancient Egypt*. New York: Harry N. Abrams, n.d.

———. "The Spreading of Christianity in Nubia." In *Ancient Civilizations of Africa*, pp. 326-40. Edited by G. Mokhtar. Vol. 2 of *General History of Africa*. Berkeley: University of California Press/London: Heinemann Educational Books/Paris: United Nations Educational, Scientific and Cultural Organization, 1981.

The Midrash Rabbah. Edited by Harry Freedman and Maurice Simon. 5 vols. New York: Soncino, 1977.

Miller, Richard Roscoe. *Slavery and Catholicism*. Durham, N.C.: North State, 1957.

"Ministry Breaks Slavery Bonds." *Christianity Today*, August 16, 1993, p. 54.

The Mishnah. Translated by Herbert Danby. London: Oxford University Press, 1933.

The Mishnah. Pointed Hebrew text, introductions, translations, notes and supplements by Philip Blackman. 7 vols. New York: Judaica, 1963.

Mitchell, Henry H. *Black Belief: Folk Beliefs of Blacks in America and West Africa*. New York: Harper & Row, 1975.

———. "The Theological Posits of Black Christianity." In *Black Theology II: Essays on the Formation and Outreach of Contemporary Black Theology*, pp. 115-32. Edited by Calvin E. Bruce and William R. Jones. Lewisburg, Va.: Bucknell University Press/Cranbury, N.J.: Associated University Presses, 1978.

Mitchell, Henry M., and Emil M. Thomas. *Preaching for Black Self-Esteem*. Nashville: Abingdon, 1994.

Mnkandla, Maureen. "Sexual Abuse." in *Our Time Has Come: African Christian Women Address the Issues of Today*, pp. 88-93. Edited by Judy Mbugua. Grand Rapids, Mich.: Baker Book House/Carlisle, U.K.: Paternoster/World Evangelical Fellowship, 1994.

Molebatsi, Caesar, with David Virtue. *A Flame for Justice*. Batavia, Ill.: Lion, 1991.

Monès, H. "The Conquest of North Africa and the Berber Resistance." In *Africa from the Seventh to the Eleventh Century*, pp. 224-45. Edited by M. El Fasi with I. Hrbek. Vol. 3 of *General History of Africa*. Berkeley: University of California Press/London: Heinemann Educational Books/Paris: United Nations Educational, Scientific and Cultural Organization, 1988.

Moody, V. Alton. *Slavery on Louisiana Sugar Plantations*. New York: AMS, 1976. (Ph.D. dissertation, University of Michigan; reprinted from *The Louisiana Historical Quarterly*, April 1924.)

Moore, Wilbert E. *American Negro Slavery and Abolition: A Sociological Study*. New York: Third Press/Joseph Okpaku, 1971.

Morgan, Timothy C. "Racist No More? Black Leaders Ask." *Christianity Today*, August 14, 1995, p. 53.

Morganthau, Tom. "What Color Is Black?" *Newsweek*, February 13, 1995, pp. 62-65.

Morgenstern, Julian. "The Ark, the Ephod and the 'Tent of Meeting.' " *Hebrew Union College Annual* 17 (1942-1943): 153-265.

Morton, A. Q., and G. H. C. MacGregor. *The Structure of Luke and Acts*. New York: Harper & Row, 1964.

Mosley, A. W. "Historical Reporting in the Ancient World." *New Testament Studies* 12 (1965): 10-26.

Moyer, James Carroll. "The Concept of Ritual Purity Among the Hittites." Ph.D. dissertation, Brandeis University, 1969.

Mukenge, Ida Rousseau. *The Black Church in Urban America: A Case Study in Political Economy.* Lanham, Md.: University Press of America, 1983.

Mumbi, Rosemary. "Battered Women." in *Our Time Has Come: African Christian Women Address the Issues of Today,* pp. 67-70. Edited by Judy Mbugua. Grand Rapids, Mich.: Baker Book House/Carlisle, U.K.: Paternoster/World Evangelical Fellowship, 1994.

Munck, Johannes. *The Acts of the Apostles.* Revised by William F. Albright and C. S. Mann. Anchor Bible. Garden City, N.Y.: Doubleday, 1967.

Murphy, James. "Teacher Expectations and Working Class Under-achievement." *British Journal of Sociology* 25 (September 1974): 326-44.

Murray, Kettehkumuehn Earl. *Oral Utterances: Philosophical, Moral/Ethical and Religious Sayings of the Ancient Griot.* Charlotte, N.C.: Kilimanjaro, 1995.

Murray, Margaret A. *Egyptian Temples.* London: Sampson Law, Marston, n.d.

———. *The Splendor That Was Egypt.* New York: Hawthorn, 1963.

Myers, David G. "Who's Happy? Who's Not?" *Christianity Today,* November 23, 1992, pp. 23-26.

Nanan, Madame. "The Sorcerer and Pagan Practices." In *Our Time Has Come: African Christian Women Address the Issues of Today,* pp. 81-87. Edited by Judy Mbugua. Grand Rapids, Mich.: Baker Book House/Carlisle, U.K.: Paternoster/World Evangelical Fellowship, 1994.

Neill, Stephen. *A History of Christian Missions.* Baltimore: Penguin, 1964.

Nelsen, Hart M., and Anne Kusener Nelsen. *Black Church in the Sixties.* Lexington: University Press of Kentucky, 1975.

Nelson, Harold H. "The Egyptian Temple." In *The Biblical Archaeologist Reader,* pp. 147-58. Edited by G. Ernest Wright and David Noel Freedman. Chicago: Quadrangle, 1961.

"Neo-Nazi Novel a Blueprint for Hate." *SPLC Report* (Southern Poverty Law Center) 25, no. 3 (September 1995): 1, 5.

Neusner, Jacob. *Judaism in the Beginning of Christianity.* Philadelphia: Fortress, 1984.

Newsweek. August 12, 1991, p. 15; September 30, 1991, p. 17; May 18, 1992, p. 47; October 12, 1992, p. 49; May 22, 1995, p. 15.

"Nigeria: Can Oil and Democracy Mix?" *Amnesty Action,* Fall 1995, pp. 1, 3.

Noble, Lowell. "Blacks and Whites: Who's Inferior?" *Urban Family,* Winter 1995, p. 34.

Nock, Arthur Darby. *Early Gentile Christianity and Its Hellenistic Background.* New York: Harper & Row, 1964.

———. "The Vocabulary of the New Testament." *Journal of Biblical Literature* 52 (1933): 131-39.

*Noll, Mark A. *A History of Christianity in the United States and Canada.* Grand Rapids, Mich.: Eerdmans, 1992.

———. "Midwives of South Africa's Rebirth." *Christianity Today,* July 17, 1995, pp. 33-34. Review of Peter F. Alexander, *Alan Paton: A Biography* (Oxford University Press), and Nelson Mandela, *Long Walk to Freedom: The Autobiography of Nelson Mandela* (Little, Brown).

Norton, Dolores G. "Diversity, Early Socialization and Temporal Development: The Dual Perspective Revisited." In *Perspectives on Equity and Justice in Social Work,* pp. 17-33. Edited by Dorothy M. Pearson. Carl A. Scott Memorial Lecture Series, 1988-1992. Alexandria, Va.: Council on Social Work Education, 1993.

Nukunya, G. K. *Kinship and Marriage Among the Anlo Ewe.* London School of Economics Monographs on Social Anthropology 37. New York: Humanities, 1969.

O'Connor, David. "Nubia Before the New Kingdom." In *Africa in Antiquity I: The Arts of Ancient Nubia and the Sudan—the Essays,* pp. 46-61. Brooklyn, N.Y.: Brooklyn Museum, 1978.

Ogebe, Mary Dija. "Social Injustice." In *Our Time Has Come: African Christian Women Address the Issues of Today,* pp. 61-66. Edited by Judy Mbugua. Grand Rapids, Mich.: Baker Book House/Carlisle, U.K.: Paternoster/World Evangelical Fellowship, 1994.

Ogot, Bethwell. "The Muslim Trade." *World Press Review,* August 1993, 23; reprinted from *Daily Nation,* Nairobi, Kenya.

Okorocha, Cyril. "The Meaning of Salvation: An African Perspective." In *Emerging Voices in Global Christian Theology,* pp. 59-92. Edited by William A. Dyrness. Grand Rapids, Mich.: Zondervan, 1994.

The Old Testament Pseudepigrapha. Edited by James H. Charlesworth. 2 vols. Garden City, N.Y.: Doubleday, 1983-1985.

Oliver, Roland. "The Riddle of Zimbabwe." In *The Dawn of African History,* pp. 53-59. Edited by Roland Oliver. London: Oxford University Press, 1961.

Oliver, Roland, and J. D. Fage. *A Short History of Africa.* New York: Facts on File, 1989.

Olmstead, A. T. *History of the Persian Empire.* Chicago: Phoenix/University of Chicago Press, 1959.

Olmsted, Frederick Law. *A Journey in the Seaboard Slave States with Remarks on Their Economy.* New York: Dix & Edwards/London: Sampson Low, Son, 1856. Reprinted in *The Slave States.* Rev. ed. Edited by Harvey Wish. New York: Capricorn, 1959.

Olsen, Edward G. "What Shall We Teach About Race and Racism?" In *Teaching in the Inner City: A Book of Readings,* pp. 356-60. Edited by James C. Stone and Frederick W. Schneider. Commitment to Teaching 3. New York: Thomas Y. Crowell, 1970.

Olsen, Glenn W. "Early Christian Nubia: Progress and Prospects of Research." *Proceedings of the PMR Conference* 6 (1981): 74-77.

Oppenheim, A. Leo. "The Mesopotamian Temple." In *The Biblical Archaeologist Reader,* pp. 158-69. Edited by G. Ernest Wright and David Noel Freedman. Chicago: Quadrangle, 1961.

O'Reilly, Kenneth. *"Racial Matters": The FBI's Secret File on Black America, 1960-1972.* New York: Free Press/Macmillan, 1989.

O'Rourke, John J. "Roman Law and the Early Church." In *The Catacombs and the Colosseum: The Roman Empire as the Setting of Primitive Christianity,* pp. 165-86. Edited by Stephen Benko and John J. O'Rourke. Valley Forge, Penn.: Judson, 1971.

The Other Side, November 1993, p. 13.

Otto, Walter F. *Dionysus: Myth and Cult.* Translated by Robert B. Palmer. Bloomington: Indiana University Press, 1965.

Owens, J. Garfield. *All God's Chillun: Meditations on Negro Spirituals.* Nashville: Abingdon, 1971.

Padgett, Alan. "The Pauline Rationale for Submission: Biblical Feminism and the *hina* Clauses of Titus 2:1-10." *Evangelical Quarterly* 59 (January 1987): 39-52.

Palestinian Talmud. *Talmud of the Land of Israel: A Preliminary Translation and Explanation.* Edited by Jacob Neusner. Chicago: University of Chicago Press, 1982- .

**Pankhurst, Richard K. Y., ed. *The Ethiopian Royal Chronicles.* Addis Ababa: Oxford University Press, 1967.

*Pannell, William. *The Coming Race Wars? A Cry for Reconciliation.* Grand Rapids, Mich.: Zondervan, 1993.

Paris, Arthur E. *Black Pentecostalism: Southern Religion in an Urban World.* Amherst: University of Massachusetts Press, 1982.

Parkes, James. *The Conflict of the Church and the Synagogue: A Study in the Origins of Antisemitism.* New York: Atheneum, 1969.

Parrot, André. "Mari." In *Archaeology and Old Testament Study.* Edited by D. Winton Thomas. Oxford: Clarendon, 1967.

Patterson, Orlando. "Going Separate Ways: The History of an Old Idea—Why Farrakhan's Obsession with Race Is Bad for Blacks." *Newsweek,* October 30, 1995, p. 43.

Payne, Daniel Alexander. *Recollections of Seventy Years.* Reprint ed. New York: Arno/New York Times, 1969.

Pedersen, Eigil, Therese-Annette Faucher and William W. Eaton. "A New Perspective on the Effects of First-Grade Teachers on Children's Subsequent Adult Status." *Harvard Educational Review* 48 (February 1978): 1-31.

Pelt, Owen D., and Ralph Lee Smith. *The Story of the National Baptists.* New York: Vantage, 1960.

Perkins, John. *Beyond Charity: The Call to Christian Community Development.* Grand Rapids, Mich.: Baker Book House, 1993.

————. *Let Justice Roll Down.* Ventura, Calif.: Regal, 1976.

*————. *With Justice for All.* Ventura, Calif.: Regal, 1982.

Perkins, Spencer. "Can Blacks and Whites Be Neighbors?" *Urban Family,* Winter 1992, pp. 21-23.

**Perkins, Spencer, and Chris Rice. *More Than Equals: Racial Healing for the Sake of the Gospel.* Downers Grove, Ill.: InterVarsity Press, 1993.

Perry, Dwight, and Ralph Hammond. "The Strategic Role of the Black Church." In *The African-*

American Consultation on Church Planting and Revitalization, pp. 101-19. Edited by Dwight Perry. Baptist General Conference Annual Meeting 1992.

Pesikta Rabbati. Translated by William G. Braude. 2 vols. Yale Judaica Series 18. New Haven, Conn.: Yale University Press, 1968.

Peters, F. E. *Muhammad and the Origins of Islam.* Albany: State University of New York Press, 1994.

Peterson, Thomas Virgil. *Ham and Japheth: The Mythic World of Whites in the Antebellum South.* American Theological Library Association Monograph 12. Metuchen, N.J.: Scarecrow/American Theological Library Association, 1978.

Petrie, W. M. Flinders. *Arts and Crafts of Ancient Egypt.* New York: Attic, 1910.

Petronius. *Satyricon, Fragment and Poems.* Translated by W. H. D. Rouse. Loeb Classical Library. London: Heinemann/New York: G. P. Putnam's Sons, 1913.

Pettigrew, Thomas F. *Racially Separate or Together?* McGraw-Hill Series in Sociology. New York: McGraw-Hill, 1971.

Pfeiffer, Charles F., ed. *The Biblical World: A Dictionary of Biblical Archaeology.* Grand Rapids, Mich.: Baker Book House, 1966.

————. *Ras Shamra and the Bible.* Grand Rapids, Mich.: Baker Book House, 1962.

————. *Tell el Amarna and the Bible.* Grand Rapids, Mich.: Baker Book House, 1963.

Philo of Alexandria. *Works.* Translated by F. H. Colson and G. H. Whitaker. Loeb Classical Library. London: Heinemann/New York: G. P. Putnam's Sons, 1929-1962. Supplementary vols. 1 and 2, translated by Ralph Marcus. Cambridge, Mass.: Harvard University Press, 1953.

Philostratus. *Life of Apollonius of Tyana.* Translated by F. C. Conybeare. 2 vols. Loeb Classical Library. Cambridge, Mass.: Harvard University Press, 1912.

Pickthall, Mohammed Marmaduke. *The Meaning of the Glorious Koran: An Explanatory Translation.* New York: Mentor/New American Library, n.d.

Pierard, Richard V. "Social Concern In Christian Missions." *Christianity Today,* June 18, 1976, pp. 7-10.

Pierce, Larry. "Where There's Faith, There's Hope for Boys." *Christianity Today,* September 13, 1993, p. 80.

Pilch, John J. "Sickness and Healing in Luke-Acts." In *The Social World of Luke-Acts: Models for Interpretation,* pp. 181-209. Edited by Jerome H. Neyrey. Peabody, Mass.: Hendrickson, 1991.

Pipes, William H. *Say Amen, Brother! Old-Time Negro Preaching: A Study in American Frustration.* New York: William-Frederick, 1951. Reprint Westport, Conn.: Negro Universities Press, 1970.

Plotinus. *Works.* Translated by A. H. Armstrong. 6 vols. Loeb Classical Library. Cambridge, Mass.: Harvard University Press, 1966- .

Plutarch. *Lives.* Translated by Bernadotte Perrin et al. 11 vols. Loeb Classical Library. London: Heinemann/New York: G. P. Putnam's Sons, 1914- .

————. *Moralia.* Translated by Frank Cole Babbitt et al. 15 vols. Loeb Classical Library. London: Heinemann/New York: G. P. Putnam's Sons, 1927-1969.

*Pobee, John S. *Toward an African Theology.* Nashville: Abingdon, 1979.

Porter, Les. "Will Your Church Become a Mosque?" *Reach Out* 7, nos. 3-4 (1994): 6-7.

Powledge, Fred. *Black Power/White Resistance: Notes on the New Civil War.* New York: Clarion/Simon & Schuster, 1967.

Pritchard, James B., ed. *Ancient Near Eastern Texts Relating to the Old Testament.* 2nd ed. Princeton, N.J.: Princeton University Press, 1955.

Proceedings of the General Anti-slavery Convention, Called by the Committee of the British and Foreign Anti-slavery Society, and Held in London from Tuesday, June 13th, to Tuesday, June 20th, 1843. London: General Anti-slavery Convention, 1843. Reprint Miami: Mnemosyne, 1969.

Quarles, Benjamin, ed. *Frederick Douglass.* Great Lives Observed. Englewood Cliffs, N.J.: Prentice-Hall, 1968.

Quintilian. *The Institutio Oratoria.* Translated by H. E. Butler. 4 vols. Loeb Classical Library. Cambridge, Mass.: Harvard University Press, 1920-1922.

Quirke, Stephen, and Jeffrey Spencer, eds. *The British Museum Book of Ancient Egypt.* London: Thames & Hudson, 1992.

**Raboteau, Albert J. *Slave Religion: The "Invisible Institution" in the Antebellum South.* New York: Oxford University Press, 1978.

"Racist Identity Sect Fuels Nationwide Extremist Movement." *Klanwatch Intelligence Report,* August 1995, pp. 1, 3, 5.

Raleigh News & Observer, September 1, 1991, p. C1.

Rankin, John. *Letters on American Slavery Addressed to Mr. Thomas Rankin.* 5th ed. Boston: Isaac Knapp, 1838. Reprint New York: Arno/New York Times, 1969.

Rashad, Adib (James Miller). *The History of Islam and Black Nationalism in the Americas.* 2nd ed. Beltsville, Md.: Writers', 1991.

*Rashidi, Runoko. "Africans in Early Asian Civilizations: A Historical Overview." In *African Presence in Early Asia,* pp. 15-52. Edited by Ivan Van Sertima and Runoko Rashidi. New Brunswick, N.J.: Transaction (Rutgers)/Journal of African Civilizations, 1988.

———. "More Light on Sumer, Elam and India." In *African Presence in Early Asia,* pp. 163-77. Edited by Ivan Van Sertima and Runoko Rashidi. New Brunswick, N.J.: Transaction (Rutgers)/Journal of African Civilizations, 1988.

Rawson, Beryl. "Children in the Roman *Familia.*" In *The Family in Ancient Rome: New Perspectives,* pp. 170-200. Edited by Beryl Rawson. Ithaca, N.Y.: Cornell University Press, 1986.

Reach Out, April 1992, p. 29; 6, nos. 1-2 (Spring 1993), whole issue.

Renfrew, Colin, and Paul Bahn. *Archaeology: Theories, Methods and Practice.* London: Thames & Hudson, 1991.

Rensberger, David. "Oppression and Identity in the Gospel of John." In *The Recovery of Black Presence: An Interdisciplinary Exploration—Essays in Honor of Dr. Charles B. Copher,* pp. 77-94. Edited by Randall C. Bailey and Jacquelyn Grant. Nashville: Abingdon, 1995.

"Report of the Symposium on the Peopling of Ancient Egypt and the Deciphering of the Meroitic Script (Cairo, January 28-February 3, 1974)." In *Ancient Civilizations of Africa,* pp. 58-82. Edited by G. Mokhtar. Vol. 2 of *General History of Africa.* Berkeley: University of California Press/London: Heinemann Educational Books/Paris: United Nations Educational, Scientific and Cultural Organization, 1981.

Reynolds, H. R. "Edesius." In *A Dictionary of Christian Biography and Literature to the End of the Sixth Century A.D., with an Account of the Principal Sects and Heresies,* p. 287. Edited by Henry Wace and William C. Piercy. Peabody, Mass.: Hendrickson, 1994.

*Rice, Gene. "The African Roots of the Prophet Zephaniah." *The Journal of Religious Thought* 36 (1979): 21-31.

Richard, R. L. "Trinity, Holy." In *New Catholic Encyclopedia,* 14:293-306. 17 vols. Washington, D.C.: Catholic University of America, 1967.

Richardson, Don. *Peace Child.* Ventura, Calif.: Regal, 1974.

Riesner, Rainer. "Education élémentaire juive et tradition évangélique." *Hokhma* 21 (1982): 51-64.

**Riggs, Marcia Y. *Awake, Arise and Act: A Womanist Call for Black Liberation.* Cleveland, Ohio: Pilgrim, 1994.

Ripley, C. Peter, ed. *Witness for Freedom: African American Voices on Race, Slavery and Emancipation.* Chapel Hill: University of North Carolina Press, 1993.

Robeck, Cecil M., Jr. "William J. Seymour and 'the Bible Evidence.' " In *Initial Evidence: Historical and Biblical Perspectives on the Pentecostal Doctrine of Spirit Baptism,* pp. 72-95. Edited by Gary B. McGee. Peabody, Mass.: Hendrickson, 1991.

Roberts, J. Deotis. *A Black Political Theology.* Philadelphia: Westminster Press, 1974.

Roberts, R. L. "The Rendering 'Only Begotten' in John 3:16." *Restoration Quarterly* 16, no. 1 (1973): 2-22.

Robinson, Armstead. "A Concluding Statement." In *Black Studies in the University: A Symposium,* pp. 216-23. Edited by Armstead Robinson, Craig C. Foster and Donald H. Ogilvie. New York: Bantam, 1969.

Robinson, Armstead, Craig C. Foster and Donald H. Ogilvie, eds. *Black Studies in the University: A Symposium.* New York: Bantam, 1969.

Robinson, Frank. "C. H. Mason and the White COGIC." Los Angeles: West Angeles Church of God in Christ tape ministry, n.d.

Robinson, Freddie. *Errors in the Bible Revealed.* N.p.: Lee T. Robinson/Transfiguration Production, 1993.

Robinson, John A. T. *Can We Trust the New Testament?* Grand Rapids, Mich.: Eerdmans, 1977.

_____. " 'His Witness Is True': A Test of the Johannine Claim." In *Jesus and the Politics of His Day*, pp. 453-76. Edited by Ernst Bammel and C. F. D. Moule. Cambridge: Cambridge University Press, 1984.

Roediger, David R. *The Wages of Whiteness: Race and the Making of the American Working Class.* New York: Verso, 1991.

Rogers, Joel A. *World's Greatest Men and Women of African Descent.* Small edition. New York: Author, 1935.

Rose, Willie Lee, ed. *A Documentary History of Slavery in North America.* New York: Oxford University Press, 1976.

Ross, Fred A. *Slavery Ordained of God.* N.p.: J. B. Lippincott, 1857. Reprint Miami: Mnemosyne, 1969.

Rowland, C. "A Man Clothed in Linen: Daniel 10.6ff and Jewish Angelology." *Journal for the Study of the New Testament* 24 (1985): 99-110.

_____. "The Vision of the Risen Christ in Rev. i.13ff.: The Debt of an Early Christology to an Aspect of Jewish Angelology." *Journal of Theological Studies* 31 (1980): 1-11.

Ruffle, John. *The Egyptians: An Introduction to Egyptian Archaeology.* Ithaca, N.Y.: Cornell University Press, 1977.

Russell, Letty M. "A Feminist Looks at Black Theology." In *Black Theology II: Essays on the Formation and Outreach of Contemporary Black Theology*, pp. 247-66. Edited by Calvin E. Bruce and William R. Jones. Lewisburg, Va.: Bucknell University Press/Cranbury, N.J.: Associated University Presses, 1978.

Safrai, Samuel. "Education and the Study of the Torah." In *The Jewish People in the First Century: Historical Geography, Political History, Social, Cultural and Religious Life and Institutions*, pp. 945-70. Edited by Samuel Safrai and Menahem Stern with D. Flusser and W. C. van Unnik. 2 vols. Assen, Netherlands: Van Gorcum, 1974 (vol. 1); Philadelphia: Fortress, 1976 (vol. 2).

_____. "Home and Family." In *The Jewish People in the First Century: Historical Geography, Political History, Social, Cultural and Religious Life and Institutions*, pp. 728-92. Edited by Samuel Safrai and Menahem Stern with D. Flusser and W. C. van Unnik. 2 vols. Assen, Netherlands: Van Gorcum, 1974 (vol. 1); Philadelphia: Fortress, 1976 (vol. 2).

Salama, P. "From Rome to Islam." In *Ancient Civilizations of Africa*, pp. 499-510. Edited by G. Mokhtar. Vol. 2 of *General History of Africa.* Berkeley: University of California Press/London: Heinemann Educational Books/Paris: United Nations Educational, Scientific and Cultural Organization, 1981.

Sandburg, Carl. *The Chicago Race Riots, July 1919.* New York: Harcourt, Brace & Howe, 1919. Reprint New York: Harcourt, Brace & World, 1969.

Sanders, Cheryl J. "Afrocentric and Womanist Approaches to Theological Educaton." In *Living the Intersection: Womanism and Afrocentrism in Theology*, pp. 157-75. Edited by Cheryl J. Sanders. Minneapolis: Fortress, 1995.

*_____. "Black Women in Biblical Perspective: Resistance, Affirmation and Empowerment." In *Living the Intersection: Womanism and Afrocentrism in Theology*, pp. 121-43. Edited by Cheryl J. Sanders. Minneapolis: Fortress, 1995.

**_____. *Empowerment Ethics for a Liberated People: A Path to African American Social Transformation.* Minneapolis: Fortress, 1995.

*_____. *Saints in Exile: The Holiness-Pentecostal Experience in African American Religion and Culture.* New York: Oxford University Press, 1996.

_____. *Slavery and Conversion: An Analysis of Ex-slave Testimony.* Ann Arbor, Mich.: University Microfilms, 1987 (Th.D. dissertation, Harvard University, 1985).

_____. *The Historical Figure of Jesus.* New York: Penguin, 1993.

Sanders, E. P. *Jesus and Judaism.* Philadelphia: Fortress, 1985.

*Sanneh, Lamin. *West African Christianity: The Religious Impact.* Maryknoll, N.Y.: Orbis, 1983.

*Sarna, Nahum M. *Exploring Exodus: The Heritage of Biblical Israel.* New York: Schocken, 1986.

_____. *Understanding Genesis.* New York: Schocken, 1970.

"Saudi Arabia—Religious Intolerance: The Arrest, Detention and Torture of Christian Worshippers and Shi'a Muslims." New York: Amnesty International, 1993.

Savage, W. Sherman. *The Controversy over the Distribution of Abolition Literature, 1830-1860.* N.p.:

Association for the Study of Negro Life and History, 1938.

Sawyer, George S. *Southern Institutes; Or, An Inquiry into the Origin and Early Prevalence of Slavery and the Slave-Trade, with an Analysis of the Laws, History and Government of the Institution in the Principal Nations, Ancient and Modern, from the Earliest Ages down to the Present Time, with Notes and Comments in Defence of the Southern Institutions.* Philadelphia: J. B. Lippincott, 1858. Reprint Miami: Mnemosyne, 1969.

Schafer, Walter, Carol Olera and Kenneth Polk. "Programmed for Social Class Tracking in High School." *Trans-Action* 12 (October 1970): 39-46.

Schapera, Isaac. *Married Life in an African Tribe.* Evanston, Ill.: Northwestern University Press, 1966.

Schedl, Claus. *History of the Old Testament.* 5 vols. Staten Island, N.Y.: Alba House, 1973.

Scherer, Lester B. *Slavery and the Churches in Early America, 1619-1819.* Grand Rapids, Mich.: Eerdmans, 1975.

Schlesinger, Arthur M., Jr. *The Disuniting of America: Reflections on a Multicultural Society.* New York: W. W. Norton, 1992.

Schneider, Gerhard. "The Political Charge Against Jesus (Luke 23:2)." In *Jesus and the Politics of His Day,* pp. 403-14. Edited by Ernst Bammel and C. F. D. Moule. Cambridge: Cambridge University Press, 1984.

Schofield, J. N. "Megiddo." In *Archaeology and Old Testament Study.* Edited by D. Winton Thomas. Oxford: Clarendon, 1967.

Schweizer, Edward. *The Good News According to Matthew.* Translated by David E. Green. Atlanta: John Knox, 1975.

Schweninger, Loren. *Black Property Owners in the South, 1790-1915.* Urbana: University of Illinois Press, 1990.

Scott, James M. "Luke's Geographical Horizon." In *Graeco-Roman Setting,* pp. 483-544. Vol. 2 of *The Book of Acts in Its First-Century Setting.* Edited by David W. J. Gill and Conrad Gempf. Grand Rapids, Mich.: Eerdmans/Carlisle, U.K.: Paternoster, 1994.

Scott, John Atwood. "The Pattern of the Tabernacle." Ann Arbor, Mich.: University Microfilms, 1978 (Ph.D. dissertation, University of Pennsylvania, 1965).

Scott, R. B. Y. *The Relevance of the Prophets.* New York: Macmillan, 1954.

Scroggs, Robin. *The New Testament and Homosexuality: Contextual Background for the Contemporary Debate.* Philadelphia: Fortress, 1983.

Seabury, Samuel. *American Slavery Distinguished from the Slavery of the English Theorists and Justified by the Law of Nature.* New York: Mason Brothers, 1861. Reprint Miami: Mnemosyne, 1969.

Seneca. *Works.* Translated by John B. Basore et al. 10 vols. Loeb Classical Library. Cambridge, Mass.: Harvard University Press, 1928- .

*Sernett, Milton C. *Black Religion and American Evangelicalism: White Protestants, Plantation Missions and the Flowering of Negro Christianity, 1787-1865.* American Theological Library Association Monographs 7. Metuchen, N.J.: Scarecrow/American Theological Library Association, 1975.

————, ed. *Afro-American History: A Documentary Witness.* Durham, N.C.: Duke University Press, 1985.

Sextus Empiricus. *Works.* Translated by R. G. Bury. 4 vols. Loeb Classical Library. Cambridge, Mass.: Harvard University Press/London: Heinemann, 1933-1949.

Shahid, Samuel. " 'Rights' of Non-Muslims in an Islamic State." *Reach Out* 5, nos. 3-4 (April 1992): 5-11.

Shapiro, Laura, with Daniel Pedersen and Marcus Mabry. "The Fundamentals of Freedom." *Newsweek,* November 15, 1993, p. 87.

Sherif, N. M. "Nubia before Napata (-3100 to -750)." In *Ancient Civilizations of Africa,* pp. 245-74. Edited by G. Mokhtar. Vol. 2 of *General History of Africa.* Berkeley: University of California Press/London: Heinemann Educational Books/Paris: United Nations Educational, Scientific and Cultural Organization, 1981.

Sherk, Robert K., ed. *The Roman Empire: Augustus to Hadrian.* Translated Documents of Greece and Rome 6. New York: Cambridge University Press, 1988.

Sherwin-White, A. N. *Roman Society and Roman Law in the New Testament.* Oxford: Oxford University Press, 1963. Reprint Grand Rapids, Mich.: Baker Book House, 1978.

Shopshire, James M. "Black Methodist Protestants, 1877-1939: Protest and Change Among African Americans Within Predecessor Organizations of the United Methodist Church." In *The Recovery of Black Presence: An Interdisciplinary Exploration—Essays in Honor of Dr. Charles B. Copher,* pp. 177-91. Edited by Randall C. Bailey and Jacquelyn Grant. Nashville: Abingdon, 1995.

Sibylline Oracles. Translated by J. J. Collins; 1:317-472 in *The Old Testament Pseudepigrapha.* 2 vols. Edited by James H. Charlesworth. Garden City, N.Y.: Doubleday, 1983-1985. Greek text in *Die Oracula Sibyllina.* Edited by Johannes Geffcken. Leipzig, 1902.

Sider, Ronald J. *One-Sided Christianity? Uniting the Church to Heal a Lost and Broken World.* Grand Rapids, Mich.: Zondervan/San Francisco: HarperSanFrancisco, 1993.

Sidey, Ken. "What's in a Word?" *Christianity Today,* February 5, 1990, pp. 40-41.

Sifre to Deuteronomy: An Analytical Translation. Translated by Jacob Neusner. 2 vols. Brown Judaic Studies 98, 101. Atlanta: Scholars Press, 1987.

Skinner, Tom. *How Black Is the Gospel?* Evangelical Perspectives. Philadelphia: J. B. Lippincott, 1970.

————. *If Christ Is the Answer, What Are the Questions?* Grand Rapids, Mich.: Zondervan, 1974.

————. *Words of Revolution.* Grand Rapids, Mich.: Zondervan, 1970.

Sleeter, Christine E., and Carl A. Grant. "An Analysis of Multicultural Education in the United States." *Harvard Educational Review* 57 (November 1987): 421-44.

Smillie, Gene R. "Adaptors to Foreign Cultures." *Mission Today 95,* 1995, pp. 4-5.

Smith, Edward D. *Climbing Jacob's Ladder: The Rise of Black Churches in Eastern American Cities, 1740-1877.* Washington, D.C.: Smithsonian Institution, 1988.

Smith, H. Shelton. *In His Image, But . . . : Racism in Southern Religion, 1780-1910.* Durham, N.C.: Duke University Press, 1972.

Smith, J. Clay, Jr. *Emancipation: The Making of the Black Lawyer, 1844-1944.* Philadelphia: University of Pennsylvania Press, 1993.

Smith, Mary B. "Alfred the Great." *Ebony,* February 1992, pp. 154-62.

**Smith, Timothy L. *Revivalism and Social Reform: American Protestantism on the Eve of the Civil War.* Baltimore: Johns Hopkins University Press, 1980.

Smith, Wallace Charles. *The Church in the Life of the Black Family.* Valley Forge, Penn.: Judson, 1985.

Smith, W. Stevenson. *The Art and Architecture of Ancient Egypt.* Vol. 14 of *The Pelican History of Art.* Edited by Nikolaus Pevsner. Baltimore: Penguin, 1958.

**Snowden, Frank M., Jr. *Before Color Prejudice: The Ancient View of Blacks.* Cambridge, Mass.: Harvard University Press, 1983.

————. *Blacks in Antiquity: Ethiopians in the Greco-Roman Experience.* Cambridge, Mass.: Belknap/Harvard University Press, 1970.

Soares Prabhu, George M. *The Formula Quotations in the Infancy Narrative of Matthew: An Enquiry into the Tradition History of Mt 1-2.* Rome: Biblical Institute Press, 1976.

Sonne, Isaiah. "The Use of Rabbinic Literature as Historical Sources." *Jewish Quarterly Review* 36 (1945-1946): 147-69.

Sparks, Jack. *The Mind Benders: A Look at Current Cults.* 2nd ed. Nashville: Thomas Nelson, 1979.

Spencer, Rev. and Mrs. Willie. *Church of God: Black Women in the Church—Historical Highlights and Profiles.* Pittsburgh: Magna Graphics, 1986.

Spencer-Byers, Alexis. "Unsung Heroes in Black History: Nannie Helen Burroughs (1883-1961)." *Urban Family,* Fall 1995, p. 36.

Stafford, Tim. "In Reluctant Praise of Extremism." *Christianity Today,* October 26, 1992, pp. 18-22.

Stambaugh, John E., and David L. Balch. *The New Testament in Its Social Environment.* Library of Early Christianity 2. Philadelphia: Westminster Press, 1986.

Stampp, Kenneth M. *The Peculiar Institution: Slavery in the Ante-bellum South.* New York: Alfred A. Knopf, 1978.

Stanton, Graham N. *Jesus of Nazareth in New Testament Preaching.* Cambridge: Cambridge University Press, 1974.

"Statement by the National Committee of Black Churchmen, June 13, 1969." In *Black Theology: A*

Documentary History, 1:37-39. Edited by James H. Cone and Gayraud S. Wilmore. 2 vols. Maryknoll, N.Y.: Orbis, 1993.

Stauffer, Ethelbert. *Jesus and His Story.* Translated by Richard Winston and Clara Winston. New York: Alfred A. Knopf, 1960.

Steele, F. R. "Sumer." In *The International Standard Bible Encyclopedia,* 4:653-62. Edited by Geoffrey W. Bromiley. 4 vols. Grand Rapids, Mich.: Eerdmans, 1979-1988.

Stennis, L. V. *The Black Church: "Why Sit We Here Until We Die?"* Seattle: Chi-Mik, 1981.

Stephens, William N. *The Family in Cross-Cultural Perspective.* New York: Holt, Rinehart & Winston, 1963.

*Sterling, Dorothy. *We Are Your Sisters: Black Women in the Nineteenth Century.* New York: W. W. Norton, 1984.

Stern, Ephraim. "A Late Bronze Temple at Tell Mevorakh." *Biblical Archaeologist* 40 (May 1977): 89-91.

Stowers, Stanley K. "The Diatribe." In *Greco-Roman Literature and the New Testament: Selected Forms and Genres,* pp. 71-83. Edited by David E. Aune. SBL Sources for Biblical Study 21. Atlanta: Scholars Press, 1988.

*Subramanian, Sribala. "The Story in Our Genes: A Landmark Global Study Flattens *The Bell Curve,* Proving That Racial Differences Are Only Skin Deep." *Time,* January 16, 1995, pp. 54-55.

"Sudan: Caught in a Vicious Cycle of Human Rights Abuses, Poverty and Political Turmoil." *Amnesty Action,* Winter 1995, pp. 1, 3.

"Sudan—the Ravages of War: Political Killings and Humanitarian Disaster." New York: Amnesty International, 1993.

*Sunderland, La Roy. *Anti Slavery Manual, Containing a Collection of Facts and Arguments on American Slavery.* New York: S. W. Benedict, 1837. Reprint Detroit: Negro History Press (P.O. Box 5129, Detroit, MI 48236), n.d.

*_____. *The Testimony of God Against Slavery: Or, A Collection of Passages from the Bible Which Show the Sin of Holding Property in Man, with Notes.* Boston: Webster & Southard, 1835.

Tacitus. *The Complete Works.* Translated by Alfred John Church and William Jackson Brodribb. New York: Modern Library, 1942.

Talib, Y., with F. Samir. "The African Diaspora in Asia." In *Africa from the Seventh to the Eleventh Century,* pp. 704-33. Edited by M. El Fasi with I. Hrbek. Vol. 3 of *General History of Africa.* Berkeley: University of California Press/London: Heinemann Educational Books/Paris: United Nations Educational, Scientific and Cultural Organization, 1988.

*Tappan, Lewis. "Disfellowshipping the Slaveholder." In *Autographs for Freedom,* 2:163-64. Edited by Julia Griffiths. Auburn, N.Y.: Alden, Beardsley, 1854.

Tarrants, Tom. "The Conversion of a Klansman." *Urban Family,* Spring 1992, pp. 22-23.

*Taylor, John H. *Egypt and Nubia.* Cambridge, Mass.: Harvard University Press/Trustees of the British Museum, 1991.

Taylor, Susie King. *Reminiscences of My Life in Camp with the Thirty-third U.S. Colored Troops, Late First South Carolina Volunteers.* Boston: Author, 1902. Reprinted as *A Black Woman's Civil War Memoirs.* Edited by Patricia W. Romero. New York: Markus Wiener, 1988.

Tertullian. *Apology.* Translated by T. R. Glover. Loeb Classical Library. Cambridge, Mass.: Harvard University Press, 1931.

The Testament of Abraham: The Greek Recensions. Translated by Michael E. Stone. Society of Biblical Literature Texts and Translations 2, Pseudepigrapha Series 2. Missoula, Mont.: Society of Biblical Literature, 1972.

Theon. *The Progymnasmata: A New Text with Translation and Commentary.* Translation and commentary by James R. Butts. Ann Arbor, Mich.: University Microfilms, 1989.

Thompson, J. A. "Incense." In *Zondervan Pictorial Encyclopedia of the Bible.* Edited by Merrill C. Tenney. Grand Rapids, Mich.: Zondervan, 1976.

*Thurman, Howard. *Jesus and the Disinherited.* New York: Abingdon, 1949. Reprint Richmond, Ind.: Friends United, 1981.

Tiénou, Tite. "The Church in African Theology: Description and Analysis of Hermeneutical Presuppositions." In *Biblical Interpretation and the Church: The Problem of Contextualization,* pp. 151-65. Edited by D. A. Carson. Nashville: Thomas Nelson, 1984.

Tiffany, Joel. *A Treatise on the Unconstitutionality of American Slavery: Together with the Powers and Duties of the Federal Government in Relation to That Subject.* N.p. [Ohio]: Author, n.d. Reprint Miami: Mnemosyne, 1969.

Tinney, James S. "William J. Seymour: Father of Modern-Day Pentecostalism." In *Black Apostles: Afro-American Clergy Confront the Twentieth Century,* pp. 213-25. Edited by Randall K. Burkett and Richard Newman. Boston: G. K. Hall, 1978.

The Tosefta. Translated by Jacob Neusner et al. 6 vols. New York: KTAV, 1977-1986.

Towns, Zanna. "Breaking Barriers." Lecture given at Christian Stronghold Baptist Church, Philadelphia, March 7, 1993.

Trigger, Bruce G. "The Ballana Culture and the Coming of Christianity." In *Africa in Antiquity 1: The Arts of Ancient Nubia and the Sudan—the Essays,* pp. 106-19. Brooklyn, N.Y.: Brooklyn Museum, 1978.

*———. "Nubian, Negro, Black, Nilotic?" In *Africa in Antiquity 1: The Arts of Ancient Nubia and the Sudan—the Essays,* pp. 26-35. Brooklyn, N.Y.: Brooklyn Museum, 1978.

Trimiew, Oliver Lee, Jr. "Paul as Prisoner: A Materialist Reading of Paul's Letter to the Philippians—An African American Perspective." Paper presented to the African American Theology and Biblical Hermeneutics Group at Society of Biblical Literature annual meeting, 1993.

Tucker, Ruth A. *From Jerusalem to Irian Jaya: A Biographical History of Christian Missions.* Grand Rapids, Mich.: Zondervan, 1983.

Tuttle, William M., Jr. *Race Riot: Chicago in the Red Summer of 1919.* New York: Atheneum, 1977.

Tutu, Desmond M. "Black Theology/African Theology—Soul Mates or Antagonists?" In *Black Theology: A Documentary History,* 1:385-92. Edited by James H. Cone and Gayraud S. Wilmore. 2 vols. Maryknoll, N.Y.: Orbis, 1993.

Urbach, Ephraim E. *The Sages: Their Concepts and Beliefs.* Translated by Israel Abrahams. 2nd ed. 2 vols. Jerusalem: Magnes/Hebrew University, 1979.

Urbana Update 6 (Winter 1991): 3, 5.

Usner, Daniel H., Jr. *Indians, Settlers and Slaves in a Frontier Exchange Economy: The Lower Mississippi Valley Before 1783.* Chapel Hill: University of North Carolina Press, 1992.

Usry, Glenn Jay. "Street Questions: A Brief Survey of Commonly Asked Questions Concerning Christianity and Islam in Urban Areas." M.R.E. thesis, Hood Theological Seminary, 1995.

Ussishkin, D. In "Notes and News." *Israel Exploration Journal* 27, no. 1 (1977): 48-51.

Valentine, Glenda. "Shades of Gray: The Conundrum of Color Categories." *Teaching Tolerance,* Spring 1995, p. 47.

Van Deburg, William S. *The Slave Drivers: Black Agricultural Labor Supervisors in the Antebellum South.* Contributions in Afro-American and African Studies 43. Westport, Conn.: Greenwood, 1979.

*———. "The Tragedy of Frederick Douglass." *Christianity Today,* January 31, 1975, pp. 7-8.

Van Leeuwen, Mary Stewart. *Gender and Grace: Love, Work and Parenting in a Changing World.* Downers Grove, Ill.: InterVarsity Press, 1990.

Van Noten, F., with D. Cahen and P. De Maret. "Central Africa." In *Ancient Civilizations of Africa,* pp. 620-38. Edited by G. Mokhtar. Vol. 2 of *General History of Africa.* Berkeley: University of California Press/London: Heinemann Educational Books/Paris: United Nations Educational, Scientific and Cultural Organization, 1981.

Vermaseren, Maarten J. *Cybele and Attis: The Myth and the Cult.* Translated by A. M. H. Lemmers. London: Thames & Hudson, 1977.

Vermes, Geza. *Jesus the Jew: A Historian's Reading of the Gospels.* Philadelphia: Fortress, 1973.

Völklein, Ulrich. "German Business Reveals Its Sins." *World Press Review,* July 1995, pp. 17-18. Translated from *Manager Magazin* (Hamburg), May 1995.

Von Rad, Gerhard. *Old Testament Theology.* Translated by D. M. G. Stalker. 2 vols. New York: Harper & Row, 1962.

Voting in Mississippi: A Report of the United States Commission on Civil Rights. Washington, D.C.: U.S. Commission on Civil Rights, 1965.

Wace, Henry. "Tertullianus." In *A Dictionary of Christian Biography and Literature to the End of the Sixth Century A.D., with an Account of the Principal Sects and Heresies,* pp. 940-53. Edited by Henry Wace and William C. Piercy. Peabody, Mass.: Hendrickson, 1994.

Wagner, Günter. *Pauline Baptism and the Pagan Mysteries: The Problem of the Pauline Doctrine of Baptism in Romans VI.1-11, in Light of Its Religio-historical "Parallels."* Translated by J. P. Smith. Edinburgh: Oliver & Boyd, 1967.

Wainwright, J. A. "Zoser's Pyramid and Solomon's Temple." *Expository Times* 91 (February 1980): 137-38.

*Walker, David. "David Walker's *Appeal.*" In *Witness for Freedom: African American Voices on Race, Slavery and Emancipation,* pp. 42-46. Edited by C. Peter Ripley. Chapel Hill: University of North Carolina Press, 1993.

Wall Paintings of the Tomb of Nefertari: Scientific Studies for Their Conservation. Cairo: Egyptian Antiquities Organization, 1987.

Walls, A. F. "Africa." In *New Bible Dictionary,* pp. 17-18. 2nd ed. Edited by J. D. Douglas. Downers Grove, Ill.: InterVarsity Press, 1982.

Walls, William Jacob. *The African Methodist Episcopal Zion Church, Reality of the Black Church.* Charlotte, N.C.: A.M.E. Zion Publishing House, 1974.

Waltke, Bruce K. "The Textual Criticism of the Old Testament." In *Biblical Criticism: Historical, Literary and Textual,* pp. 47-82. Grand Rapids, Mich.: Zondervan, 1978.

Warmington, B. H. "The Carthaginian Period." In *Ancient Civilizations of Africa,* pp. 441-64. Edited by G. Mokhtar. Vol. 2 of *General History of Africa.* Berkeley: University of California Press/London: Heinemann Educational Books/Paris: United Nations Educational, Scientific and Cultural Organization, 1981.

Washington, Booker T. *Up from Slavery: An Autobiography.* New York: Doubleday, 1901. Reprint Boston: Americanist Library, 1965.

*Washington, James Melvin, ed. *Conversations with God: Two Centuries of Prayers by African Americans.* New York: HarperCollins, 1994.

————. *Frustrated Fellowship: The Black Baptist Quest for Social Power.* Macon, Ga.: Mercer University Press, 1986.

Washington, Joseph R. *Black Religion: The Negro and Christianity in the United States.* Boston: Beacon, 1964.

Waters, John W. "When the Vultures Are Finished, Can There Be Life? The Valley of Dry Bones and the Future of the Black Church." In *The Recovery of Black Presence: An Interdisciplinary Exploration—Essays in Honor of Dr. Charles B. Copher,* pp. 95-106. Edited by Randall C. Bailey and Jacquelyn Grant. Nashville: Abingdon, 1995.

*Weary, Dolphus, with William Hendricks. *I Ain't Comin' Back.* Wheaton, Ill.: Tyndale House, 1990.

Weems, Renita J. *Just a Sister Away: A Womanist Vision of Women's Relationships in the Bible.* San Diego, Calif.: LuraMedia, 1988.

————. "Womanist Reflections on Biblical Hermeneutics." In *Black Theology: A Documentary History,* 2:216-24. Edited by James H. Cone and Gayraud S. Wilmore. 2 vols. Maryknoll, N.Y.: Orbis, 1993.

Wenham, David, and Craig Blomberg, eds. *The Miracles of Jesus.* Vol. 6 of *Gospel Perspectives.* 6 vols. Sheffield, U.K.: JSOT Press, 1986.

*West, Cornel. *Race Matters.* Boston: Beacon, 1993.

" 'What Martin Luther King Jr. Means to Me.' " *Ebony,* January 1994, pp. 21-25.

White, Gayle. "Colorblind Calling." *The Atlanta Journal & Constitution,* November 3, 1991, pp. M1, 4.

"Wilberforce, William." In *The New Encyclopaedia Brittanica,* 12:654. 15th ed. Chicago: University of Chicago Press, 1992.

Wilkins, William. "The Concept of a Self-Fulfilling Prophecy." *Sociology of Education* 49 (April 1976): 175-83.

*Williams, Chancellor. *The Destruction of Black Civilization: Great Issues of a Race from 4500 B.C. to 2000 A.D.* Illustrated by Murry N. DePillars. Chicago: Third World Press, 1987.

Williams, Delores S. "Afrocentrism and Male-Female Relations in Church and Society." In *Living the Intersection: Womanism and Afrocentrism in Theology,* pp. 43-56. Edited by Cheryl J. Sanders. Minneapolis: Fortress, 1995.

Williams, Leon F. "Revisiting the Mission of Social Work at the End of the Century: A Critique." In *Perspectives on Equity and Justice in Social Work,* pp. 51-64. Edited by Dorothy M. Pearson.

Carl A. Scott Memorial Lecture Series, 1988-1992. Alexandria, Va.: Council on Social Work Education, 1993.

Williams, Trevor. "Teacher Prophecies and the Inheritance of Inequality." *Sociology of Education* 49 (July 1976): 223-36.

Williamson, H. G. M. *1 & 2 Chronicles.* New Century Bible Commentary. Grand Rapids, Mich.: Eerdmans/London: Marshall, Morgan & Scott, 1982.

Willis, Rev. Dr. "The Bible vs. Slavery." In *Autographs for Freedom,* 2:151-55. Edited by Julia Griffiths. Auburn, N.Y.: Alden, Beardsley, 1854.

**Wilmore, Gayraud S. *Black Religion and Black Radicalism: An Interpretation of the Religious History of Afro-American People.* 2nd rev. ed. Maryknoll, N.Y.: Orbis, 1983.

Wilson, John A. *The Culture of Ancient Egypt.* Chicago: University of Chicago Press, 1951.

Wilson, Monica. *Rituals of Kinship Among the Nyakyusa.* London: Oxford University Press, 1957.

Wimby, Rekhety. "The Unity of African Languages." In *Kemet and the African Worldview: Research, Rescue and Restoration,* pp. 151-66. Edited by Maulana Karenga and Jacob H. Carruthers. Los Angeles: University of Sankore Press, 1986.

Winkle, R. E. "The Jeremiah Model for Jesus in the Temple." *Andrews University Seminary Studies* 24 (1986): 155-72.

Wiseman, D. J. "They Lived in Tents." In *Biblical and Near Eastern Studies: Essays in Honor of William Sanford Lasor,* pp. 195-200. Edited by Gary A. Tuttle. Grand Rapids, Mich.: Eerdmans, 1978.

Wiseman, P. J. *Ancient Records and the Structure of Genesis: A Case for Literary Unity.* Updated by D. J. Wiseman. Nashville: Thomas Nelson, 1985.

Witherington, Ben, III. *The Christology of Jesus.* Minneapolis: Fortress, 1990.

————. *The Jesus Quest: The Third Search for the Jew of Nazareth.* Downers Grove, Ill.: InterVarsity Press, 1995.

————. *Jesus the Sage: The Pilgrimage of Wisdom.* Minneapolis: Fortress, 1994.

Woldering, Irmgard. *The Art of Egypt: The Time of the Pharaohs.* New York: Greystone, 1963.

Wood, Peter H. *Black Majority: Negroes in Colonial South Carolina from 1670 Through the Stone Rebellion.* New York: Alfred A. Knopf, 1974.

Woods, Donald. *Biko.* New York: Random House, 1978.

Woodson, Carter G. Introduction. In *Addresses Mainly Personal and Racial,* pp. vii-xxii, vol. 1 of *The Works of Francis J. Grimké.* Edited by Carter G. Woodson. 4 vols. Washington, D.C. Associated Publishers, 1942.

————. *The Mis-education of the Negro.* Washington, D.C.: Associated Publishers, 1933. Reprint Trenton, N.J.: Africa World Press, 1990.

*Woodward, C. Vann. *The Strange Career of Jim Crow.* New York: Oxford University Press, 1957.

Woolman, John. *Some Considerations on the Keeping of Negroes 1754; Considerations on Keeping Negroes 1762.* Philadelphia: James Chattin, 1754. Reprint New York: Grossman/Viking, 1976.

World Press Review, March 1989, pp. 28-29; June 1991, p. 36; March 1994, p. 31.

Wright, G. Ernest. *Biblical Archaeology.* 2nd ed. Philadelphia: Westminster Press, 1962.

Wright, N. T. *Who Was Jesus?* Grand Rapids, Mich.: Eerdmans/London: S.P.C.K., 1992.

Wright, Sarah E. *A. Philip Randolph: Integration in the Workplace.* Englewood Cliffs, N.J.: Silver Burdett/Simon & Schuster, 1990.

Yamauchi, Edwin M. *The Stones and the Scriptures: An Introduction to Biblical Archaeology.* Grand Rapids, Mich.: Baker Book House, 1972.

Yates, Walter L. "The God-Consciousness of the Black Church in Historical Perspective." In *Quest for a Black Theology,* pp. 44-61. Edited by James J. Gardiner and J. Deotis Roberts Sr. Philadelphia: Pilgrim, 1971.

"Young 'Slaves.'" *World Press Review,* January 1992, p. 33.

Yoyotte, J. "Pharaonic Egypt: Society, Economy and Culture." In *Ancient Civilizations of Africa,* pp. 112-35. Edited by G. Mokhtar. Vol. 2 of *General History of Africa.* Berkeley: University of California Press/London: Heinemann Educational Books/Paris: United Nations Educational, Scientific and Cultural Organization, 1981.

"Zaire—Violence Against Democracy." New York: Amnesty International, 1993.

Zana, Mehdi. "A Kurd's Tale of Turkish Prison." *World Press Review,* July 1995, pp. 13-15. Translated from *Libération* (Paris), January 21-27, 1995.

Zayed, A. Hamid. "Egypt's Relations with the Rest of Africa." In *Ancient Civilizations of Africa,* pp. 136-54. Edited by G. Mokhtar. Vol. 2 of *General History of Africa.* Berkeley: University of California Press/London: Heinemann Educational Books/Paris: United Nations Educational, Scientific and Cultural Organization, 1981.

Zilversmit, Arthur. *The First Emancipation: The Abolition of Slavery in the North.* Chicago: University of Chicago Press, 1967.

Index of Names & Subjects

Index of Primary References